THE POLITICS OF WINE]
FRANC

In the late fifteenth century, Burgundy was incorporated into the kingdom of France. This, coupled with the advent of Protestantism in the early sixteenth century, opened up new avenues for participation in public life by ordinary Burgundians and led to considerably greater interaction between the elites and the ordinary people. Mack P. Holt examines the relationship between the ruling and popular classes from Burgundy's reincorporation into France in 1477 until the Lanturelu riot in Dijon in 1630, focusing on the local wine industry. Indeed, the vineyard workers were crucial in turning back the tide of Protestantism in the province until 1630 when, following royal attempts to reduce the level of popular participation in public affairs, Louis XIII tried to remove them from the city altogether. More than just a local study, this book shows how the popular classes often worked together with local elites to shape policies that affected them.

MACK P. HOLT is Professor of History at George Mason University, Virginia. From 1998 to 1999 he served as Co-President of the Society for French Historical Studies, and from 2009 to 2011 as the President of the Society for Reformation Research. In 2005 and 2014, he was Visiting Professor of History at the École des Hautes Études en Sciences Sociales in Paris, and in 2018 Visiting Fellow Commoner at Trinity College, University of Cambridge.

NEW STUDIES IN EUROPEAN HISTORY

Edited by

PETER BALDWIN, University of California, Los Angeles
CHRISTOPHER CLARK, University of Cambridge
JAMES B. COLLINS, Georgetown University
MIA RODRÍGUEZ-SALGADO, London School of Economics
and Political Science
LYNDAL ROPER, University of Oxford
TIMOTHY SNYDER, Yale University

The aim of this series in early modern and modern European history is to publish outstanding works of research, addressed to important themes across a wide geographical range, from southern and central Europe, to Scandinavia and Russia, from the time of the Renaissance to the present. As it develops the series will comprise focused works of wide contextual range and intellectual ambition.

A full list of titles published in the series can be found at:
www.cambridge.org/newstudiesineuropeanhistory

THE POLITICS OF WINE IN EARLY MODERN FRANCE

Religion and Popular Culture in Burgundy, 1477–1630

MACK P. HOLT

George Mason University

CAMBRIDGE
UNIVERSITY PRESS

CAMBRIDGE
UNIVERSITY PRESS

University Printing House, Cambridge CB2 8BS, United Kingdom

One Liberty Plaza, 20th Floor, New York, NY 10006, USA

477 Williamstown Road, Port Melbourne, VIC 3207, Australia

314–321, 3rd Floor, Plot 3, Splendor Forum, Jasola District Centre, New Delhi - 110025, India

79 Anson Road, #06-04/06, Singapore 079906

Cambridge University Press is part of the University of Cambridge.

It furthers the University's mission by disseminating knowledge in the pursuit of education, learning and research at the highest international levels of excellence.

www.cambridge.org
Information on this title: www.cambridge.org/9781108456814
DOI: 10.1017/9781108620017

First published 2018
First paperback edition 2020

A catalogue record for this publication is available from the British Library

Library of Congress Cataloging in Publication data
NAMES: Holt, Mack P., author.
TITLE: The politics of wine in early modern France : religion and popular culture in Burgundy, 1477–1630 / Mack P. Holt, George Mason University.
DESCRIPTION: Cambridge, United Kingdom ; New York, NY, USA : Cambridge University Press, 2018. | Series: New studies in European history | Includes bibliographical references and index.
IDENTIFIERS: LCCN 2018015241 | ISBN 9781108471886 (hardback)
SUBJECTS: LCSH: Burgundy (France) – Church history. | Burgundy (France) – Religious life and customs – History. | Popular culture – Religious aspects – Christianity. | Wine industry – Political aspects – France – Burgundy – History. | BISAC: HISTORY / Europe / General.
CLASSIFICATION: LCC BR847.B85 H65 2018 | DDC 944/.41–dc23
LC record available at https://lccn.loc.gov/2018015241

ISBN 978-1-108-47188-6 Hardback
ISBN 978-1-108-45681-4 Paperback

For Gisèle Baridon

And in memory of Michel Baridon

Contents

Figures

Tables

Acknowledgments

Any author who has taken as long as I have to produce a book will naturally acquire a number of debts – financial, social, and intellectual – which I wish to acknowledge here. An Andrew W. Mellon Faculty Fellowship at Harvard University in 1986–1987 allowed me to make an efficient start on reading the printed sources. Summer stipends from the National Endowment for the Humanities, the American Philosophical Society, the American Council of Learned Societies, West Texas State University, Vanderbilt University, and George Mason University allowed me to spend every summer in Dijon from 1986 to 1994 to work in the archives. A fellowship from the National Endowment for the Humanities in 1994–1995 allowed me to complete the archival research in Burgundy, and a John Simon Guggenheim Memorial Fellowship in 1996–1997 allowed me to make a systematic start on writing the book. I obviously am indebted to all these institutions for their financial largesse, and the book could never have been written without their generous financial support.

My personal debts to a variety of different individuals over the years are gargantuan, and I cannot possibly list them all here. Nevertheless, I cannot help but single out some of the most important contributors. That I decided to focus on the province of Burgundy at all is the result of a very productive suggestion made by Myron Gutmann over lunch at a Tex-Mex restaurant in Austin. It was he who first alerted me about the very copious archives in Burgundy for the sixteenth and seventeenth centuries, and I cannot thank him enough for this suggestion. At about the same time, I discovered that Jim Farr had recently completed a Ph.D. dissertation on artisans in premodern Dijon, and I had the good fortune to meet him shortly thereafter. Not only did he confirm for me the richness of Dijon's archives, but he personally introduced me to them and to the relevant archivists in the summer of 1986. We shared many successive summers together working in the Dijon archives, and his friendship and encouragement have been appreciated throughout this project. I am also grateful to Jim for introducing me to a wonderful couple in Dijon that first summer in 1986, Gisèle and Michel Baridon, whose intellectual stimulation, warm hospitality, and friendship made every successive trip to Dijon both pleasurable and rewarding.

Indeed, I can say that without the hospitality of the entire extended Baridon family the research and writing of this book would not have been possible. Four generations of this generous family gave up their beds, flats, or homes over the years to provide my wife and me a place to stay whenever we were in France. My deepest regret in not finishing this book sooner is that Michel did not live long enough to see the finished product. As an academic and expert on so many things himself, he taught me much about Dijon's past as well as the history of *mentalités*. And I also learned just about everything I know about Burgundy's wines from drinking it on so many occasions at his and Gisèle's dining room table, as well as accompanying them on numerous visits to various *vignerons* of the Côte d'Or for a *dégustation*. It is to Gisèle and to the memory of Michel that I dedicate this book.

A number of other Dijon friends and colleagues have also extended their hospitality to us over the years, and I wish to thank them all: Nicole and Lucien Cherchi, Chantal and Claude Jeannot, Claire Pasquier, Michele and Didier Perrin, and Claudette and Raymond Prost. I am also grateful to the staff of the archives and municipal library in Dijon, as they warmly welcomed a foreigner who was uncomfortable in their language and a complete stranger to their archival holdings. I also wish to acknowledge the assistance of the staff at the Archives départementales de la Côte-d'Or, as well as the staff at the Bibliothèque municipale de Dijon, who made the wonderful printed sources and manuscripts in its collection as well as its microfilm service available to me.

I also learned a great deal from the audiences at the many universities on both sides of the Atlantic where I was invited to share my work, and I thank them all for their invitations, criticisms, and suggestions. And I have benefited enormously from many individuals over the years who have helped me in various ways, especially Megan Armstrong, Marie Barral-Baron, Sara Beam, Bill Beik, Phil Benedict, Stuart Carroll, Jack Censer, Jim Collins, Olivier Cristin, Denis Crouzet, Hugues Daussy, Natalie Davis, Marion Demossier, Robert Descimon, Jon Dewald, Barbara Diefendorf, Jim Farr, Mark Greengrass, Arlette Jouanna, Bob Knecht, Nicolas Le Roux, Andrew Pettegree, Jonathan Powis, Virginia Reinburg, Penny Roberts, Brian Sandberg, and Julian Swann. And I also wish to acknowledge posthumously the great assistance I received early on from the late Sharon Kettering, Russell Major, Nancy Roelker, John Salmon, Bob Scribner, and Thierry Wanegffelen.

Two local institutions closer to home have also been very helpful. I have learned a great deal and have appreciated feedback from all the participants in a variety of seminars at the Folger Shakespeare Library in Washington DC. And I also thank the members of the Washington DC-Baltimore Old Regime Study Group, who warmly welcomed me into its community when I first arrived in the Washington area in 1989. Everyone in the group has been helpful to me, but I especially want to acknowledge Katherine and Tom Brennan, Jack Censer, Jim Collins, the late Sharon Kettering, Robbie Schneider, and Orest Ranum. My colleagues and students at George Mason University have also been very helpful in a number of ways, and I want to thank them all for their support and encouragement. I am especially grateful to two graduate students who served as my research assistants at various times – Elena Rozlogova and Eric Rose – both of whom taught me more than they realize about how to use spreadsheets and databases. My good friend Philippe Loustaunau has offered constant support, encouragement, and his passion for French food and wine for nearly thirty years.

Finally, I can only inadequately thank my wife, Meg, who has accompanied me nearly every step of the way on this long journey through the cities, towns, and vineyards of Burgundy. I could not have done it without her, and every day I realize more and more how lucky I have been to have her by my side. I can also say that no one is happier to see this book finished than she is.

Abbreviations and Translations

ADCO	Archives départementales de la Côte d'Or, Dijon
AMD	Archives municipales, Dijon
BMD	Bibliothèque municipale, Dijon
BNF	Bibliothèque nationale de France, Paris

All quotations from the Bible are from the New Revised Standard Version unless otherwise noted.

All other translations given in English are the author's own translations unless otherwise noted.

Units of Currency and Measurement in Dijon

Currency

    1 *livre tournois* = 20 *sous* = 240 *deniers*
    1 *sou* = 12 *deniers*
    1 *franc* = 1 *livre* = 20 *sous*
    1 *gros* (one-twelfth of a *livre*) = 1 *sou* and 8 *deniers* = 20 *deniers*
    1 *blanc* (one-fourth of a *gros*) = 5 *deniers*

Capacities for Wine (Generally in Wooden Barrels)

    1 *queue* = large barrel of approximately 456 liters
    1 *muid* = medium barrel of approximately 228 liters
    (a *muid* is also sometimes referred to as a *poinçon, tonneau,* or *pièce*)
    1 *feuillette* = smaller barrel of approximately 114 liters

Capacities for Cereal Grains and Other Dry Goods

    1 *muid* = approximately 29.2 hectoliters = 2,920 liters
    1 *quarteranche* (one-hundredth of a *muid*) = 1 *boisseau* = approximately
       29.2 liters
    1 *picotin* (one-eighth of a *boisseau*) = 3.65 liters
    1 *quintal* = one hundred weight = 100 pounds = 48.95 kg
    1 *bouteau* (one-eighth of a *quintal*) = 12.5 pounds = 6.12 kg

Area of Vineyards and Arable Land

    1 *perche* = 9.5 square meters
    1 *are* = 107 square meters
    1 *ouvrée* = 4 *ares* = 428 square meters
    1 *journal* = 8 *ouvrées* = 3,424 square meters

Introduction

I am the true vine and my Father is the vinegrower. He removes every branch in me that bears no fruit. Every branch that bears fruit he prunes to make it bear more fruit. You have already been cleansed by the word that I have spoken to you. Abide in me as I abide in you. Just as the branch cannot bear fruit by itself unless it abides in the vine, neither can you unless you abide in me. I am the vine, you are the branches. Those who abide in me and I in them bear much fruit, because apart from me you can do nothing. Whoever does not abide in me is thrown away like a branch and withers: such branches are gathered, thrown into the fire, and burned.

John 15: 1–6

Because God, by his divine mercy and goodness, has provided a ready and certain means to men of goodwill to serve together with him, such that they are all made as the bones of his bones, the flesh of his flesh, and the limbs of his limbs, between the two of them [they compose] one same bread and one same body, Him being the vine, vine-shoots, and branches of the same by the high and wonderful sacrament of the altar, which is the spiritual and invisible weapon of all good and virtuous Catholics, by which they defend against the attacks and transgressions of the devil, of the world, and of the flesh. In this holy faith we have promised and do promise that each year on All Saints' Day, after having prepared for confession and being absolved of all our transgressions and sins, we shall present ourselves in church to receive the holy sacrament and communion, the precious body of our savior and redeemer Jesus Christ at the time of the Mass, in order to be fortified and strengthened with the same heart and will against the gates of Hell and the ruses and tricks of Satan and all his minions and every undertaking that the enemies of God's faith and church can make against the said city [of Dijon], and against us, our brothers, allies, and friends. We also promise to conduct and govern ourselves in this world as true and natural-born citizens and soldiers of the city of God and of his armies, and that after having strived to live a godly and steadfast life in his faith and law in the time it has pleased

him to keep and preserve us here on earth, we shall at last be able to
reach his holy kingdom to be placed and counted among the number
of the blessed in his church triumphant.

Oath of association sworn by the leading
citizens of Dijon, January 7, 1571[1]

When the leading inhabitants of the Burgundian capital of Dijon took an
oath in January 1571 to join a lay confraternity, they chose to do so in
language that explicitly linked together the sacrament of the Eucharist, the
salvation of their souls in the next world, their opposition to Protestantism,
their loyalty to the French crown, and the material life of so many of the
city's inhabitants, the latter indicated by the Biblical metaphor of the
grapevine. This melding together of politics, religion, and material life
into one homogenous culture forms the methodology of this book. To say
that the resulting narrative is cultural history, then, may possibly be true,
but hardly adequate to describe the kind of book I have tried to write. It is
neither a history of high culture nor a history of exclusively popular
culture, but a history of the relations between the elites and the popular
classes. Thus, this book is not primarily about texts, discourses, and language
representations, a kind of cultural history that tends to limit itself to the
educated elites and usually omits material life altogether. If my insistence on
including an analysis of material life in this study leads some to suggest that
this is more a social history than a cultural history, then this is a criticism I can
happily embrace. Though very few historians would still insist that ideas and
social practices are derived from or historically determined by social relations
and/or material conditions, one of the goals of this book is to demonstrate that
they are nevertheless related in some way and are best treated together rather
than analyzed independently. Moreover, materiality necessarily includes material objects, whether they be ecclesiastical monuments, a wooden board with
Bible verses painted on it used by the city council as a symbol of their
authority, or vineyards and vine-pruning hooks. In our constant efforts as
historians to valorize texts, manuscripts, and archives over material objects as
sources of the past, we need to remember that these texts too are material
objects when we encounter them. So, I hope the book can also be in some way
an antidote to what Alexandra Walsham and others have referred to as "the

---

[1] AMD, B 117, fols. 120–125, January 7, 1571 (quote on fols. 123–124): "*Articles de société et fraternité jurez
et affermez par plusieurs notables habitans de la ville de Dijon par maintenir la religion catholique,
apostolique et romaine et conserver ceste ville de Dijon sous l'auctorité et souveraineté du roy.*" The articles
of the oath are also printed (with a few minor transcription errors) in Edmond Belle, *La Réforme à
Dijon des origins à la fin d ela lieutenance générale de Gaspard de Saulx-Tavanes, 1530–1570* (Dijon:
Damidot; Paris: Henri Champion, 1911), 215–219 (quote on 217–218).

denigration, suspicion and distrust of material culture that modern historians have inherited from the post-Reformation era."[2]

Moreover, this book eschews terms such as political culture, religious culture, and material culture, because contemporaries in the premodern world did not and could not experience politics, religion, and material life as independent cultural entities with their own disparate spheres of meanings. Instead, they understood them as melded together through their lived experiences as part of a cultural whole. Thus, I am aiming for a "cultural historical approach that focuses on differentiated practices and contrasted uses."[3] Like Roger Chartier, I fully agree that any model "that has long made the unequal distribution of objects the primary criterion of the cultural hierarchy must be replaced by a different approach that focuses attention on differentiated and contrasting uses of the same goods, the same texts, and the same ideas."[4] I eschew any model that assumes learned culture and folk tradition were normally in opposition in some kind of cultural default setting. The depictions of print culture versus oral culture or of a dominant elite culture suppressing and acculturating a more spontaneous popular culture are simplistic models at best and totally misleading at worst.

What has been called the acculturation thesis was first championed by scholars as diverse as Pierre Chaunu, Jean Delumeau, Robert Muchembled, and Peter Burke over the last 40 years.[5] All of them in various ways tended to see culture as a struggle between the elites and the masses, or to employ Peter Burke's memorable phrase, a culture caught in the battle between Carnival and Lent, with the Carnival culture of the popular classes getting suppressed by the Lenten culture of the learned elites. But the acculturation model has seen its popularity wane of late. Even if in the longer term there is unquestionably a kernel of truth in it, this model tends to underplay both resistance to any top-down cultural

---

[2] Alexandra Walsham, "The Pope's Merchandise and the Jesuits' Trumpery: Catholic Relics and Protestant Polemic in Post-Reformation England," in Jenifer Spinks and Dagmar Eichberger, eds., *Religion, the Supernatural and Visual Culture in Early Modern Europe* (Leiden: Brill, 2015), 370–409, quote on p. 400.

[3] Roger Chartier, *Cultural History: Between Practices and Representations*, trans. Lydia G. Cochrane (Ithaca, NY: Cornell University Press, 1988), 13.

[4] Roger Chartier, "Texts, Printing, Readings," in Lynn Hunt, ed., *The New Cultural History* (Berkeley, CA: University of California Press, 1989), 171.

[5] See Pierre Chaunu, *Les Temps des Réformes de l'Eglise: L'Eclatement* (Paris: Fayard, 1974); Jean Delumeau, *La Peur en Occident (XIVe–XVIIIe siècles): Une cité assiégée* (Paris: Fayard, 1978); Robert Muchembled, *Popular Culture and Elite Culture in France, 1400–1750*, trans. Lydia G. Cochrane (Baton Rouge, LA: Louisiana State University Press, 1985); and Peter Burke, *Popular Culture in Early Modern Europe* (London: Morris Temple Smith Ltd., 1978).

pressures and the impact of bottom-up cultural contributions to the whole. In fact, Muchembled and Burke themselves soon recognized that the acculturation thesis was too simplistic and ignored the symbiotic interaction between the learned and folk traditions.[6] So, I fully ascribe to Chartier's view that "describing a culture should thus involve the comprehension of its entire system of relations – the totality of the practices that express how it represents the physical world, society, and the sacred."[7] Thus, to claim that the acculturation model is no longer as popular as it once was is to claim something that is so common as to be a historical cliché. What is much more difficult is to offer a convincing example of extended interaction between the learned elites and the masses in the premodern world, one that demonstrates the totality and integrated nature of the political, social, and religious practices that made up that world. I hope this book will be a modest step in that direction.

* * * *

This book addresses one principal question. What was the range of relations between the learned elites and the popular classes from the late fifteenth to the early seventeenth centuries in Dijon, and how did they change over time? I aim to explore the parameters of these relations in a period in which the incorporation of the duchy of Burgundy into the French crown in 1477, the advent of the Reformation in the 1540s, the outbreak of the French Wars of Religion in 1562, and the rise of absolute monarchy in the early seventeenth century all impacted the relations between the elites and the masses. And more specifically, I want to know how ordinary people, and especially those working in the local wine industry, understood and engaged in the political and religious struggles of the period. Invariably, many ordinary people were the audiences for and often participants with the elites in many different cultural practices, especially in the realm of politics, religion, and material life. While there certainly were areas of premodern life where there was explicit confrontation and opposition between the elites and the masses, as this book will demonstrate, this does not exhaust the entire gamut of their relationships. For a start, neither elites nor ordinary people usually spoke with one

[6] For example, see Muchembled's revision of his own model in his *L'Invention de l'homme moderne: Culture et sensibilités en France du XVe au XVIIIe siècle* (Paris: Pluriel, 1994); and see Burke's revision of his ideas in the introduction to the revised edition of *Popular Culture in Early Modern Europe* (Aldershot: Scolar Press, rev. edn. 1994). Also see Burke's *The Historical Anthropology of Early Modern Italy: Essays on Perception and Communication* (Cambridge: Cambridge University Press, 1987).
[7] Roger Chartier, *The Cultural Uses of Print in Early Modern France*, trans., Lydia G. Cochrane (Princeton, NJ: Princeton University Press, 1987), 11.

common voice, so any oppositional model, such as the acculturation thesis, not only blurs and disguises divisions and tensions arising from within the elites and within the popular classes, but it also makes it next to impossible to see the lively cultural interaction going on between elites and ordinary folk. What this book will demonstrate is that their relationship was often symbiotic, with contributions made by those from above as well as below. Above all, I shall try to show that ordinary people did not always oppose or resist their social betters – that is, they were not always wielding "weapons of the weak" – and politics and religion were two particular areas of Burgundian life where this can easily be demonstrated.[8]

By politics, I mean a very broad spectrum of negotiations about the distribution of power by all those who claimed to have a stake in it. I do not claim that ordinary people ever wielded political power or even claimed to do so. But I take seriously their claims to have a stake in Burgundian society as well as their efforts to negotiate with those who did wield power in order to influence the policing and ordering of their community, whether participating in formal and ritualized political settings such as elections and royal entries, or in less formal settings such as work, home, and the tavern. And by religion, I mean all the religious beliefs and practices that made up the Christian experience for most lay Burgundians, both inside and outside the parish church. Thus, my goal here is not to make some vague and ambiguous claim of agency for ordinary people, but simply to make their voices heard in places where they are not usually heard.

If there is one unifying argument in the book that underscores the significant changes over time in the relations between the elites and popular classes, it is this: Burgundy's incorporation into the kingdom of France in the late fifteenth century as well as the advent of Protestantism in the first half of the sixteenth century opened up new avenues for participation in public life by ordinary Burgundians – especially by the vignerons[9] and others of the popular classes in the period of the Wars of Religion.

---

[8] See James C. Scott's *Weapons of the Weak: Everyday Forms of Peasant Resistance* (New Haven, CT: Yale University Press, 1985) as well as his *Domination and the Arts of Resistance: Hidden Transcripts* (New Haven, CT: Yale University Press, 1990). I fully accept Scott's very useful models, but I am arguing that not all cultural tools wielded by ordinary people were necessarily weapons aimed at resisting the powerful.

[9] The French word *vigneron* has no good English translation. While it is sometimes translated as vinegrower or vinedresser, these terms disguise the fact that in the sixteenth century a vigneron was involved in both viticulture – the growing of the grapes and the tending of the vines – and viniculture – the making of the wine from the harvested grapes. Thus, I have chosen to stick with the French word, which conveys both functions. And since I use it so often, I have normally not italicized it in the text.

Their repertory of actions expanded considerably in this period, which led to even greater interaction between elites and ordinary people. After the civil wars drew to a close, however, especially in the reign of Louis XIII (1610–1643), royal attempts to reduce the level of popular participation in public affairs increased in earnest. These efforts resulted in divisions and tensions within both the elites and the popular classes and transformed the relationship between crown and province that had existed since 1477.

* * * *

The book is divided into three chronological sections, with Part I focusing on the period following the murder of the last Valois Duke of Burgundy up to the outbreak of the religious wars following the emergence of Calvinism in the province (1477 to ca. 1560). Chapter 1 examines the political processes and means of wielding political power in Dijon after Burgundy's reincorporation into the French crown after 1477, showing how the evolution of the mayoral elections in the city reflected a growing participation by the vignerons and other non-elites in public affairs. Chapter 2 analyses the religious life of lay Burgundians on the eve of the Reformation. It examines two particular touchstones of Christian belief and practice in this period – the Eucharist and the Virgin Mary – and concludes with an analysis of the religious experiences that mattered most to lay Christians both inside and outside the parish church. The parish of St. Michel, one of seven parishes in Dijon and where so many of the city's vignerons lived and worshipped, takes center stage in this chapter. Chapter 3 examines the material life of the region and especially emphasizes the impact of the local wine industry. The chapter begins with an analysis of the origins of wine production in Burgundy, goes on to analyze the *métier* of a vigneron, and concludes with an analysis of urban life in the parish of St. Michel, examining in some detail the inhabitants on one particular street in the parish, Rue Vannerie, using tax rolls, market prices, and other sources to build up a picture of the structures of material life in the city.

Part II focuses on the period of the Wars of Religion in Burgundy, ca. 1560 to ca. 1595. Chapter 4 examines the advent of Protestantism in Burgundy and how the church, the city council, the sovereign courts, and the lay Catholics of the region responded to this challenge. It suggests that the consistently harsh treatment of Protestants – seizure of property and imprisonment or banishment – resulted in a province relatively free of religious violence. Unlike so many other similar cities such as Rouen, Lyon, Toulouse, and Bordeaux where Calvinism also took firm root, there was no serious effort by Protestants to seize Dijon by force in the early 1560s, nor was there a St. Bartholomew's massacre in Dijon in 1572. Chapter 5 begins by examining Burgundy's role as a bastion of the Catholic League from 1584 to 1595 and argues for a corrective to the traditional view that the Catholic League was an entirely polarizing and divisive organization run by its most militant members. It concludes by analyzing the ways in which the civil wars impacted the material lives of most Burgundians in the period, with an analysis of how a moral economy was supposed to work to insure stability and availability of foodstuffs as well as equilibrium in the economic sector, as well as another look at the Rue Vannerie and the ways in which the civil wars disrupted the material lives of many despite this moral economy. In Chapter 6 Dijon's parish records suggest that many of the most powerful voices among both the Leaguer and royalist camps were in fact moderates looking for a means of reconciliation and that they maintained the close ties they enjoyed with each other via marriage and god-parentage both before, during, and after the struggle of the early 1590s.

Part III focuses on the period from the end of the Wars of Religion up to the popular uprising known as the Lanturelu Riot of 1630. Chapter 7 addresses how the city of Dijon's generally positive relationship with the crown under Henry IV began to go awry from the very beginning of the reign of the young Louis XIII over the issue of mayoral elections, and how ordinary Burgundians coped with these changes. It also looks at the beginnings of systematic Catholic reform in Burgundy, with particular attention paid to the visit of François de Sales, who preached a series of Lenten sermons in Dijon in 1604, as well as his impact on the daughter of one of the presiding judges in Dijon's Parlement, the recently widowed Jeanne Frémyot, baroness de Chantal. Chapter 8 analyzes the further deterioration of relations between the crown and the city, beginning with the tensions created by Louis XIII's royal entry in January 1629 and ending in the popular uprising known as the Lanturelu riot in February–March 1630, a demonstration aimed specifically against Louis's tax policies and imposts on wine in Burgundy. Finally, I offer some general conclusions about politics, religion, and material life over the previous century and a half in the province, and how ordinary Burgundians' participation in public life – especially the vignerons – expanded rapidly during the Wars of Religion and then contracted sharply in the period immediately afterward.

PART I

Burgundy after the Valois Dukes
(1477 to ca. 1560)

CHAPTER I

Guarding the Gospels
Elections and Politics

When Charles the Bold, the last Valois duke of Burgundy, was found dead, lying in a ditch, beheaded, and impaled on a Swiss pike in January 1477 on a battlefield near Nancy in Lorraine, his ambitious efforts to resurrect the House of Burgundy were over. He was unable to restore this recently cobbled-together state to its former glory and influence that it had enjoyed under his predecessor, Duke Philip the Good. And due to his death without a male heir, the Burgundian state was soon to be divided up between the King of France and the Holy Roman Emperor. Indeed, Charles's only heir was his unmarried 19-year-old daughter, Mary, whom many Burgundians immediately proclaimed as their new sovereign duchess. King Louis XI of France wasted little time, however. On January 12, 1477 – just days after receiving news of the Burgundian defeat at Nancy – a royal army surrounded the city of Dijon and readied its artillery. The French king sent out peace feelers and promised to uphold all Burgundian liberties and privileges in return for recognizing his authority. "You know that you are part of the crown and kingdom [of France]," Louis reminded Etienne Berbisey, the mayor of Dijon.[1] In Ghent, the daughter of Charles the Bold wrote to the quickly assembled estates of Burgundy and urged them to hold out and resist the French king, claiming that "the duchy of Burgundy was never part of the domain of the French crown."[2] Above all, she appealed to their Burgundian loyalties, which many

---

[1] Joseph Garnier, ed., *Correspondance de la mairie de Dijon extraite des archives de cette ville*, 3 vols. (Dijon: Rabutot, 1868–1870), 1: 192, letter from Louis IX to the mayor and magistrates of Dijon, January 9, 1476/77.

[2] Mary of Burgundy and her supporters claimed that the duchy of Burgundy was a fief and not part of the royal domain, and thus inheritable by her from her father, Charles the Bold. This ran counter to the views of Louis XI, who claimed that the duchy of Burgundy was part of the royal domain and was given as an *apanage* by King John to the Valois dukes, and thus should revert back to the crown automatically upon the death of Charles the Bold. The legal situation was complex, however. See Paul Saenger, "Burgundy and the Inalienability of Appanages in the Reign of Louis XI," *French Historical Studies*, 10 (Spring 1977): 1–26.

contemporaries referred to simply as their *foy de Bourgogne*. When the
mayor of Dijon, Etienne Berbisey, and the president of Charles the Bold's
council, Jean Jouard, both recommended submission to the French king,
many of the popular classes in the duchy's capital demonstrated openly in
favor of rebellion and disobedience. French troops marched into Dijon,
nevertheless, only a fortnight later on February 1, 1477, accompanied by
open rebellion all over the duchy and county of Burgundy. The free county
of Burgundy – Franche-Comté – was the first to rebel, led by Jean de
Chalon, prince of Orange, as the towns of St-Jean-de-Losne and Auxonne
declared for Mary of Burgundy. By early spring the resistance had spread to
the duchy itself, as Autun, Nuits, Tournus, Avallon, and the Chalonnais
rallied to the cause of the *foy de Bourgogne*. The presence of royal troops in
Dijon itself prevented any outburst of anti-French sentiment there
until June, when a four-day demonstration of support for Mary of
Burgundy by artisans and vignerons turned violent. The so-called *mutemaque* of June 26–29 resulted in the assassination of Jean Jouard, who had
helped negotiate the submission to the king only five months earlier. And
although Dijon remained loyal to the French king despite the *mutemaque*,
other Burgundian towns were more recalcitrant. In 1478 uprisings in
support of Mary of Burgundy appeared in Beaune, Châtillon, and
Semur. Thus, Louis XI discovered that he would somehow have to reckon
with the *foy de Bourgogne*.[3]

The French king appeased the elites, most of whom supported the
overtures of Berbisey and Jouard in Dijon, with the announcement that
he would create a permanent Parlement and other sovereign courts in the
Burgundian capital. When Mary of Burgundy announced her engagement
to Maximilian of Austria in spring 1477, most Burgundians who were still
undecided quickly came to the conclusion that reintegration into the
French state offered far more benefits than domination by the
Habsburgs.[4] Two years later, in the summer of 1479, Louis XI made his
own royal entry into Dijon. He issued patent letters maintaining all their
traditional privileges, publicly swearing an oath in front of the high altar in

---

[3] AMD, B 164, fols. 84–85, January 1476/77; André Leguai, *Dijon et Louis XI, 1461–1483* (Dijon, 1947),
50–55; André Leguai, "La conquête de la Bourgogne par Louis XI," *Annales de Bourgogne*, 49 (1977):
87–92; Pierre Champion, *Louis XI*, 2 vols. (Paris: Honoré Champion, 1927), 2: 281–289; Dom
Urbain Plancher, *Histoire générale et particulière de Bourgogne*, 4 vols. (Dijon: Antoine De Fay,
1739–81), 4: 268–274; A. Voisin, "La mutemaque du 26 juin 1477: Notes sur l'opinion à Dijon au
lendemain de la Réunion," *Annales de Bourgogne*, 7 (1935): 337–356; and Pierre Gras, ed., *Histoire de
Dijon* (Toulouse: Privat, 1987), 101.
[4] Leguai, "La conquête de la Bourgogne par Louis XI," esp. 92; and Marie-Josèphe Reynes-Meyer,
"Dijon sous Charles VIII," *Annales de Bourgogne*, 50 (1978): 85–102.

the abbey church of St. Bénigne to maintain "all the privileges accorded to the inhabitants of Dijon par the former dukes of Burgundy, and he received in turn an oath of fidelity from all those assembled there."[5] The following year, in 1480, the king authorized the creation of a new Parlement in Burgundy, which would be situated in Dijon, to replace those of the Valois dukes, along with another sovereign court, the Chamber of Accounts (*Chambre des comptes*). Realizing that the magistracy who filled the highest offices in these courts would be beholden to him personally as royal officers, Louis sought to create his own clientele of loyal servants. And his successor Charles VIII did the same for municipal offices in 1491 when he granted the mayor of Dijon the right to the title of *vicomte-mayeur*, accompanied by the right of automatic ennoblement, though this title was only valid during the mayor's term in office and was not inheritable by his heirs.[6] Tensions would still remain between the duchy and the crown in the sixteenth century, tensions that would be exacerbated by the Reformation and Wars of Religion. It will be seen, however, that the root cause of these tensions was neither provincial particularism nor any difficulty in assimilating a distinctly Burgundian identity – the *foy de Bourgogne* – into a French identity.

For the elites of the duchy – the mayors and city councilors (*échevins*) of the major towns such as Dijon and Beaune, not to mention the new judges in the Parlement and other new sovereign courts – the key to Burgundy's loyalty to the crown was to build and maintain a strong alliance with the popular classes, that is, with the merchants, artisans, and vignerons who made up the bulk of the duchy's population. That job became easier in September 1513 when an imperial army of Swiss troops in the pay of both the Pope and Emperor Maximilien I lay siege to the city of Dijon, hoping to reunite the duchy with the county of Burgundy under the Emperor's jurisdiction as the legacy of his wife, Mary of Burgundy. The siege began on September 9, and for four solid days artillery shells rained down on the city, destroying numerous homes and buildings, and causing serious damage to the parish church of St. Michel as well as the nearby abbey of St. Etienne. The siege only ended on September 12 when the royal governor of Burgundy, Louis II de la Trémoïlle, a count, viscount, baron, and seigneur of various lands all over France, authorized a ransom of 400,000 *écus* (over a million *livres*) to be paid to the Swiss

---

[5] AMD, B 2, cote 45, "Confirmation des privilèges par Louis XI," July 31, 1479.
[6] AMD, B 11, cote 7 (carton), October 1491, "Lettres patentes de Charles VIII données à Laval par lesquelles, pour recompenser la ville de Dijon de son affection et de sa fidelité, il lui accorde l'annoblissement de tous les maires présans et àvenir."

commander, with 26,000 *livres* in the form of a tax levy as the city's part of her huge sum, with the rest to be paid by the king.[7] La Trémoïlle had to provide a number of hostages to the Swiss commander, including his own nephew and four *échevins* from Dijon's city council, to guarantee the payment. Although a religious procession of an eleventh-century wooden statue of the Virgin Mary by the clergy of Notre-Dame parish the day before on September 11 would in the years to come overshadow the ransom payment in the memory of the siege by the popular classes and even some of the city's elites, it was the survival experience that helped forge a common bond between Dijon's elites and popular classes.[8] But it would take more than a siege by a foreign army to maintain a common trust and build a longer term alliance between Dijon's elites and popular classes. Exactly how the city's elites forged such an alliance, and how the popular classes came to play a vital role in local politics in the first half of the sixteenth century form the focus of this chapter.

1.1   The Burgundian Capital

The origins of the city of Dijon are unusually murky. The first surviving description of the city, indeed the very first detailed mention of the city and its origins, appeared in Gregory of Tours's *History of the Franks* in the late sixth century:

> It is a fortress girded round with mighty walls and set in the centre of a pleasant plain. Its lands are fertile and so productive that after a single ploughing, when the fields are sown, a rich harvest soon follows. On its southern side it has the River Ouche, which teems with fish. A smaller stream runs down from the north [the River Suzon], entering through one gateway, running under a bridge and then flowing out again through another gate. This stream washes all the fortifications with its gentle waters

---

[7] The principal sources are AMD, B 168, fols. 267r–70v, September 6–11, 1513; Chabeuf, *Dijon: Monuments et souvenirs*, 81–87; Gras, ed., *Histoire de Dijon*, 106–107; Claude Courtépée and Edme Béguillet, *Description générale et particulière du duché de Bourgogne*, 4 vols. (Avallon: F. E. R. N., 3rd edn. 1967) 1: 225–227; and especially Jules Thomas, *La délivrance de Dijon en 1513 d'après les documents contemporains* (Dijon: Chez tous les libraires, 1898). These last three books make heavy use of two contemporary accounts of the siege written by Michel Boudet, bishop of Langres, and Pierre Tabourot, an auditor in the *Chambre des comptes* and a future mayor of Dijon. Also see Kathryn A. Edwards, *Families and Frontiers: Recreating Communities and Boundaries in the Early Modern Burgundies* (Leiden: Brill, 2002), 301–315; Laurent Vissière, *Louis II de la Trémoïlle (1460–1525): Sans poinct sortir hors de l'ornière* (Paris: Honoré Champion, 2008); and what is now the best overall survey of the siege, Laurent Vissière, Alain Marchandisse, and Jonathan Dumont, eds., *1513 l'année terrible: Le siège de Dijon* (Dijon: Éditions Faton, 2013).

[8] More about the siege of 1513 and its religious significance will be explained in Chapter 2.

and turns the mill-wheels round at wondrous speed outside the gate. The four entrances to the town are placed at the four quarters of the compass, and thirty-three towers adorn the circuit of the walls, which are made of squared stones rising to a height of twenty feet, with smaller stones placed above to reach in all some thirty feet, the whole being fifteen feet thick. Why Dijon is not elevated to the dignity of a bishopric I cannot imagine. Round about are excellent springs of water. To the west the hills are covered with fruitful vines, which yield so noble a Falernian-type wine that the inhabitants have been known to scorn a good Mâcon. The ancients say that Dijon was built by the Emperor Aurelian [emperor AD 270–275].[9]

Thus, even Gregory was forced to admit that the city's origins were based on hearsay. Nevertheless, he did visit Dijon often, and his sixth-century description of the city, replete with a reputation for good wine, would have been recognizable to sixteenth-century inhabitants. Gregory called Dijon a fortress (*castrum*) in his history, and it was the Latin form that was still in use in the sixteenth century to refer to the walled interior of the older city. By 1500 Dijon had expanded well outside the walls of the original *castrum*, which enclosed a square space of barely more than 300 meters on a side. In June 1137 a devastating fire destroyed virtually everything within the *castrum* and much outside as well. The Duke of Burgundy constructed a new and much larger fortified wall around the rebuilt *castrum* in 1153, increasing Dijon's size by nearly eight times to roughly one and a half square kilometers.[10] In 1478 King Louis XI insisted on adding a fortified enclosure with towers to the city walls, to enable Dijon to withstand an attack or siege. Called the Château by contemporaries, this fortification was constructed along the northwest side of the city wall. It was basically a large rectangle about 75 meters long, with four massive circular towers on the corners, the whole surrounded by a wide moat. With one side overlooking the city and the other overlooking the vast countryside beyond, the Château housed and safeguarded the city's arms and munitions.[11] The citizens of Dijon were levied a special tax of 6 *blancs* on each household within the city walls and 1 *gros* on each household outside the city walls in order to pay for its construction.[12] A map of the city drawn in 1574 by Edouard Brédin (see Figure 1.1) shows the relative dominance of the city by

[9] Gregory of Tours, *The History of the Franks*, trans. Lewis Thorpe (Harmondsworth, Middlesex: Penguin, 1974), 182–183.

[10] Pierre Gras, ed., *Histoire de Dijon* (Toulouse: Privat, 1987 edn.), 42–43.

[11] Henri Chabeuf, *Dijon: Monuments et souvenirs* (Dijon: Damidot, 1894), 101–112.

[12] AMD, B 165, fols. 28v–29r, December 23 and 30, 1478. One *gros* equaled one-twelfth of a *livre tournois* (or 1 *sous* 8 *deniers*). One *blanc* equaled one-fourth of a *gros* (or 5 d.).

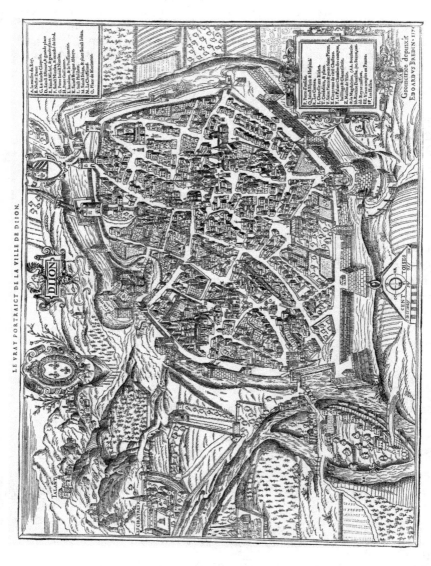

Figure 1.1 Engraving of a bird's eye view of the city of Dijon by Edouard Bredin, "Le vrai portraict de la ville de Dijon," 1574, courtesy of BMD

the Château, and it also helps explain why Dijon was able to withstand the siege of the Swiss in 1513.[13]

Brédin's map also shows how much Gregory of Tours's description of Dijon in the sixth century was still more or less accurate in the sixteenth century. The city walls had expanded all the way out to the River Ouche, which flowed in from the west and continued southward on its journey to the Sâone. The River Suzon is also visible flowing from the north through the middle of Dijon, until it went underground and then emptied into the Ouche in the southwest corner of the city. The vast areas of vineyards that Gregory described are still visible west of town, rising up to the village of Talant on a hill overlooking Dijon, as well as southward along the west bank of the Ouche. By the sixteenth century, Brédin's map also shows that there were vineyards on the eastern outskirts of Dijon. Also prominent is the Carthusian monastery, the Chartreuse de Champmol – labeled as *Les Chartreux on* Brédin's map – due west of the city, where the Valois dukes of Burgundy were buried in elaborately decorated tombs designed by the Flemish sculptors Claus Sluter and Claus de Werve as well as the Aragonese sculptor Jean de la Huerta.[14] What stands out above all on Brédin's map, however, is how by the sixteenth century Dijon had become a principal fortified town on the French frontier, with the massive Château dominating the city's fortifications.

Inside the walls, several edifices both sacred and secular dominated Dijon's skyline. Perhaps most impressive of all was the former Palace of the dukes of Burgundy with its striking tower in the very heart of the city. Referred to as the *Maison du Roi* following the incorporation of Burgundy into the French crown after 1477, it stood side by side with the Valois dukes' former chapel, the Sainte Chapelle, the official meeting place of the order of the Golden Fleece. After the royal palace and the Sainte Chapelle, the two most dominating structures in Dijon were the abbey churches of St. Bénigne, a Benedictine abbey in the extreme western quadrant of the city, named after the saint who was believed to have brought Christianity to Dijon in the second century, and St. Etienne, just across from the Sainte

[13] Edouard Brédin's map was originally produced for François de Belleforest's French translation of Sebastian Münster, *La Cosmographie universelle de tout le monde* (Paris: Nicolas Chesneau and Michel Sonnius, 1575). The printer Nicolas Chesneau also included it a few years later in Pierre de Saint-Julien, *De l'origine des bourgognons, et antiquité des estats de Bourgongne, deux livres* (Paris: Nicolas Chesneau, 1581). I have consulted copies of the latter in the BMD and in the Folger Shakespeare Library, Washington, DC. It is also online on Gallica: http://gallica.bnf.fr/ark:/12148/bpt6k1249377.

[14] The tombs of John the Fearless and his wife Margaret of Bavaria and that of Philip the Bold are now located in the Musée des Beaux Arts in Dijon.

Chapelle, which housed the cathedral chapter of the bishop of Langres when he often resided in Dijon. Brédin's map also clearly shows the seven parish churches of the city: St. Nicolas in the far northeastern corner; St. Michel in the extreme eastern quadrant of the city; St. Pierre, just inside the city wall in the southeastern quadrant; St. Philibert and St. Jean, both of which stood in the shadow of the abbey church of St. Bénigne in the extreme western part of the city; and in the city center the parish churches of Notre Dame, just behind the royal palace, and St. Médard, just south of the palace in the parish of the Parlement, the Chamber of Accounts, and the Bureau of Finances (see Figure 1.2). The parish churches of Notre Dame and St. Michel were the largest and most prominent. The former housed the famous statue of the Virgin that played such a prominent role in the siege of Dijon in 1513. The latter was rebuilt in the first three decades of the sixteenth century, replacing a much older and deteriorating medieval church.[15] Other prominent sites in Dijon shown by Brédin that would certainly have been well known to all inhabitants were the marketplace (*Les Halles*) in St. Nicolas parish and the Place du Morimont, the site of public executions, in St. Jean parish.

What is also striking is that Brédin's map also delineates the major social and occupational cohorts that made up the majority of Dijon's inhabitants. Dijon's tax rolls show that at the beginning of the sixteenth century there were 2,753 lay households in the city.[16] Members of the clergy and the nobility were not required to pay the *taille* or *taillon*, nor were a number of exempt elites; so, they are not included in this number.[17] But an approximate total population of around 12,000 inhabitants can be extrapolated from these figures, rising to about 15,000 inhabitants over the course of the sixteenth century. Brédin's map shows the sovereign courts of Parlement and the Chamber of Accounts in the city center, and along with the bailiwick courts and the Bureau of Finances, the legal profession and royal officers were well represented among Dijon's population. With upward of six presiding judges (*présidents*) and forty lesser judges (*conseillers*) in each of the sovereign courts, smaller though still significant numbers of judges in the lesser courts, perhaps fifty barristers (*avocats*) and a dozen solicitors (*procureurs*) licensed to present cases in each court, more

---

[15] For a closer look at the parish church of St. Michel, see Chapter 2.

[16] AMD, L 163, tax roll for 1500.

[17] The *taille* was a tax assessed on personal property in Burgundy, like taxes in most of northern France. The *taillon* was a supplemental tax introduced in 1549, specifically designed to prevent the billeting of troops on a town. Both were progressive taxes, and they provide a rough index of relative personal wealth in Dijon.

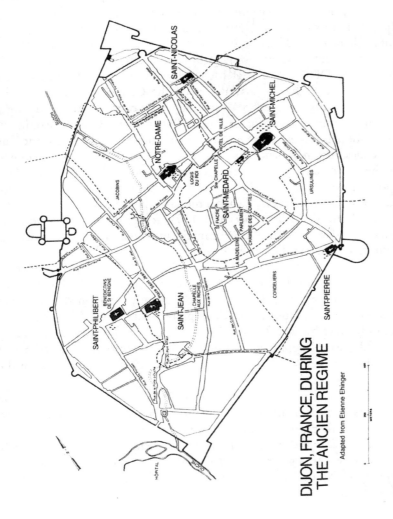

Figure 1.2 Parishes in sixteenth-century Dijon. © James R. Farr, *Hands of Honor: Artisans and Their World in Dijon, 1550–1650* (Ithaca: Cornell University Press, 1988), 82

than forty notaries in the city, along with countless other fiscal and administrative officials, the parish of St. Médard was heavily populated by the legal profession and royal officers. A second significant cohort of Dijon's population indicated by Brédin's map was the large number of clergy and other religious staff, despite the fact that Dijon was not the seat of a bishopric, a fact already lamented by Gregory of Tours nearly a thousand years earlier. Nevertheless, in addition to the two abbeys, the Sainte Chapelle, and the seven parish churches – each with its own ecclesiastical staff – there were a number of chapels, monasteries, and convents in Dijon. A collegial chapel with a hospital, founded by Dominique Le Riche in 1182 and called the Chapel aux Riches in the sixteenth century, housed a dean and nine canons. An even larger Dominican convent was founded in Dijon in 1237. Called Jacobins in France, because their first house was founded in Paris on the rue St. Jacques, its members had one of the largest and most decorated churches in the city, located near the parish church of Notre Dame. This Jacobin convent was also the site of Dijon's annual mayoral elections. In 1295 the Franciscans established a monastic house of Grey Friars in the city called the Cordeliers, because of the recognizable girdle worn by Franciscan friars. It had a large church and holdings in the parish of St. Pierre just inside the city walls in the extreme southern sector of the city. There was also a Carmelite order of White Friars in the parish of St. Jean, where the Berbisey family had its family tomb. Finally, just outside the city walls to the west was the already mentioned Carthusian monastery, the Chartreuse de Champmol, where the Valois dukes of Burgundy were buried. Thus, Dijon and its environs had an unusually large ecclesiastical population for a city without a bishopric. In theory at least, all these clerics and religious staff were under the jurisdiction of the bishop of Langres.[18]

A third major cohort of inhabitants in Dijon included wealthy textile merchants, professionals such as doctors of medicine and bankers, and surgeons, apothecaries, booksellers, and other major retailers. Collectively referred to as *bourgeois* by contemporaries, these inhabitants were relatively few in number, though they wielded considerable economic and political influence in Dijon. They tended to reside in the parishes of Notre Dame and St. Jean, which were the two wealthiest parishes in the city. Also

---

[18] See Chabeuf, *Dijon: Monuments et souvenirs*, 161–165 for the abbey of St. Etienne, 176–191 for the abbey of St. Bénigne, 207–217 for the Sainte Chapelle, 231–261 for the seven parish churches, and 261–278 for the other convents, chapels, and monasteries.

involved in trade and commerce was a fourth cohort: the numerous prosperous artisans in the various craft trades. Most of the master artisans had formed guilds in the Middle Ages, when Dijon became a *ville jurande*, a town regulated by incorporated cohorts of workers, or sworn trades. Each year in Dijon the newly elected mayor would appoint several master artisans from each trade as a *juré*, or sworn, member of his particular guild (only the goldsmiths and pastry cooks elected their own *jurés*). These *juré* artisans swore an oath to regulate and police their particular trade guild, and each master artisan was required to swear an oath to maintain the regulations of the guild, including the policing of their métier by the *jurés*. In return, the mayor gave the guild of each trade a monopoly to sell the particular product it manufactured or the service it rendered, and the *jurés* got to keep a portion of the fines they levied in the policing of their own trade.[19] Artisans, in fact, made up the single largest cohort of Dijon's population. As the city's tax rolls make clear, by the mid-sixteenth century more than a third of all known heads of households in Dijon were artisans.[20] Moreover, in terms of wealth they were widely distributed across the socioeconomic spectrum. Since both the *taille* and the *taillon* were based on personal wealth, the city's tax rolls give a fair indication of how artisans' wealth compared to the rest of the city. In 1556 for example, the tax rolls show that 35.1 percent of all Dijon's artisans ranked in the bottom 40 percent of the population based on their personal wealth. Nearly half of the artisans – 47.2 percent – ranked between the 41st and the 80th percentile; while 17.8 percent of the city's artisans ranked in the top 20 percent of the population based on wealth. As James Farr has noted, economically speaking, Dijon's artisans were "a middling sort."[21]

Finally, a fifth major cohort that made up Dijon's population was the large number of vignerons, who worked in the vineyards outside the city wall and then made the wine from their harvest. In the early sixteenth century vignerons made up roughly one quarter of all lay heads of

---

[19] James R. Farr, *Hands of Honor: Artisans and Their World in Dijon, 1550–1650* (Ithaca, NY: Cornell University Press, 1988), 16–17 and 29–31; Henri Hauser, "L'Organisation du travail à Dijon et en Bourgogne au XVIe et dans la première moitié du XVIIe siècle," in Hauser, ed., *Les débuts du capitalisme* (Paris: Alcan, 1927).

[20] Farr, *Hands of Honor*, especially 76–86; and the same author's "Consumers, Commerce, and the Craftsmen of Dijon: The Changing Social and Economic Structure of a Provincial Capital, 1450–1750," in Philip Benedict, ed., *Cities and Social Change in Early Modern France* (London: Unwin Hyman, 1989), 134–173.

[21] Farr, *Hands of Honor*, 91–92; and AMD, L 170, tax roll for 1556. One should keep in mind, however, that most of the very wealthiest inhabitants were exempt from the *taille* and *taillon*. In 1556, 148 heads of household out of 2,652 (5.6 percent) were exempt and not included in the percentiles shown in this section. They were far wealthier than even the wealthiest master artisans.

household in the city: 718 out of 2,753 households in 1500 (26.1 percent) and 606 out of 2,493 households in 1523 (24.3 percent).[22] The vignerons' numbers remained pretty constant as the city grew throughout the sixteenth century. So, though their overall percentage of the total number of lay households declined to about 20 percent by the time of the religious wars, it is clear that viticulture and viniculture were important to Dijon's economy, as both Gregory of Tours's description and Edouard Brédin's map suggest.[23] The tax rolls also make clear that, like Dijon's artisans, the vignerons were widely spread across the economic spectrum. Although nearly half (47.6 percent) of Dijon's vignerons ranked in the bottom 40 percent of the population based on their personal wealth, a further 43.3 percent ranked between the 41st and the 80th percentile, and 9.1 percent ranked in the top 20 percent of Dijon's population based on wealth.[24] While many of the poorer vignerons tended to congregate in St. Philibert parish, some of the most wealthy and prosperous lived in St. Michel parish.[25] And as would become clear once Protestantism emerged in Burgundy, the most politically militant and religiously conservative vignerons were those who resided in St. Michel parish. Like the artisans, the vignerons were also incorporated as a sworn trade, though without a guild. The newly elected mayor appointed *jurés* vignerons each year just as with the other artisanal trades, and they helped the Hôtel de Ville police and maintain the vineyards under Dijon's jurisdiction outside the city walls. Their duties became especially important as the *vendange*, or grape harvest, approached each September.[26]

The capital city of Burgundy, then, was a city of roughly 12,000 inhabitants at the beginning of the sixteenth century. Located on the Ouche River, which flowed into the Sâone, and only 35 km overland from the source of the Seine, Dijon served as a major crossroads in the major trade and commercial routes between Lyon and Paris. It was also the gateway from France to Franche-Comté, Savoy, and Geneva. Though dominated predominantly by elites – lawyers, royal officers, some influential clergy, and wealthy bourgeois merchants – the city also contained significant numbers of artisans and vignerons, who made up more than half its population. How these two groups interacted, the elites on the one hand and the artisans and vignerons on the other, was a key determinant in

---

[22] AMD, L 159, tax roll for 1500 and L 164, tax roll for 1523.
[23] Also see Claude Tournier, "Le vin à Dijon de 1430 à 1560: Production et commerce," *Annales de Bourgogne*, 22 (1950): 7–32.
[24] AMD, L 170, tax roll for 1556; and Farr, *Hands of Honor*, 92.   [25] See Chapter 3.
[26] For more about the grape harvest, see Chapter 3.

maintaining the polity of the city. While virtually all the political authority in Dijon was wielded and controlled by the elites through the Hôtel de Ville, the lowers classes both participated in and believed they had a role to play in the political process. If politics can be defined as the negotiation of power by those who claimed to have a stake in the polity, then the artisans and vignerons in Dijon were clearly just as much a part of the world of politics as royal officers, judges in the king's sovereign courts, and the mayor and *échevins* who served in the Hôtel de Ville. Understanding the functions and inner workings of the Hôtel de Ville, in fact, is the key to understanding what kinds of political participation the lower classes enjoyed in Dijon in the sixteenth century.

1.2   The Authority of the Hôtel de Ville

According to Bernard Chevalier, Dijon was one of 190 towns and cities in the kingdom in the sixteenth century, out of a total of 435 (43 percent), which were governed by a *corps de ville*, or a small body of men who governed and policed the city on behalf of the whole. In the north of France, as in Dijon, these men were usually called *échevins* (aldermen), while in the south they were often called consuls, though in many places they were referred to as *prud'hommes* (prudent men), *bonnes hommes* (good men), or *conseillers* (councilors). Many, though not all, also had a mayor, or, as in Paris, a *prévôt des marchands*. In this sense, Dijon was very much like many other towns and cities all across France.[27]

The public symbol of political authority in the sixteenth century for Dijon's Hôtel de Ville – that is, the mayor and *échevins* – was not a mace, a coat of arms, a seal, or any other secular symbol. There was, to be sure, an official seal of the commune of Dijon, but few inhabitants of the city were likely to see it unless they were called into the Hôtel de Ville for official business. Much better known to all the city's residents, however, was something called the Book of Gospels (*Livre des évangiles*), a decorated and hand-painted image of the first fourteen verses of the gospel of St. John, painted on sheepskin glued to two hinged pieces of chestnut wood (see Figure 1.3). Commissioned by the mayor and *échevins* in February 1488, this image of the gospels was designed and created by Hennequin Cougny.[28] Measuring roughly 31 cm high and 22 cm

[27] Bernard Chevalier, *Les bonnes villes de France du XIVe au XVIe siècle* (Paris: Aubier, 1982), 199–202.
[28] AMD, B 95 (*carton*), February 16, 1487/88; Yolanta Zaluska, *Manuscrits enluminés de Dijon* (Paris: Centre Nationale de la Recherche Scientifique, 1991), 264–265; and Chabeuf, *Dijon: Monuments et souvenirs*, 319. This icon is now housed in the Archives municipales in Dijon, where it is occasionally on public display.

Figure 1.3 The gospel of St. John, late fifteenth century, courtesy of AMD

wide folded up, when opened this icon of the gospel of St. John revealed two striking religious images. On the left-hand side was a hand-colored painting of Christ on the cross, flanked by a mourning Virgin Mary and St. John the Evangelist. On the right-hand side was an equally striking depiction of the Virgin of Pity, holding the dead body of Christ in her arms. Surrounding these two images was the text of the first fourteen verses of the Gospel according to St. John in the Latin of the Vulgate Bible, opening with the words, *"In principio erat Verbum et Verbum erat apud Deum et Deus erat Verbum.* (In the beginning was the Word, and the Word was with God and the Word was God.)" The only clue that this artifact was indeed a symbol of secular political authority was the presence of two small and inconspicuous red chevrons less than 2 cm high at the bottom of each page: the coat of arms of the commune of Dijon. This enfolding together of political and religious authority was commonplace in sixteenth-century Europe, as political leaders of every rank and estate, not just kings and princes at the top of the social and political hierarchy, legitimated their authority by association with the Almighty. If the Duke of Burgundy's or the king's joyous entry into Dijon could be accompanied by someone dressed up as Jesus Christ, then the mayor and city councilors could certainly justify their own authority through reference to painted images of Christ's dead body, both on the cross and in his mother's arms. The underlying message was that God mandated both the state and public order: to oppose this authority was to oppose God. Thus, religion and politics were explicitly linked in the premodern world. It was impossible for any contemporary, of whatever social rank or estate, to make sense of one without recourse to the other. In sixteenth-century France politics was by necessity couched in religious terms, and it was both practiced and understood through religious rituals. After 1520, in fact, the mayor and *échevins* began each meeting of the city council with a Mass, designating a special chapel and altar at the Hotel de Ville and paying a chaplain for this very purpose.[29] Thus, the mixing together of the spiritual and the political was both intentional and inevitable in the premodern world. And the public display of the city's chief political artifact, the Book of the Gospels, in a religious procession, for example, or at the annual elections for mayor, expressed urban authority through religious iconography. It was a subtle yet unmistakable way of perpetuating the idea that public order was also godly order. This icon, then, became very familiar to the inhabitants of the city of Dijon because of the numerous public events at which it was displayed.

The Book of Gospels was prominently displayed in each of the three principal spheres in which Dijon's mayor and city council wielded authority: administration, criminal justice, and the military. These powers were originally granted to the mayor and *échevins* in a charter granted by Hugues III, Duke of Burgundy, and confirmed by King Philip Augustus in 1183. And in April 1187 this charter was presented to the city council, outlining their various privileges and liberties.[30] The mayor wielded the greatest authority on the council, as he was obviously the chief administrator, judge, and military captain for the entire commune of Dijon.[31] Although each of these three areas was important, the administration and jurisdiction of the city, what contemporaries called *police*, occupied the most time and energy of the members of the Hôtel de Ville. As has already been mentioned, the *échevins* oversaw and administered the various artisan trades in the city through the *juré* artisans of each trade guild, whom they appointed at the beginning of each new administrative year in June. The council enforced both the guilds' lucrative monopolies in their respective trades and the rules each member was required to uphold. The council's policing of the local

[29] AMD, B 170, fol. 14v, November 16, 1520.
[30] AMD, B 1 (carton), Charter of Dijon (1183); also see Thierry Dutour, *Une société de l'honneur: Les notables et leur monde à Dijon à la fin du Moyen Age* (Paris: Honoré Champion, 1998), 62; and Gras, ed., *Histoire de Dijon*, 48–49.
[31] Joseph Garnier, ed., *Correspondence de la mairie de Dijon*, 3 vols. (Dijon: Rabutot, 1868–1870), 1: xi.

economy was most visible in the ways in which they intervened in the
workshops of Dijon's bakers and butchers to insure that there was enough
food for all its citizens to eat. For a start, the city councilors set the bread
prices for what the standard one-pound loaf of white bread could be sold for
in the local bakeries; the less desirable brown bread, or *pain bis*, was usually
sold in two-pound loaves. This was done through an assize, in which the
councilors periodically – though not often enough to suit most of Dijon's
bakers – assessed the cost of various grades of wheat and other cereal grains,
then after allowing a certain margin for the baker's costs and profit, determined what a loaf of bread should cost.[32] The problem for the bakers,
however, was not only that the assizes were infrequent, but that the city
council also tried to keep the cost of a one-pound loaf stable despite
fluctuating and usually rising costs for rent, fuel, and wheat. For example,
a one-pound loaf of white bread was set at 4 d. in 1535, yet it was still set at 4 d.
per loaf more than twelve years later.[33] In order to survive in a period of rising
inflation, bakers were forced to undertake various measures of deception.
The most common was selling loaves that were several ounces light (*pains
legers*), for which bakers were fined repeatedly. Even though the fines were
usually significant – between 10 s. and 40 s., or the price of 120–480 loaves of
white bread[34] – they were not enough of a deterrence, as nearly every baker in
the city was fined at one time or another. On August 22, 1550, for just one
example, twenty-nine bakers were arrested and fined for selling underweight
bread. This was not unusual, however, as many bakers were fined over and
over again, suggesting that the city council's fines were not enough of
a deterrence. Nicolas Roze, for example, who was one of the twenty-
nine bakers fined in August 1550, was fined again in August 1554 and
in May and July 1557 for selling underweight bread. Thus, it seems that
the gains outweighed the fines for contravening the rules set by the city
council.[35] So the policing of the sale and distribution of bread in the city,
while well intentioned, was not always as efficacious as it was supposed
to be.

   The authority of the Hôtel de Ville to regulate commerce in Dijon was
nevertheless a vital part of the councilors' responsibilities. Much more
severe fines were levied against anyone who was caught practicing a trade
before they were admitted to the appropriate guild. In 1553, for example,
the vigneron Claude Begin thought he could make his own wine barrels

---

[32] See Farr, *Hands of Honor*, 38.
[33] AMD, B 179, fol. 56v, November 6, 1535, and B 186, fol. 16r, July 1, 1548.
[34] AMD, B 189 fol. 42r, June 27, 1551; B 191, fols. 47r and 51r, July 13 and 18, 1553.
[35] AMD, B 188, fols. 66r–67v, August 22, 1550; also see Farr, *Hands of Honor*, 40.

cheaper than the asking price of the master barrel-makers. When he was caught using the illicit barrels, he was fined the sum of 100 s. Later that same year he was also accused of doctoring his wine.[36] Butchers were also fined as often as bakers. They were often cited for disposing of the blood and entrails of their slaughtered animals in the Suzon River, which flowed through the butchers' quarter of the city. The councilors insisted that butchers take all their refuse and dispose of it outside the city walls.[37] The most egregious contravention of the rules set by the city council, however, was the butchers' refusal to sell meat by the pound. Instead, they preferred to sell portions of meat by the piece cut from the carcass, which they could individually price themselves. Like the bakers selling light-weight loaves, butchers selling meat by the piece rather than by the pound was a persistent problem that fines alone could never completely eliminate.[38]

The Hôtel de Ville also policed Dijon's wine trade. Although much more about the day-to-day growing and tending of the vines as well as the making and distribution of wine will be analyzed in later chapters, suffice it to say that Dijon's mayor and *échevins* were involved in virtually every step of the process. If the grapes were threatened during the growing season – whether by the weather, by disease, or by various pests, including various insects as well as birds – the council invariably asked the city's clergy to organize religious processions to deal with the problem. And the councilors often participated in these processions themselves. And because certain insects called *écrivains* (because they left their written signatures on the grape leaves they feasted upon) as well as caterpillars attacked the vines almost like clockwork every spring and summer, these religious processions were regular occurrences.[39]

The city council also controlled the *vendange*, or wine harvest, every September. Indeed, in the weeks preceding the harvest, the *juré* vignerons met with the council and advised them as to the exact dates on which each parcel of vines surrounding the city should be harvested. The Hôtel de Ville appointed a large number of guards called *vigniers* to

---

[36] AMD, B 191, fol. 65v and 130r, August 8 and December 19, 1553.

[37] AMD, B 189, 75r, July 24, 1551; and B 190, fols. 217v–218r, April 7, 1553.

[38] Farr, *Hands of Honor*, 41–43.

[39] See for example, AMD, B 189, fols. 222r–v, June 8 and 10, 1552. Also see AMD, D 11 (*liasse*), June 10, 1540; B 181, fols. 151v–152r, July 27–30, 1540; B 190, fol. 258v, June 9, 1553; B 191, fol. 185v, April 10, 1554; and B 191, fol. 214r, June 5, 1554, among numerous other examples. The deliberations of the city council demonstrate that nearly every year religious processions were ordered as a remedy against insects or other natural threats to the vines. For more on the beasts that plagued the vines, see Chapter 3.

watch over the vineyards day and night leading up to the wine harvest, and they announced the exact dates on which harvesting could commence. These dates, called the *bans de vendange*, were strictly enforced. Anyone caught harvesting too soon or otherwise contravening the bans was fined, publicly humiliated, or even beaten.[40] Just one example among many that could be cited is that of Perrenot Chambellan, who was found guilty of stealing grapes from a vineyard during the banns. In addition to giving him a stiff fine, the executor of high justice paraded Chambellan through the city wearing a hat made of grapes and forced him to sit atop two wine barrels for three hours, further increasing the public ridicule against him.[41] In 1538 a monk from the priory of Larrey was fined 90 *livres* for harvesting grapes from a vineyard before the banns allowed, and for using a soldier to threaten one of the *vigniers* guarding the vines.[42] After the grape harvest was completed the council then regulated the price for which wine could be sold, just like bread and meat.

The Hôtel de Ville's administrative powers to intervene into the lives of ordinary inhabitants of the city extended well beyond regulating the food and wine trades. They fined inhabitants for putting garbage and human waste into the street or throwing it into the river.[43] Whenever the plague broke out, as it frequently did, the councilors could quarantine the entire city – preventing anyone from entering or exiting. They also quarantined individual residences housing plague victims and required their owners to display a black and white cross on the exterior as a sign of contamination.[44] If particularly serious cases broke out in individual households, the city could even order the inhabitants to leave town, as happened in 1553 to a vigneron and his wife and children who lived on the rue du Champs-Damas. His entire family was expelled from Dijon for six weeks "on pain of being hanged and strangled."[45] The councilors also decided who could be armed in the city. Only nobles and soldiers were allowed to carry "swords, daggers, knives, pistols, or any other *bâtons*" within the city on pain of confiscation of the weapon and a fine of 100 s.[46] In 1555 the councilors even

---

[40] See AMD, B 165, fols.65–7r; B 167, fols. 138r–v, September 12, 1498; B 168, fols. 14v–5r, August 1, 1500; and B 185, fols. 69v–71v, August 10, 1547 for some specific examples, but the city council deliberations record that *vigniers* were appointed and the *bans de vendange* were publicly announced every year in a formal ceremony. For more on this ceremony, see Chapter 7.

[41] AMD, B 173, fol. 71v, September 16, 1529.   [42] ADCO, B II 360/32, August 31, 1538.

[43] AMD, B 188, fol. 203v, May 12, 1551; and B 189, fols. 76v–77r, July 28, 1551 among many others.

[44] AMD, B 190, fol. 248r, May 16, 1553; B 191, fol. 226, June 9, 1554; B 192, fols. 16v, 88r, and 268r, June 22, and July 10, 1554 and March 10, 1554/5; B 193, fols. 34r and 42v, July 16 and 23, 1555; and B 196, fols. 130r–132r, March 1, 1558/9 among many others.

[45] AMD, B 190, fol. 213r, March 24, 1552/3.   [46] AMD, B 189, fol. 67v, July 17, 1551.

required all householders to build a latrine in their homes for better sanitation and the prevention of disease. If they did not already have one, they were given ten days to build the latrine or risk a whopping fine of 10 *livres tournois*.[47] And while the councilors did not have the authority to tax Dijon's citizens on their own – that belonged, in theory at least, to the *élus* of the provincial estates of Burgundy and the king – the Hôtel de Ville did, in fact, supervise the collection of taxes in the city and had a great deal of influence in deciding who was exempt from taxation at both the poorest and the wealthiest ends of the social scale. When the king asked the mayor for a donation toward the fortification of the city, for example, it was up to the councilors to assess and collect the monies.[48] In short, their administration and policing of the city extended to virtually every part of urban life. And as the Protestant Reformation emerged in the first half of the sixteenth century, this purview would also begin to extend into the Church.

The second major area of the Hôtel de Ville's authority was in civil and criminal justice. The dukes of Burgundy had long since given the power of seigneurial justice to the mayor and *échevins* within the city of Dijon and its outlying villages, and this arrangement continued after 1477 when Burgundy was restored to the jurisdiction of the French crown. As such, the city council was the court of first instance for all criminal cases in the city, and this included capital cases such as murder. Although all capital cases that resulted in conviction were automatically appealed to the Parlement of Dijon, the council's role as the gateway to the criminal justice system in the city gave it powers of enforcement that went well beyond its administrative powers. To be sure, most of the council's judicial functions dealt with the usual variety of petty crime and urban violence, with theft being the most common crime. Punishment for these crimes could nevertheless be severe. Ritual public shaming and banishment from the city was the normal punishment. An apprentice cobbler named Petit Jean stole the key to his master's wine cellar and raided it on several occasions. When he had confessed to this, the councilors sentenced him to be bound on the scaffold for four hours on a Saturday morning, and then banished from the city for two years.[49] Repeat offenders were dealt with even more severely, as they could be banished for terms of ten or twenty years, or in the most egregious cases, forever.[50] Banishment was hardly a severe punishment, however, for nonnatives who were caught stealing in Dijon. One

---

[47] AMD, B 193, fols. 101v–102r, October 25, 1555.
[48] AMD, B 194, fol. 34r–v, July 3, 1556, when the king asked the mayor to levy the sum of 450 *livres* for the city's defenses.
[49] AMD, B 168, fol. 45r, January 26, 1501/2.   [50] AMD, B 168, fols. 46r–47r, February 24, 1501/2.

outsider from St. Symphorien, for example, who was convicted of multiple thefts, was sentenced to be "thrashed and beaten with birch-rods throughout the city, then to be banished forever from Dijon and its environs after having one ear cut off."[51] And if thieves violated the sacred spaces of Dijon's churches, the punishment was still more severe. When a goldsmith named Jean Richard was convicted of various thefts and "sacrileges" in two churches in Dijon, for example, he was condemned "to be hanged and strangled on the gibbet in Dijon."[52]

Brawling and fighting were other common forms of violence that came before the council, with convictions resulting in steep fines. When three vignerons from St. Philibert parish beat up one of their companions named Jean Colasson in 1537, for example, they were fined 10 *livres* each, or nearly twice their monthly wages.[53] That same year three other vignerons were fined 50 *livres* each for attacking and beating up a *vignier* named Humbert Boissière, leaving him injured.[54] Cases like this of simple assault were very common in the council's court. Often the victims and the accused were close acquaints, either neighbors living on the same street or comrades who worked together. Many of the accused claimed that they were only trying to get the victims to pay back money that had been lent to them.[55]

Women were also occasionally tried in the criminal court of the city council, though usually not for fighting. They were most often accused of either procuring for prostitution or infanticide, and if found guilty the consequences were serious. Prostitution itself was not illegal in Dijon until 1561, when it was finally outlawed all over France by a royal ordinance of the young king Charles IX.[56] The city ran its own municipal brothel, in fact, called the Grande Maison on the rue du Grand Champs de Mars in St. Nicholas parish, which was closed for good in 1563 due to the royal ban. Moreover, there were seven municipal bath-houses where prostitution also flourished. All told, Dijon had somewhere in the region of 100 prostitutes working in the city at the beginning of the sixteenth century. As the historian Jacques Rossiaud has noted, "prostitution had a function" that was both social and moral, since it "contributed to the defense of collective order."[57] It was clearly illegal to attempt to procure girls or

---

[51] AMD, B 166, fol. 67r, March 28, 1487/8.   [52] AMD, B 166, fol. 59r, September 3, 1487.
[53] ADCO, B II 360/32, June 29, 1537.   [54] ADCO, B II 360/32, November 11–13, 1537.
[55] ADCO, B II 360/32, April 13, 1533/4 and October 29, 1537 for other examples.
[56] James R. Farr, *Authority and Sexuality in Early Modern Burgundy, 1550–1730* (Oxford and New York, 1995), 139–140.
[57] See the work of Jacques Rossiaud, the historian who has studied prostitution in Dijon most thoroughly: *Medieval Prostitution*, trans. Lydia Cochrane (Oxford: Blackwell, 1988), esp. 4–10 and 32–63 (quote on 42–43); as well as the same author's "Prostitution, Youth, and Society in the Towns of Southeastern France in the Fifteenth Century," in Robert Forster and Orest Ranum, eds.,

young women into prostitution, however, and the city councilors made every effort to try to crack down on such activity. The crime of *maquerelage*, or pimping, was not just a male preserve, and women were just as frequently found guilty of this crime. Punishment was swift and such women were usually banished from the city and its environs for a period of ten years.[58] Women found guilty of infanticide, however, were usually dealt a more lethal punishment. Given the legality of prostitution, unwanted pregnancies were hardly uncommon. Moreover, combined with high infant mortality, still-births, and abandoned babies who died before being found, the mayoral court often had difficulty in determining whether the mother of a dead newborn was guilty of infanticide or not. And the records suggest that the punishment was especially harsh, because the unfortunate murdered infants never had a chance to be baptized. A typical example is a woman in 1506 who was condemned "to be decapitated" and to have her head and body exposed on the gibbet for public display. Moreover, all her goods and property were confiscated "for having thrown her baby into the latrines without being baptized."[59]

More women were victims of crime, however, than were accused. And the most common crime committed against women was sexual violence. Jacques Rossiaud has demonstrated that only a fraction of the rapes that occurred in fifteenth- and sixteenth-century Dijon ever got reported. Either out of fear or shame, or because of a private settlement with the attacker, most women simply failed to make an official complaint. Rossiaud estimates that perhaps only one-fourth to one-fifth of all crimes of sexual violence ever got reported to the authorities. What did get reported, and thus what shows up in the criminal records in Dijon, is an average of about 20 "public" rapes per year, public in the sense that there were witnesses who could testify against the attackers. And the overwhelming majority of these – 80 percent of the total – were gang rapes committed by between two and fifteen attackers. These men were almost always unmarried, from Dijon rather than outsiders, overwhelmingly the sons of respectable citizens from every social level but especially artisans, and most were between 18 and 25 years of age. Only about one-tenth of them were truly classified as thugs or outlaws.[60] Their female victims were overwhelmingly widows, wives temporarily separated from their husbands, or young unmarried girls. Most were between the ages of 15 and 30, that is,

Deviants and the Abandoned in French Society: Selections from the Annales, vol. 4, trans. Elborg Forster and Patricia Ranum (Baltimore, MD: Johns Hopkins University Press, 1978).

[58] AMD, B 168, fol. 91v, July 12, 1504.   [59] AMD, B 168, fol. 120v, September 4, 1506.

[60] Rossiaud, *Medieval Prostitution,* 11–26; and the same author's "Fraternités de jeunesse et niveaux de culture dans les villes du sud-est à la fin du moyen âge," *Cahiers d'histoire,* 1–2 (1976): 67–102.

of marriageable age, and unlike their male attackers they were overwhelmingly from the least affluent groups: servant girls or the wives or daughters of day laborers.[61]

What motivated such behavior, especially given that legal prostitution in Dijon allowed for more legitimate sexual activity for young, unmarried men? According to Rossiaud, these gang rapes were committed by members of unmarried men's brotherhoods, or youth abbeys, which "were institutions for conserving and passing on the most traditional sort of misogyny. They contributed to keeping women subservient, at least in the middle and lower levels of society ... Anonymously and thorough violence, they embodied a true counter-force controlling marriage."[62] The mayoral court treated these young men much like municipal prostitutes, who served a social and moral function to help maintain public order. Their punishment was typically light, small fines without any public humiliation or banishment from the city. Although they often committed unspeakable acts of brutality against their female victims, the members of the court tended to accept that these young men never intended to maim or kill their victims.[63] What concerns us here, however, is that the members of the Hôtel de Ville spent much of their time and expended much of their authority in regulating and policing criminal justice in Dijon, all part of an effort to uphold a viable notion of public order. Criminal behavior of all types was perceived as a significant threat to that order, and as a result, all mayors and *échevins* in Dijon took their judicial responsibilities very seriously.

The third and final principal area in which the Hôtel de Ville wielded its authority was as head of the local militia (*la milice bourgeoise*). The mayor was automatically captain of the local militia in Dijon in the absence of the royal governor and lieutenant-general, which was most of the time, and this gave him the power to enforce both administrative and judicial decisions, as well as to maintain order both in wartime as well as peacetime. The militia was composed of able-bodied male citizens of Dijon, not professional soldiers, and it was organized at the parish level, with each parish having a captain, a lieutenant, and an ensign. The mayor could muster the militia at any time, whether to defend the city from enemies from without, or to quell a riot or maintain order within the city walls. More routinely, the male inhabitants who made up the militia also served

---

[61] Rossiaud, *Medieval Prostitution*, 27–28. For more on youth abbeys, see Natalie Z. Davis, "The Reasons of Misrule," in her *Society and Culture in Early Modern France* (Stanford, CA: Stanford University Press, 1975), 97–123.
[62] Rossiaud, *Medieval Prostitution*, 25–26.   [63] Ibid., 12, n. 4.

as night-watchmen on guard duty. Again, their function was not just to be on the lookout for attackers from outside, but also to maintain order within the city. Nighttime crime was always a problem, and the night-watch was often all that stood between the inhabitants and the theft or destruction of their property. Members of the militia were responsible for maintaining their own arms, though during wartime the city council sometimes provided arms for the inhabitants.[64] Nobles, clergymen, and older males were generally exempt from militia and night-watch duty, but in times of war all such exemptions were abandoned, with even the elderly and the retired having to pitch in for the security of the city.[65] All these efforts required the city council to keep track of arms, gunpowder, and munitions within the city, with regular inventories of inhabitants' arms a necessity, again especially in wartime.[66]

This authority did not give the mayor and *échevins* autonomous military authority in Dijon, however, as the recently constructed Château was outside their jurisdiction. The royal governor of Burgundy,[67] a powerful nobleman, appointed the captain of the Château, who theoretically answered only to the king through the royal governor, or in the governor's absence, the lieutenant-general of Burgundy. All the arms, powder, and munitions in the Château belonged to the king. And while Louis XI originally constructed the Château as a means of defending Dijon as well as the French frontier against the Habsburgs, the Hôtel de Ville had no authority over this fortification. To be sure, the captain of the Château and the mayor usually worked closely together in times of duress; the siege of Dijon by the Swiss in September 1513 was a case in point. As long as the city and the king were pursuing common policies, the relationship was generally a cordial one. There was always the possibility of disagreement, however, as both the king and the Hôtel de Ville would soon discover during the civil wars of the second half of the sixteenth century. Ultimately, the inhabitants of Dijon would demand that the king tear down this fortification, as it seemed as much of a threat as a protector to those who lived in the city.[68]

---

[64] AMD, B 195, fols. 112r and 143r, October 25, 1557 and January 18, 1557/8.

[65] AMD, B 195, fols. 62r, 90v, and 130v, August 17, September 27, and December 17, 1557.

[66] AMD, B 195, fol. 132v, December 28, 1557.

[67] Philippe Chabot, seigneur de Brion, was governor from 1526 to 1543; Claude de Lorraine, count of Guise, was governor from 1543 to 1550; Claude de Lorraine, duke of Aumale, was governor from 1550 to 1573; and Charles de Lorraine, duke of Mayenne, was governor from 1573 to 1595. These last three were members of the powerful Guise family.

[68] For such disagreements, see Chabeuf, *Dijon: Monuments et souvenirs*, 115–125.

1.3   Mayoral Elections in Dijon

How, then, did these urban officials who wielded the authority of administrators, judges, and military captains come to occupy their positions? How were mayors and *échevins* in Dijon selected, and what does the process of selection say about the polity of the city? Who had the right to be elected, and who had the right to do the electing? What did participating in such an election mean for the participants? Why is it significant that premodern participants gave their "voices" rather than their "votes" to candidates? And why was the sharing of food and drink both before and after each election so important that an act of Parlement was required to protect these almost sacred rituals? Above all, why did Dijon's system of electing its own mayor change in the early sixteenth century from one in which the people gave their unanimous assent, which accented communal solidarity, to one of competition and adversarial politics, which threatened that very community? The answers to all these questions tell us much more about the social relations within the city as well as its polity than a focus on elections might at first suggest. One of the reasons is that premodern elections were not about democracy or representative government at all. In fact, they were not even primarily about voters choosing one candidate or one set of policies over another. The emphasis was less on the outcome of elections, and any resulting prospects for policy change, than on the process of *participating* in elections. The act of participating in elections was so significant because mayoral elections conferred honor on the elected mayor. Although the office of mayor was not a venal office, from 1491 it did confer nobility on its holder, though only for his term of office.[69] Ever since the late thirteenth century, in fact, all who were elected to this title styled themselves as *vicomte mayeur* (viscount mayor) in Dijon rather than just mayor, a clear sign that they had long had noble pretensions and felt that their social estate was on par with those of the lesser nobility.[70] To be sure, the title of *vicomte mayeur* and noble status itself were strongly contested by the aristocracy. Moreover, Dijon's mayors presided over the third estate rather than the second in Burgundy's own provincial estates. And the same was true if any of Dijon's mayors were ever elected to the Estates-General, as they were forced to assemble with the third estate rather than the other nobles who made up the second estate. Thus, the mayors'

---

[69] AMD, B 11, cote 7 (carton), October 1491, "Lettres patentes de Charles VIII données à Laval par lesquelles, pour recompenser la ville de Dijon de son affection et de sa fidelité, il lui accorde l'annoblissement de tous les maires présans et àvenir."

[70] Gras, ed., *Histoire de Dijon*, 50–51.

noble status was clearly recognized as a limited one, even more limited than those royal officers who acquired a noble title when they purchased or inherited a venal office, as at least those offices could be inherited, unlike the office of *vicomte-mayeur*. Nevertheless, if a mayoral election still conferred honor on the one who was elected, then it also conferred honor on whoever participated in the election. In short, the premodern election was just a metaphor for the ideal harmony that was supposed to exist between the elites, who produced the candidates, and the people, largely artisans and vignerons in Dijon, who gave their voices to them so that they could be elected to govern in a hierarchical society. But this ideal soon came to be undermined in the early sixteenth century, as we shall see.

Mark Kishlansky has used Shakespeare's drama *Coriolanus* to illustrate how Parliamentary elections functioned in seventeenth-century England.[71] But *Coriolanus*, based largely on the accounts of Roman elections by the historians Plutarch and Livy, also reveals much about mayoral elections in Dijon after the regime of the Valois dukes of Burgundy. In Shakespeare's Rome, the highest political achievement was to be selected consul, one of two chosen annually as the chief civil and military magistrates in Rome during the period of the Republic (509–44 BCE). The process was twofold. First, the Senate met and unanimously endorsed a candidate; then, this candidate presented himself to the people for their assent and approbation, which they also gave unanimously. In the case of Shakespeare's anti-hero, Caius Marcius Coriolanus, the process came unglued because Coriolanus refused to abide by the traditional rituals and verities of the election process. He spurned the assent of the people and asked the Senate to allow him to dispense with such a debasing ritual. That he eventually discharged his obligation to the people backfired nevertheless, as he did so only grudgingly and with obvious scorn for the plebeians of Rome. Coriolanus failed to win his consulship because, despite the unanimous backing of the Senate, he failed to win the approbation of the people. As Shakespeare made so plainly clear to his audiences, Coriolanus's banishment from Rome, his attempt at revenge, and his ultimate fall resulted entirely from his contravention of the norms of consular selection. In the end, he could not lower himself to behave humbly toward the people whose assent he was required to seek. Instead, he mocked the "voices" that would have made him consul:

---

[71] Mark A. Kishlansky, *Parliamentary Selection: Social and Political Choice in Early Modern England* (Cambridge: Cambridge University Press, 1986), 3–9.

> Most sweet voices!
> Better it is to die, better to starve,
> Than crave the hire which first we do deserve.
> Why in this woolvish toge should I stand here,
> To beg of Hob and Dick that does appear
> Their needless vouches?[72]

In this ideal vision of Republican Rome, the selection of a consul took place without a choice. The Senate bestowed the gift of nomination upon Coriolanus unanimously. The people's role was to give their assent, not their consent, to the Senate's nomination. They had no veto power over the Senate, and all they could really do was to bring the process to a halt if a candidate should disdain the "needless vouches" of every Hob and Dick. Dissent was alien to this system, as it robbed it of the honor bestowed on consul, senators, and the people alike. This was a politics of consensus rather than conflict. The selection of a consul was thus a ritual that expressed the harmony of the state: that which bound patricians and plebeians together in an otherwise hierarchically divided society.[73]

Dijon's mayoral elections were similarly ideal visions of social and political harmony. They occurred during the annual four-day celebration of midsummer's eve, June 21–24, culminating in the feast of St. John the Baptist on June 24, a special feast day in the liturgical and social calendar marked with fireworks and bonfires.[74] The feast of St. John the Baptist also marked the first day of the administrative New Year, when the mayor, the échevins, and the juré artisans and vignerons were all sworn in for the next year's work. Thus, the mayoral elections were part of a celebration of political, religious, and social cohesion and harmony. The language used by contemporaries to describe these events reinforces this sense of community and sociability. While the term "election" was commonly used during the reigns of the Valois dukes of Burgundy and after, the Hôtel de Ville's own descriptions of these elections commonly used the phrase "création et institution" of their mayors, making clear the active role of the inhabitants of the city in a process of consensus.[75]

Hugues IV, Duke of Burgundy, had originally granted to the male heads of household of the commune of Dijon the right to select their own mayor in 1235. They were entitled to reelect a mayor as often as they wished,

---

[72] William Shakespeare, *The Tragedy of Coriolanus*, act II, scene iii, lines 114–119.

[73] Kishlansky, *Parliamentary Selection*, 5–7.

[74] See Arnold van Gennep, *Manuel de folklore français contemporain*, part I, vol. 4 (Paris: Picard, 1949), 1727–1906 for an analysis of the observation of this holiday period.

[75] AMD, B 165, fols. 1v, 21v, 35v, 56v, 73r, 92v, and 128v, June 1577–June 1583.

"provided that he was competent and faithful to the city."[76] The charter of the duke also spelled out that no fathers and sons, and no brothers, were allowed to serve on the Hôtel de Ville at the same time. The format and procedure to be observed in these elections were also spelled out, and they changed hardly at all in the intervening centuries. Each year in mid-June just prior to the upcoming election, the mayor would hand over his symbol of office, the aforementioned Book of the Gospel of St. John, to one of the *échevins* specially chosen to be the Keeper of the Gospels (*Garde des évangiles*), who would supervise the upcoming mayoral election. The traditional election day was always June 21 each year, unless that date happened to fall on a Sunday, in which case the election was held the previous day, on Saturday, June 20. The mayor, *échevins*, and all male heads of household who wished to participate assembled in the Jacobin convent near the parish church of Notre Dame at six o'clock in the morning to cast their "voices" for the new mayor. By the beginning of the sixteenth century it was customary for the governor of Burgundy, or his deputy, the lieutenant-general of the province, to cast the first voice. If both were absent, then a deputy from the Chamber of Accounts would usually cast the first voice "in the name of the king." After this ritualistic blessing from the king, each of the twenty *échevins* – and from 1533 the four ecclesiastical *échevins* as well[77] – then proceeded to give his voice for mayor. Finally, each of the heads of household in Dijon then filed into the convent one at a time to give his voice orally in front of the assembled council. After all the assembled participants had cast their voices for mayor, a process that could last well into the afternoon or even into the evening in years of a heavy turnout, the *Garde des évangiles* then announced the election of the new mayor. The newly elected mayor was then conducted back to his own house, where he was expected to provide food and drink for all those who had participated in the election. In a ritualistic feast

[76] AMD, B 12, cote 31 (carton), "Reglement pour l'election du Maire," November 1235. For full details of the charter see Ferdinand Amanton, "Précis historique et chronologique sur l'établissement de la commune et des vicomte mayeurs ou maires de Dijon," *Mémoires de la Commission des Antiquités du département de la Côte-d'Or*, 8 (1873): 1–142.

[77] Joseph Garnier and Ernest Champeux, *Chartes de communes et d'affranchissements en Bourgogne* (Dijon: Rabutot and Garantière, 1918), 320. These ecclesiastical *échevins* were nominated by the clergy: One member was always from the Sainte Chapelle; one was selected from the abbeys of St. Etienne, St. Bénigne, and Cîteaux on a rotating basis, the latter located about 10 kilometers from Dijon; and two were chosen from the lower clergy, consisting of the staff of the seven parish churches, the Chapelle aux Riches, the priory of Val des Choux, and the priory of Larrey, the latter located outside Dijon. The ecclesiastical *échevins* met with the rest of the Hôtel de Ville for all matters except the mayoral court cases. See AMD, B 19, cotes 7 and 8 (liasses), and B 20, cote 11 (carton), for how the ecclesiastical *échevins* were nominated.

of communal solidarity, the consensus choice of the Hôtel de Ville, having been given the people's assent in the form of their voices, was duly celebrated as the mayor for the coming administrative year.

Two days later on June 23, the eve of the feast day of St. John the Baptist, the newly elected mayor would supervise the selection of the twenty *échevins* for the coming year in the Hôtel de Ville. According to the Duke of Burgundy's original charter of 1235, the mayor was required to select six *échevins* who had served from the previous year, and then those six plus the new mayor selected the other fourteen to make up the complete complement of twenty. Moreover, this selection was complicated by the fact that all 20 *échevins* had to be chosen proportionally, based on the number of households, from the seven parishes of the city: six from the parish of Notre Dame, three each from the parishes of St. Jean and St. Michel, and two each from the parishes of St. Nicolas, St. Médard, St. Pierre, and St. Philibert. The newly elected mayor and newly selected *échevins* then supervised the traditional holiday bonfire in the Place St. Jean that evening. The following day, the feast day of St. John the Baptist, the new mayor and *échevins* returned to the Jacobin convent for Mass, after which they proceeded to the cemetery of the abbey of St. Bénigne, where the election results were formally approved. The *Garde des évangiles* then gave the Gospels to the new mayor, who was in charge of them until just before the next year's election. Then, the entire troupe moved on to the parish church of Notre Dame. Before the high altar the mayor and each of the *échevins* in turn then proceeded to take his oath of office with one hand on the Gospels and "in the presence of the precious body of Our Lord Jesus Christ, being in the hands of the priest who was holding it for this very purpose."[78]

That Dijon's mayoral elections were supposed to follow this idyllic script of unanimity and common popular assent is evident in the way the elections were recorded in the Hôtel de Ville's deliberations. The account of the election of Jean Aigneault is a typical example. First elected mayor in 1493, Aigneault was reelected in 1494, 1495, 1496, 1497, and again in 1498. Each year the recording secretary at the Jacobin convent wrote down the names of the elites – mainly the *échevins* and members of the Chamber of Accounts – who gave their voices to Aigneault, after which the secretary

---

[78] AMD, B 11, cote 2 (carton), June 24, 1446. For the continuity of the format and structure of the elections from the days of the Dukes of Burgundy prior to 1477 to the early sixteenth century, see also AMD, B 19, cote 1, fols. 6v–7r, June 24, 1485 and 9v–10v, June 24, 1495; AMD, B 168, fol. 283r, June 16, 1514; and Garnier and Champeux, *Chartes de communes et d'affranchissements*, 312–330.

added "and many other inhabitants of the said city of Dijon in the number of 1000 to 1200 persons,"[79] or an even more generic phrase such as "and many other inhabitants of the said city assembled in great number."[80] The point was that the selection of Aigneault each year was unanimous and without any rancor or conflict among the electorate, as the deliberations for his reelection in 1498 spelled out even more explicitly: "Because the inhabitants of the city of Dijon have from good and ancient custom the right to elect each and every year the viscount-mayor to rule over and govern the said city and commune in good order and administration (*en bon ordre et police*) . . . the said *échevins* . . . and the said gentlemen of the [Chamber of] Accounts. . . are of the advice and opinion that the said Jean Aigneault is competent and sufficient to exercise and discharge the said office [of mayor] this current year." The secretary listed the 33 names of the notables who gave their voice for Aigneault, "and many others in great number, all of whom with one common mind and opinion have named and elected without any contradiction the said Jean Aigneault viscount-mayor of the said city."[81] Thus, the election of the mayor of Dijon was supposed to be a ritual that emphasized the unanimity and common assent of both the elites and the people, one that reflected that perfect harmony of the state in a hierarchical society. And in many years this appears to be more or less the way the selection process worked.

Already by 1498, however, there were signs that this ideal of unanimity and universal assent was just a model to be strived for rather than a regimen that governed how mayors were chosen in Dijon. In 1485, for example, there was no unanimity at all, as Etienne Berbisey, who had been mayor in Dijon since the death of Charles the Bold, the last Duke of Burgundy, in 1477, was defeated by Philippe Martin, seigneur de Bretenières: 55 voices to 3. A third candidate, Pierre Bouscal, received 14 voices.[82] The city council's deliberations suggest that this was a singular exception, however, as in every year for the next couple of decades the recording secretary listed the names of the elites who gave their voices, then added a phrase such as "and many other inhabitants of the said city in the number of 100 or 120 people, all of whom have been of the same mind and opinion that the said Bénigne de Cirey is elected viscount-mayor of this city of Dijon for the coming year, and there [in the Jacobin convent] they have given their voices for the welfare of the King and the said city."[83] There might be occasional differences in

---

[79] AMD, B 167, fol. 2r–v, June 24, 1495.   [80] AMD, B 167, fol. 35r–v, June 24, 1496.
[81] AMD, B 167, fols. 119r–120r, June 21, 1498.
[82] AMD, B 13, cote 48 (liasse), June 21, 1485; and B 166, fol. 1r, June 24, 1485.
[83] AMD, B 168, fol. 153r, June 21, 1508.

language from one year to the next, sometimes echoing the emphasis on unanimity used in describing the election of Jean Aigneault in the 1490s: "and many other persons numbering about a hundred, all inhabitants of the said city of Dijon, who have advised and deliberated without any contradiction that the said Bénigne de Cirey was still to continue in the estate and office of viscount-mayor."[84] Or when Pierre Sayve was reelected in 1516, the secretary noted "many other inhabitants of the said city . . . assembled in great number, all of whom were of one and the same assent (*dung mesme c[on]santement*)."[85] It would certainly appear, then, that the Hôtel de Ville as well as the inhabitants were doing their best to live up to the ideal of unanimity and common assent traditionally associated with the selection of Dijon's mayors.

This tradition changed abruptly in the 1520s, however, as in 1523 the deliberations of the Hôtel de Ville stated without further comment that "many inhabitants of the said city in great number" had chosen Pierre Sayve to be mayor for the next year by the "plurality" of their voices.[86] That a plurality of voices had replaced the unanimous common assent "without contradiction" of previous years without any comment whatsoever suggests that the ideal electoral vision later to be espoused by Shakespeare in *Coriolanus* was not quite as hegemonic as the deliberations of the Hôtel de Ville would lead us to believe. In fact, just a few years later the electoral process nearly broke down completely as division and bitter contestation replaced the ideals of unanimity and popular assent.

The elections of 1527, 1528, and 1529 broke with the traditional norms of civility and sociability associated with the selection process in Dijon, and a personal rivalry between two former mayors, Pierre Sayve and the incumbent, a doctor of law named Jean de Noel, seigneur de Bierne, was the principal cause.[87] When Bierne was reelected for a second term as mayor in June 1527, Sayve complained that the mayor had packed the Jacobin convent with paid supporters from the ranks of the vignerons to sway the vote, and Sayve complained to the royal governor of Burgundy about it.[88] The following year Sayve got his revenge, when he was elected over the incumbent Bierne, though not without a major disturbance during the election itself. When the secretary recorded the names of the

---

[84] AMD, B 168, fol. 176r, June 21, 1510.   [85] AMD, B 169, fol. 68r, June 18, 1516.

[86] AMD, B 170, fol. 150r, June 22, 1523.

[87] Pierre Sayve was elected mayor in 1514, 1515, 1516, 1517, and again in 1523. Jean Noel, seigneur de Bierne, was elected mayor in 1526 and 1527. Bierne was thus the incumbent in the election of 1528.

[88] AMD, B 172, fol. 61r–72v, June 1528. Also see E. Nolin, "Épisodes de la lutte des classes à Dijon au XVIe siècle," *Annales de Bourgogne*, 36 (1964): 270–275.

elites in the Hôtel de Ville's deliberations on June 22, 1528, he added that there were also in attendance "a great number of other men who were impossible to record because of all the noise and tumult." The election began with the lieutenant-general of Burgundy, the sieur de la Boullaye, reading aloud a letter from the royal governor, Philippe de Chabot, seigneur de Brion and Admiral of France: "He [the governor] beseeches them [the notables] and all the other inhabitants of the said city to favor the election of Monsieur Pierre Sayve, seigneur de Flavignerot, as their viscount-mayor for the forthcoming year, and in doing this they will be serving the pleasure of the King and of my lord the Admiral."[89] The governor was clearly trying to influence the outcome of the election, in effect naming Sayve as the officially backed candidate. The traditional gravity of the election was disrupted, however, when a noisy demonstration broke out in the midst of the voting, "in which many vignerons and others from the lower orders [*menu people*] from the city, who were in the convent in great numbers, began to cry out in a loud voice, some shouting the words 'Sayve! Sayve!' and others in even greater number shouting the words 'Bierne! Bierne!'" The seigneur de Bierne's supporters continued to demonstrate and some of them put Bierne upon their shoulders and took him out of the convent, "always crying in a loud voice the name Bierne, saying that they would elect him for their mayor."[90] Nothing could have been further from the mythical ideal of unanimity and popular assent in Dijon's mayoral election. Pierre Sayve then got up and begged all those still assembled "to observe the accustomed manner of holding the election of the viscount-mayor in Dijon for which they were assembled, and that they had to elect from among them the person who in their consciences they knew to be the most competent and profitable for the public good of the city of Dijon."[91] Then each of the elites, beginning with the master of the Chamber of Accounts and the prior from the abbey of St. Etienne, gave his voice for the former mayor Pierre Sayve. Ignoring the chants for Bierne still resonating around the hall, the *échevins* endorsed the royal governor's wishes, refrained from collecting any further voices, and abruptly left the convent.[92] The Hôtel de Ville arrested three vignerons for taking part in the disruptions and questioned them thoroughly. One of them, Simon Haron, aged 30, claimed that no one had coerced him to support Bierne. And when asked if he had planned the demonstration to whisk Bierne away by force during the election, he claimed that "it was more the artisans than

---

[89] AMD, B 172, fol. 110r–v, June 22, 1528.   [90] AMD, B 172, fols. 110v–111r, June 22, 1528.
[91] AMD, B 172, fol. 111r, June 22, 1528.   [92] AMD, B 172, fol. 112r, June 22, 1528.

the vignerons, and the artisans had more affection for him than the vignerons." Another vigneron, Pierre L'Heretier, aged 21, was also asked why he went to the convent that day. "He said it was because it was raining and he didn't know where else to go." And when a third vigneron named Lambert Lesnaves, aged 21, was asked why the vignerons hated Pierre Sayve so much, "he said it was because he had ordered the beating of a vigneron from St. Michel when he was mayor."[93] Only the barest façade of unanimity and popular assent remained in the electoral process.

The following year's election in 1529 was equally divisive, as once again the appearance of unanimity and common assent was undermined by divisiveness and contention. After the previous year's debacle, the mayor Pierre Sayve urged all those who assembled to vote on June 21, 1529 to refrain from any "misdeed . . . outburst or tumult (*meffait . . . bruit ou tumulte*)."[94] After all the elites had cast their voices – all for Sayve – the recording secretary stopped writing down the names of the voters after the first 16 names, "because he could not tell who the men were due to the pressure of the crowd, and also that he did not know the names of the vignerons and other tradesmen who were first [in line] and in front of the others."[95] Sayve then ordered the voting to resume, with two sergeants supervising the entry in the convent. But a vigneron named Denis Marquet then spoke up and told the mayor "that he did not have to wait [to hear the rest of the voices], since each of them wanted him to be the viscount-mayor." Accompanied by more than two hundred other voters, most of them vignerons, Marquet was attempting to make the selection of Sayve appear to be unanimous. When the throng followed Sayve out of the convent to his home, however, a small group of about 20 vignerons, masons, and other artisans rushed up to the recording secretary, Pierre Fenovier, shouting the name of Pierre Tabourot several times. A smaller group of about ten of them surrounded Fenovier and claimed that he had not recorded their choice for mayor. He replied that because the gentlemen of the Hôtel de Ville had already departed, he no longer had any authority to record their voices. They remonstrated with him that the royal governor and the king should not decide who was to be chosen as the next mayor, and that he had better record their voices, "saying that they wanted to make someone else mayor other than Monsieur Pierre Sayve."[96] The poor secretary managed to escape only by insisting that the recalcitrant voters go on to the home of Pierre Sayve, where the mayor and his supporters were already celebrating. When Fenovier got there himself, he

---

[93] ADCO, B II 360/29, July 5–8, 1528.   [94] AMD, B 173, fol. 43r, June 21, 1529.
[95] AMD, B 172, fol. 44r, June 21, 1529.   [96] AMD, B 173, fol. 45r–v, June 21, 1529.

discovered the dissidents had already joined in. "They wined and dined in the accustomed manner, and there were more than six hundred people there, such that both courtyards of the said house were completely full of people. Apart from this no one said anything against the said election."[97] The vigneron Marquet and the rest of Sayve's supporters obviously were trying to maintain the mythical ideal of unanimity and common assent, and the communal eating and drinking in the mayor's home reinforced that ideal. But although their voices were never recorded in the official results of the election, at least twenty voters strongly dissented from the collective decision. They may have been willing to share a meal with the mayor and his supporters afterward, but the illusion of a united community giving its popular assent to the new mayor was impossible to maintain.

Similar outbursts and demonstrations during the mayoral elections continued to occur, however, with the royal governor making his choice known, the elites selecting their candidate, and the masses of the people voicing their own choices. Thus, a rowdy demonstration by the vignerons helped to select Pierre Tabourot, seigneur de Veronnes, as mayor in 1532. Tabourot was also the elites' choice, though he was not the selection of the royal governor, the Admiral de Brion.[98] An even more severe disruption, with rival groups of vignerons attempting to outshout each other at the convent, caused the election of 1545 to be temporarily disbanded for two days. In the midst of the voting, different groups of vignerons shouted out the names of their preferred candidates: some for Benigne Bryet, some for Etienne Jaquotot, and others for Jean Jaquot. Because of all the "noise and clamor" the *échevins* and the *Garde des évangiles* were forced to abandon the convent without a result. The next day they decided to issue an ultimatum to the city's voters:

> Because some vignerons and mechanics come to the elections for mayor more to go drinking in the home afterwards of the one who is elected than for any other reason, it has been decided that at the sound of the trumpet the elected viscount-mayor or anyone else will henceforth be prohibited from giving either drink or food to the said vignerons and said men on the day of the said election . . . under penalty of an arbitrary fine.[99]

They went on to note that anyone who interrupted any future election "will be corporally punished as an example to all others."[100] When the

---

[97] AMD, B 173, fol. 45v, June 21, 1529.   [98] AMD, B 175, fols. 145r–147r, June 21, 1532.

[99] AMD, B 183, fols. 1r–7v, June 20–22, 1545, quote on fols. 4v–5r. Also see AMD, B 13, cote 59 (*liasse*), June 20, 1545.

[100] AMD, B 183, fol. 5r, June 21, 1545.

voting resumed at the convent on June 22, the voices of the inhabitants were split among seven candidates. When the voices from the two days of voting were tabulated, 258 voters had participated, with Etienne Jaquotot getting 172 voices, a clear majority, against Jean Jaquot's 39 voices and Bénigne Bryet's 28 voices. Four other candidates received a total of 19 voices.[101] The Hôtel de Ville had clearly discovered evidence that candidates were soliciting voters to turn up at the convent to vote for them, with Bryet being the most serious offender. One of his friends, Jean Bernard, was fined 20 *livres tournois* a few days later for having tried to influence the election.[102] Thus, it was not so much the vignerons or mechanics who were to blame for destroying the ideal of unanimity and common assent in the mayoral elections in Dijon; it was certain members of the Hôtel de Ville itself who brought about the division and contention of the elections in their efforts to secure the position of viscount-mayor of the city. By promising a little food and drink after the voices were counted, they believed that they could manipulate the elections in their favor. But this celebratory practice was partly responsible for the discord sown during the elections themselves, as demonstrations of vignerons and artisans interrupted the proceedings, fueled by promises of food and drink from the candidates. Multiple candidates were also the norm after 1545 rather than the exception, and the masses could hardly be blamed for sowing seeds of dissension if the *échevins* themselves were unable to agree on one candidate to select unanimously as mayor each year. The irony is that notwithstanding all the Hôtel de Ville's rhetoric against the rowdy vignerons and artisans during the elections, it was their own candidates for mayor who were responsible for such demonstrations.

Despite the prohibition by the Hôtel de Ville of the celebratory feast afterward by the winning candidate – and the fine for holding this ritual was changed from an arbitrary fine to a fine of 500 *livres tournois* in 1546[103] – election tensions remained. In 1553, for example, a man insulted the mayor, Guillaume Berbisey, and accused him of buying votes in order to be elected, claiming that "the day of the election of the said Berbisey as viscount-mayor, Berbisey had a band of vignerons in his garden, to whom he gave dinner, and that without this he would not have been elected viscount-mayor."[104] There were also assemblies of potential voters on the morning of the election the following year in June 1554, prompting the Parlement of Dijon to issue an *arrêt* prohibiting such assemblies:

---

[101] AMD, B 183, fols. 5v–7v, June 22, 1545.   [102] AMD, B 183, fol. 10r, June 26, 1545.
[103] AMD, B 184, fol. 2v, June 21, 1546.   [104] AMD, B 191, fol. 110r, November 3, 1553.

The court being advertised of the popular assembly this morning at the Jacobin convent of the city of Dijon, and seeing the results of it, has prohibited and does prohibit explicitly all inhabitants of the city from participating in any assemblies, undertakings, demonstrations, or uprisings, either on account of the election of the city's officers or for any other reason, on pain of a public beating.[105]

Thus, Parlement was forced to act because mayoral candidates were still organizing assemblies of potential voters on the sly to give them food and drink, or at least to promise them food and drink at some later date. But given that the selection of mayors in Dijon took place during the celebration of the feast of St. John the Baptist, it should hardly be surprising that food and drink played a major role in the rituals of the elections.

In fact, food and drink were so important to the feast day itself (June 24) that the inhabitants in Dijon filed suit in Parlement to maintain one of the oldest rituals associated with it. In their efforts to eliminate the celebratory meal in the home of the newly elected mayor on election day, the *échevins* had also decided to eliminate a symbolic gift of food and wine to the seven parishes after the new mayor was sworn in and took his oath of office on the feast day itself. Traditionally, the newly sworn-in mayor had always distributed a basket of cherries, a butt of wine, a leg of lamb or a ham, and some bread to each of the seven parishes as a sign of his affection as well as a symbolic gesture toward the feast so important to the feast day. In 1558, however, the vignerons of the city complained to the Parlement of Dijon that the Hôtel de Ville had usurped their "right (*droit*)" to have "the bread, wine, and cherries that they ought to have on the day of the confirmation of the viscount-mayor ... following that which had always been done in the past by the newly elected viscount-mayors after their confirmation: the butts of wine, bread, cherries, and other accustomed tributes."[106] Though the judges of Parlement had done their best to suppress all the demonstrations and interruptions of the elections with threats of fines and beatings, they upheld the "right" of the people to receive their gift of food and drink on the feast day of St. John the Baptist.

> The vignerons and laborers [who are] inhabitants of Dijon ... have remonstrated that after the confirmation and oath of office taken by the newly elected viscount-mayor of Dijon on the feast day of St. John the Baptist,

---

[105] AMD, B 12 cote 32 (carton), June 25, 1554.

[106] AMD, B 196, fols. 35r–36r, July 23, 1558: "*de droit du pain, vin et serizes quilz doibvent avoir le j[ou]r de la confirmation du vicomte maieur ... suyvant que du passé avoit tousiours este faict p[ar] les esleuz vicomte maieurs après leurs confirmations, les thenes de vin, pain, serizes et aultres droitures accoustumees.*"

they have always had the right of taking and having from the said newly elected mayor for his recognition seven butts of wine, seven dozen loaves of bread, seven hams, and seven baskets of cherries, as they have always received in the past and which was customarily eaten in the marketplace of the said city. Yet by order of this court it has been ordered that that the said seven butts, etc. will be divided and dispersed accordingly to each parish.[107]

When the *échevins* recorded this *arrêt* in their deliberations, one of them, former mayor Guillaume Berbisey, noted in the margin that the chamber's decision to limit the dispersion of food to the parishes on the feast day was only "in consideration of the intrigues and scandals that are perpetrated every year at the election of the viscount-mayor of this city of Dijon."[108] Thus the mayoral elections in Dijon and the eating and drinking so commonly associated with a major feast day on the liturgical calendar were so enfolded together that both the Hôtel de Ville and the Parlement of Dijon found it impossible to separate them. The very social rituals of eating and drinking together after an election that were supposed to underscore the ties of sociability that bound the community together in divine harmony had become sites of division, contention, and disorder.

In summary, the selection of Dijon's mayors tells us a lot about the polity and social relations within the city. For nearly half a century after the duchy of Burgundy's incorporation into the French crown, the inhabitants of Dijon selected their mayors more or less according to the traditional ideals of unanimity and common assent. Whatever competition existed was contained within the Hôtel de Ville, as in most years there was only one candidate who emerged to submit himself to the selection process, and he appears to have been endorsed by elites and commoners alike in the late fifteenth and early sixteenth centuries. Although we only have the official deliberations and minutes of the secretary of the city council as sources to what happened during the selection process – and these records are certainly biased in favoring the very ideals of unanimity and common assent that dominated the culture of elections in Dijon – they do show a city trying its best to live up to the lofty and almost mythical ideals that Shakespeare outlined in *Coriolanus*. By the 1520s, however, the cracks and fault-lines in the foundation of these ideals began to become more visible, as competition among the elites trickled out of the closed confines of the Hôtel de Ville and into public view. Collective rituals of community and common assent soon took a back seat to competition and divisiveness, as

[107] AMD, B 196, fol. 37r, July 23, 1558.   [108] AMD, B 196, fol. 38r, July 23, 1558.

the selection process itself became tainted, with some elections even being disrupted and temporarily suspended. These changes also challenged the way that the elites thought about their electoral ideals, as the unanimity of voices of Dijon's citizens quickly and almost unremarkably gave way in the 1520s to a mere plurality of voices. And the elections of Guillaume Berbisey in 1553 with 116 out of 328 voices (35.4 percent) and Jean Maillard in 1560 with 68 out of 234 voices (29.1 percent) show just how small those pluralities could sometimes be.[109] To modern eyes a shift from unanimity to sometimes less than a third of the electorate endorsing the winning candidate seems like a constitutional change of the highest order. Perhaps we need to be reminded again, however, that premodern elections were not about democracy and constitutions so much as participation. Even if the result or outcome of the process was not quite as self-evident as it was before the 1520s, the new mayor was always a member of the ruling class of elites who was also endorsed by some significant segment of that ruling cohort.

The most explicit beneficiaries of the new competitive spirit that emerged in the electoral process in Dijon in the 1520s were what the *échevins* often referred to in their official deliberations as "mechanics" and "men of lowly estate," particularly the vignerons and journeymen artisans who made up so much of the city's population. Many of their names were actually recorded in the deliberations of the elections for the first time in 1540 when they delivered their voices in Dijon's Jacobin convent, and from 1545 each and every head of household who turned up to cast his voice for mayor had his name and occupation systematically recorded in the Hôtel de Ville's official deliberations. Thus, the organized demonstrations and electoral disruptions of the late 1520s soon led to the vignerons and others of "lowly estate" having their names entered alongside those of the elites in the records of these annual electoral rituals. Moreover, the respective candidates targeted these men of the popular classes for their voices, often accompanied by promises of food and drink either before or after the election. It is thus an irony that the increased competition among the elites of the city to be elected viscount-mayor was the principal cause of the increase in participation and importance of these "mechanics of lowly estate" whom they otherwise scorned. As the figures in Table 1.2 show, vignerons hardly dominated the voting as the Hôtel de Ville's deliberations might seem to suggest. Only in specific years when they were explicitly solicited by one of the candidates, as they were in 1557 by

---

[109] AMD, B 191, fols. 1r–9v, June 21, 1553, and B 198, 1r–7v, June 21, 1560. Also see Table 1.1.

Table 1.1 *Dijon mayoral elections, 1545–1560*

Year	Elected mayor	Total voices	Voices for winning candidate	Percent of total voices
1545	Etienne Jaquotot	258	172	66.7
1546	Etienne Jaquotot	82	73	89.0
1547	Jean Jaquot	138	84	60.9
1548	Jean Jaquot	—	—	—
1549	Jean Jaquot	164	105	64.0
1550	Jean Jaquot	—	—	—
1551	Chrêtien Godran	299	166	55.5
1552	Chrêtien Godran	82	80	97.6
1553	Guillaume Berbisey	328	116	35.4
1554	Jean Robin	357	158	44.3
1555	Chrêtien Godran	118	104	88.1
1556	Chrêtien Godran	52	50	96.2
1557	Bénigne Martin	252	181	71.8
1558	Bénigne Martin	121	118	97.5
1559	Bénigne Martin	224	130	58.0
1560	Jean Maillard	234	68	29.1

Source: AMD, B 183–198. Details of the elections of 1548 and 1550 are missing from the deliberations.

Bénigne Martin, did vignerons turn out in large numbers. In that particular year vignerons made up 42.5 percent of the total number of those who participated in the election, providing nearly half of Martin's total of voices in his first election as mayor. Martin was easily reelected the following year in a nearly unanimous vote – all but three participants cast their voices for him – and he easily won again the year after an election that was not as close as the figures in Table 1.1 might suggest.[110] In 1560, however, Martin was defeated in an extremely close election in which none of the candidates made any appeal to the vignerons. In an election contested by a greater than usual number of candidates – eleven different men received voices in this election – Martin was narrowly defeated by the *échevin* Jean Maillard, who had been serving as the *Garde des évangiles* during the election. Maillard won with 68 voices, Martin received 60 voices, and none of the other nine candidates received more than 31 voices. Martin received only eight vigneron voices from his own parish

[110] AMD, B 197, fols. 1r–7v, June 21, 1559. Martin received 130 voices; André Machers, his nearest rival, received 43 voices; and five other candidates received the remaining 51 voices.

Table 1.2 *Vignerons in Dijon's mayoral elections, 1555–1560*

Year	Vigneron voices	Percent of total	Vignerons for winning candidate	Percent of winner's total	Percent of vignerons for winner
1555	16	13.6	16	15.4	100.0
1556	14	26.9	14	28.0	100.0
1557	107	42.5	89	49.2	83.2
1558	24	19.8	24	20.3	100.0
1559	48	21.4	33	25.4	68.8
1560	21	9.0	4	5.9	19.0

Source: AMD, B 193–198. The figures in this table are to be used in conjunction with those in Table 1.1.

of St. Michel, and none at all from the other vigneron stronghold, the parish of St. Philibert.[111] Thus, he obviously made little effort to turn out the vignerons to support him as he had when he was first elected in 1557. Nevertheless, a perusal of the list of those who gave their voices every year shows overwhelmingly that vignerons and artisans usually made up the majority of those who participated. But were Dijon's mayoral elections from the 1520s onward primarily a social struggle between the haves and the have-nots, as some historians have argued? Did these rituals of social cohesion really threaten to break down the ideal harmony between the elites and the masses?

When a fight broke out between nobles and commoners during the bonfire celebrations on the eve of the feast day of St. John the Baptist on June 23, 1527, it certainly seemed as if violence between the haves and the have-nots was about to explode. A cloth shearer named Guillaume de Mothe was dancing with the fiancée of a merchant when he was interrupted by a nobleman, Charles Baissey, seigneur de Beaumont. Beaumont tried to cut in on the tradesman and exclaimed "that he [the tradesman De Mothe] was lowering himself (*quil se mist plus bas*)" by dancing with someone from a higher estate than he. De Mothe quickly replied "that he was as honorable a man as he [Beaumont] was to dance with her (*quil estoit aussi homme de bien que luy pour la mener*)." Things escalated even further, however, when the nobleman "placed his hand on his sword." A bourgeois named Pierre Fourneret tried to intervene and wrestled the tradesman to the ground. When others jumped in to help De Mothe,

Beaumont joined in to aid Fourneret with "his sword drawn." The popular mayor, Jean Noel, seigneur de Bierne, had just been reelected for another term as mayor two days before, and he intervened to calm things down and restore order.[112] But was this incident evidence of a possible class war of vignerons against the elites? At least two historians have claimed it was and that it was also tied to Dijon's elections for mayor. Claiming that Jean Noel, seigneur de Bierne, represented the interests of the vignerons and that Pierre Sayve represented the interests of the elites of the city, these historians insist that the elections from 1526 to 1538 were a "class war (*lutte des classes*)," in which "the common people, always faithful to their same candidate (a noble besides, as they always supported Jean Noel, seigneur de Bierne), made him the winner five times. Meanwhile, the opposing faction, also faithful to its own candidate Pierre Sayve, seigneur de Flavignerot, won six times."[113] Even if it is patently obvious that the ideal social harmony between the elites and the masses was only an ideal, and that social tensions were a quotidian part of the premodern world, it seems somewhat simplistic to suggest that candidates for mayor represented class interests in the elections of the sixteenth century.

As this discussion has made clear, candidates competed among themselves for support from the masses, but when the masses gave their support to a candidate, or withheld it from another, class was not the vital factor. First of all, concerning the election of 1527, Jean Noel, Seigneur de Bierne, had been overwhelmingly reelected with just one dissenting vote among those who participated.[114] Bierne was thus a consensus candidate who obviously represented the elites as much as the popular classes. In the next election in 1528, in which so many vignerons supported Bierne unsuccessfully against former mayor Pierre Sayve, the city council deliberations make it very clear that "some vignerons and others of humble estate of the said city present in the convent in great number were taken to crying in loud voices these words: Sayve! Sayve! Others in even greater number: Bierne! Bierne!"[115] Thus, vignerons and artisans from the popular classes supported both candidates; they were willing to support most candidates who appealed for their voices and clearly did not see Jean Noel, seigneur de Bierne, as the candidate of the vignerons and Pierre

---

[112] ADCO, B II 360/29, June 25–26, 1527.

[113] E. Nolin, "Episodes de la lutte de classes à Dijon," 275. Also, see Henry Heller, *Iron and Blood: Civil Wars in Sixteenth-Century France* (Montreal: McGill-Queen's University Press, 1991), 16–17 and 29, who relies exclusively on Nolin's article for his view that the political enmity between Sayve and Bierne was based on "the conflict between notables and plebians" (29).

[114] AMD, B 172, fol. 36r, June 21, 1527.   [115] AMD, B 172, fols. 110v–111r, June 22, 1528.

Sayve as the candidate of the elites. And the following year, in 1529, a demonstration of vignerons estimated to be between 300–400 persons supported Sayve again in his reelection for mayor.[116] If there was a vigneron candidate in 1529, it was clearly Pierre Sayve, not the seigneur de Bierne.

Again, I would stress that in general the members of the popular classes were so keen to take part in these elections not because of any particular interest, but because they saw this as a chance to participate in a process that deflected honor upon them. It validated their participation in the body social more than in the body politic. As one vigneron made clear, he might choose to oppose Sayve because his opponent had ordered the beating of a vigneron in the past, but this was in no way a signal of any class interest. Vignerons and artisans could easily divide their support among several candidates, and they could also support a candidate one year and support his opponent the next. At least until religion became an issue in the mayoral elections in 1561, Dijon's citizens did not generally support or advocate a particular interest or policy when they cast their voices; they were legitimating their social standing in the community. By participating in a process that cast honor on the one who was elected viscount-mayor, they were also reaping the residual honor that necessarily reflected on themselves as vital participants. As Coriolanus himself discovered so tragically, the role of the people was essential to the political process. The power and authority of the elites depended on the participation and the assent of the masses. While not always so harmonious in practice as the mythical ideal would pretend, this fundamental relationship between the rulers and the ruled was a vital part of the polity in the premodern state.

a kind of 'moral economy' [handwritten marginal note]

But how did Dijon's system of elections compare with other French towns governed by a *corps de ville*? Again, Bernard Chevalier notes that nearly all of these towns had some formal process whereby new *échevins* or consuls replaced those leaving their posts, but "the power they held did not come from any electoral mandate, even though they generally submitted to an annual ballot for renewal [of their posts]." In fact, as Chevalier notes, their power was given to them to coopt and choose their own successors: "this choice always comes back to a co-optation and this process is never mistaken for a proclamation of a result from a ballot." In other words, the Hôtel de Ville was virtually a self-perpetuating oligarchy of elite families.[117] And, as in Dijon, the mayor and *échevins* whose terms were up every June

---

[116] AMD, B 173, fol. 44v, which describes a demonstration of support for the mayor, Pierre Sayve.
[117] Chevalier, *Les bonnes villes*, 203–204.

alone had the power to decide who could appear on the ballot, and the names on the ballot almost always came from a relatively small coterie of fifty or so elite families in the city. Details of the format of the elections might vary from one town to another, but the underlying principle of cooptation by the cities' elites was fundamental to the entire process. The two largest towns in the Free County of Burgundy across the Rhône River are good examples of this. In Dôle and Besançon annual elections operated in a similar manner to that in Dijon, though the details varied to some degree. In Dôle, for example, the mayor and fifteen outgoing councilors – they were called *conseillers* rather than *échevins* in Dôle – met together with a group of 16 "notables" chosen by the city's male heads of household. This group of 32 then chose the new mayor and 15 new councilors, with the outgoing mayor always being selected as a councilor in the year after his term as mayor to provide continuity. In Besançon, the process was even more complex, as it was an imperial city of the Holy Roman Empire. Thus, its mayor was not elected at all, but chosen by the imperial governor of the county, and the choice was usually an outsider and a nobleman rather than a resident of the city from one of the leading families. These families were represented and dominated the town council, and like in Dijon and Dôle, they were a self–perpetuating oligarchy there.[118] Only in Dijon, however, had the artisans and vignerons come to play such a prominent role in the annual election rituals, and in the process forged a closer relationship with the city's elites. That relationship and the polity itself, however, would be sorely tested by the emergence of Protestantism in 1561, when Dijon, like so many other towns in France, exploded in religious violence.

---

[118] Kathryn A. Edwards, *Families and Frontier: Re-Creating Communities and Boundaries in the Early Modern Burgundies* (Boston, MA, and Leiden: Brill, 2002), 195–196 and 213–214.

CHAPTER 2

Protected by the Virgin Mary
Lay Religious Experiences

Any analysis of religious belief and practice on the eve of the Reformation must take account of the fact that not all Christians understood or perceived the tenets of faith and ritual practices of devotion in exactly the same way. While it is no doubt true that on some level the educated elites were more likely to meet the clergy's expectations in their knowledge of the subtleties of theology and the fundamentals of basic doctrine, it is equally true that religion was one of the principal aspects of premodern life where the educated and nonliterate had significant contact and social interaction. Whether inside the parish church on Sundays or outside the church at a religious procession on feast days, Christianity served as an astringent to bind the community together in specific ways. Although he may have exaggerated the cohesiveness of this community in some ways, John Bossy's vision of a social community of believers bound together by their beliefs and practices of rituals and sacraments rings true to a certain extent. And even if the precise space where one prayed inside the parish church, whether in a private family chapel or in the nave with the rest of the congregation, as well as the order one marched in a religious procession outside it were both explicit indicators of social rank and estate, there is no question that religious life offered a unique intermingling of the social orders, in which all members considered themselves a part of a single body of believers: a community.[1] In short, religion has always been about belonging.

The purpose of this chapter is to analyze the foundations and diversity of religious experiences for most lay Burgundian Christians on the eve of the Reformation. Although this cannot possibly be a comprehensive survey of all aspects of doctrinal beliefs and lay practices of late medieval Christianity, I will try to sketch out the principal components that made up the foundation of most Christians' religion on the eve of the

[1] John Bossy, *Christianity in the West, 1400–1700* (Oxford: Oxford University Press, 1986).

53

Reformation. Moreover, I shall also try to highlight some of the most recent changes to religious experience on the eve of the Reformation to illustrate the larger contention that Christianity was constantly being made and remade. The chapter will begin with an analysis of perhaps the two most important components of traditional religion, which contemporaries perceived as being at the center of their religious experience: the Eucharist and the Virgin Mary. Both of these elements also show how impossible it was for contemporaries to separate, much less distinguish, between belief and practice, as the central doctrine of each was linked and intertwined with its respective ritual practices. First, the Eucharist, or Mass, as it was commonly referred to, was the central rite of late medieval Christianity. In both doctrine and practice the Mass incorporated everything that was crucial to the lay Christian. As both sacrament and sacrifice, it embodied the flesh and blood of Christ from the most basic elements of human subsistence, bread and wine. It also symbolized the collective sense of spiritual cohesiveness and social affinity that defined the community of Christ. Above all, however, the ingestion of the consecrated flesh and blood of Christ in the Eucharist imparted divine grace and was thus firmly linked with Christian salvation. So, even though parishioners did not normally receive the Eucharist except on Easter Sunday, it remained the central rite of their religious experience precisely because it made possible life after death. The other religious motif singled out here for discussion is the prominent role played by the Virgin Mary in late medieval Christianity. As both intercessor in the next world and protector in this world, the Virgin had only recently evolved into a much more important figure in the lives of most members of the laity than she had been for early Christians. And while the rise of the cult of the Virgin was evident throughout the Christian West on the eve of the Reformation and would only reach its zenith in the seventeenth century in many parts of Christendom, it had a particular resonance for Burgundians due to their perception of the Virgin's role in protecting them and coming to their aid during the Swiss siege of Dijon in 1513.

Given that so much of religious experience was perceived through the senses, especially through the visual, the chapter then turns to an analysis of what ordinary Christians on the eve of the Reformation would have seen in practicing their religion. Although it is impossible to get inside the heads of ordinary lay Christians in this period without explicit documentation, which is rare, we can nevertheless assess what these Christians would have seen and visualized with their own eyes in their day to day religious practices. And because so much of the material fabric of the parish churches of the sixteenth century still remains intact today, the main entry into this visual world of late medieval Christianity will focus on a virtual walking tour of a parish church, in particular, the parish church of St. Michel in Dijon, which was rebuilt in the early sixteenth century and whose interior and exterior remain largely unchanged despite the ravages of the French Revolution. Although my analysis has been informed by a great deal of theoretical and practical scholarship from the discipline of art history, this will not be primarily an iconographic tour of the church, but rather an attempt to see what sixteenth-century Christians would have seen and to try to understand the range of meanings that they might have given to the various images they saw.[2] Finally, the chapter will conclude by moving outside the church to explore several specific religious rituals in which the laity participated, again with the intent of exploring the range of meanings and understandings that contemporaries would have attached to their participation in them. This chapter is not intended to be a comprehensive survey of religious life for the laity, as it ignores what, for lack of a better term, I call private religion, such as prayers and the reading of Scripture at home for those who were literate. Fortunately, Virginia Reinburg has recently explored this aspect of premodern religion very comprehensively.[3] Taken as a whole, however, the chapter aims to show how closely integrated the principal doctrines of the church were with the social and cultural practices that emanated from these doctrines. It is impossible to speak of one without the other. Moreover, both the doctrines and the practices underscored the community shared by the elites and the masses alike. Indeed, both inside and outside the church, the practice of their religion brought both groups into frequent and regular contact and produced many shared religious experiences despite the social distance separating them.

2.1 Meanings of Lay Piety: The Mass and the Virgin Mary

Although the Eucharist was technically only one part of the larger liturgy of the Mass in which it featured so prominently, the two terms came to be

---

[2] Of the many works from art history that I have relied on, the following, covering a wide range of approaches, have been especially useful: Michael Baxandall, *Painting and Experience in Fifteenth-Century Italy* (Oxford: Oxford University Press, 1972); Keith Moxey, *The Practice of Theory: Poststructuralism, Cultural Politics, and Art History* (Ithaca, NY: Cornell University Press, 1994); Patricia Fortini Brown, *Venetian Narrative Painting in the Age of Carpaccio* (New Haven, CT: Yale University Press, 1988); and Emile Mâle, *Religious Art in France, the Late Middle Ages: A Study of Medieval Iconography and Its Sources*, eds. Harry Bober, trans. Marthiel Mathews (Princeton, NJ: Princeton University Press, 1986).

[3] Virginia Reinburg, *French Books of Hours: Making an Archive of Prayer, c. 1400–1600* (Cambridge: Cambridge University Press, 2012).

used almost interchangeably by both Protestants and Catholics in the sixteenth century. The word "Mass" (*messe* in French) comes from the words
missa est at the very end of the Eucharistic Mass. Lee Wandel is certainly right
to point out, however, that this usage is problematic. Although the Eucharist
was at the center of the Mass, not every Mass contained the Eucharist. Indeed,
as Wandel makes very clear, the liturgy of the Mass varied from place to place
and from time to time throughout Christendom until the order of the Mass
was codified and regularized at the very end of the Council of Trent, with the
first Tridentine missal not appearing in print until 1570. Even in the same
place, the order of the Mass varied considerably over the course of the
liturgical calendar, with an Easter Mass being very different from a Mass on
any other Sunday. So, to speak of the Mass as one single ritual is a misnomer,
as it varied considerably over time and space and was always changing in the
context of the liturgical calendar. Moreover, the most complex Masses performed in clerical communities, whether in a monastery or cathedral chapter,
involved many more participants and was more textured than the simple Mass
celebrated by a single priest and witnessed by most lay Christians in their
parish church.[4] The history of the Mass's evolution from its inception as an
early Christian rite to its various forms on the eve of the Reformation has been
well established by scholars such as Karl Young, Joseph Jungmann, and many
others, and it need not be recounted here.[5] Suffice it to say, however, that in all
its forms and multiple variations there was a unity and commonality to the
Eucharistic experience on the part of the laity.

If the complete Mass were being celebrated by the local clergy in a parish
church, it would have contained a number of constituent parts, which were
divided into three main sections: Fore Mass (preparation), Offertory (oblation), and the Eucharist (consecration and celebration).[6] The main innovation in the Mass in France on the eve of the Reformation occurred in

---

[4] Lee Palmer Wandel, *The Eucharist in the Reformation: Incarnation and Liturgy* (Cambridge:
Cambridge University Press, 2006), 14–19.

[5] In addition to the book by Wandel, see especially Karl Young, *The Drama of the Medieval Church*, 2
vols. (Oxford: The Clarendon Press, 1933), 1: 15–43; Joseph A. Jungmann, *The Mass of the Roman Rite:
Its Origins and Development*, trans. Francis A. Brunner, 2 vols. (Allen, Texas: Christian Classics, 1986;
orig. edn. 1951–1955); Miri Rubin, *Corpus Christi: The Eucharist in Late Medieval Culture*
(Cambridge: Cambridge University Press, 1991); Gregory Dix, *The Shape of the Liturgy* (London:
Dacre Press, 1945); Hans Lietzman, *Mass and Lord's Supper: A Study in the History of the Liturgy*, trans.
Dorothy H. G. Reeve (Leiden: Brill, 1979); T. Klauser, *A Short History of the Western Liturgy*, trans.
J. Halliburton (Oxford: Oxford University Press, 1969); John Bossy, "The Mass as a Social
Institution, 1200–1700," *Past & Present* 100 (1983): 29–61; and Virginia Reinburg, "Liturgy and the
Laity in Late Medieval and Reformation France," *Sixteenth Century Journal* 23 (1992): 526–547.

[6] I have adapted this discussion of the Mass from the slightly differing versions in Jungmann, *Mass of
the Roman Rite*, 1: 261–494 and 2: 1–459; Young, *Drama of the Medieval Church*, 1: 19; Rubin, *Corpus
Christi*, 12–82; and Reinburg, "Liturgy and the Laity," 547.

the second part, the Offertory, when the congregation would bring loaves of bread to the altar to be blessed by the priest and then distributed at the end of the Mass to the poor in the city. Led by the men, followed by the women, and with the clergy bringing up the rear, the entire congregation would proceed to the altar carrying bread (and sometimes wine), candles, and alms for the poor. In this procession every lay Christian was actively participating in the sacrament by enacting the rite's central themes of sharing and giving. This communal almsgiving further underscored the lay Christian's perception of the Mass as a sacred exchange: all must give materially in order to receive the body of Christ physically and spiritually.[7] The bread that was collected was generally not used for the communion itself by the sixteenth century, as the clergy of the parish usually provided their own thin wheat wafers referred to as the Host that would be consecrated in the final part of the Mass. The bread from the Offertory was blessed as *pain bénit* and would be distributed to the poor in the local community by one of the local confraternities after the Mass had ended, further underscoring the sharing and giving of Christian charity to each other as well as the oblation to God. As Barbara Diefendorf has reminded us, the distribution of blessed bread to the poor at the end of the Mass was a peculiarly French custom and was not part of the official Roman rite. And it was certainly distributed in Dijon, as the city council sometimes made donations to cover the cost in the parish of St. Michel where the Hôtel de Ville was located.[8] Indeed, the bulk of the *pain bénit* was distributed to the city's poor, and this distribution of blessed bread was much more common in France than anywhere else in the Roman church. Originally introduced in Frankish times throughout the West to be distributed to noncommunicants, the practice died out in German-speaking lands and elsewhere by the twelfth century, surviving primarily in France, and as Jungmann notes, blessed bread was especially popular in Burgundy.[9] By the time a new Hôtel de Ville was built in the parish of St. Michel in 1501, the church's records show that the city council regularly funded the distribution of this blessed bread to the poor. And from January 1560 the members of the confraternity of the Three Kings, who had a chapel in the parish church of St. Michel, undertook to distribute *pain bénit* every Sunday.[10] For the laity, then, "the large, fine loaves of holy bread shared

---

[7] Jungmann, *Mass of the Roman Rite*, 2: 1–26; and Reinburg, "Liturgy and the Laity," 532.

[8] AMD, D 21 (liasse). Also see Etienne Metman, *L'Eglise Saint-Michel de Dijon* (Dijon: Ratel-Cotosset, 1914), 67–70.

[9] Jungmann, *Mass of the Roman Rite*, 2: 452–455.

[10] Jean Rigault, "L'ancienne confrérie des Rois à Saint-Michel de Dijon," *Mémoires de l'Académie des sciences, arts et belles-lettres de Dijon* 117 (1969): 82.

out each week among the congregation were a more accessible symbol of community than the thin, dry, and rarely partaken communion wafer."[11]

What has been suggested here, and what I wish to further underscore, is that while the experience and understanding of most of the laity during the Mass was markedly different from that of the clergy and the educated elites, this was a ritual in which the popular classes and the clerical and secular elites of the city were all active participants in the social and spiritual drama of the Mass. Moreover, we should not think that because most of the sacrament was in Latin that the experience had very little meaning for the majority of congregants. For them it was a sacred drama, a reenactment of the Last Supper and the Passion of Christ. It was a performance in which they were actively involved as participants, not simply as a passive audience. Even if they did not understand all the words, they were certain that God did and were hardly put off, much less distanced, from the rite, because it was in a foreign tongue. They had to learn their lines and follow the stage directions of the priest, knowing when to stand, kneel, genuflect, and process to the altar. The drama was composed of sounds – the bells and singing of the celebrant and the chorus, not to mention the bedes and the sermon in their own language – as well as smells – the aromas of burning incense – and tastes – the sensation of the consecrated Host and the blessed but unconsecrated wine in their mouths. Above all, however, the climax of the drama for the majority of the laity was visually seeing the Host elevated by the priest, bringing the body of the living God directly into their presence: seeing was participating. And what illuminated this seeing of the Host were the special torches, candles, and tapirs near the altar during the Eucharist.[12] Finally, the distribution of *pain bénit* at the end of the sacrament was one final reminder for the laity that the entire Mass was about the community's bonding together in Christian charity. For lay Catholics, it was a ritual of giving, receiving, sharing, and uniting together in the bonds of Christian charity through the body of Christ. And the sharing of blessed bread with the communicants and distributing it to the poor had evolved by the eve of the Reformation into a potent symbol of that ideal community. This certainly did not guarantee that Dijon's elites and masses would always live together in an ideal community, but they shared a common ideal. And everyone from the wealthiest elite to the poorest vigneron knew that their participation in this sacred drama was

[11] Barbara B. Diefendorf, *Beneath the Cross: Catholics and Huguenots in Sixteenth-Century Paris* (New York, NY: Oxford University Press, 1991), 32.
[12] See Catherine Vincent, *Fiat Lux: Lumières et luminaires dans la vie religieuse du XIIIᵉ au XVIᵉ siècle* (Paris: Cerf, 2004), 221–241.

a vital part of belonging to that community. And that ideal would prove potent when Protestantism threatened to disrupt that community in the 1540s.

Shifting away from the Eucharist, the Virgin Mary was the single most important figure in late medieval piety apart from her son Jesus. That had not always been the case, however, and the rise of the cult of the Virgin in the fourteenth and fifteenth centuries was one of the most visible ways that Christianity was constantly making and remaking itself. Although the cult of the Virgin would not reach its apex until the seventeenth century in many parts of Europe, the growing popularity and increasing importance of the Holy Family in general and of Marian devotions in particular for late medieval Christians stemmed from a growing need to understand God in human terms. Though Jesus was both human and divine, what made him real to lay Christians was that he had human kin, just like themselves, and of all those kin, the closest was his mother, Mary. And because Mary was entirely human herself, lacking the divine nature of her son, in some ways she may have been even more approachable to ordinary lay Christians than Jesus. So, while the Virgin Mary certainly occupied a very special status in the church on the eve of the Reformation, it was overwhelmingly because of her human characteristics rather than her spiritual traits.[13]

Nevertheless, the Virgin Mary came to occupy a significant place in the history of Christianity by the late Middle Ages, even though she is only mentioned in about a dozen passages in the entire New Testament, and most of those only in passing. In the gospel of Mark, for example, the oldest of the four gospels, she is only mentioned once (Mark 6:3). In the Acts of the Apostles, the oldest record of the first generation of Christians, she is again mentioned only once (Acts 1:14). And finally, in the first four centuries of the early church Mary was neither venerated nor celebrated. In fact, it was not until after Mary was declared to be *Theotokos*, or the "Mother of God" by the Council of Ephesus in 431 C.E. that a popular Marian devotion started to emerge, reaching its apex in the seventeenth

[13] On this point see Larissa Taylor, *Soldiers of Christ: Preaching in Late Medieval and Reformation France* (New York, NY: Oxford University Press, 1992), 110–113; Donna Spivey Ellington, *From Sacred Body to Angelic Soul: Understanding Mary in Late Medieval and Early Modern Europe* (Washington, DC: Catholic University of America Press, 2001), 47–101; and Bossy, *Christianity in the West*, 5–11. For an introduction to the literature on the cult of the Virgin, the place to start is Miri Rubin, *The Mother of God: A History of the Virgin Mary* (New Haven, CT and London: Yale University Press, 2009). Also see Jaroslav Pelican, *Mary Through the Centuries: Her Place in the History of Culture* (New Haven, CT: Yale University Press, 1996); Dominique Iogna-Prat, Eric Palazzo, and Daniel Russo, eds., *Marie: Le culte de la Vierge dans la société médiévale* (Paris: Beauchesne, 1996); and Bruni Maes, *Le Roi, la Vièrge et la nation: Pèlerinages et identité nationale entre guerre de Cents Ans et Révolution* (Paris: Editions Publisud, 2003).

century.[14] As already suggested, one of the reasons for Mary's popularity in the late Middle Ages was that as both virgin and mother she was fully human. And her humanity was further accented around 1260 by Jacobus de Voragine in his compilation of saints' lives called *The Golden Legend*, as he filled in the many gaps about Mary's family and kin that were left out of the New Testament. Whereas the gospels of Matthew and Luke spell out the lineage of Joseph tracing generation to generation all the way back to David, and then further back to Adam, Voragine noted that Mary was also descended from the royal lineage of David, but through his other son Nathan, rather than through his son Solomon, as Joseph was. Thus, Voragine traced Mary's ancestors directly from David, through his son Nathan, all the way down to Mary's father Joachim.[15] Although this lineage had been first constructed much earlier, probably in the apocryphal book, *The Protogospel of James* in the second century,[16] Voragine's version gained a much wider audience in the late Middle Ages. He also sorted out the confusion of Marys mentioned in the gospels of Jesus's resurrection: the Virgin Mary, Mary Magdalene, Mary Cleophas, and Mary the mother of the apostles James and John. Voragine explained that the latter two and the Virgin Mary were all half-sisters, since Mary's mother Anne had three husbands: Joachim, Cleophas, and Salome, remarrying after the deaths of the first two, all of whom produced daughters named Mary. It was Anne's first husband, Joachim, who sired the Virgin Mary.[17] All these kin only further established the humanity of the Virgin Mary on the eve of the Reformation.

For lay Christians Mary served a variety of different functions. She was at the same time virgin, mother, queen, bride, intercessor, and protector. It was these last two roles in particular, however, that seemed to be the most important to most Christians on the eve of the Reformation. As intercessor and mediator, Mary assumed the predominant role of all the saints as the one who could most easily intervene with her son on the behalf of any Christian. Just as few had direct access to the King of France, one had to go through intercessors. And because God was even busier than the King, one had to go through inter-locutors such as Mary and the saints. In both image and text, the late medieval imagery of Mary as *Mediatrix* emanated directly from the Mary of Sorrows

---

[14] Michael P. Carroll, *The Cult of the Virgin Mary: Psychological Origins* (Princeton, NJ: Princeton University Press, 1986), 4–5, and Pelikan, *Mary through the Centuries*, 55–65.

[15] Jacobus de Voragine, *The Golden Legend: Readings on the Saints*, trans. William Granger Ryan, 2 vols. (Princeton, NJ: Princeton University Press, 1993), 2: 149.

[16] Rubin, *Mother of God*, 8–12.

[17] Voragine, *Golden Legend*, 2: 150. Also see Katherine Ludwig Jansen, *The Making of the Magdalen: Preaching and Popular Devotion in the Later Middle Ages* (Princeton, NJ: Princeton University Press, 2000), 29.

associated with the Passion of Christ. This was the image of the Virgin painted on the gospel of St. John used by the Dijon city council as its symbol of political authority (see Figure 1.3), with the Virgin Mary standing at the foot of the cross watching her son suffer and eventually die. But, Mary's sorrow and anguish at her son's suffering on the cross were also tempered by her happiness at knowing that her son was also her savior. For late medieval Christians Mary was Jesus's only blood kin, who felt sorrow and anguish over her son's death like any mother would, but at the same time, due to her special relationship with him, she could also intercede and mediate with him on their behalf when their own time for death approached. In this way the Mary of Sorrows also became the principal mediator and intercessor above all other saints. Like the Mary of Sorrows, who intervened with God to better prepare their journey to the next world, the Mary of Mercy could protect late medieval Christians from God's vengeance in this world, as well as comfort and succor those who were already so afflicted.

Images of the *Pièta* were extremely popular in the province of Burgundy in general, and in the region of Dijon in particular, on the eve of the Reformation. From the number of surviving examples, it might seem that nearly every parish church had a *Pièta* carved from stone (see Figure 2.1). These examples will be discussed in more detail later, but suffice it to say here that this particular ecclesiastical monument was extremely popular in Burgundy in the early sixteenth century. Three parish churches in Dijon have survived with their interior fabrics more or less intact: Notre-Dame and St. Michel inside the city walls and Talant high on the hill just outside the city walls. And though one might expect a parish church named after the Virgin to contain a number of representations of her inside, both St. Michel and Talant parish churches also contained images of the *Pièta* in stone (see pp. 72–73). As for images of the Virgin of the Cloak, the Virgin Mary had long had particular associations with the Cistercian order founded just outside Dijon at Cîteaux in the twelfth century. Although the Cistercians certainly did not invent this image – it predates the order's founding by several centuries in the Byzantine east – the order certainly adopted the image of the Virgin Mary as their principal protector explicitly as early as the 1220s, as detailed by a Cistercian in the diocese of Cologne. The Cistercians adopted the Virgin of the Cloak as part of their official seal and coat of arms, and this was evident in a manual written by the Cistercian Jean de Cirey in 1491, one of the earliest printed books to be published in Dijon.[18]

---

[18] Ibid., 261–268. Also see Paul Perdrizet, *La Vierge de miséricorde: Etude d'un thème iconographique* (Paris: Albert Fontemoing, 1908), 16–29.

Figure 2.1 Sculpture of *Pièta* in the parish church of St. Michel, Dijon, sixteenth century

The main reason all these images of the Virgin Mary resonated so acutely in the city of Dijon on the eve of the Reformation, however, was the recent memory of the role of the Virgin in protecting the city from the siege by the Swiss army in 1513, as described in Chapter 1. For many in the city, notwithstanding the fact that the city council had promised the Swiss the enormous sum of 400,000 *écus* to end the siege, it was the Virgin herself who had intervened to save and protect the city from destruction. Marielle Lamy has recently argued that it was not until one year later in 1514, when the mayor and city councilors decided to commemorate the lifting of the siege of the Swiss the year before with a religious procession, that the inhabitants of the city began to credit the Virgin Mary for the defeat of the Swiss armies.[19] Thus, in September 1514, the mayor, Pierre Sayve, and two *échevins*, Bénigne de Cirey and Thomas Berbisey, proposed to the clergy of the city that they lead a procession with the black wooden statue of the Virgin (see Figure 2.2) each year on the first Tuesday after the Feast of the Nativity of the Virgin Mary (September 8) to commemorate the salvation of the city, "at which the members of the *Chambre de ville* and all the inhabitants of the city would assist." The mayor also promised to provide twelve torches (each with two pounds of wax) for the procession, as well as sergeants to carry them. Lastly, he declared that every year the city would "sanctify this day as a feast day."[20] Moreover, David El Kenz has also suggested that it was not until several years later, when a special tapestry depicting the religious procession of the chaplains of the parish of Notre-Dame was commissioned by the *échevin* Philippe Godran, that the link between the statue of Our Lady and the deliverance of Dijon from the Swiss siege was finally linked in the popular imagination. Godran was one of the hostages turned over to the Swiss in 1513 as security for the payment promised by La Trémoïlle, and he commissioned this tapestry, which was made in Flanders and completed by 1520.[21] And as El Kenz shows, the belief that the Virgin Mary miraculously saved the city became entrenched in the memory of Dijon's elites and popular classes thereafter.

Lest we think that this was merely a few cynical city fathers attempting to keep the people in line by propping up the popular notion that it was the Virgin Mary who had saved the city rather than their own reluctant political decision to buy off the captain of the Swiss army the

---

[19] Marielle Lamy, "Une siege levé par l'intervention de Marie? La dévotion à Notre Dame de Bon-Espoir," in Jonathan Dumont, Alain Marchandissel, and Laurent Vissière, eds., *1513 L'année terrible: Le siege de Dijon* (Dijon: Faton, 2013), 212–217.

[20] AMD, D 2 (*liasse*), September 12, 1514: ". . . de sanctifier ce jour comme un jour ferié." Also see AMD, B 169, fols.12v-16r, September 6–12, 1514; Jules Thomas, *La délivrance de Dijon en 1513 d'après les documents contemporains* (Dijon: Chez tous les libraries, 1898), 196–204; and Chabeuf, *Dijon: Monuments et souvenirs*, 87.

[21] David El Kenz, "Une mariophanie martiale a Dijon," *Annales de Bourgogne* 87 (2015): 47–57. Also, see Gabriel Peignot, *Nouveaux details historiquessur le siège de Dijon en 1513, sur le traité qui l'a terminé et sur la tapisserie qui le représente* (Dijon: Douvillier, 1837); and Pierre Quarré, "La tapisserie du siege de Dijon en 1513," *Plaisir de France* 431 (July–August 1975): 44–77. For several centuries the tapestry hung in the chamber of the Hôtel de Ville in Dijon, and it is currently displayed in the Salle de Garde of the Musée des Beaux Arts in Dijon.

Figure 2.2 The Black Virgin, parish church of Notre-Dame, Dijon

previous year, the sources suggest that the city fathers were just as much indebted to the protection of the Virgin Mary as the people of the city. Thomas Berbisey, in particular, seems to have been persuaded that without the Virgin's intervention during the siege of 1513 neither money nor political persuasion would have convinced the Swiss army to withdraw.[22] Berbisey was the son of Etienne Berbisey, the mayor of Dijon who had first recognized King Louis XI after the death of Charles the Bold in 1477. Further insight into his own personal piety is evident from a wooden pillar

---

[22] AMD, B 169, fols. 12v–16r, September 6–12, 1514.

Figure 2.3 Wooden sculpture of Christ and St. Thomas, sixteenth century, Hotel Berbisey, Dijon

he had built in the entry courtyard of his house on which was sculpted the tree of knowledge at the base, leading up to the figures of Christ and St. Thomas at the top (see Figure 2.3). The intricately carved wooden pillar depicts Christ on the right, touching the wound in his side from the sword thrust into his chest during the crucifixion. Thomas on the left, who doubted the news of Jesus's resurrection as told him by his fellow disciples, is in the process of seeing, touching, understanding, and believing, as depicted in the gospel (John 20:26–29).

What is striking is that Thomas Berbisey chose to depict this particular scene of his own patron saint and namesake in the courtyard entering his house off the street, no. 19 rue de la Parcheminerie, and he paid an unknown craftsman to carve this pillar in the main entryway of his house.[23] Although this carving was also doubtless a social marker indicating his wealth and affluence as the head of one of the city's elite families and would have been noticed as such by most who entered into his townhouse through this courtyard, it was also a marker of Thomas Berbisey's piety. So, it seems clear that the religious faith in the Virgin's ability to protect Dijon was equally robust among both the elites such as Thomas Berbisey as well as the popular classes of the city. The mayor Sayve and the city council sought permission from the bishop of Langres to hold an annual procession commemorating the miracle of the intervention of the Virgin each year thereafter. And the bishop readily agreed, noting that "it was now confirmed throughout the entire world" that Dijon had been saved the previous year by the miraculous intervention of the Virgin Mary.[24] Finally, even Louis de la Trémoille, the very military commander who negotiated with the Swiss army and paid them to retreat the previous year, was equally convinced that without the miracle of the Virgin's intervention, this payoff would not have been successful. "The General de la Trémoille invoked the aid of the Holy Virgin," noted a contemporary account, "and it is said that it was as if he was inspired from above to propose to the besiegers the terms of the treaty."[25] So, out of devotion to the Virgin, the elites and popular classes together participated in a special religious procession in September 1514 commemorating the Virgin's role in relieving the siege of the Swiss the year before "to render praise to God the creator, to his glorious mother, and to all the saints above because it has pleased them to liberate and take away the said city [of Dijon] from the great captivity of the Swiss who had held them captives, and that by God's will they have lifted the said siege Tuesday the thirteenth day of September

[23] Eugène Fyot, *Dijon, son passé évoqué par ses rues* (Dijon: Damidot, 1927), 248–251; and Chabeuf, *Dijon: Monuments et souvenirs*, 413. Today rue Parcheminerie is called rue Berbisey, in honor of the street's most famous family.

[24] Quoted in Thomas, *La Délivrance de Dijon*, 237–238. Also see Kathryn A. Edwards, *Families and Frontiers: Recreating Communities and Boundaries in the Early Modern Burgundies* (Leiden: Brill, 2002), 312–317.

[25] BMD, Fonds Bossuet, Ms. 139: "Le general de la Tremoille invoqua le secours de la saincte vierge. On dit quil fut comme inspire den haut de proposer aux assiegeants un jour de treve et dentrevue."

by divine means and inspiration."[26] And on the first Tuesday after the Feast of the Nativity of the Virgin every September thereafter until the ritual was finally ended in the seventeenth century, the people and leaders of Dijon continued to remember the day the Virgin protected them in September 1513 and "to sanctify this day as a feast day."[27] Moreover, at least one historian has claimed that by the beginning of the sixteenth century there was already a growing sense that the Virgin Mary was linked politically to the French nation as a whole, not just in Dijon, as a protector and defender.[28] However widespread this link was in the rest of the kingdom, it seems clear that in Dijon the reimagination of the Virgin's role in ending the siege of 1513 demonstrates clearly how the elites and the popular classes in the city were constantly remaking the function of the Virgin to suit their own local needs.

2.2 Exploring a Parish Church: St. Michel

Although many Christian practices and rituals occurred outside the church, for Christians in the late Middle Ages some of the most significant of their religious experiences took place inside their parish church. The church was where they were baptized, where they confessed their sins, where they took communion with their neighbors, where they encountered what they believed to be actual relics of Jesus and the saints, and ultimately where they confronted the physical body of Christ in the Mass and experienced personally the ultimate sacrifice of the crucifixion. As such, for the majority of Christians their parish church was the holiest and most sacred place in which they were ever likely to set foot. This had not always been the case, however. Indeed, as medieval historians have reminded us, the physical fabric of the church was not considered sacred or a special place of refuge in the early centuries of Christianity, as the term *ecclesia* still reflected its original Greek meaning of an assembly of people rather than a building or institution. The sanctification and sacralization of

---

[26] AND, B 169, fol. 14r, September 9, 1514: "*pour render louange a Dieu le createur a sa glorieuse mere et aux saincts et sainctes de parades de grace quil lui pleust faire a ladicte ville que de les liberer et oster de la grande captivitie ou les Suisses les tenoyent assieyes et que par le vouloir de Dieu ilz partirent et leverent ledict siege le mardi xiiie jour de septembre par le bon moyen et inspiration divine.*"

[27] AMD, D 2 (*liasse*), September 12, 1514: "*de sanctifier ce jour comme un jour ferié.*" The procession was repeated every year thereafter until 1640, when the clergy of Dijon decided to discontinue it, partly because the judges of the Parlement had decided not to take part any longer. See ADCO, G 44, fol. 154.

[28] Maes, *Le Roi, la Vièrge et la nation*, 109–131.

the interior space of the church really only began in the ninth century.[29] Yet by the late Middle Ages, as Dominique Iogna-Prat has recently shown, every Christian in the West understood that to be a member *of* the church meant that one had to be *in* the church. This transformation of interior space also resulted in the sanctification of the ecclesiastical monuments of the church in which "God became stone."[30] Given that so much of this stone fabric of the sixteenth-century church has survived intact to the present, an exploration and analysis of this fabric can shed much valuable light not only on how the themes of the Mass and the Virgin Mary reverberated and made sense to those sixteenth-century Christians who ventured inside its sacred spaces, but also how the elites of the city as well as the popular classes worshipped together. In the discussion that follows we shall focus on one such church in the city of Dijon, the parish church of St. Michel, one of the largest and most diverse parishes in the city.

The church in the parish of St. Michel was originally only a small chapel constructed just outside the wall of the Roman *castrum* between 889 and 897, funded by a parcel of grape vines donated by a preacher named Amalbert from the nearby abbey of St. Etienne. A larger church in Romanesque style was constructed on the same site in the eleventh century by Garner de Mailly, abbot of St. Etienne. Its most noted ecclesiastical monument was a stone statue of the Virgin Mary carved by the well-known Flemish sculptor Claus Sluter, employed in Dijon in the late fourteenth century by Philip the Bold, Duke of Burgundy.[31] The present-day church was constructed in the early sixteenth century, as the growth of the city and the parish, not to mention the decay of the eleventh-century church, required a larger church for the parish. On July 17, 1497 the parish clergy formally decided to build a new church on the same site, and the city council of Dijon and mayor Jean Aignault gave formal approval for construction to begin on August 6, 1499.[32] The church was constructed in stages, took thirty years to complete, and was formally dedicated on July 29, 1529. It was the second largest church in the city, measuring 61 meters in length, 29 meters in width, and nearly 21 meters in height. By comparison the Benedictine abbey church of St. Bénigne was the largest

[29] See Samuel W. Collins, *The Medieval Debate Over Sacred Space* (New York, NY: Palgrave Macmillan, 2012).

[30] Dominique Iogna-Prat, *Maison Dieu: Une histoire monumentale de l'Eglise au Moyen Age* (Paris: Seuil, 2006), especially 443–486 (quote on 443).

[31] Metman, *L'Eglise de Saint-Michel*, 8–15. Sluter's statue of the Virgin Mary survived in the church until the Revolution, when it was destroyed.

[32] AMD, B 167, fols. 85r–88v, August 6, 1497. Also see Metman, *L'Eglise de Saint-Michel*, 19; and Chabeuf, *Dijon: Monuments et souvenirs*, 250–251.

church in the city, measuring 66 meters long, 27 meters wide, and 23 meters high.[33] The church was constructed in flamboyant Renaissance gothic style and was more Italianate in design than most French churches of the period. A richly decorated porch was added to the west entrance soon after the dedication between 1537 and 1551. Under the direction of Nicolas de la Court, a sculptor from Flanders, the three arches of the porch depicted the Last Judgment with a striking statue of St. Michael himself as the focal point, with the Latin inscription *"Millia millium erat numerus eorum* (A thousand thousand was their number)" taken from Revelation 5:11, referring to the number of angels who would descend at the Last Judgment. The two towers that rise above the porch on the west end of the church today were not begun until 1570 and not completed until the later seventeenth century. So, on the eve of the Reformation the parish church of St. Michel was very much like the one depicted in a sketch made in the 1660s (see Figure 2.4).

The completion of the porch with its three large arches surrounding the three principal doors of the church drew explicit attention to the connection between the patron-saint of the parish, the archangel Michael, and the Last Judgment.[34] In the central arch was a life-size statue of the archangel Michael standing on a pedestal and holding up a sword. This depiction was based on the account of the archangel in the Biblical account of the Last Judgment: "And war broke out in heaven; Michael and his angels fought against the dragon. The dragon and his angels fought back, but they were defeated, and there was no longer any place for them in heaven. The great dragon was thrown down, that ancient serpent who is called the Devil and Satan, the deceiver of the whole world – he was thrown down to the earth, and his angels were thrown down with him."[35] Jacobus de Voragine further elaborated upon the role of St. Michael in the Last Judgment in his well-known thirteenth-century *Golden Legend*: "In the time of the Antichrist Michael will rise up and stand forth as defender and protector of the elect. He it was who fought with the dragon and his angels and expelled them from heaven, winning a great victory ... At the sound of the voice of the archangel Michael the dead will rise, and it is he who will present the cross, the nails, the spear, and the crown of thorns at the Day of Judgment"[36] (see Figure 2.5).

---

[33] Metman, *L'Eglise de Saint-Michel*, 22–24.

[34] The fullest description of the decorated porch on the church of St. Michel is Henri David, *De Sluter à Sambin: Essai critique sur la sculpture monumentale en Bourgogne au XVe et au XVIe siècles*, 2 vols. (Paris: Leroux, 1933), 2: 260–314. Also see Eugène Fyot, "L'Architecture à Dijon sous la Renaissance: Hugues Sambin," *Revue de Bourgogne* 12 (December 1925): 5–27.

[35] Revelation 12:7–9.   [36] Voragine, *The Golden Legend*, 2: 201.

Figure 2.4 Sketch of parish church of St. Michel, Dijon, seventeenth century.
Etienne Metman, *L'Eglise Saint-Michel de Dijon* (Dijon: Ratel-Cotosset, 1914), 55

Figure 2.5 The Last Judgment, porch of St. Michel, Dijon, sixteenth century

Behind the statue of the archangel Michael, the Last Judgment was depicted in sculpted stone. On God's right-hand side (the viewer's left) were the elect being received into Heaven, and on God's left-hand side (the viewer's right) were the damned being received into Hell, a scene recounted by Jesus just before his crucifixion in the famous parable of how God will separate the saved from the damned just as a shepherd separates the sheep from the goats (Matthew 25:31–46). Those to be saved were those who gave food to the hungry, drink to the thirsty, shelter to the needy, clothes to the naked, and care to the sick, while those who denied such Christian charity, even to "the least of these," were banished into damnation. "And these will go away into eternal punishment, but the righteous into eternal life," as the passage concluded. Thus, any lay parishioner walking into the main entrance of the church of St. Michel in Dijon would almost certainly have known that the elect and the damned being divided on the right and left by Christ and the archangel Michael were receiving their just rewards. The stone depiction of the Last Judgment reminded them of this each Sunday as they entered the church, just as their receiving the blessed bread (*pain bénit*) after Mass reminded them of it as they exited.

One other very visible motif that the lay Christians of St. Michel parish would have noticed upon entering the church, however, was the preponderance of grape vines decorating the capitals of the columns in each of the three portals of the porch. As was demonstrated in Chapter 1, St. Michel parish was the home of the most militant and most political cohort of Dijon's vignerons, who tended the vines outside the city walls. Unlike most churches in France, which depicted the entire gamut of the vegetable world in its ecclesiastical decorations, in Burgundy "one plant in particular stands out above all others . . . it is the vine."[37] When the church of St. Michel was rebuilt in the early sixteenth century, the capitals of the columns surrounding the three magnificent portals of the western end of the church were decorated with the *pinot noir* vines of Burgundy so familiar to the vignerons who worshipped there (see Figure 2.6). Moreover, these vines were placed at eye level as the parishioners entered the church, so they were clearly meant to be seen as part of the monumental fabric of the church. It cannot have escaped them that just as the columns supported the depiction of the Last Judgment on the façade of their new church, the fruit of their labor as vignerons, chosen above everything else by God to become Christ's blood in the Mass, supported and sustained the Catholic faith.[38]

---

[37] David, *De Sluter à Sambin*, 2: 260.
[38] Mack P. Holt, "Wine, Community and Reformation in Sixteenth-Century Burgundy," *Past & Present* 138 (February 1993): 58–93, especially 89–90.

Figure 2.6 Columns of the western portals of the parish church of St. Michel, Dijon,
sixteenth century

Upon entering the church of St. Michel from the porch (see the plan of the
church, Figure 2.7) parishioners would have been struck by a stone sculpture of
the *Pièta* and another of Christ's body being laid in the tomb off to the right as
they entered the western portal (see Figures 2.1 and 2.8). As already mentioned,
the *Pièta* was one of the most evocative images of the Virgin Mary, the grieving
mother holding her dead son in her arms after he was taken down from the
cross after his crucifixion. Both the *Pièta* and the depiction of Christ's body
being laid in the tomb were very common in parish churches in the city in the
sixteenth century, and examples abound in nearby churches just outside the
city.[39] What is most striking about both works is that they managed to link the
lay Christians' understanding of both the Mass and the Virgin Mary as
protector and defender. In both the *Pièta* and the *Mise au tombeau* (Laying
in the Tomb) Christ's body, although dead, fulfilled the promise of the Last
Supper and was thus a direct link to the Mass. The Virgin Mary fulfilled the
protector's role of the Mary of Mercy in the *Pièta* as she grieved for her son's
death. In the *Mise au tombeau*, she was still grieving, but more serene and

[39] For example, see the parish church in the village of Talant on the hill overlooking the city walls in the
       sixteenth century. The large *Mise au tombeau* sculpture in this church is one of the best in all of
       Burgundy.

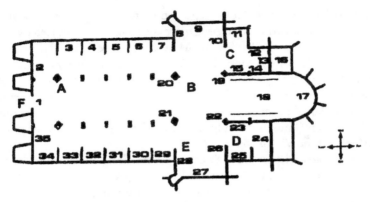

Figure 2.7 Plan of the parish church of St. Michel, Dijon, sixteenth century. As shown in brochure *Eglise Saint-Michel* (Dijon: J. & P. C. / Paroisse Saint-Michel, 1995)

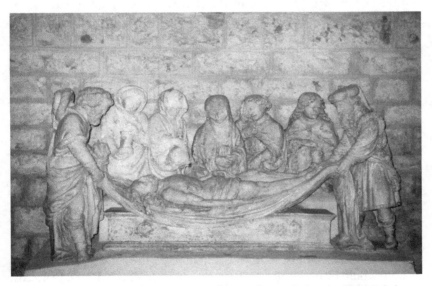

Figure 2.8 Sculpture of the *Mise au tombeau* in the parish church of St. Michel, Dijon, sixteenth century

accepting, knowing that her son's death was necessary for the salvation of the world and that his resurrection was still to come. According to Jean Gerson around 1400, Mary alone was able "to behold the secrets of God in mystical contemplation" prior to the resurrection on Easter Sunday.[40] Here, obviously, with her hands crossed in front of her in prayer she was comforted by Joseph of Arimathea, John the Evangelist, Mary Magdelene (with the long hair), along with her half sisters Mary the mother of James and Mary Cleophas, and Martha. In their different ways both these sculptures reminded parishioners of the sorrow and pain associated with the death of Christ and the suffering of the Virgin Mary, but they also represented the promise of joy and salvation of the resurrection. Thus, both sculptures reminded parishioners of the power of the Mass and the Virgin Mary.

If they followed past these two sculptures along the south side of the nave and looked up just beneath the stained-glass windows, they would have seen a number of stone plaques commemorating masses for the dead. They would have been too high up to be able to read them, but local residents would have recognized them for what they were because of the two very visible and legible plaques located at ground level just inside the vestibule of the southern door of the church. Here were two large stone plaques spelling out the foundation of masses for the dead put up in the sixteenth century (see Figures 2.9 and 2.10). The smaller of the two on the right was established in 1557 by a laborer of the parish requesting God's protection of the grape harvests. In a similar vein, the larger of the two on the left read as follows:

> To the honor of God, the venerable priests and chaplains of the church of St-Michel within are perpetually obliged to say a low mass at the high altar every day, which will be sounded for half an hour at three o'clock in the morning from the feast of Candelmas [February 2] to the feast of St-Remy [October 1], and at four o'clock in the morning from the feast of St-Remy to the feast of Candelmas; and on Sundays to present the blessed bread and holy water; to say the Passion of Christ from the first day of April until the feast of St-Remy, and on any other times and occasions when there is bad weather, heavy rain, hailstorms, or ice.

The foundation went on to spell out that a high mass for the dead, with vespers, canonical hours, matins, penitential psalms, and a religious procession, would be performed on the feasts of St. Michel (May 8), Pentecost (the seventh Sunday after Easter), and Corpus Christi (Thursday after Pentecost Sunday), as well as on each Sunday after the feasts of St. Luke (October 18) and All Saints (November 1). The foundation included funds for candles and torches for all these masses, and was paid in the form of a *rente* on the principal of 1,274 *livres*. The contract was drawn up by a royal

---

[40] Quoted in Ellington, *From Sacred Body to Angelic Soul*, 98.

Figure 2.9 Foundation of masses, church of St. Michel, Dijon, sixteenth century

Figure 2.10 Foundation of masses, church of St. Michel, Dijon, sixteenth century

notary, Jean Dubois, on April 28, 1566. The foundation ends with the list of 40 donors, all of them vignerons, who had the foundation inscribed in the vestibule of the church in 1577, replete with the traditional skulls and bones.[41] This particular foundation is striking for a number of reasons. First, it was a collective foundation of 40 individual vignerons who lived in the parish. Second, it was funded by a *rente* secured by wine futures; the overwhelming majority of foundations in Burgundy were funded with wine. A sample of six parishes over the course of the fifteenth, sixteenth, and seventeenth centuries – the urban parish of St. Michel in Dijon, and the nearby villages of Fontaine-lès-Dijon, Fixin, Marsannay, Gevrey, and Couchey along the Côte d'Or south of Dijon – reveals that of a total of 314 such foundations, 287 (91 percent) were funded by wine futures; that is, in return for perpetual masses for the dead the local churches in question were paid after the wine harvest each year in wine from a specified parcel of vines.[42] For Burgundians in the sixteenth century, then, it is no exaggeration to say that wine sustained them in death as well as in life.

Much of what we know about masses to the dead and testamentary donations of property to the church on the eve of the Reformation we owe to Jacques Chiffoleau's *La Comptabilité de l'au-delà*.[43] This massive study of over 3,000 such donations in the region of Avignon in the fourteenth and fifteenth centuries examined the origins and growth of the practice of establishing masses for the dead, which began in the decades preceding the outbreak of the Black Death. Chiffoleau argued that these Christians were principally responding to the pressures of urbanization and a rising individualism. As many French men and women found themselves cut off from their rural roots and ancestral identities, he argues, the enclosed spaces of the cities generated a greater sense of individualism. "It is urbanization, which in unraveling the traditional links which united the living and the dead, in imposing new familial relations, in giving to the individual

---

[41] The carved image is approximately 1.5 meters by 2.5 meters and is located just on the left inside the vestibule of the south door of the parish church of St. Michel, Dijon. The actual contracts on which these monuments were based are located in ADCO, G 3573 to 3581 and AMD, D 38 for the parish of St. Michel. This particular foundation contract was signed on April 28, 1566 by the notary Jean Dubois.

[42] See ADCO, G 3573 to 3581 (parish of St. Michel in Dijon), G 3947 and 3948 (village of Couchey), G 3975 and 3976 (village of Fixin), G3984 (village of Fontaine-lès-Dijon), G 3996 (village of Gevrey-en-Montagne, today Gevery-Chambertin), and G 4044 (village of Marsannay-La Côte). Also, see Dominique Viaux, *La Vie paroissiale à Dijon à la fin du Moyen Age* (Dijon: Editions Universitaires de Dijon, 1988), 181–198; and the same author's article, "Eglises rurales en Bourgogne aux XVe et XVIe siècles," *Annales de Bourgogne* 60 (1988): 111–137.

[43] Jacques Chiffoleau, *La Comptabilité de l'au-delà: Les hommes, la mort et la religion d'Avignon à la fin du Moyen Age, vers 1320-vers 1480* (Rome: Ecole française de Rome, 1980).

a greater and greater role, explains the birth of a new image of death."[44] This new image of the "death of the self (*mort de soi*)" manifested itself in masses for the dead. Cut off from the living in this world, Christians in the fourteenth and fifteenth centuries attempted to forge new ties in the next world. Thus, Chiffoleau argues, Christians came to focus more and more on what he called "the bookkeeping of the beyond," a process exacerbated by the demographic crisis of the century between 1350 and 1450.

While it is undeniable that individuals who donated money or property to the church in return for masses for the dead believed in their efficacy, and that this is also a direct reflection of a nearly universal acceptance of the doctrine of purgatory, it also seems clear that these masses served other more terrestrial social functions. Given that in Burgundy wine was the common link between the living and the dead, I wish to suggest that these masses were as much about the here and now as they were about the beyond. This in no way contradicts Chiffoleau's thesis, whose large data base of masses for the dead were almost entirely testamentary foundations made in wills, many just prior to death. My data base is composed almost entirely of foundations made in the prime of life by individuals who had dual goals: the prophylactic protection of the vineyards, such as the collective foundation in in the parish church of St. Michel described earlier, as well as the perpetual masses for the salvation of their souls. Thus, it hardly comes as a surprise to discover that these foundations were as much about social links in this world as they were about future ties in the next. Not only is my data base much smaller than Chiffoleau's but my goals are very different. Unlike him, I am not trying to measure piety in any quantitative way; rather I am attempting to analyze the social links the contents of the foundations reveal. Thus, I am much more interested in the language of the foundations and what the masses were linked to socially in the context of the local community, which is much more difficult to quantify than the overall level of piety measured in numbers of masses or amounts invested.

If we look back at the foundation in the parish church of St. Michel in Dijon by the 40 vignerons, several factors stand out. First, it is clear that whatever new communal links were being forged in the beyond, social links in this world were at least as important. Forty vignerons from one parish funding a collective foundation was unusual, to be sure. It was quite common, however, for various social links – familial and kinship ties, and friendship networks being most common – to be explicitly underscored in

---

[44] Ibid., 480.

such contracts. The one here funded by 40 vignerons reveals that not only
were they all from the same parish, but 33 of the 40 lived in the same
neighborhood in the parish on adjoining streets.[45] Thus, this foundation
was about reinforcing already existing social ties among a group of affluent
vignerons in a Dijon neighborhood. That they collectively contributed
a sum of 1,274 *livres* – an average of 31 *livres* 17 *sous* each – indicates they had
strong social ties extending from the neighborhood streets where they
lived, to the vineyards outside the city walls where they journeyed
each day for work. So, this foundation was not so much about establishing
new ties in the beyond as it was about reinforcing those in the here and
now.[46]

The collective foundation of the 40 *vignerons* in the parish church of
St. Michel also demonstrates that the masses were intended to benefit the
vineyards supporting them as much as the souls of the founders. They
required the chaplains of the parish of St. Michel "to say the Passion of
Christ from the first day of April until the feast of St-Remy [October 1],
and on any other times and occasions when there is bad weather, heavy
rain, hailstorms, or ice."[47] Any vigneron would have recognized the reference to "bad weather, heavy rain, hailstorms, or ice," which were the
enemies of his craft, and would have understood how the efficacy of
these masses for the dead was also meant to continue the support of the
living. More evidence for this point appears in the number of times that
Burgundian founders, especially vignerons, declared that their anniversary
masses would be said not on the anniversary of their death but on or
around the feast of St. Remy [October 1]. Not only did it fall at the time of
the grape harvest, but popular understanding of St. Remy, whatever it was,
was based on two things. As the thirteenth-century *Golden Legend* made
clear, St. Remy was obviously remembered as the bishop who baptized
Clovis into the Christian faith, but he was also known for his Christ-like
miracle involving wine: "Once when he was a guest in the house of
a certain matron and her supply of wine was running short, Remy went
to the cellar and made the sign of the cross over the wine cask; and after he
had prayed, the wine overflowed the cask and half-filled the cellar."[48] Is it
any surprise, then, that nearly 40 percent of all the masses for the dead

---

[45] For the tax roll of the parish of St. Michel for 1566 see AMD, L 198, fols. 1–38, which shows that 33 of
the donors of this foundation lived on adjoining streets: rue Vannerie, rue de Roulotte (today rue de
l'Ecole), and rue Chanoine (today rue Jeannin).
[46] See my article, "Wine, Life, and Death in Early Modern Burgundy," *Food and Foodways:
Explorations in the History and Culture of Human Nourishment* 8 (Fall 1999): 73–98.
[47] See Note 41.   [48] Voragine, *The Golden Legend*, 1: 86.

founded in Burgundy from my sample – 119 out of 314 (38 percent) – included at least one on the feast of St. Remy? And among vignerons the proportion was even higher: 91 out of 186 (49 percent). Thus, it would appear that these masses for the dead were just as much prayers for the grape harvest as they were for the souls of the donors.[49]

What these foundations show is that in Burgundy on the eve of the Reformation wine futures largely funded the numerous masses for the dead. The foundations were contracts in which wine from specific parcels of vines were designated as payment at each grape harvest for the perpetual masses for the dead outlined in the contracts. In practical terms it meant that many parish clergy became wine brokers as they sold the wine from these parcels in order to pay for their services. Much more will be said about the logistics of the local wine industry in Burgundy in the next chapter, but suffice it to say here that this collective foundation by 40 vignerons in the parish of St. Michel established in 1566 makes it very clear that the religious and spiritual experiences of the people were inherently tied to the conditions of material life. There was certainly no structural or mono-causal relationship between the two, but these foundations remind us that we cannot understand the religious experience of the laity unless we understand that for them life in this world and life in the next were inextricably linked and that there were significant forms of communication and translation between the two.

Once parishioners moved past the monument of the foundation of masses at the south vestibule of the church of St. Michel, they would eventually arrive at the eastern end of the nave where they would see the entrance to the choir flanked by two chapels on either side. Neither the original altar table nor the other accoutrements of the choir from the sixteenth century have survived, as they were replaced in 1763.[50] But this is the same space where the priest celebrated Mass and where the laity of the parish would have assembled to receive the Host on Easter Sunday. Of all the spaces in the church, this was the most sacred. It is where the Host was elevated and displayed each Sunday by the parish clergy, and

[49] Holt, "Wine, Life, and Death," 84–88. The sample comes from, ADCO, G 3573 to 3581 (parish of St. Michel, Dijon), G 3947 and 3948 (village of Couchey), G 3976 (village of Fixin), G3984 (village of Fontaine-lès-Dijon), G 3996 (village of Gevrey-en-Montagne), and G 4044 (village of Marsannay-La Côte). The collective sample thus consists of a medium-sized urban parish in Dijon of ca. 350 households, several large rural villages of 50–100 households, and several smaller rural villages of fewer than 50 households for greater diversity. The rural parishes were selected because of their close proximity to Dijon, all within 20 km of the city. Dates covered are from the mid-fifteenth to the early eighteenth centuries.

[50] Metman, *L'Eglise Saint-Michel*, 100–101.

as already explained, also where the ritual of the Mass was performed. Though the present decorations at the entrance of the choir and the altar area itself at the far end of the choir are all modern, the importance of this space in the church was nevertheless clear. One had to go up two steps to reach the elevated space of the choir, and it was explicitly marked off from the rest of the church by the choir screen. It was also probably the least visited space in the church by the majority of lay Christians, though in some ways that helped it to retain its sacred status.

The other spaces in the parish church that most lay Christians would also probably not have experienced were the many private chapels scattered throughout the church. With a total of sixteen chapels in all, these spaces were occupied and decorated by some of the most elite families in the parish, with a few being reserved for parish confraternities, such as the confraternity of the Three Kings, whose chapel was just off the south vestibule opposite the foundation of masses by the 40 vignerons. Looking at the plan of the church, there were six chapels along both the north and the south walls of the nave, with a further four at the eastern end of the church, two flanking each side of the choir. The chapels founded by elite families in the parish of St. Michel included the Fyot and Cirey family chapels on the south side near the choir. And along the north aisle of the nave were the family chapels of the Gagne, Martin, and La Verne families. Members of all of these families served the city of Dijon as mayors, city councilors (échevins), judges in the Parlement, or royal officers during the course of the sixteenth century. In the Gagne family chapel there is some sixteenth-century stained glass depicting the crucifixion painted by the Dijon artist Edouard Brédin. Next to it was the Martin family chapel, where Bénigne Martin, who served several terms as mayor of Dijon in the mid-sixteenth century, was buried under the floor in 1573. This chapel was founded by his father, Etienne Martin, and his mother, Michelle Valrans, in 1527: "They founded a resurrection chapel in the church of St. Michel for themselves, their children, parents, in-laws, brothers and sisters, as well as all other ancestors and close relatives, including those to come. They also founded five low masses to be performed each week . . . and they donated several foundations for the endowment of this chapel."[51] And just next to it was the La Verne family chapel, perhaps the most decorated and ornate in the entire church. Jacques La Verne was not only one of the most con-troversial mayors of Dijon during the Wars of Religion (see Chapter 5), but

[51] ADCO, G 3573, April 11, 1527.

his family was one of the wealthiest nonaristocratic families in the entire parish of St. Michel. Their family chapel contained a small statue of the Virgin Mary carrying the Christ-child in her arms on the altar from the school of Claus Sluter. Above the altar was a painting commissioned by Jacques La Verne in 1588 of the death of the Virgin Mary. Painted by the well-known Flemish artist Nicolas de Hoey, who had emigrated to Dijon the decade before, this mural decorated the vaulted ceiling of the family chapel. It depicted the Trinity at the top looking down on the Virgin Mary on her deathbed, surrounded by the apostles (see Figure 2.11).[52] There was nothing else quite like this mural in the entire church at the time, and obviously the La Verne family members were attempting to demonstrate their wealth and sense of taste as well as their piety in commissioning such a painting. On the other hand, that Jacques La Verne chose to depict the death of the Virgin in his family chapel indicated how powerfully the image of the Virgin Mary resonated among lay Christians in the sixteenth century.

This brief tour of one of Dijon's parish churches helps us better understand the many different ways that lay Christians in the sixteenth century might have experienced their religious faith and piety. Their understandings of the theology of salvation hinged on the knowledge that entrance into the kingdom of heaven ultimately required Christian charity on their part, as evidenced in the Last Judgment and repeated in many elements of the rite of the Mass. In addition, they knew in some way that God's own grace was required and was imparted to them in the Eucharist. They trusted implicitly in the Virgin Mary's ability to protect them in this world, as she did in 1513 during the siege of Dijon. Moreover, they believed in the efficacy of masses for the dead, not only for satisfying their sins and reducing time in Purgatory in the next life, but also for protecting the grape harvests on which their livelihood depended in this life. Indeed, it is clear that their most sacred and pious religious experiences that occurred inside the parish church were visibly connected to their everyday lives outside the church. Moreover, the making and remaking of these religious experiences, especially in the appropriation of the Virgin Mary and the investment by ordinary vignerons in masses for the dead, demonstrates how late medieval Christians in Burgundy understood their own roles in surviving the perils of this world as well as salvation in the next.

---

[52] Metman, *L'Eglise Saint-Michel*, 126–128. For more on De Hoey, see Marguerite Guillaume, *La Peinture en Bourgogne au XVIe siècle* (Dijon: Musée des Beaux-Arts de Dijon, 1990), 137–144.

Figure 2.11 Painting by Nicolas De Hoey of "The Death of the Virgin," 1588, in the church of St. Michel, Dijon, La Verne Chapel, sixteenth century

2.3   Religious Practices Outside the Church

As already suggested by Dominique Iogna-Prat, in the late Middle Ages lay Christians understood that to be a member *of* the church, they also had to be *in* the church on a regular basis. This did not mean, however, that their religious practices were restricted to the interior spaces of the parish church: "being in the church implied one could also be outside" the church.[53] Indeed, religious experiences for lay Christians outside the church were so numerous and varied that it is impossible to recount them all here. I shall limit my focus in this section to three broad categories of extramural religious practices: religious processions, the celebration of feast days, and participation in confraternities, though these categories were obviously not mutually exclusive, such as the celebration of the feast day of Corpus Christi with a special procession of the Host with various confraternities participating.

We have already encountered one sort of religious procession, the one organized by the clergy of the parish church of Notre Dame in September 1513 with the statue of the Black Virgin to seek the Virgin Mary's protection during the siege of Dijon by the Swiss. Spontaneous religious processions such as this one organized by the clergy, or very often requested by the mayor and city council to seek relief from some immediate danger or threat to their safety or livelihood, were very common. In fact, there were probably more religious processions organized by the clergy and/or city council to deal with harsh weather conditions affecting the local grapevines than for any other reason. Virtually every year like clockwork, for example, Dijon's city council, as its deliberations attest, made regular efforts to organize religious procession to protect the grape harvest from drought, too much rain, hail, or the seasonal insects and vermin that destroyed the grapes. Much more will be said about these natural ravages to the vines and the Burgundians' efforts to deal with them in Chapter 3, but a religious procession was the most common remedy chosen to combat them. And the primary reason for this was that most Burgundians associated any attacks on their grape vines from bad weather or insects as divine punishment for their own sins. Moreover, these remedies were by no means just the product of popular beliefs and unlearned culture; they were the collective attempts of the humblest vignerons, wealthy vineyard owners, the clergy, urban officials, and even the bishop of Langres to alleviate and ameliorate what they perceived to be collective punishment for their sins.

There were many other types of religious processions, however. Every April 23 – the feast day of St. George – there was a religious procession from Dijon to the chapel at St. Jacques-des-Vignes and to the priory of Larrey outside the city walls. And every year on the first day of May – the feast day of St. James and St. Philip – there was a procession to the Cross of

---

[53] Iogna-Prat, *Maison Dieu*, 479–480, quote on p. 479.

Charmotte in the village of Fontaine just outside the city.[54] There was another annual procession outside the city walls to the cross at the priory of Epoisses on June 6 every year.[55] And finally, after 1531 there was an annual procession every year inside the city on the eve of the feast day of St. Anne, the mother of the Virgin Mary, on July 25.[56] All these processions usually departed at seven o'clock in the morning from one of the parish churches or from the Sainte-Chapelle. There would always be several clergy present, one of whom would preach a sermon upon arrival at the destination, as well as numerous servants carrying large amounts of food, wine, pots for reheating the food, wood, table linens, glasses, and a butt of water that would be blessed by one of the clergy and distributed as holy water (*l'eau bénite*) after the sermon and prayers. All of this was organized by Dijon's vignerons, whose specific duty it was to supervise the food and wine. The food would then be reheated over a fire and everyone shared a meal together. Although the records of these processions cannot tell us how many people participated, we can get a general sense of numbers by the amount of provisions that the vignerons provided. Clearly these were not large processions: 2 dozen loaves of bread, 2 dozen pints of wine, 3 hams, 2 legs of mutton, 3 pounds of lard (though sometimes butter instead), several veal tongues, 2 haunches of venison, unspecified amounts or oranges, salt, nutmeg and other spices, eggs, and sometimes fish (a whole salmon in 1587).[57] With the consumption of so much food and drink, there was certainly a social and commensal aspect to the event. But it is much harder to say exactly who and how many participated.

By far the best-attended religious procession, however, was the one that took place inside the city of Dijon every year to mark the feast of Corpus Christi, a special feast day honoring the Eucharist that was established in the thirteenth century.[58] It was not on a fixed date, as it was tied to the date of Easter every year, being celebrated on the Thursday after Pentecost Sunday, which was the seventh Sunday after Easter. Thus, Corpus Christi could fall between May 21 and June 24 inclusive. Mervyn James and Barabra Diefendorf have analyzed the Corpus Christi Day processions in detail in England and Paris, respectively, and the processions in Dijon shared many elements with the practices in these other places.[59]

[54] AMD, D 4 (liasse).   [55] AMD, D 3 (liasse).   [56] AMD, B 185, fol. 57r, July 21, 1547.
[57] AMD, D 4 (liasse), expenses for processions to Larrey and Fontaine, 1571, 1578, 1587, 1604, and 1618.
[58] The best introduction is Rubin, *Corpus Christi*, especially 243–271. Also, see Wandel, *The Eucharist in the Reformation*, especially 39–44.
[59] Mervyn James, "Ritual, Drama and Social Body in the Late Medieval English Town," *Past & Present* 98 (February 1983): 3–29, reprinted in the same author's *Society, Politics and Culture: Studies in Early*

The procession in Dijon almost always took place on a Sunday, usually the first Sunday after the Feast of Corpus Christi. The route varied from year to year, but it invariably began at the Sainte Chapelle and went from the center of town to one of the main gates on the city walls, then back to the Sainte Chapelle where Mass was celebrated.[60] As was the case elsewhere in Europe, the Corpus Christi procession was both a ritual of religious piety and a visual reminder of the social hierarchy of the city's political and religious elites. Some scholars such as Mervyn James have stressed the functional nature of Corpus Christi processions as playing a critical role in the development and perpetuation of *communitas*. Drawing heavily from the discipline of anthropology – especially Claude Levi-Strauss, Mary Douglas, and Victor Turner – James notes that the processions served to reaffirm a civic notion of community, "to express the social bond and to contribute to social integration ... Social wholeness was the central emphasis."[61] Miri Rubin, on the other hand, finds the ritual fulfilled more of a political than a social function. On the one hand, she argues that a ritual that excluded most of the working population of the city, not to mention women, children, and servants, expressed a very elitist notion of community and hardly a mirror of the community itself. "By laying the hierarchy bare," she notes, "it could incite the conflict of difference ever more powerfully sensed in a concentrated symbolic moment."[62] In other words, the ritual could foment conflict and disorder as easily as community and harmony. On the other hand, she agrees with James that the ritual also served to reinforce magisterial authority in the community, though she finds this function more powerful than the social function of community building.

> What emerges, then, is the penetration of the secular and the civic-political into the eucharistic procession in two hardly separable ways. First, the symbolic meaning of eucharistic practices, and the eucharisitc public pro-cession, attracted those whose claims to power and privilege could be re-expressed, and celebrated on this special event. Second, as the event devel-oped, and impinged on political relations, law, and order, a controlling and regulating function was required from the town officials ... Majesty was the theme of the eucharistic procession.[63]

Modern England (Cambridge: Cambridge University Press, 1986), 16–47; and Barbara B. Diefendorf, *Beneath the Cross: Catholics and Huguenots in Sixteenth-Century Paris* (New York, NY: Oxford University Press, 1991), especially 32–48.
[60] AMD, D 4 (liasse).   [61] James, *Society, Politics and Culture*, 17 and 25.
[62] Rubin, *Corpus Christi*, 266.   [63] Ibid., 259.

Corpus Christi processions in Dijon in the sixteenth century certainly exhibited both the social and political functions described by James and Rubin, though I suspect that Barbara Diefendorf is closer to the mark when she suggests that the political, social, and religious elements of such processions were all enfolded together, with none taking precedence over the other two. This was especially true when the king himself participated in the procession. She notes that such Corpus Christi processions in Paris "ritually enacted a vision in which civic, monarchical, and Catholic symbols merged; the body social, the body politic, and the body of Christ were so closely intertwined as to be inseparable."[64] The king appeared in Dijon's Corpus Christi procession only once in the sixteenth century, when Henry IV remained in the Burgundian capital specifically to march in the procession after the city surrendered to him at the end of the civil wars in June 1595 (see Chapter 5). The other major difference between Corpus Christi processions and those described above to Larrey, Fontaine, and Epoisses was that all the city's elites marched in the Corpus Christi processions and nearly all the towns inhabitants also turned out to line the route of the procession to watch. Indeed, the inhabitants of the parish through which the processional route passed each year were required to clean the streets in front of their houses and decorate their homes with tapestries. So, in many ways the Corpus Christi processions in Dijon were community affairs. The city fathers – mayor and échevins – plus the judges in the Parlement and other royal officers, as well as the leading clergy of the city all participated in the annual ritual to celebrate the Eucharist, organized according to their rank and dignity: Indeed, the entire city turned out to see the Host and King Henry IV in 1595, but even in other years in which the king was not present, the city celebrated this feast day collectively. The inhabitants lining the processional route to get a glimpse of the consecrated Host were just as necessary a part of the ritual drama of Corpus Christi as the marchers in the procession itself. So, despite Miri Rubin's contention that the ritual did not include most working men, women, children, and servants, these groups were clearly all present, just not in the procession itself. But their participation was just as vital as those who did march before them, and their participation in the ritual was just as active as the marchers'. It was the body of Christ that was processing before them, after all, the consecrated Host they had turned out to see. And as noted earlier in connection with the Eucharist inside the church, seeing and participating went hand in hand outside the church as well.

[64] Diefendorf, *Beneath the Cross*, 48.

To be sure, Rubin is correct that this was a powerful *political* assembly of notables. But their presence also emphasized the importance of the Host that they were accompanying. For the lay people of the city of Dijon, they obviously noticed all the pomp and circumstance of the assembled elites. But they also knew that the main reason for which they had turned out was to celebrate, contemplate, and gaze upon the body of Christ. If seeing and ingesting the consecrated Host at Mass imparted God's grace to an individual Christian, then processing the Host through the parishes of the city could equally be seen as imparting God's grace to the entire community. Thus, the Corpus Christi procession was a religious ritual with political and social implications, as Rubin and James, respectively, rightly note. But it was still overwhelmingly a religious experience for contemporaries; even the presence of the king could not disguise that fact. And a final point to note is that special religious processions such as the one marking the feast of Corpus Christi also drew in hundreds of villagers from nearby communities, who came to line the streets and observe the consecrated Host. A vigneron named Jean Robert from the village of Couchey, for example, wrote in his family record book (*Livre de raison*) that in June 1583 some 364 of his fellow vignerons from the villages of Morey, Gevrey, Brochon, Fixin, Fixey, Couchey, and Marsannay marched to Dijon dressed in white and carrying banners and crosses to participate in the collective ritual of Corpus Christi with the inhabitants of the city of Dijon.[65] Indeed, 1583 was an especially eventful year, as the Corpus Christi processions set off a wave of numerous processions throughout eastern France as well as the capital of Paris throughout the summer that lasted until October, in which penitents dressed all in white marched together carrying crosses, banners, and singing the *Ave Maria* and *Stabat Mater*. As a contemporary noted, "this year [1583] the people of France and especially in this region [of Champagne, north of Burgundy] are greatly stirred up with devotion, such that each of the towns and villages organized great processions . . . the people being dressed in white, always in good order."[66] And in Dijon, vignerons participated in these processions alongside the clergy and their social betters.

---

[65] "Le livre de la famille Robert: Notes sur le village de Couchey," in Charles Oursel, ed., *Deux livres de raison bourguignons* (Dijon: Mémoires de la Société bourguignonne de géographie et d'histoire, 1908), 358.

[66] Quoted in Denis Crouzet, *Les guerriers de Dieu: La violence au temps des troubles de religion, vers 1525- vers 1610*, 2 vols. (Seyssel: Champ Vallon, 1990), 2: 297–298. Also see Crouzet's "Recherches sur les processions blanches, 1583–1584," *Histoire, économie et société* 1 (1982): 511–563.

In addition to the variety of religious processions already discussed, another major category of religious experience outside the church was the celebration of special feast days. The number and varieties of feast days in early modern France were so disparate that it might seem churlish to select a single one to illustrate the lay religious experience of a feast day. Moreover, there is nothing like the astute summary and analysis of the liturgical calendar for France as David Cressy and Ronald Hutton have produced for early modern England, which might make such a selection more palatable.[67] Nevertheless, I want to focus on one feast day in particular to illustrate the ways in which religious practice, sociability, and politics could be combined in the celebration of a religious festival, with both the city's elites and popular classes taking part: the feast of St. John the Baptist on June 24, also known all over Western Europe as the midsummer festival. According to Peter Burke, in northern Europe this feast day was especially important. Celebrating midsummer's eve has a long history in northern Europe, and like its midwinter counterpart, Christmas, it looks as if the medieval church simply superimposed one of its principal feasts on preexisting pagan celebrations. "Just as the Midwinter festival on 25 December came to be celebrated as the birthday of Christ, so the Midsummer festival came to be celebrated as the forerunner of Christ."[68] This feast day had also long been celebrated with the lighting of bonfires and the carrying of torches going back to pagan festivals. By the time the *Golden Legend* of saints' lives was compiled by Jacobus de Voragine in the mid-thirteenth century, the lighting of bonfires and carrying of torches had become firmly linked to this saint's feast day:

> There are people who on this day burn the bones of dead animals, collected wherever they are found ... Since this was usually done around the time of Saint John's feast day, some people continue to observe the custom ... Lighted torches are also carried around this bonfire, because John was a burning and a shining torch, and a wheel is spun because the sun then begins to be lower in its cycle.[69]

---

[67] See David Cressy, *Bonfires and Bells: National Memory and the Protestant Calendar in Elizabethan and Stuart England* (Berkeley and Los Angeles, CA: University of California Press, 1989); Ronald Hutton, *The Rise and Fall of Merry England: The Ritual Year, 1400–1700* (Oxford: Oxford University Press, 1994); as well as Hutton's more comprehensive *The Stations of the Sun: A History of the Ritual Year in Britain* (Oxford: Oxford University Press, 1996). For France, the best place to start is still Arnold van Gennep, *Manuel de folklore français contemporain: Part 1*, 8 vols. (Paris: A. and J. Picard, 1943–1988). Despite its title, there is a great deal here relating to the early modern period.

[68] Peter Burke, *Popular Culture in Early Modern Europe* (Aldershot: Scolar Press, 1994 rev. edn.), 181 and 195 (quote on 181).

[69] Voragine, *The Golden Legend*, 1: 335–336.

And a century before Voragine, Jean Belathus, a twelfth-century theologian at the University of Paris, noted that the lighting of bonfires on the eve of the Feast of St. John the Baptist was already a popular custom. And by the sixteenth century bonfires were being set all over Europe on the eve of the feast of St. John the Baptist, and Burgundy was no exception.[70] In Dijon, however, what made this particular feast day resonate so acutely in the liturgical calendar was that it was linked to the city's annual elections for mayor (see Chapter 1). Every year on June 23, the eve of the feast day, the new mayor, twenty *échevins*, and all the *juré* artisans and vignerons were sworn in and took their oaths of office. Thus, the festive eating, drinking, dancing, and all the bonfires and torches accompanying the celebration of the feast day later that evening were also celebrations marking a new political régime in the city and either the reelection of the former mayor or the installation of a new mayor. Normally each parish would conduct special prayers and services in the parish church, followed by a large bonfire celebration in the plaza just outside the parish church of St. John. Singing, dancing, and the requisite eating and drinking normally accompanied the bonfire, as the festivities moved from the sacred space inside the church to the profane space outside in the plaza. The transition from the sacred to the profane part of the festivities was not always clear-cut, however, as in June 1555 the singing, dancing, and general merriment actually began inside the parish church of St. John before the bonfire was even lit. There was so much noise and commotion, in fact, that complaints were registered in nearby parishes (the parish church of St. Philibert, for example, was barely 100 meters away). And the Parlement of Dijon issued an immediate prohibition of such behavior in the future. "The said court [of Parlement] has forbidden and does so forbid all persons of whatever, estate, rank, or condition on pain of imprisonment and an arbitrary fine from singing licentious songs or of creating any scandal, commotion, or mockery when they gather at the said [parish] churches for celebrating the eve of the feast day. Thus, the court has ordered and does so order them to focus instead on the prayers and sermons that honor God and his saints in such devotion and reverence that is expected of them."[71] It was recounted in Chapter 1 how easily a fight could break out and tempers could flare amid all the drinking and festivity surrounding the bonfire on the eve of St. John the Baptist's Day. The principal point here, though, is that a major

---

[70] Hutton, *Stations of the Sun*, 311–331; and Hutton, *The Rise and Fall of Merry England*, 37–40. For Burgundy, see Van Gennep, *Manuel de folklore français contemporain: Part I*, 4: 1755.

[71] Quoted in Joseph Garnier, *Le feu de la Saint-Jean à Dijon* (Dijon: Jobard, 1890), 10–11.

religious feast marking a major turning point in the astronomical calendar, complete with services and prayers led by the clergy inside the church, was accompanied by political rituals and rites of sociability outside the sacred spaces of the church, which were just as important for the city and its citizens.

One final arena of religious experience outside the parish church for many citizens of Dijon – at least for the males – was the confraternity. Dozens of these brotherhoods existed in Dijon, as in most major towns, and by the sixteenth century most of them were virtually indistinguishable from the city's craft guilds, where membership was obligatory for master artisans if they intended to practice their trade in the city. Each artisanal craft had its own guild as well as a spiritual brotherhood, or confraternity. As James Farr has shown, these two overlapping corporations merged together into one organization by the late Middle Ages, with the guild policing the economic activities of its members while the confraternity looked after their spiritual needs.[72] Not all confraternities were composed of masters of the same craft guild, however, and we have already encountered one of these in the parish church of St. Michel, where the Confraternity of the Three Kings helped to distribute the *pain bénit* after Mass each Sunday. This confraternity had its own chapel in the church, adorned with a stone relief of the Adoration of the Magi, to which its members were devoted. Founded originally in Cologne and coming to Dijon by way of Franche-Comté, the confraternity's funeral chapel was established in 1550 by Bénigne de Cirey and his wife Marguerite Gros. The confraternity had 60 members at its founding, though it expanded considerably during the Wars of Religion in the second half of the sixteenth century to 99 members by 1583 and to 208 members by 1606. Once women were admitted in 1607, the group grew even faster, to 327 members by 1618 (of which 59 were females) and to 492 members by 1650. Even though the Confraternity of the Three Kings had its chapel in the parish church of St. Michel, its members came from every parish in the city. Moreover, unlike the craft guilds, the members of the Confraternity of the Three Kings came from all the artisanal crafts: vignerons, gardeners, butchers, tailors, shoemakers, etc. The highest social rank of any of its members at its founding was a doorkeeper (*huissier*) in the law courts, so for

---

[72] James R. Farr, *Hands of Honor: Artisans and Their World in Dijon, 1550–1650* (Ithaca, NY: Cornell University Press, 1988), 242–246; as well as the same author's *Artisans in Europe, 1300–1914* (Cambridge: Cambridge University Press, 2000), 228–235.

the most part this was a confraternity whose membership was drawn largely from the popular classes.[73]

As its name would suggest, the confraternity was devoted to the feast of the Epiphany at Christmastide. Every December 27 the confreres would elect one of their members as the "King," who, on January 5, the eve of the Feast of the Kings – or Twelfth Night – was conducted from his house to the parish church of St. Michel for vespers. Then the following day, January 6, on the feast day itself there was a high mass with all the members present, each holding a candle. The elected "Kings" for the three preceding years, symbolically representing the Three Magi, then led the newly elected "King" to the altar to receive the Eucharist. Afterwards, the entire corporation led the newly installed "King" back to his own house, where he offered dinner and wine to his fellow confreres, much as the newly elected mayors of the city did after they were elected each June 21.[74] As already noted, however, their most visible and most significant extramural activity in Dijon was their aiding and supervising the distribution of blessed bread (*pain bénit*) after church each Sunday. Like so many other aspects of religious experience, those that took place outside the parish church were just as important as those that occurred within.

This brief survey of religious beliefs and practices on the eve of the Reformation in Dijon has attempted to make explicit that the variety of religious experiences of pre-Reformation Christians was neither fixed and static nor imposed exclusively from above by an authoritative clergy upon an unthinking and uncomprehending laity. On the contrary, pre-Reformation Christianity – or Catholicism, if you will – was constantly being made and remade by both its clerical and lay members. Nor should pre-Reformation Catholicism be considered in any way as a default religion, that is, as a religion that French men, women, and children simply became members of without any deliberate choice or even conscious intellectual engagement. Above all, this chapter has tried to make clear that pre-Reformation clergy and lay Catholics in Dijon took it for granted that their salvation was not solely the result of individual effort, but was the product of collective effort, by both clergy and laity, as well as by the living and the dead. The protection and mercy offered by the Virgin Mary as well as the grace of God offered through the Eucharist were two of the principal foundations of their understanding of salvation. And as Chapter 4 will

---

[73] Jean Rigault, "L'ancienne confrérie des rois à Saint-Michel de Dijon," *Mémoires de l'Académie des sciences, arts et belles-lettres de Dijon* 117 (1969): 81–85; and Farr, *Hands of Honor*, 246.
[74] Rigault, "L'ancienne confrérie des rois," 82.

demonstrate, when both the Virgin Mary and the Eucharist came under attack by Calvinists in the 1540s and 1550s, Dijon's Catholics, both the city's elites and the popular classes, demonstrated just how significant and relevant their religion was to them. Indeed, the city's vignerons served as a bulwark against the new religion, working hand in hand with the city's clerical and secular elites. But, to understand that reaction in context, we first need to examine more closely the ways in which their religion was intimately bound to their material lives.

CHAPTER 3

Beasts in the Vines
Wine and Material Life

High up the famed slope of the Côte d'Or, just a few miles west of the villages of Meursault and Auxey-Duresses south of Beaune, lies the settlement of Saint-Romain. Divided between an upper village at the very summit of the wine slopes and a lower village where most of the villagers lived, the small community was dominated in the sixteenth century, as in the twenty-first, by viticulture. And when the parishioners erected a new limestone pulpit in their parish church in the upper village in 1619, they underscored a vital link between their faith and their material life. The stone pulpit was built by two brothers in the village, and they carved their names at the base of the stone: "Pierre and Philibert Barolet, brothers and property owners in common, have made this pulpit. Above all birds I am king [and] I can fly so high that I can see next to the sun. Happy are those who will see God."[1] Indeed, the new pulpit depicted in graphic carved relief the very targets of so many prayers uttered from that same pulpit. A grapevine ran the entire length of the staircase leading to the pulpit, and on it were depicted the principal beasts that threatened not only the villagers' livelihoods but also their salvation. Caterpillars and snails came in waves every spring in April and May and gorged themselves on the young vine shoots (see Figure 3.1). Those shoots that survived were then plagued in late May and June by the insects the locals called *écrivains* (Figure 3.2). Finally, as the fruit began to ripen in late summer, the vines fell prey to birds that feasted on the grapes, picking clean whatever the other vermin had left behind (Figure 3.3). Images such as these not only help us understand four hundred years later how much life in early modern Burgundy depended on the wine harvest for its survival, but also how securely viticulture bound together the material and the spiritual

---

[1] Parish church of upper St. Romain, Burgundy, stone pulpit constructed in 1619: "*Pierre et Ph[ilibe]rt Barolet frères et communs en biens ont facit faire ceste chaire. Sur tous oyseus ie suis le roy voller ie peus en si hault lieu que le soleil de pres je voyt. Heureux sont ceux qui verront dieu.*"

Figure 3.1 Stone pulpit in the parish church of upper St. Romain depicting
caterpillars, 1619

components of Burgundian culture. Thus, battling these bestial plagues, as
well as the usual vagaries of the weather, depended heavily on pleas to God,
most often in the form of prayers and religious processions described in the
previous chapter. That a stone pulpit carved in 1619 would depict such
beasts in the vines only underscores how closely tied religion was to the
material existence of the parishioners. And it is this material life of
premodern Burgundians that serves as the focus of this chapter, with the
local wine industry, which provided for both the spiritual and material
needs of the community, featuring prominently. The principal argument
of the chapter is not only that wine played a significant role in the material
lives of most Burgundians – not just for those who tended the vineyards
and then made the wine after the grapes were harvested – but that the
material circumstances of their lives were so thoroughly integrated into

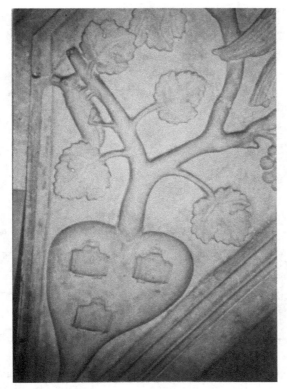

Figure 3.2 Stone pulpit in the parish church of upper St. Romain depicting *écrivains*, 1619

their politics and religious experiences that we cannot fully understand the latter without at least a cursory glance at the former.

3.1 Wine in Burgundy

Grapes for wine have probably been grown in Burgundy at least since the time of Roman Gaul, and there is archeological evidence to suggest that the Celts were drinking wine in the region even before the Romans annexed Gaul in 51 BCE.[2] Although there is little corroborating evidence, few historians would dispute the claim of Gregory of Tours in the sixth

[2] E. Thévenot, "Les origines du vignoble bourguignon d'après les documents archéologiques," *Annales de Bourgogne* 23 (1951): 253–266.

Figure 3.3 Stone pulpit in the parish church of upper St. Romain depicting birds, 1619

century, mentioned in Chapter 1, that Dijon was already known for producing a good local wine at that time: "To the west [of Dijon] the hills are covered with fruitful vines, which yield so noble a Falernian-type wine that the inhabitants have been known to scorn a good Mâcon," the highest praise possible from a sixth-century Latinist.[3] But there is really little documentation of the extent of Burgundy's wine industry until the High Middle Ages, when the Church in general and the Cistercians in particular initiated a period of dramatic growth in viticulture and viniculture.[4] Although the Cistercians under Bernard of Clairvaux (1090–1153)

[3] Gregory of Tours, *The History of the Franks*, trans. Lewis Thorpe (Harmondsworth, Middlesex: Penguin, 1974), 183. Falernian wine was the most famous and most sought after wine produced by the Romans, grown from Aglianico grapes planted on the slopes of Mt. Falernius near the border of Latium and Campania. It was a white wine of high alcoholic content. See Hugh Johnson, *The Story of Wine* (London: Mandarin Paperbacks, 1991), 59.

[4] The best general histories of wine in France are Roger Dion, *Historie de la vigne at du vin en France aux origins au XIXe siècle* (Paris: Flammarion, 1990 ed., orig. edn. 1959); Gilbert Garrier, *Histoire sociale et culturelle du vin* (Paris: Bordas, 1995); and Marcel Lachiver, *Vins, vignes et vignerons: Histoire du vignoble français* (Paris: Fayard, 1988). In English, in addition to Hugh Johnson's *The Story of Wine*, Rod Phillips, *A Short History of Wine* (London: Penguin Press, 2000); Phillips's more recent *French Wine: A History* (Oakland, CA: University of California Press, 2016); and Tim Unwin, *Wine and the Vine: An Historical Geography of Viticulture and the Wine Trade* (London: Routledge, 1991) are additional historical studies that are very useful.

have usually received most of the credit for generating the growth of viticulture in Burgundy in the twelfth century, other monastic orders had already laid the groundwork in the province. The abbey of St. Germain des Prés, a powerful Benedictine abbey in Paris, for example, had owned a significant parcel of vines in the village of Gilly near Vougeot since the Merovingian period, as well as vineyards in Corton, Beaune, Chambolle, Beaune, Fixin, Pommard, Vosne, Nuits, and Meursault. And another Benedictine house thirty kilometers northeast of Dijon, the abbey of Bèze, owned vineyards in the villages of Gevrey, Marsannay, Fixin, Couchey, and Vosne.[5] It was the arrival of Bernard at the recently founded abbey of Cîteaux in 1112, however, along with 30 other Burgundian noblemen, that not only resulted in a new monastic order but also initiated an unprecedented period of growth in Burgundian viticulture. The new order was the Cistercians, named after its founding house at Cîteaux near Dijon, and its explicit policy of acquiring vineyards through purchase and donation was to enable these rural and isolated monastic houses to remain economically viable and as self-sufficient as possible in order to accentuate the cloistered experience. The Cistercians wore white habits to distinguish themselves from the Benedictines, who traditionally wore black habits, but they also sought to distinguish themselves from the older order by secluding themselves in rural retreats and becoming self-sufficient and more rigorous. In Burgundy, this meant relying on income from vineyards to maintain and support the white monks of Cîteaux through a long-term policy of donation, purchase, and exchange.

The abbey of Cîteaux's first vineyard, a parcel in Meursault, was donated at its founding by the Duke of Burgundy, Eude I, on Christmas Day 1098.[6] Other donations quickly followed, however, and by the middle of the twelfth century the monastery had acquired vineyards in Beaune, Chambolle, Dijon, Fixin, Gilly, Meursault, Morey, Vosne, and Vougeot.[7] And by the time of Bernard's death and canonization in 1153,

---

[5] Jean Richard, "Le vignoble et les vins de Bourgogne au Moyen Age: un état de la recherche," *Annales de Bourgogne* 73 (2001): 9–17; Hannelore Pepke-Duix, "L'économie des vignes et du vin autour de Dijon au Moyen Âge," in Jean-Pierre Garcia and Jacky Rigaux, eds., *Vignes et vins du Dijonnois: Oubli et renaissance* (Clemencey: Terre en Vues, 2012), 57–63; and Johnson, *The Story of Wine*, 132.

[6] Marcel Lebeau, *Essai sur les vignes de Cîteaux aux origins à 1789* (Dijon: Académie de Dijon, 1986), 64.

[7] Jean Marlier, ed., *Charetes et documents concernant l'abbaye de Cîteaux, 1098–1790* (Rome: Cistercienses, 1961). Also see Jean Marlier, "Le vin de Cîteaux au XIIe siècle," *Mémoires de l'Académie des sciences, arts et belles lettres de Dijon* (1943–46): 267–272; Béatrice Bourély, *Vignes et vins de l'abbaye de Cîteaux en Bourgogne* (Nuits St. Georges: Editions de Tastevin, 1998); Aline Lagrandré, "Les vignerons de Cîteaux dans la Côte de Beaune au Moyen Age," *Annales de Bourgogne* 73 (2001): 95–101; and Lachiver, Vins, vignes et vignerons, 78.

the new order of white monks had grown to more than four hundred monastic houses all over Western Europe, and the monks practiced viti-culture in virtually every one of them. Indeed, one of the Cistercian's original plots in the village of Vougeot had been expanded so much by 1336 that the monks decided to enclose it with a stone wall, still visible today, and the resulting vineyard – the Clos de Vougeot – was, at 50 hectares, the single largest plot of land devoted to viticulture in the entire province of Burgundy.[8] But the monks had already been producing high quality wine from their vineyards at least two centuries before they enclosed the parcel at Vougeot. They brought a sense of devotion and respect to winemaking, as part of a larger belief in perfecting as best they could what they saw as one of God's creations. Thus, the Cistercians experimented and did practical research in the different ways that soil types, climatic conditions, different vine plants, differences in pruning and tying the vine shoots, and wine-making techniques affected the overall quality of their wine. And even though virtually all wine in Europe at this time was drunk young, within a year of the harvest – there were no glass bottles with airtight stoppers until the late seventeenth century – the Cistercians were among the first to associate specific parcels of land with distinctive and definable tastes and qualities of wine, which only later in the modern world would come to be defined as *terroir*. In fact, the Cistercians' wine was deemed to be of such high quality by 1171, less than two decades after the death of Bernard of Clairvaux, that Pope Alexander III exempted the abbey at Cîteaux from paying the tithe, a church tax, on their vines, and King Louis VII of France also exempted them from paying any duty normally charged to those transporting and selling their wines in cities and towns.[9]

Not only the wines made by the Cistercians but all the wines that came from the vineyards around the town of Beaune had developed a reputation outside of Burgundy for being of extremely high quality in the later Middle Ages. Some even believed it to be the best red wine in Europe. Once the Valois dukes of Burgundy set up their court in Dijon in 1363, the fame of the region's wines – especially its red wines made largely from the *pinot noir* grape – expanded considerably. This was especially true in the dukes' northern holdings in the Netherlands, and Duke Philip the Bold (1363–1404), the first Valois duke of Burgundy, was perhaps the wine's finest champion. Not only did he disseminate Burgundian wine throughout his holdings in Franche-Comté and the Netherlands but he also dispatched

---

[8] Phillips, *Short History of Wine*, 96.
[9] Ibid., and Bourély, *Vignes et vins de l'abbaye de Cîteaux*, 101–102.

wine southward to the Avignon popes. In 1371, for example, he sent Pope Gregory XI a gift of 36 *queues* of wine (a *queue* was a barrel with a capacity of about 450 liters), and he sent another gift of 10 *queues* of Burgundian wine to Pope Benedict XIII in 1395.[10] One of his successors, Duke Philip the Good (1419–1467) even touted himself as "the lord of the best wines in all Christendom."[11] By the sixteenth century, then, the ultimate gift anyone could present to kings, popes, and princes was a barrel of red wine from Burgundy. When King Charles IX of France was preparing to visit Dijon in 1564 as part of his royal tour of his kingdom, the mayor ordered a special commission "to go to Beaune to buy the finest wine that can be found to present to the king upon his arrival."[12] Perhaps the Burgundian lawyer Barthélemy de Chasseneux, a barrister in the Parlement of Dijon from 1525, best summed up the most discriminating opinion in verse in his encyclopedic compendium of knowledge, the *Catalogus gloriae mundi*: "*Vinum belnense, super omnia recense*," or roughly, "The wine of Beaune stands all alone."[13] This assessment of the quality of the wine from Beaune was also apparently shared by Chasseneux's contemporary François Rabelais, himself a connoisseur of good wine. Near the end of Book 5 of his *Gargantua and Panegruel*, when the priestess Babuc asked the travelers to guess which wine they were tasting from the fountain, Panurge responded first: "By God, this is the wine of Beaune, and the best I have ever tasted!"[14] Thus, by the sixteenth century, drinkers of Burgundian wines had created a strong export market throughout France and much of Western Europe, and viticulture had established itself as a principal component of the local Burgundian economy.[15]

In the Burgundian capital of Dijon, the presence of the wine industry was everywhere evident in the sixteenth century, especially in the parishes of St. Philibert, St. Nicolas, St Pierre, and St. Michel where the overwhelming majority of vignerons lived. By the end of the fifteenth century vignerons made up about a quarter of all the heads of household in the city

[10] Dion, *Histoire de la vigne*, 291–292.
[11] Quoted in Garrier, *Histoire sociale et culturelle du vin*, 45: "réputé seigneur des meilleurs vins de chrétienté."
[12] AMD, B 200, fol. 189v, April 20, 1564: "pour aller a beaulnes acheter des vins plus exquis quil pourra trouver pour faire p[rese]nt a la venue du roy."
[13] Bartélemy de Chasseneux, *Catalogus gloriae mundi* (Lyon: Vicentius, 1546), 315; quoted in Dion, *Histoire de la vigne*, 299.
[14] François Rabelais, *Oeuvres de Rabelais*, 2 vols., ed. Louis Moland (Paris: Garnier Frères, 1926), 2: 326: "Par Dieu, c'est icy vin de Beaune, meilleur qu'onques jamais je beus."
[15] Claude Tournier, "Le vin à Dijon de 1430 à 1560: Ravitaillement et commerce," *Annales de Bourgogne* 22 (1950): 7–32 and 161–186.

whose occupations are known from the tax rolls. This had not always been the case, as in the late fourteenth and early fifteenth centuries vignerons usually comprised less than 10 percent of the population.[16] This coincided with a period of agrarian crisis, continued outbreaks of the plague, and the ravages of troops from the Hundred Years' War.[17] By the second half of the fifteenth century, however, one sign of recovery was the growth of Dijon's vignerons. As Table 3.1 makes clear, as the city's overall population increased, so did the city's households headed by vignerons. At the turn of the sixteenth century in the year 1500, for example, the tax rolls show that 718 of the city's 2,753 households were headed by vignerons, or 26.1 percent.[18] And as Dijon's population continued to expand throughout the sixteenth century, the number of vignerons remained relatively stable or even declined slightly. Thus, the percentage of total households headed by vignerons did diminish somewhat over the course of the century. By 1553 vignerons headed 541 of 2,888 households – 18.7 percent – and for the rest of the century this percentage remained fairly stable.[19] By 1643 there were only 373 households headed by vignerons, a decline of nearly one-third from a century earlier.[20] The sharpest drop in the number of vignerons living in Dijon occurred in the second half of the seventeenth century, however, when the local wine industry experienced a serious crisis due to overcultivation in the region around Dijon during the reign of Louis XIV. When a depression in the wine trade occurred between 1670 and 1685, many vignerons, who were already in significant debt, were denied any further capital from their creditors and went bankrupt.[21] Many were forced into market gardening or other areas of agricultural labor simply to survive. By 1750 the number of households headed by vignerons had shrunk to just 165, or a mere 6 percent of the total population.[22] The point here is that the turn of the sixteenth century was a highpoint for the presence of

---

[16] Anne Galanaud and Henri Labesse, "Les vignerons à Dijon au début du XVIe siècle," *Cahiers d'histoire de la vigne et du vin* 3 (2002): 82.

[17] Rosalind Kent Berlow, "The 'Disloyal' Grape: The Agrarian Crisis of Late Fourteenth-Century Burgundy," *Agricultural History* 56 (1982): 426–438; and Hannelore Pepke-Durix, "Les raisins de la crise: Vignes et vin en Bourgogne aux XIVe et XVe siècles," *Cahiers d'histoire de la vigne et du vin* 1 (2000): 23–49.

[18] AMD, L 163, fol. 1r–219v.

[19] AMD, L 192, fol. 1r–224v and L 193, fol. 45r–92r and 213r–237v.

[20] AMD, L 234, fol. 1r–254v; and James R. Farr, *Hands of Honor: Artisans and Their World in Dijon, 1550–1650* (Ithaca, NY: Cornell University Press, 1988), 78.

[21] Vignerons' debts and how they borrowed money to finance their vineyards are discussed later in this chapter.

[22] James R. Farr, "Consumers, Commerce, and the Craftsmen of Dijon: The Changing Social and Economic Structure of a provincial Capital, 1450–1750," in Philip Benedict, ed., *Cities and Social Change in Early Modern France* (London: Unwin Hyman, 1989), 134–173, especially 143–144; and

Table 3.1 *Vignerons in Dijon's population, 1464–1523*

Year	Total hearths	Vignerons	Percent of total
1464	2,336	472	20.2
1479	2,313	546	23.6
1500	2,753	718	26.1
1523	2,493	606	24.3

Sources: AMD, L 159 (1464), L 131 (1479), L 163 (1500), L 164 (1523).

vignerons in the city in terms of their percentage of the total population, with the result that their influence on municipal affairs – both political and religious – between 1500 and 1650 was also at its apex. As the Burgundian historian Gaston Roupnel has noted, this meant that in this period "the history of the vine was intimately connected to the history of the city."[23]

There was also a significant and regular wine market in Dijon held every week in the sixteenth century, called the *étape* (a rough translation might be warehouse), which took place outdoors in the Place St. Jean every Friday. Wine was sold here in bulk, normally in wooden barrels, so this was solely a wholesale market. More will be said about the prices of wine and its different levels of perceived quality and places of origin later in this chapter, but suffice it to say here that wine played a prominent role in the local economy. Wine could also be purchased by the pot or pint on a retail basis in three distinct and regulated kinds of urban spaces in Dijon: (1) inns (*hostelleries*), where rooms for overnight stay and food were available, and in theory at least, places which were supposed to be off limits to inhabitants of the city, though fines of innkeepers for serving local males were so frequent that it is clear that Dijon's inhabitants frequented them on a regular basis; (2) cabarets, which were open to all and where drinkers could sit down and usually get beverages other than wine and also some light food such as savory pies and tarts; and (3) taverns, where only wine was sold and it was drunk standing up on bare ground. It was the middle group – cabarets – that grew and expanded in the sixteenth century, filling a growing market for wine. Cabarets became so numerous, in fact, that an act of the Parlement of Dijon on March 18, 1559 required the city council to regulate and reduce the number of cabarets in the

Gaston Roupnel, *La Ville et la campagne au XVIIe siècle: Etude sur la populations du pays dijonnais* (Paris: Armand Colin, 1955), 156 and 227–249.
[23] Roupnel, *La Ville et la campagne*, 157.

city.[24] This in turn led to the expansion of the inns, which grew from around 30 in 1530 to more than 70 in 1594.[25] These three categories were very fluid, however, and also difficult to police, as the many fines of the proprietors of inns in the period attest.[26]

In all of these venues, however, the price of wine, whether purchased in bulk from the weekly wholesale market or by the pint in a cabaret, was set by the city council. For just one example, in 1535 the council set the tariff of a pint of ordinary old wine, that is, any wine older than that from the most recent harvest, at 2 s., a pint of better quality old wine at 2 s. 6 d., a pint of ordinary new wine (the current vintage) at 1 s., and a pint of better quality new wine at 1 s. 3 d.[27] Thus, old wine commanded a higher retail price – double that of new wine – because of the added storage costs as well as its perceived quality. This also meant that unscrupulous cabaret owners might occasionally, or even more than occasionally, pass off new wine as old, or more likely, mix old and new wine to get a higher price for the more abundant recent vintage.

Edourd Brédin's map of Dijon in 1574 (Figure 1.1) gives only a partial glimpse of the extent of the vineyards under the jurisdiction of the city of Dijon. Not only did Dijon's vineyards extend extramurally to those surrounding the hamlets of Talant to the north, Larrey to the west, and Chenôve to the south, all visible on Brédin's map, but they continued a further six kilometers all the way to the villages of Ruffey to the north-east, Plombières to the northwest, and Marsannay to the southwest.[28] All this wine was sold as "Dijon wine" in the local wine market, even though much of it came from vineyards six kilometers outside the city. And it was this wine – much more humble in quality than the more celebrated wine from the region around Beaune – that was largely purchased and consumed by most of the city's inhabitants. But there was also a good deal of wine sold and consumed in Dijon from farther afield. From 1428 the Duke of Burgundy – and after 1477 the King of France – always enjoyed the right of free entry to bring any outside wine into the city. So did any inhabitant who regularly paid taxes to the city. And those who were not residents could still bring in wine other than Dijon wine if they paid a tax called the *octroi*. And others – such as

[24] Tournier, "Le vin à Dijon de 1430 à 1560," 163–167.
[25] Henri Drouot, "Hostelleries dijonnaises en 1593," *Revue de Bourgogne* 3 (1915): 473–476.
[26] See, for example, the list of *cabaretiers* fined in 1552–53 in AMD, I 130 (liasse).
[27] AMD, B 179, fol. 56v, November 6, 1535.
[28] Maurice Chaume, "Le finage et la banlieue de Dijon," *Mémoires de la Commission des Antiquités de la Côte-d'Or* 21 (1939–1941): 342–344. Also see Thomas Labbé, "Le vin de Dijon du XIVe au XVIIIe siècle: trajectoire historique d'un cru (presque) disparu," in Garcia and Rigaud, eds., *Vignes et vins du dijonnois*, 81–87.

lawyers in the Parlement and other royal officers who were not residents, or the bishop of Langres – were often given temporary passports to bring in outside wine without paying the tax. So, there was always a good deal of outside wine being sold and consumed in the city, even if most of its inhabitants considered their own wine to be superior to all outside wine, which they categorized as "very slight and poor wines (*très petits et povres vins*)." Ironically, most of this imported wine that was considered such poor quality in the sixteenth century came from villages farther south outside the city's jurisdiction: from villages such as Couchey, Fixin, Gevrey, Chambolle, Vougeot, and Nuits, where some of the best wines were produced in the nineteenth and twentieth centuries. The *octroi* was first established in 1428 at the rate of 20 *sous* per queue (a barrel of approximately 450 liters), though it was often reduced in times of extreme shortage when outside wine was necessary to make up what was needed for local consumption. Nevertheless, inflation in the sixteenth century reduced the value of the 20 *sous octroi* considerably. By 1500 wine merchants in Dijon were importing more than 1,000 *queues* of outside wine per year, and this could increase dramatically in times of shortage, such as 1522 and 1523 when more than 2,500 *queues* of outside wine was imported into the city.[29] If we assume that Dijon's population was roughly 12,000 people at this time, this works out to almost 100 liters per person – man, woman, and child – per year of just imported wine, not counting the more copious quantities of local "Dijon wine" consumed. Obviously, much of this wine was consumed by nonresidents of Dijon, some coming to town on a regular basis for the local markets, others just passing through. Nevertheless, it seems clear that wine in sixteenth-century Dijon mattered in a variety of ways and was a significant part of the material life of its inhabitants.

3.2 *Écrivains* and Other Beasts

Chapter 2 has already introduced the religious processions organized by Dijon's political elites and clergy to combat the various enemies that plagued the annual grape harvest, some of which decorated the stone pulpit in the parish church of St. Romain depicted at the beginning of this chapter. And the engraved foundations of masses for the dead in the

---

[29] Tournier, "Le vin à Dijon de 1430 à 1560," 9–29 (quote on p. 23). Also see AMD, G 248 (liasse), accounts for the local wine market (*étape*). The *octroi* was still set at 20 *sous* per queue for importing wine into Dijon as late as 1616 (BMD, Ms. 1012, p. 127, July 1616).

parish church of St. Michel also demonstrate that such masses offered prayers not only for the souls of the dead but also for the grapevines of the living. Depicting images of and references to the various enemies of Burgundy's vines in ecclesiastical monuments in parish churches only reinforces the connections and links between religious and material life in the sixteenth century. Remission of sins and the good health of the vignerons' vines thus went hand in hand. So, it is hardly a surprise that vignerons in sixteenth-century Burgundy considered many of the common threats to the vineyards produced by ordinary climatic conditions, especially if they were extensive or long-lasting, to be divine retribution and punishment for their sins. The records of Dijon's city council are full of lamentations about too little rain, too much rain, strong winds, flooding, a late Spring freeze just when the grape buds were beginning to germinate, and especially hail, which could destroy an entire year's crop in a matter of minutes. These maladies were so frequent and so common, in fact, that we might be tempted to think that the vignerons of the sixteenth century had learned to deal with them both stoically and uncomplainingly. Each time some new threat to the vines emerged due to bad weather or other adverse climatic conditions, however, the typical reaction from most vignerons was that their own sins and shortcomings were ultimately responsible for these divine punishments. And the usual remedy, as has already been recounted in Chapter 2, was to ask the city's clergy to organize a religious procession and prayers to God to appease his anger and to ask for his grace and forgiveness. In November 1542, for example, too much rain caused the River Ouche and River Suzon to flood much of the city: "Because of the calamity that the waters of the Suzon and the Ouche have made against the walls of this city as well as the Chevres Bridge, as well as other misfortunes that can arise from flooding, the gentlemen of the clergy will say prayers and make pleas to God the Creator to appease his wrath."[30] An extended drought in the summer of 1540, for yet another example, resulted in these very remedies: "In order to grant and receive the grace of our Creator as well as to procure rain, and following the discussions with the gentlemen of the church, a religious procession will take place next Monday from [the abbey of] St. Etienne and another next Thursday from the Ste. Chapelle, in which the holy and sacred Host will be carried."[31] That same summer when various insects invaded the vineyards, the clergy of the city organized yet another religious procession and special prayers to beg God "to drive out the insects and vermin destroying the vines and their fruit, which has come

[30] AMD, B 170, fol. 122r-v, November 16, 1522.   [31] AMD, B 181, fol. 152r, July 30, 1540.

about because of numerous sins and blasphemies."[32] Another remedy was ringing the church bells of the city during the night. In order "to appease the weather" in May 1538, for example, the city council ordered the night watchmen to ring all the church bells in the city in a particular pattern of three bells "due to the request made in writing by Dijon's vignerons to counter the dangers of hail, storms, winds, and lightening."[33] Thus, it seems pretty clear that in the sixteenth century both bad weather and beasts in the vines were most often interpreted as punishment from God that required ecclesiastical intervention.

A new and seemingly even greater threat to the vines emerged in the first half of the sixteenth century, however: the small insects known locally as *écrivains* or *gribouris*. Burgundians were familiar with other insects such as *cancouaires*, the larvae of the common maybug that attacked the new grape buds of the young vine plants, and *hurebers*, a red-colored beetle similar to a weevil, whose larvae fed on the young vine leaves. These insects were both pretty common each spring in the fifteenth and early sixteenth centuries, and while annoying and potentially dangerous to the grape harvest, they were more of a nuisance than a threat, as they normally did not permanently injure the vine plants they fed on. The appearance of a new insect in 1529 – the so-called *écrivains*, because the trail of their devastation as they feasted on the leaves of the vine plants resembled handwriting – was more of a threat, however, as their attacks often destroyed the fruit of an entire plant. The larvae of this beetle lived on the roots of the plants all winter and emerged in spring to eat the young grape buds as soon as they appeared. Although they first appeared in 1529, these *écrivains* spread more widely and became much more numerous starting in the spring of 1540. They appeared every year from 1549 to 1554, with the spring of 1554 marking the apogee of this new insect.[34] The usual remedies were introduced, with Dijon's mayor and city council asking the local clergy in June 1546 "to organize a general procession to appeal to God's good graces so that it will please him to expel and extirpate the small insects that one calls *écrivains*."[35] Just one week later the city council noted that "for the previous four years they [Dijon's vignerons] have not made any profit from their vines because of an insect that one calls *écrivains*, which have damaged and eaten not only the buds but also the wood of the said vines, with their losses being so great

---

[32] AMD, D II (liasse), June 10, 1540.
[33] AMD, B 180, fol. 368r, May 31, 1538. Also, see Lachiver, *Vins, vignes et vignerons*, 194–198.
[34] Claude Tournier, "Notes sur la culture de la vigne et les vignerons à Dijon," *Annales de Bourgogne* 24 (1952): 145–146.
[35] AMD, B 183, fol. 295v, June 1, 1546.

that numerous poor vignerons have been unable to recover and have resorted to begging."[36]

But what were these new insects called *écrivains*? Not formally identified until 1758 by the Swedish botanist and taxonomist Carl Linnaeus, these small beetles of about 5 mm in length and black and brown in color were members of the Chrysonelidae family. Formally named *Adoxus obscurus* or *Bromius obscurus*, these *écrivains* – known today as the western grape rootworm in English and as *coupe-bourgeons* (budcutters) in French – were a new threat to Burgundian vineyards, because they could ruin an entire harvest by eating all the new grape buds when they appeared in the spring.[37] As already noted, complaints about *écrivains* first appeared in the deliberations of Dijon's city council in 1529, and the insects quickly developed into a real threat to the grape harvest by the late 1540s. At the height of the crisis in June 1554 Dijon's mayor and city council asked the bishop of Langres, in whose diocese Dijon lay, to perform an exorcism of the marauding insects. Philippe Berbis, the vicar-general of the bishop of Langres, exclaimed to all the clergy of the city that although God was tormenting the city with the beasts in the vines in order to correct ungodly living, prayer was the only remedy against these vermin and that prayer alone was the sole means of appeasing divine wrath. He then gave a prayer of his own: "I curse and issue a sentence of damnation and anathema on all these insects, *écrivains*, and other vermin that are destroying the buds and the substance of our vines."[38] But prayers by the clergy seemed to be no more efficacious than the vignerons' efforts to combat these insects by trying to kill them by hand.

Although the annual attacks of these *écrivains* did diminish somewhat in subsequent years, their intensity and regularity were still so acute twenty years later that the mayor and city council declared that Dijon's clergy would organize a special religious procession every year on the feast day of St. George (April 23) "so that it pleases God to drive out and destroy the tiny beasts who have inundated the vines of the vineyards around Dijon."[39] And in fact, the *écrivains* remained a continual threat for the rest of the

---

[36] AMD, B 183, fol. 305r–v, June 9, 1546.
[37] Jean Lafon, Pierre Couillaud, and Roger Hyde, *Maladies et parasites de la vigne*, 2 vols. (Paris: Baillière et Fils, 3rd edn., 1966–1970), 2: 75–77; Pierre Galet, *Les maladies et parasites de la vigne*, 2 vols. (Montpellier: Galet, 1977–1982), 2: 1420–1428; Lachiver, *Vins, vignes et vignerons*, 196–197; H. J. Quale, "A New Root Pest of the Vine in California," *Journal of Economic Entomology* 1 (June 1908): 175–176; and A. J. Winkler, J. A. Cook, W. M. Kliewer, and L. A. Lider, *General Viticulture* (Berkeley, CA: University of California Press, 2nd edn. 1974), 547–548.
[38] AMD, B 191, fol. 214r, June 5, 1554 (text in Latin).
[39] AMD, B 210, fol. 144v, March 27, 1573.

sixteenth and early seventeenth centuries. As such they remained a fact of life for Burgundy's vignerons every spring and provided yet another threat to their already perilous subsistence.

3.3   The *Métier* of a Vigneron

How did those in Burgundy's wine industry manage to eke out a living, then? Other than fighting the various enemies of the vine, what kinds of work did a vigneron perform, and how did this labor vary over the harvest year? Much depended, of course, on whether vignerons owned the vine-yards they worked in, or if they were simply day laborers, hired – and usually paid a daily wage – by those who did own the vineyards. While a majority of vignerons living in the city of Dijon probably were just day laborers (*journaliers*) or sharecroppers (*métayers*) who did not own any vines, some certainly did. Indeed, there were three main categories of vignerons in the sixteenth century. Simple day laborers were the least skilled and were paid the lowest daily wage, and more about their wages will be explained later in this chapter. More skilled vignerons could sign contracts for sharecropping, getting to keep up to half of the crop they tended and harvested in the fifteenth century, which diminished to a third and eventually just a quarter by 1560. Though they did not own the vines they worked, they had a much more reliable and regular income than did simple day laborers. At the top of the vigneron hierarchy came those who owned their own vines. It is clear not only from the foundation of masses for the dead that we saw in the last chapter but also from numerous contracts for long term loans that many vignerons in the city, and maybe even a majority of vignerons in some of the rural villages outside Dijon along the route to Beaune, clearly did own some vineyards.[40] They often used income from these vineyards to fund not only masses for the dead, but also for other purposes, such as to pay rent for accommodation. Most owned their vineyards through a contract called a *cens*, which gave them perpetual use of a specified parcel of vines (called the *censive*). In many ways a *cens* was like perpetual rental of property.[41] Normally, one paid the *cens* to the lord, or landlord, under whose jurisdiction one lived. For just one example, a vigneron named Etienne Malechart signed a contract with the

---

[40]   See, for example, the scores of vignerons in the villages of Couchey, Fontaine-les-Dijon, Marsannay, and Gevrey who owned vines and used the income from them to pay for the foundation of masses, in ADCO, G 3947–3948, 3984, 3996, and 4044, all dates between 1435 and 1611. For the parish of St. Michel within Dijon itself, see ADCO, G 3573–3581.

[41]   Tournier, "Notes sur la culture de la vigne," 152–155.

canons of the Sainte Chapelle, the Duke of Burgundy's private chapel, in February 1417 for half of a parcel of vines of seven *quartiers* (or one and three-quarters *arpents*, about six tenths of a hectare), for which he was required to pay "an annual and perpetual assessment indefinitely . . . of 20 *sous* and one *gros*" to the clergy of the Sainte Chappelle.[42] These *cens*, being perpetual contracts, could be passed on to heirs or sold, almost as if vignerons such as Malechart actually owned the vineyards outright, and the notarial archives in Dijon are full of examples of this kind of transaction. Indeed, either Malechart or his heirs did sell this parcel of vines at some point, as it was owned by a merchant named Jean Mathieu who sold it to another merchant in April 1506 for 15 *livres tournois*. The new buyer, like all previous owners of the *cens*, had to continue to pay the customary 8 s. 4 d. of *cens* annually to the clergy of the Sainte Chappelle.[43] These duties, while seemingly a small though not insignificant amount, were typical of the Old Regime in that even though the holders of a *cens* enjoyed exclusive rights to the property and all it produced, they remained a constant irritant and often proved to be a financial burden, especially in a poor harvest year. Moreover, they were emblematic of the variety of feudal dues that a great many landholders in France still owed their social betters or the church, if the land they paid for was originally part of a seigneurial or ecclesiastical estate.[44]

To be sure, the three categories of day laborer, sharecropper, and vineyard owner were not strictly separated, as many vignerons living in Dijon often overlapped these divisions. For example, it was possible for a vigneron to work as a sharecropper in some vineyard parcels while working as a day laborer in others. Moreover, a vigneron with a *cens* for a small parcel might need to work as a sharecropper or even as a day laborer in another vineyard to make ends meet until the annual grape harvest in the fall allowed him to sell his grapes or finished wine for income. On the other hand, a simple day laborer who only knew how to prune vines and harvest grapes would have been unable to move up the vigneron hierarchy without also acquiring the skills and knowledge actually to make wine from the harvested grapes. Thus, the incomes and standards of living of the three different types of vigneron varied considerably, much depending on the

---

[42] AMD, B 445, fols. 283–284, February 8, 1416 [old style, i.e. 1417].
[43] AMD, B 445, fol. 297, April 3, 1506.
[44] For more on the *cens* and *censive*, see Guy Cabourdin and Georges Viard, eds., *Lexique historique de la France d'Ancien Régime* (Paris: Armand Colin, 1978), 54; and William Beik, *A Social and Cultural History of Early Modern France* (Cambridge: Cambridge University Press, 2009), 26.

skills, knowledge, and basic material conditions of the individual vignerons.[45] So, what kinds of work did they do?

Without a doubt the most complete contemporary description of the
vigneron's world of work in sixteenth-century France was the massive
treatise on agriculture written by Olivier de Serres, seigneur de Pradel
(1537–1619) first published in 1600: *Le Théâtre d'agriculture et mesnage des
champs.*[46] Its eight major divisions covered much more than viticulture
and viniculture, however, including all the necessary instruction for the
growing of cereal grains, the raising of animals, livestock, and poultry, as
well as how to maintain a constant supply of garden vegetables, wood,
and water, not to mention instruction on hunting and fishing. The one
hundred and seventy pages of Book 3 "On the Culture of the Vine"
contained all the basic information any vigneron would need to know to
plant, grow, and harvest grapes, as well as the necessary instruction for the
pressing, fermentation, and production of those grapes into wine. To be
sure, De Serres was no Burgundian, as he lived on his estate of Pradel in
the Vivarais region of France farther south in the Ardèche. Moreover,
unlike most vignerons, he was both a noble and also a Huguenot. And he
also attended university and received a humanist education. He was
invited to Paris by King Henry IV in 1599 to organize the planting of
mulberry trees in the Tuilleries gardens as well as at the royal estate at St.
Germain-en-Laye, which led to a treatise on producing silk worms. So,
De Serres was far from a typical Burgundian vigneron – or indeed any
vigneron – in nearly all respects. He was best known, however, for his *Le
Théâtre d'agriculture et mesnage des champs*, which, despite his origins and
knowledge of the wine in the south of France, he intended as a national
manual on agriculture for the entire kingdom.[47] He dedicated the work
to Henry IV, and in his dedication he made it very clear that the knowledge the book contained was for all the king's subjects and for the
flourishing of his entire kingdom.[48] So this was no local or even regional

[45] Tournier, "Notes sur la culture de la vigne," 152–155.
[46] Olivier de Serres, *Le Théâtre d'agriculture et mesnage des champs, dans lequel est représenté tout ce qui est
requis et nécessaire pour bien dresser, gouverner, enricher et embellir la maison rustique* (Paris: Abr.
Saugrain, 1600). It was reprinted several times before the author's death in 1619, and numerous times
thereafter in the seventeenth century. I have cited throughout this study a modern edition: Olivier de
Serres, *Le Théâtre d'agriculture et mesnage des champs*, ed. Hubert Nyssen (Arles: Actes Sud, 1996).
[47] There is no reliable and complete scholarly biography of De Serres. For what is available, see A.-H.
Vaschalde, *Olivier de Serres, seigneur de Pradel: Sa vie et ses travaux* (Paris: Plon, 1886); Fernand
Lequenne, *La vie d'Olivier de Serres* (Paris: Réné Julliard, 1945); Fernand Lequenne, *Olivier de Serres:
Agronome et soldat de Dieu* (Paris: Berger-Levrault, 1983); and Henri Gourdin, *Olivier de Serres:
Science, expérience, diligence en agriculture au temps de Henri IV* (Arles: Actes Sud, 2001).
[48] De Serres, *Le Théâtre d'agriculture* (1996 edn.), 7–9.

manual. And even though there is no evidence that De Serres ever visited
Burgundy, unless he passed through on his way to Paris, he commented
on wines of other regions in France outside his native Vivarais, including
the delicate wines of Beaune and Sens in Burgundy.[49] And despite the
fact that he was anything but a typical vigneron, *Le Théâtre d'agriculture*
is nevertheless the best and most complete source we have for the world of
work in sixteenth-century viticulture – the planting, tending, and harvesting of grapes in the vineyard – and viniculture – the process of
turning those grapes into wine in the vigneron's cellar.

The noted historian of wine Marcel Lachiver has recently summed up
the vigneron's work in the vineyards of Old Regime France: "Whether
good or bad, harsh or mild, the viticultural year always began with the
pruning and ended with the harvest. In every vineyard this [the wine
harvest], as is still true today, was the most important moment of the
year, the one which determined abundance or misery, the one which had
the greatest human impact."[50] Olivier de Serres, like vignerons everywhere,
certainly agreed about the importance and significance of the harvest,
though for him the viticultural year actually could begin even earlier
than the start of pruning if new vine plants needed to be sown. Indeed,
once planted, grape vines could produce quality fruit for wine for decades,
but they did eventually need to be replaced.[51] De Serres was obviously
familiar with both the ancient and contemporary varieties of grape that had
historically been planted in France, listing 27 ancient varieties and 38 "and
infinite others" among the modern varieties. Already by the sixteenth
century in Burgundy, however, the pinot noir grape dominated among
red grape varieties. And despite the ban originally imposed on growing the
gamay grape in Burgundy – Duke Philip the Bold ordered all gamay vines
to be ripped out in 1395 because he felt it was an inferior variety – the more
abundant and cheaper gamay was still being grown in small quantities and
occasionally blended or substituted for the more expensive pinot noir, as is
clear from the few vignerons who were caught and fined for this practice.[52]
In terms of white grape varieties, the chardonnay grape was already
dominant in sixteenth-century Burgundy, though it is not listed by name

---

[49] Henri Hauser, "Olivier de Serres et la Bourgogne," *Annales de Bourgogne* 13 (December 1941):
306–307.
[50] Lachiver, *Vins, vignes et vignerons*, 198: "*Bonne ou mauvaise, dure ou clémente, l'année viticole,
commencée avec la taille, se termine avec la vendange. Dans tous les vignobles c'est, comme aujourd'hui
encore, le moment de l'année le plus important, celui qui concrètise l'abondance ou la misère, celui qui
rassemble les effectfs humains les plus grands.*"
[51] De Serres, *Le Théâtre d'agriculture* (1996 edn.), 243–244.
[52] For the ducal ban on gamay see Rosalind Kent Berlow, "The 'Disloyal' Grape," 426–438.

by De Serres, though the pinot blanc and gouais varieties from which it was cloned are mentioned. For the most part, then, except for the planting of new grape plants, the viticultural year usually did always begin with the pruning of the old canes. But when exactly did this occur?

In Burgundy, pruning traditionally never started before the feast day of St. Vincent, patron saint of vignerons, on January 22.[53] In reality, though, pruning usually did not begin in earnest until February. The purpose of pruning was to direct, control, and regulate the growth and vegetation of the vine plant so that the resulting fruit would be more concentrated and abundant. The idea was to control the plant's growth so as to produce as many new shoots and new buds as possible each year from the same plant. As Olivier de Serres pointed out, "you would no more allow it [a grape vine] to go according to its own will than you would a young colt."[54] So pruning was essential and had to be started during the cold winter months before the new vine shoots started to grow. As a result, pruning with frozen fingers and then tying up the newly pruned vine canes, which could be used as fuel, were probably the most arduous and distressing tasks a vigneron had to perform.[55] Burgundian vignerons pruned their vines with a semi-circular pruning hook called a *serpe*, which had a sharp point at both ends of the blade.[56] This was the essential tool of vignerons every-where, who used it for pruning, cutting, and chopping as well as digging throughout the year.[57]

After the pruning was complete in February or early March, the vigner-ons had to aerate the soil in the vineyards, usually done "by robust men with spades or hoes," according to De Serres, which took place in late March or early April.[58] This was hard work, but was necessary to prevent weeds or other unwanted vegetation from restricting the roots of the vine plants. And by late May, depending on the weather, it was usually time to set out the vine stakes – called *paisseaux* in Burgundy – wooden stakes of up to six or seven feet in length to which the vines would eventually be tied. Further weeding throughout the summer continued the vigneron's labors

[53] Sylvain Pitiot and Jean-Charles Servant, *Les vins de Bourgogne* (Paris: Presses universitaires de France, 11th edn. 1992), 33.
[54] De Serres, *Le Théâtre d'agriculture* (1996 edn.), 261.   [55] Ibid., 262.
[56] Lachiver, *Vins, vignes et vignerons*, 189. A variety of these *serpes* have survived from the sixteenth century, and a good collection of them is on display in the Musée du Vin de Bourgogne in Beaune. Drawings and pictures of them are also in André Lagrange, "Musée du Vin de Bourgogne à Beaune: Salles des travaux de la vigne et du vin et des métiers auxiliaires," *Arts et traditions populaires* 13 (1965): 107–180.
[57] De Serres, *Le Théâtre d'agriculture* (1996 edn.), 261–262.
[58] Ibid., 265. Also see Lachiver, *Vins, vignes et vignerons*, 190–191.

right up to the harvest.[59] Battling the vagaries of the weather as well as the beasts in the vines described earlier in the chapter, however, was a year round occupation, especially drought and hail, which could attack at any time of the year.[60]

When the first shoots began to appear from the pruned vine branches – usually sometime in April, though this could vary with the arrival of warmer weather – this was also the time, according to De Serres, to put down manure or other natural fertilizer around the base of the plants. This practice was not common everywhere in France, and in some areas it was actually forbidden, though in Burgundy it was up to the vigneron and usually depended on the supply of manure available. The very best for the vines, again according to De Serres, was either chicken or pigeon dung, something most vignerons did not have access to in large quantities, though some wealthier vineyard owners they worked for probably did.[61] Controlling the amount of pruning and manuring in early spring were the most effective ways a vigneron had at his disposal to regulate both the quantity and quality of his harvest. And the quality of the wine produced was more than just a material concern for vignerons, as De Serres and others were very explicit "that one was esteemed to be a worthy man (*homme de bien*) who has good wine."[62] And this same sentiment was expressed by the anonymous author of "The Monologue of the Good Vigneron," written by an unknown vigneron who lived near Auxerre in northern Burgundy sometime in the sixteenth century. "God protects the worthy vigneron . . . [and] everyone wants to be a vigneron in order to drink, it is said, good wine."[63] Thus, producing good wine provided more than just a living for a vigneron's family; it also served to cement his social standing in the community.

If there was ample – but not too much – rain in the spring, and lots of warm sun in the summer, and if the vineyards survived the annual infestation of *écrivains* and other threats such as hail, then the grapes would begin to mature by late August. This was when the *juré* vignerons appointed by the mayor of Dijon each year would begin their rounds of all the vineyards administered by the city, up to 6 km outside the city walls, to determine when the grapes were ripe enough to pick. The mayor and city council would then announce the *bans de vendange*, that is, the exact dates when picking could commence in each parcel of vineyards administered by the city. This was all

[59] De Serres, *Le Théâtre d'agriculture* (1996 edn.), 271–292.   [60] Ibid., 299.   [61] Ibid., 267.
[62] Ibid., 301.
[63] "Le monologue du bon vigneron sortant de sa vigne, et retournant soupper en sa maison," in Charles Moiset, ed., "La poésie auxerroise au XVIe siècle," *Annuaire historique du department de l'Yonne* 21 (1857): 63–83 (quotes from 74 and 77).

done "for the general interest of the entire community," as De Serres was quick to note.[64] Suffice it to say here that the *juré* vignerons visited the vines in every part of the city's jurisdiction and decided a specific date, usually in late September or early October, when the picking of the harvest could begin, and dates were often different for each vineyard as some parcels of vines ripened sooner than others. Each of them was paid a fairly substantial sum of 4 *livres* "for their efforts as well as for the loss of two entire days' work for each of them." This sum remained constant at 4 *livres* throughout the first half of the sixteenth century, even though by 1532 the work required took four days rather than two.[65] They would also select a team of monitors, called *vigniers*, from among the city's vignerons to station themselves in each vineyard to make sure that the date of the bans was enforced. The *vigniers* would thus stand watch and report anyone trying to contravene the bans by picking grapes early. The number of *juré* vignerons and *vigniers* increased over the course of the sixteenth century as the city's vineyards expanded, requiring more supervision and policing. In the late fifteenth and early sixteenth centuries, for example, the mayor named only two *juré* vignerons each year after his election. This increased to three by mid-century,[66] to four beginning in 1557,[67] to six starting in 1569,[68] and finally to seven – one named from each of the city's seven parishes – beginning in 1579.[69] There are no records at all indicating how the *juré* vignerons were chosen by the newly elected mayor each year, though clearly there was a great deal of continuity. For example, the same vignerons were selected for long periods, such as Denis Simmonet, called Pintet, who was named a *juré* vigneron in 1550 and served until June 1564.[70] Pierre Bouletet served even longer, from 1553 to 1571, though he was not named in every one of those years.[71] There was also considerable familial continuity, as many sons followed in their fathers' footsteps by being appointed as *juré* vignerons. For example, Philippe Arbelot served as a *juré* vigneron from June 1557 to June 1559, while his sons Jean (June 1572–June 1573) and Bénigne Arbelot (June 1579–June 1580 and June 1586–June 1587) also served in the same capacity.[72] Jean Bryet served as *juré* vigneron from

---

[64] De Serres, *Le Théâtre d'agriculture* (1996 edn.), 311–312.
[65] AMD, I 152 (liasse), especially those for October 27, 1502 and February 27, 1531/32.
[66] AMD, B 188, fol. 18v, June 1550.   [67] AMD, B 195, fol. 17v, June 1557.
[68] AMD, B 206, fol. 16r, June 1569.   [69] AMD, B 217, fol. 13v, June 1579.
[70] See AMD, B 188, fol. 18v for his appointment in June 1550, and AMD, B 200, fol. 11v for his last appointment of a one-year term in June 1563.
[71] See AMD, B 191, fol. 21v, for his first appointment in June 1553, and AMD, B 207, fol. 26v for his last appointment in June 1570.
[72] For the Arbelot appointments see AMD, B 195, fol. 17v (June 1557); AMD, B 210, fol. 17v (June 1572); and AMD, B 217, fol. 13v (June 1579).

June 1560 to June 1561, while his son Simon served in the same capacity even longer, from June 1575 to June 1585.[73]

Once the harvest officially began on the announced day for each vineyard, the vignerons worked in earnest to get the grapes picked as quickly as possible. In general, it took twenty vignerons one full working day to pick the grapes from one hectare of vines.[74] The length of duration of the grape harvest averaged about thirteen days in the first half of the sixteenth century, after which it began to shorten to generally no more than three days, so that all of Dijon's vineyards began to be harvested more or less simultaneously after the Wars of Religion.[75] The cutting of the bunches of grapes from the vine branches with the *serpe*, then carrying the harvested grapes in large baskets on backs to a temporary storage site until they could be carried to a wine press, was hard work. As Olivier de Serres pointed out, the harvest was a vital period in the community's welfare, as so much labor expended over the previous year could be lost if the grape harvest was not brought in when the grapes were at their ripest. Even the Parlement took an annual break from its ordinary day to day business "from the beginning of the [harvest] holidays of September until the feast day of St. Martin [November 11]."[76] Getting the grapes to a wine press as quickly as possible was essential before the grapes could begin to rot or dry out. Wine presses were obviously expensive items that were often used only once per year after the grape harvest, so most were owned by the wealthy.[77] There are two surviving examples of wine presses from the sixteenth century that form part of the museum at the Clos de Vougeot (see Figure 3.4). These presses were extremely large and were constructed by the Cistercian monks of the abbey at Cîteaux who owned the vineyard. Presses of this size were used to press grapes from all the vineyards in the village of Vougeot, not just those from the Cistercians' vineyards, and even grapes from neighboring villages. While nobles, ecclesiastical orders, and perhaps a very few individuals might own presses, most vignerons certainly did not, and even most vineyard owners did not own their own presses, paying a fee to have their grapes pressed each harvest by those who did own presses. We know from the notarial records of sales of property and inventories after death

---

[73] For the Bryet appointments see AMD, B 198, fol. 16v (June 1560); and AMD, B 213, fol. 17r (June 1575).

[74] Lachiver, *Vins, vignes et vignerons*, 213–214.

[75] Thomas Labbé and Fabien Gaveau, "Les dates de bans de vendange à Dijon: Établissement critique et révision archivistique d'une série ancienne," *Revue historique* 657 (2011): 19–51.

[76] De Serres, *Le Théâtre d'agriculture* (1996 edn.), 301.

[77] Lachiver, *Vins, vignes et vignerons*, 198–199.

Figure 3.4 Wine press at the Clos de Vougeot, sixteenth century

that many wealthy elites, largely members of the Parlement and other royal officers, owned their own wine presses and kept them in their stables or courtyards inside the city walls. In fact, though none of these wine presses have survived, at least eleven of them show up in the archives, and they were rented out to those who had no press of their own at harvest time.[78] Much more will be said about vigneron income and wages later in this chapter, but the point here is that even if a vigneron owned some grape-vines, usually through one of these perpetual contracts, it was unusual for him to own a wine press. It was, of course, possible to make wine without a press at all, using the traditional method of stomping on the grapes with bare feet, though this was a much less efficacious way to extract the juice from the grapes, resulting in a significantly lower yield of juice. And while this method of pressing (*pigeage*) could work for red wines, where the juice, skins, and seeds were allowed to ferment together, it was unsatisfactory for white wines, where all the juice had to be separated from the skins and seeds before fermentation. So, whether they grew grapes for red or white

[78] Agnès Botté, *Les Hôtels particuliers à Dijon au XVIIe siècle* (Paris: Editions A. and J. Picard, 2015), 87–89.

wine, vignerons who were share-croppers or who owned their vines almost always preferred to take their grapes to a winepress to extract the juice, as this produced more wine, and also more profit even with the fees paid to press the grapes.[79] This was yet another way in which the elites and the vignerons interacted socially and commercially during the period on a regular basis.

The actual vinification process was much simpler in the sixteenth century than it is today, so simple in fact, that De Serres spends almost no space at all on it. The pressed grape juice just seemed to ferment magically on its own. In the making of red wine the skins, seeds, and stems were all left to ferment together after the crush, with the skins giving the red wine its color and the skins, stems, and seeds providing tannin. For white wines, the skins, stems, and seeds were separated from the colorless grape juice and discarded, while the juice fermented on its own. Once the juice was pressed out of the grapes, it was collected in wooden barrels, oak or walnut if it was available, as De Serres counselled against using pottery containers like the ancient Romans had done.[80] A variety of natural yeasts in the air and on the grapes eventually turned the sugar in the grape juice to alcohol (ethanol) and carbon dioxide, the latter evaporating into the air. Depending on the amount and types of yeasts on the grapes and the amount of time the juice was left to ferment, the alcoholic level of the resulting wine could vary considerably. Moreover, unlike contemporary wine makers, who allow enough time and introduce special bacteria to produce a secondary (malolactic) fermentation, a bacterial process that converts malic acid in the fermented grape juice to lactic acid, cutting down the acidic level and softening the wine considerably, sixteenth-century vignerons, even those as knowledgeable as De Serres, knew nothing about this process and were anxious to get their wine to market as quickly as possible.[81] This secondary fermentation could occur naturally by chance if there was enough uncultivated lactic acid bacteria present in the pressed grape juice, but most vignerons in the sixteenth century would not have allowed the wine to continue to ferment in barrel long enough for this to occur. And as most wines were drunk within a year of the harvest, the harsh tannins in the red wines – the same bitter flavor you get if you bite into a grape seed – would also not have had time to soften as is the case with contemporary wines today. What all this means is that most six-teenth-century wines tasted nothing like their counterparts today.

---

[79] Ibid.   [80] De Serres, *Le Théâtre d'agriculture* (1996 edn.), 303–311.
[81] Lachiver, *Vins, vignes et vignerons*, 214–226.

Although we can only guess, sixteenth-century wines were almost certainly more bitter and acidic than today's wines. Although some wines might have been more alcoholic than the standard 11–14 percent alcohol by volume drunk today, most were probably less alcoholic than that. Moreover, it would have been completely oxidized, as glass bottles and airtight stoppers were only introduced in the late seventeenth century. In any case, wine was drunk in the sixteenth century more as a beverage for calories as part of the daily diet, for socializing with friends and neighbors, and for some, for getting inebriated. Thus, wine provided various pleasures in the premodern world, but it was a distinctly different beverage than what we are used to today.

All this discussion of wine almost making itself naturally might lead us to think the vinicultural skills of the vigneron did not matter very much. On the contrary, knowing how long to leave the grape juice to ferment, the skill of removing the pulp (pressed skins, stems, and seeds) from the juice after fermentation, and how to store the wine after fermentation was completed, were all highly developed skills. This required vignerons to know a bit about barrel-making for storage, at least enough to repair aging or damaged barrels. Barrel-making was itself a highly developed skill and sixteenth-century coopers worked hand in hand with vignerons at harvest time. Indeed, De Serres knew very well that heat was the enemy of wine, and that the best storage was always completely underground. This required good quality barrels, however. Moreover, De Serres urged vignerons to construct a good quality wine cellar to store the wine until it was sold or drunk. And if they could not afford a proper cellar, then they should simply bury their barrels of wine in the woods.[82] Vignerons who were simply day laborers, of course, did not have to concern themselves with any of this. But for those who did, how did they earn enough money to survive and how did they finance their vineyards?

To begin with, for vignerons whose principal income was a daily wage earned from working in the vineyards as a day laborer, their income was seasonal and depended on both the weather and their own health and ability to work as well as demand for their labor. Their wages also depended on which specific jobs in the vineyard they performed, which was also seasonal. Those who simply weeded and collected dead wood and debris from the vineyards earned the least, between 24 d. and 30 d. per day in 1530. Those who pruned the vines, the most physically demanding job, earned not quite double that, 50 d. per day. While those who actually tied

[82] De Serres, *Le Théâtre d'agriculture* (1996 edn.), 340–341.

the young vine shoots to the wooden stakes, requiring more skill than the other jobs in the vineyards, earned up to 60 d. per day. Any vignerons from the neighboring villages or others who were not residents of Dijon earned 10 d. less for each of these tasks. And women were paid roughly half what men earned for the same task.[83] But all these wages were seasonal, so vignerons would not be working, or being paid, every working day of the year. And after the harvest in late September until pruning began in February, they might not be paid at all. During the late fall and winter months, then, many vignerons had to do other work simply to subsist.

As for vignerons who were either sharecroppers or who owned some vines via a *cens*, how much income did they make through selling their wine? Because the city council of Dijon did not begin systematically keeping records of market prices of wine sold in bulk at the weekly *étape*, or wholesale market, until the 1560s, we can only estimate what vignerons would have earned selling their wine at the wholesale market from the retail prices of a pint of wine, which the local city fathers did keep track of pretty scrupulously from the mid-fifteenth century. This was because, like the price of a one-pound loaf of bread, the price of a pint of wine was regulated by the city council throughout the city in order to prevent vignerons with larger holdings from undercutting the prices of vignerons with smaller holdings and driving them out of business. They recorded the prices of wine sold at three different levels of quality: basic, medium, and best. What is immediately clear from the retail prices, however, is that prices were usually closely tied to the supply of wine from the previous harvest. To be sure, a steady inflation of all prices in sixteenth-century Europe contributed to a longer term rise in wine prices, and much more will be said about inflation in Chapter 5. Nevertheless, as we have already seen, bad weather and the various beasts in the vines resulted in significant fluctuations in the amount of wine produced in any harvest year.[84]

But even these prices are like a snapshot, capturing just one moment in a year of constantly fluctuating prices, with the fluctuations caused by supply and demand at any time of the year. For example, on December 31, 1547 the council recorded the mean retail price of a pint of the best wine as 6 d.[85] But six months later when King Henry II made his "joyous entry" into the

[83] For all these figures, see Tournier, "Notes sur la culture de la vigne," 159 and the sources from the Dijon archives cited there. Also see Golanaud and Labesse, "Les vignerons à Dijon," 86, whose figures are also based on Tournier's.

[84] These prices are taken from the registers of Dijon's city council, with references for each year's price printed in Tournier, "Le vin à Dijon," 186.

[85] AMD, B 185, fol. 158v, December 31, 1547.

Table 3.2 *Retail price of a pint of medium quality wine in* deniers *on December 31 in Dijon, 1480–1550*

1480	3.3	1495	6.6	1515	6.0	1541	8.0
1481	11.6	1499	5.0	1517	9.0	1542	8.0
1482	13.3	1500	5.0	1518	5.0	1543	16.0
1483	1.6	1505	2.0	1522	8.0	1544	20.0
1486	10.0	1506	5.0	1528	8.0	1545	15.0
1487	10.0	1507	10.0	1529	12.0	1546	10.0
1489	10.0	1508	10.0	1530	15.0	1547	6.0
1490	6.6	1509	5.0	1531	10.0	1548	9.0
1491	12.0	1510	5.0	1534	9.0	1549	10.0
1493	10.0	1511	6.0	1538	12.0	1550	8.0

Source: Tournier, "Le vin à Dijion," 186.

city, the council recorded the retail price of a pint of the best wine sold as 12 d.[86] And six months after that the price of a pint of the same wine dropped to 10 d.[87] What all this suggests is that income from wine, despite long-term inflation, fluctuated dramatically over time, demonstrating how vital the weather and beasts in the vines served as a constant threat to the livelihoods of vignerons and their families. Thus, even those vignerons who were fortunate enough to own some vineyards could not rely on a steady and stable income from their grapes, as a bad harvest resulted in a significant loss of revenue. How, then, did they stay afloat, and how could they possibly finance the purchase of additional parcels of vines or the improvement of their holdings?

The short answer is that they did so like vignerons still do today: They borrowed against their potential for future earnings. Without a system of credit and debt, the wine industry in the sixteenth century would never have been able to meet expanding market demands caused by demographic growth as well as increased demand from afar for Burgundy's best wines. There were a variety of different kinds of credit, or loans, available to sixteenth-century vignerons living in Dijon, primarily because the city had a critical mass of wealthy elites from merchants to royal officers and judicial officials connected with the royal courts. These affluent individuals often had spare cash to invest in the wine industry, and they were anxious to do

[86] AMD, B 186, fol. 16r, July 1, 1548.   [87] AMD, B 186, fol. 91r, December 31, 1548.

so, especially because of one particular form of loan called a *rente*. Like every form of monetary transaction, a *rente* provided benefits as well as risks to both parties. But much like the *cens* described earlier, which allowed vignerons to control and administer their own vines, *rentes* were heavily weighted toward the elite lenders, who could benefit financially much more significantly than simply lending money at a fixed rate of interest. This kind of loan was hardly new in the sixteenth century, as *rentes* had been a fundamental part of viticulture in Burgundy at least since the fourteenth century.[88] They worked as follows: An investor provided a significant sum up front to a potential borrower, who agreed in return to pay the investor a small sum of interest, usually about one-sixteenth of the principal (6.25 percent) on a certain date each and every year in perpetuity, with all his heirs inheriting this same obligation. The *rente* actually referred to the annual interest paid each year to the investor, so the borrower was technically referred to in contracts such as this as the vendor of the *rente*, selling the rights to collect interest for a much larger loan payment up front. For elite investors, the only real risk was that the borrower might default and be unable to pay the annual *rente* due to him, or that even if he could, he might die heirless and thus prevent any significant return on the lender's investment.[89] But in order to understand the *rente*'s significance and how it operated in Burgundian viticulture, it is necessary to examine one of these agreements in detail:

> On the twelfth day of November 1611 before noon in Dijon in my office and in the presence of me, Nicolas Guenot, royal notary and record-keeper, established and living in Dijon, rue de la Verrerie, and also in the presence of the witnesses listed below, are standing before us Louis Joyot, vigneron living in the village of Talant, the principal, and Pierre Joyot, vigneron, [his father] also living in Talant and in the house of the said Louis Joyot, his co-signer and nevertheless co-principal, who, both the one and the other and each of them alone as well as together without any distinction, have sold an annual *rente*, which by this [contract] is binding on them and their heirs, to noble Master Philibert Boulier, barrister in the court of the Parlement of Dijon, who is acquiring also perpetually for him and his heirs the annual and perpetual *rente* of six *livres* and five *sous tournois*. This sum is payable each year without exception to the said Mr. Boulier in his house in Dijon and to his heirs on the same day every year as

---

[88] Thierry Dutour, *Une société de l'honneur: Les notables et leur monde à Dijon à la fin du Moyen Age* (Paris: Honoré Champion, 1998), 277–278.

[89] For more on the *rente*, see Cabourdin and Viard, eds., *Lexique historique de la France d'Ancien Régime*, 281–282; and Bernard Schnapper, *Les Rentes au XVIe siècle: Histoire d'un instrument de crédit* (Paris: S.E.V.P.E.N., 1957).

today, the twelfth of November, so that one year from today in 1612 the first payment will be due, continuing from each year to the next without exception, in return for the sum of one hundred pounds *tournois*, which is being paid, counted, and delivered to the said constituents [the Joyots], along with the sum of 21 s. 4 d. owed to the notary and witnesses, 16 s. of which they are currently holding in coins and consider payment in full that the said Mr. Boulier has provided. By this contract the said sellers and constituents [the Joyots] have assigned and do so allocate the [payments of the] said *rente*, for both the principal as well as any other charges, to fall upon each and all of their heirs for the present and in the future if they should ever have recourse to default on the payments for one or more terms of the said *rente* of six *livres* and five *sous*, as well as for any additional costs or reasonable expenses. They promise by the terms of the loan to agree forever to pay each year the amount of six *livres* and five *sous* without exception to the said gentleman [Boulier], on the date and at the place stated above, on pain of all costs plus interest, the security of which they have firmly pledged and are obliged to pay from all their property and that of their heirs, including both moveable and immoveable property, both at present and in the future, to be enforced by the Chancellery court of the Duchy of Burgundy and any other royal courts which may judge this contract. And they renounce all claims to the contrary, even the law that says a general renunciation is not valid unless the purchaser [Boulier] predeceases the said parties [the Joyots]. Made, read, and agreed on the date and at the place specified above in the presence of Simon Gouhan, merchant living in Fontaine-lès-Dijon, and George Simon, vigneron living in Talant, as the required witnesses, as well as the notary.[90]

Thus, in the legal language of the *rente* a vigneron "sold" the right to an annual payment of 6.25 *livres tournois* to a barrister in the Parlement of Dijon for the "purchase price" of 100 *livres tournois*. This clearly represented the transaction through the eyes of the investor. Seen through the eyes of the borrower, however, the transaction looked very different: A vigneron borrowed a sum of money from a wealthy lawyer and agreed to pay it back at a rate of fixed interest, with each and every annual payment only counting as interest, the principal never being paid off. In effect, the vigneron was *renting* the principal in return for this annual interest payment in perpetuity. To be sure, the borrower could pay off the entire principal of the *rente* at any point, plus the interest owed for that particular year, thereby discharging his debt. But this so seldom ever happened that it was not even written into the contract. Moreover, the

---

90 ADCO, E 2225 (notaires), fol. 9v–10v, November 12, 1611.

lender of the principal sum never intended that the debt would be discharged, as he fully expected that he and his heirs could enjoy their annual income in perpetuity. Indeed, he would never have invested his money if he believed the vigneron intended to pay it off quickly. This, of course, was how a *rente* was supposed to work in theory. In the messier practice of daily life the specific terms of the contract might temporarily be abandoned or even dissolved altogether for a variety of reasons: One or both parties might die without any heirs, either party could move away, the borrower might default through poverty without any significant property to secure the loan, or the lender or his heirs might simply refuse to prosecute a borrower in default. Ultimately, however, *rentes* were a way for many vignerons who had some vineyards of their own to raise capital in order to increase their holdings and ultimately raise their standard of living. For others, they were a means of survival. And they were relatively popular too, given the numbers that are recorded in the notarial archives of Dijon. As such, these kinds of loans made it possible for some of the most prosperous vignerons to expand their holdings and purchase addi- tional vines, even if through a *cens*. And prosperous vignerons were exactly the kind of borrowers that would-be investors were looking for, as they offered the least risk for their investment. And although a more detailed examination of the relationship between Dijon's vignerons and its elites will follow in several chapters, suffice it to say here that the *rente* provided one of the more common relationships that some vignerons had with the city's elites. And even if this relationship consisted of a face to face encounter only once per year, the necessity to prepare for that annual encounter by producing the cash to cover the annual payment served as a stark and constant reminder of the social gulf separating even the most wealthy and prosperous of vignerons from men such as the lawyer, Philibert Boulier. Moreover, *rentes* such as this one illustrate very expli- citly how much the premodern economy depended on debt in order to function.[91] Both wealthy vignerons and investors such as Boulier staked their families' futures on debt. Thus, one can say without too much exaggeration that the system of loans and debts at work in the premodern economy tied the fortunes of the wealthy elites to the fortunes of the more prosperous vignerons in a systematic way.

---

[91] For two somewhat different views of the role of debt, both stressing the significance of debt to the functioning of the premodern economy, see Laurence Fontaine, *The Moral Economy: Poverty, Credit, and Trust in Early Modern Europe* (Cambridge: Cambridge University Press, 2014); and Jeff Horn, *Economic Development in Early Modern France: The Privilege of Liberty, 1650–1820* (Cambridge: Cambridge University Press, 2015).

3.4   Anatomy of Urban Life: Rue Vannerie

In order to fully understand how vignerons lived and interacted with their neighbors when they were not working in the vineyards, it is necessary to set them in the context of the urban setting in which they lived. And just as in Chapter 2, where we took a virtual tour of the parish church of St. Michel to try to understand the religious beliefs and practices of the parish's inhabitants, an analysis of one particular street in this parish and everyone who lived on it can give us a much better idea of the material lives of these same inhabitants. The street selected for this close examination was one of the longest streets in the parish, the Rue Vannerie, so-called because in the late Middle Ages it was the street where a number of basket-weavers resided, and a few still did in the sixteenth century. It ran directly from the plaza on the north side of the parish church due north all the way to the parish boundary near the parish church of St. Nicolas (see Figure 3.5). Originally it had been divided into three sections, each with a separate street name. The bottom section nearest the parish church of St. Michel was originally called Rue Serrurerie, presumably because a locksmith resided there. The middle section – running between present-day Rue Jeannin and Rue d'Assas – had always been called Rue Vannerie. And the top end, running from present-day Rue d'Assas all the way to the parish church of St. Nicolas, was called Rue Derrière Saint-Nicolas.[92] In the middle section of Rue Vannerie a cross-street called Rue Roulotte bisected it – Rue Roulotte is the present-day Rue du Lycée – and for the purposes of this study all the inhabitants who lived on the Rue Roulotte are being combined with those living on the Rue Vannerie, as did many of the tax assessors in the sixteenth century when going door to door to record tax assessments of all the inhabitants of Dijon by street name. Thus, when referring to Rue Vannerie in the discussion that follows, I am actually referring to a cross-shaped street, with the three sections of Rue Vannerie forming the longer vertical section of the cross and Rue Roulotte forming the shorter horizontal section. Another reason for selecting this street is that it contained a true cross-section of the city's population as a whole, from nobles to paupers, as well as a very good cross-section of Dijon's vigneron population, from poor day laborers to property owners who owned some vines. Dijon's poorest vignerons tended to live as a group in the parish of St. Philibert, and it is this parish that is usually referred to as

---

[92] For a good overview of the history of Rue Vannerie, see Eugène Fyot, *Dijon: Son passé évoqué par ses rues* (Dijon: Damidot, 1927), 466–482.

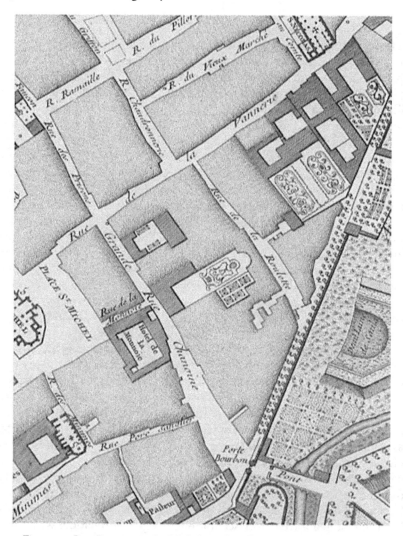

Figure 3.5 Rue Vannerie in St. Michel parish, Dijon (map from Mikel in the
eighteenth century)

the parish of the vignerons in Dijon in many contemporary accounts.[93] A more
representative sample including some of the wealthiest vignerons in the city
lived in St. Michel, however, and it is to the street where many of this cohort of
vignerons lived in the sixteenth century that we now turn.

[93] Henri Chabeuf, *Dijon: Monuments et souvenirs* (Dijon: Librairie Damidot, 1894), 261.

Tax rolls from the period list each inhabitant by name and occupation as well as the amount of tax assessed, except for those who were exempt from paying tax because of their social status, such as nobles, or extreme poverty. As in many sixteenth-century towns, rich and poor often lived side by side, as they did in the parish of St. Michel. While the wealthiest merchants and professionals tended to congregate in the parishes of St. John and Notre-Dame, and the judges, lawyers, and notaries tended to live near the Parlement in the parish of St. Médard, the parish of St. Michel was inhabited by a very good cross-section of the city's population. A number of important families lived in the parish, such as the Bouhier, Des Barres, Frasans, La Verne, and Martin families, all of which provided some of Dijon's mayors, *échevins*, judges, and lawyers in the Parlement, and other royal officers throughout the course of the sixteenth century. And just on the Rue Vannerie alone, the noble Saulx family owned two properties. Jean de Saulx, sire de Courtviron, a judge in the Parlement of Paris and also a councilor of the Duke of Burgundy, constructed the house at the present-day no. 15 in 1412. His great-grandson Gaspard de Saulx, sieur de Tavanes (1509–1575), was born in this house. He served at the court of King Francis I and as marshal of France in the king's army during the Habsburg–Valois wars in Italy in the 1540s and 1550s, after which he was named the king's lieutenant-general in Burgundy (see Chapter 4). His heirs would later construct a second house at present-day no. 35, with a cadet branch of the family remaining in the old house, which they then rebuilt in 1667.[94] Another important family also lived on Rue Vannerie in the sixteenth century, the Le Compasseur family. Their house at present-day no. 66 was probably constructed in the late fifteenth century, and by the middle of the sixteenth century the noble Bénigne Le Compasseur, seigneur of Jancigny, occupied the house. He was a royal officer in the Chamber of Accounts in Dijon, the royal court that adjudicated financial cases and tax disputes. His son, Claude Le Compasseur, was a master in the Chamber from 1573 and later became a treasurer-general of France and the president of the Bureau of Finances in Burgundy. He had married Michelle Frémyot in 1567, the daughter of another important elite family in Dijon, and sometime between 1570 and 1580 had a balcony and turret constructed on the façade of his house in an ornate Renaissance design. Attributed to the famous Dijon architect, engraver, and sculptor of stone and wood, Hugues Sambin (ca. 1520–1601), this stone turret jutted out into the

---

[94] Fyot, *Dijon: Son passé*, 481.

street like a military sentry box and gave the house an almost military look despite the very artistic and ornate stone work.[95] As such, it was not just a symbol of wealth and affluence but it also served as a marker of the family's noble status, despite the obvious fact that the family's wealth and influence came from the sovereign courts rather than military service.

But living cheek by jowl with families such as the Saulx and Le Compasseur families were also vignerons, merchants, artisans of virtually all trades, widows, and even paupers. Table 3.3 gives a good overview of the diversity of wealth of the inhabitants of rue Vannerie. These figures come from the tax assessment rolls of the *taille*, the personal property tax imposed on all goods and property in Dijon. In 1523 there were a total of 489 households in the parish of St. Michel, of which 180 were headed by vignerons. Thus, while vignerons made up between 20 and 25 percent of all households in the city of Dijon in the sixteenth century, in the parish of St. Michel vignerons made up 37 percent of all households. Excluding four exempt households, three of which were exempt for holding royal offices and one for extreme poverty, the mean or average tax assessment in the entire parish in 1523 was 10.26 *sous*.[96] The mean tax assessed to the vigneron households was lower, only 7.24 *sous*. So, the vignerons as a group fell below the mean for the entire parish. If we focus on Rue Vannerie specifically, we see a similar pattern: 82 total households of which 38 (46.3 percent) were headed by vignerons. The mean tax assessment on Rue Vannerie was 9.34 *sous*, while the vignerons on Rue Vannerie were assessed a mean of 7.34 *sous*, again, below the mean for the entire street. This disguises the fact that many wealthy vignerons lived on rue Vannerie, however. Based on the tax assessment for 1523, the sixth highest assessment on the entire street – more than 25 *sous* – was paid by the widow of a vigneron, Girard Gagnière. And seven other vignerons paid between 11 and 15 *sous*, all above the mean for the entire parish: Simon Noirot, Mathieu La Vielle, Pierre Jacquelin, Jean Malnourry, Thibault Nault, Jean Quarrey, and Guiot Horry. As a cohort, the vignerons on Rue Vannerie ran the gamut of the entire social spectrum, however, as there was 1 in the highest quintile (the top 20 percent of all households on the street), 11 in the next quintile, 7 in the middle quintile, 14 in the next quintile, and 5 in the bottom 20 percent.

---

[95] Ibid, 467. For more on Sambin, see Noël Garnier, *Contribution à l'histoire de Hugues Sambin* (Dijon: Darantière, 1891), and Henri David, *De Sluter à Sambin: Essai critique sur la sculpture et le décor monumental en Bourgogne au XVe et XVIe siècle*, 2 vols. (Paris: Presses Universitaires de France, 1933).
[96] AMD L 164, fols. 20–212. The tax assessments in the documents are given in *francs, gros*, and *blancs*, all of which I have converted to *sous* for comparison. For rates of conversion, see p. xvi.

Table 3.3 *Tax assessments in the parish of St. Michel, Dijon, 1523 and 1552 (all tax values are given in sous tournois)*

Year	Total households	Mean tax	Vigneron Households	Vigneron Mean tax	Rue vannerie Households	Vannerie Mean tax	Vannerie Vignerons	Van. vign. Mean tax
1523	489	10.26	180	7.24	82	9.34	38	7.34
1552	614	9.48	164	7.78	90	7.37	34	7.85

Source: AMD, L 164, fols. 20–212 (1523) and L 189, fols. 68–284 (1552).

If we move to the 1552 tax assessment nearly three decades later, we see that the vignerons had become a little wealthier in relation to their neighbors on Rue Vannerie. For example, while the mean tax assessment for the entire parish in 1552 was 9.48 *sous*, the vignerons in the parish as a group were assessed a mean of 7.78 *sous*, which was much closer to the parish mean than their counterparts of 1522.[97] Moreover, the mean tax assessment on Rue Vannerie was 7.37 *sous*, while the vignerons on the street were assessed an average of 7.85 *sous*, which was higher than the mean for the entire street. Indeed, six of the ten highest tax assessments on the entire street were vignerons, including both Thibault Nault and Jean Malnourry from the 1552 tax roll. Broken down by quintile, there were 7 vignerons in the top 20 percent, 8 in the next quintile, 8 in the middle quintile, 5 in the next quintile, and 5 in the bottom 20 percent of households on the street. So even though the vignerons made up a smaller percentage of the total population of the parish in 1552 (26.7 percent) compared to 1523 (36.8 percent), those vignerons still living on Rue Vannerie had increased their net worth, not just in relation to their neighbors on the street, but in relation to the entire parish.

But who else lived on Rue Vannerie besides these vignerons? Besides the elites, who were exempt, there were other well-to-do fiscal officers, professionals such as doctors and notaries, and just about every kind of artisanal trade imaginable: barrel makers, wood workers, turners, carpenters, bakers, butchers, vinegar makers, drapers, dyers, tanners, cloth cutters, barbers, pastry makers, tilers, builders, roofers, masons, locksmiths, weavers, wool carders, and so on. And what is most striking is that all these trades were evenly distributed throughout the street regardless of income and wealth. As the tax assessors went door to door, we can clearly see that rich and poor lived side by side. It was very common for someone in the top quintile of wealth to have neighbors on both sides in the bottom quintile. For example, a poor widower paying less than 1 *sous* in tax lived next door to a clerk of the court who paid 30 *sous* in tax, and a wealthy vigneron paying 25 *sous* in tax lived next door to a pauper who paid nothing. This was the rule rather than the exception, as the exterior of the house often gave no indication at all what kind of person lived within it. The amounts and kinds of furnishings inside, however, were much surer indicators of the social hierarchy.

But what kinds of houses did these vignerons live in? We have already seen that fairly complete descriptions of the hôtels of elites such as the

---

[97] AMD L 189, fols. 68–284.

Saulx and the Le Compasseur families have survived because of the expense and decoration invested in their houses in order to make them stand out. There is much less documentation for those below the elites, however. What we can say is that most vignerons, like a majority of the inhabitants of the city, rented their houses. The terms of these agreements were usually only two to three years, and sometimes even less, even for families that occupied the same house for long periods of time.[98] But the tax rolls also make it clear that some families moved within the parish and even to other parishes fairly regularly, as the names of the heads of household make clear. The elites who built their impressive residences for long-term occupation obviously owned their own houses, but most residents of the city lived in rented accommodation. But what do we mean by a house? Most of the literature on vigneron houses refers to those living in the rural villages, not the urban vignerons such as those living in Dijon, where they owned small farm houses and sometimes a barn for animals, with a separate wine cellar.[99] In the city, this was not possible, and we know a lot more about where vignerons lived in the city because of the tax rolls than we do about the kind of houses they lived in.[100] A household on the tax rolls may in fact refer only to a couple of rooms, or in some cases, a single room in a multi-room townhouse. It is equally clear, however, that some of the wealthiest vignerons were owners of their own homes, or at least owners of a *cens* entitling them to permanent residence in their homes. Thibault Nault, for example, already mentioned as one of the most prosperous vignerons living on Rue Vannerie, did own the rights to his home thorough a *cens*. He lived on the part of the street known as the Rue Roulotte, and in May 1519 he first acquired the *cens* for a house on the street that required him to pay an annual payment of 6 s. and 8 d. to the clergy of the parish church of St. Michel, who owned the house outright. The house remained in the Nault family until 1652, when Louise de la Grange, widow of Pierre Nault, vigneron, remarried to a man named Nicolas Baittent. At this time the *cens* and the house were divided, with half going to the son of Louise de la Grange, a parchment maker named also Pierre Nault, and the other half going to the heirs of Baittent.[101]

In addition to paying for their housing, all inhabitants of the city had to buy basic provisions and foodstuffs. While the basic retail prices of a one-

[98] See Farr, *Hands of Honor*, 118–121 on the homes Dijon's artisans.
[99] See, for example, Lachiver, *Vins, vignes et vignerons*, 231–236.
[100] Golenaud and Labesse, "Les vignerons à Dijon," 87–96.
[101] ADCO, G 3579 (liasse), May 6, 1519, April 7 and October 15, 1652.

Table 3.4 *Prices of provisions in Dijon, 1535 and 1548 (all prices listed in* sous *and* deniers)

	1535	1548
Bread (loaf of 16–17 ounces)	4 d.	4 d.
Wine (pint of best quality)	1 s. 3 d.	1 s.
Wine (pint of medium quality)	1 s.	10 d.
Wine (pint of basic quality)	—	9 d.
Wine (pint of previous vintage)	2 s. 6 d.	—
Oats (one bushel, measure of Dijon)	1 s. 8 d.	2 s. 6 d.
Firewood (one cord)	25 s.	20 s.
Lard (pound of best quality)	—	2 s. 6 d.
Lard (pound of medium quality)	—	2 s.
Lard (pound of basic quality)	—	1 s. 8 d.
Candle wax (pound)	2 s.	2 s. 6 d.
Mutton (quarter)	—	10 s.
Veal (quarter)	—	12 s. 6 d.
Flour (cartranche)	—	9 s. 2 d.
Butter (pound)	—	3 s. 4 d.
Capon (with feathers)	—	5 s.
Capon (larded)	—	6 s.
Hen (with feathers)	—	3 s.
Hen (larded)	—	4 s.
Chicken (with feathers)	—	1 s. 8 d.
Chicken (larded)	—	2 s.
Pigeon	—	1 s. 6 d.

Source: AMD, B 179, fol. 56v (1535), and B 186, fol. 16r-v (1548).

pound loaf of bread and a pint of wine were recorded regularly in the city council's deliberations, other prices were recorded only periodically in this period. We have complete records for 1548 only, because the king made a royal entry into Dijon in July of that year.

The city council only began recording complete prices of foodstuffs and provisions every year in 1578. So, what we have before that date is a mere snapshot rather than annual figures over a long period of time. And what these prices in these two years cannot show, moreover, is the impact of long-term inflation going on throughout Western Europe in the sixteenth century, about which more will be said in Chapter 5. Even so, it is clear that a vigneron who was a simple day laborer earning only 30–40 d. per day would be hard-pressed to afford to buy even a pint of the most basic wine he produced; he could rarely purchase meat, and he would never be able to buy a cord of firewood. So, simple subsistence was always under threat, and the possibility of a poor wine harvest could mean starvation was always just around the corner. Wealthier vignerons and artisans, even if their day-to-day subsistence was rarely under threat, still felt the impact of unstable prices and fluctuating standards of living. Only the city's wealthiest elites could weather most economic crises without suffering unduly. But economic crises occurred regularly and were hardly unanticipated. The regular and periodic travails of the beasts in the vines, for example, were largely accepted by most as God's will, as punishment for their own shortcomings. As we have already seen, it was far too common in the first half of the sixteenth century for the city fathers to order a religious procession and prayers so that God "will drive out the beasts and vermin destroying the fruits of our vines, which is happening because of our many sins and blasphemies."[102]

By mid-century, however, a far different crisis emerged in Burgundy, which for many inhabitants was even more threatening to their livelihoods than the beasts in the vines. This was the advent of religious reform from Calvin's Geneva, beliefs and practices that most in Burgundy believed to be heresy. Indeed, the beasts in the vines that threatened their subsistence and the heretical beliefs and practices that seemed to threaten their salvation often melded into one common enemy. As the city council's deliberations recorded in 1562, "tomorrow at six o'clock in the morning a solemn and general religious procession will take place, whose purpose is to pray to God the Creator, as much for the extirpation of heresy and the conservation of the goods and fruits of the earth, as for the health and prosperity of the people."[103] Moreover, the advent of the Reformation and ensuing religious wars in the second half of the century would ultimately come to challenge the very foundations of the political stability constructed in Burgundy since the province's incorporation into the kingdom of France three quarters of a century earlier. As a result, both the clerical and lay elites discovered that they would need to forge new alliances with the popular classes if they hoped to defeat the perceived dangers emanating from the establishment of the new religion.

---

[102] AMD, D II (liasse), June 10, 1540.
[103] AMD, D II (liasse), 1562 (exact date torn off with corner of the page).

PART II

The Wars of Religion in Burgundy
(ca. 1550 to 1595)

CHAPTER 4

The Reformation in Burgundy

It is difficult to pinpoint exactly when the Reformation first made inroads in Burgundy generally and in Dijon in particular, though it is clear that books thought to be suspect or even heretical were circulating as early as the 1530s. On October 22, 1535, for example, the mayor announced to the members of the city council in Dijon that a man named Jean de Vaulx had been arrested and imprisoned, because he was discovered to be trying to sell three books by Erasmus. The mayor did not name the books, but said they were suspected of containing heresy, and he recommended that one of the books be sent to the Cardinal of Givry, who was the Bishop of Langres in their diocese, and a second be sent to the monks at the monastery in Cîteaux, for their inspection. The third was kept by the city councilors for their own perusal.[1] Almost a month later, they received word that the books were indeed "suspect" and should not be returned to the still imprisoned De Vaulx.[2] He got off lightly, however, as in 1549 another would-be purveyor of suspect books named Jean Haynon was "beaten and flogged with sticks until his blood flowed," before his books were burned in his presence.[3] There are numerous other references throughout the 1550s of books being seized and burned by the city fathers and other local magistrates, mostly books coming from and printed in Geneva, and the stakes were raised even higher for those caught trying to sell illicit or banned books in the city. In February 1561, two young men named François Hébart and Philippe Barrey, a 21-year-old cobbler and 18-year-old baker, respectively, from Caen in Normandy, were stopped when they tried to enter the city, and their belongings were searched. They were found to be carrying copies of the New Testament in French from the print shop of Jean Crespin, copies of the Psalms of David also printed by Crespin, copies of a child's catechism in French printed in Geneva, and a letter addressed to

---

[1] AMD, B 179, fol. 52v, October 22, 1535.   [2] AMD, B 179, fol. 62v, November 17, 1535.
[3] AMD, B 194, fol. 227v, undated except for the year 1549.

the authorities in Geneva seeking permission to reside there. The two young men were quickly arrested and interrogated separately. Ten days later they were pronounced to be "seditious" and were condemned "to be hanged and strangled at the sign of the sinister place in Dijon," that is, the Place Morimont, where executions took place.[4] Because all capital offenses were automatically appealed to the Parlement of Dijon, there is no way of knowing if this brutal sentence was actually carried out, since those records have not survived, though it seems unlikely given that there is no further mention of these men in the city council deliberations. All these "suspect" books coming into Dijon, however, are clear indications that there was a market for them in the city, and there is no doubt that a small reformed community had emerged there by the early 1550s.[5] But how large was it? What new ideas were those of this new religion actually trying to propagate? And why were city officials so frightened by their presence in the community? This chapter will try to answer these questions, as well as explain how Dijon's mayor and city council, along with a fair bit of help from other elites in the city as well the city's vignerons, managed to suppress the growth of the new religion by 1572 without significant violence or bloodshed. Given that cities such as Paris and a dozen other provincial towns were rocked by the violence of the St. Bartholomew's massacres in the summer and fall of 1572, it is worth exploring how Dijon managed to enforce religious uniformity while avoiding the collective bloodshed of those other places.

4.1   The Success and Failure of the Reformed Religion in Dijon

What was this new religion that appeared in Burgundy in the 1540s and 1550s? In 1554 one very alarmed member of Dijon's city council, Didier La Verne, reported that "the rumor was going around that two-thirds of the city were Lutherans."[6] This was clearly a gross exaggeration, as the city had approximately 12,000 residents at that time. Moreover, the term

---

[4] AMD, B 198, fol. 100r, February 4, 1560/61; and AMD, D 65 (liasse), February 4 and 13, 1560/1. Also see Edmond Belle, "Les libraires dijonnais et les débuts de la Réforme à Dijon," *Bulletin de la Société de l'histoire du protestantisme français* 59 (1910): 481–495.

[5] For the origins of the Reformation in Dijon, see Edmond Belle, *La Réforme à Dijon des origins à la fin de la lieutenance générale de Gaspard de Saulx-Tavanes, 1530–1570* (Dijon: Damidot, 1911), 1–18; Jacques Fromental, *La Réforme en Bourgogne aux XVIe et XVIIe siècles* (Paris: Les Belles Lettres, 1968), 9–29; James R. Farr, *Hands of Honor: Artisans and Their World in Dijon, 1550–1650* (Ithaca, NY, and London: Cornell University Press, 1988), 224–236; and Mack P. Holt, "Wine, Community and Reformation in Sixteenth-Century Burgundy," *Past and Present* 138 (1993): 58–93.

[6] AMD, B192, fol. 92v, July 17, 1554.

"Lutheran" was simply a catch-all for any variety of suspect believer. But if they were not Lutherans, then what kind of new religion were they trying to practice? And what new religious ideas were beginning to circulate in the Burgundian capital to warrant such a reaction by Didier La Verne in 1554? Although it is nearly impossible to trace the origins of ideas that by definition were propagated clandestinely, it seems equally clear that the form of the new religion that so frightened La Verne and others was an offshoot of the Reformed tradition that was first established by Matthias Zell, Martin Bucer, and Wolfgang Capito in Strasbourg in the 1520s, by Pierre Viret in Lausanne in the 1530s, and later by Guillaume Farel and John Calvin in Geneva in the 1530s and 1540s. It was a religion that contrasted sharply with the traditional form of Christianity that had evolved over the centuries, described in Chapter 2. Above all, Calvin, much like Martin Luther in Saxony before him in the 1520s, had constructed a theology of salvation – based largely on his interpretation of certain passages in Paul's epistles to the Romans and Ephesians – that denied any role to Christian charity or good works of any kind, that claimed the community of saints had no power whatsoever to intercede with God on anyone's behalf, and that rejected the notion that God's grace was imparted to individual Christians during the Mass. For Calvin, God had predestined some for salvation and others for damnation at the time of the creation. Those who were predestined for salvation – the elect – were saved entirely through God's grace, and no human works of Christian charity nor any intercession by the Virgin Mary or any of the saints could alter that. Although Calvin had many other quarrels with the traditional church over the authority of the Pope, the powers of bishops, and a host of other issues, it was his notion of salvation that had the most serious implications for sixteenth-century Christians. For Burgundians in particular, the idea that the Virgin Mary's intervention was useless, that all the masses for the dead funded by their wine were inefficacious, and that their participation in the Mass, where they encountered Christ in the flesh, was, to use Calvin's own words, just "buffonnery" and "farce,"[7] may have been attractive ideas for some, but for many others, such as the *échevin* Didier La Verne in 1554, they were cause for concern and alarm.[8] The Reformed

---

[7] John Calvin, "Short Treatise on the Holy Supper of Our Lord and Only Saviour Jesus Christ," in J. K. S. Reid, ed. and trans., *Calvin: Theological Treatises* (Philadelphia, PA: The Westminster Press, 1954), 161.

[8] For an introduction to Calvin's church in Geneva, his theology, and his efforts to send out pastors into French-speaking areas to found new churches, see E. William Monter, *Calvin's Geneva* (New York, NY: Wiley, 1967); Robert M. Kingdon, *Geneva and the Coming of the Wars of Religion in*

church's rejection of the doctrine of transubstantiation in the Eucharist in particular, especially its denial that the Mass imparted divine grace upon those who participated in it, was particularly divisive. Moreover, as Christopher Elwood has shown, Reformed rhetoric and printed propaganda about the Eucharist quickly led to many Protestants rejecting traditional views about political authority and power as well as the proper relations between the sacred and society as a whole.[9] The competing doctrines over the Mass remained a principal fault line – and maybe the single most significant obstacle that divided not only Protestants from Catholics, but also divided Protestants themselves – for the duration of the Reformation.[10] This was certainly the case in Burgundy.

Small groups of Protestants began forming in Burgundy as early as 1524 according to Jacques Fromental, and they met with resistance and opposition nearly everywhere.[11] They cannot have been very great in number, as there is virtually no mention of them whatsoever in the city council's deliberations over the next two decades.

Nevertheless, by the late 1550s it has been estimated that as many as 500–600 Protestants – largely Calvinists rather than Lutherans – had either converted or settled in the Burgundian capital.[12] The deliberations of the city council throughout this period are replete with reports of "heretics" who attempted "to break, efface and stain the effigy, image and remembrance of the holy and sacred host," or incidents where the "unfaithful (*mal de foy*)" hurled abuse and insults at a religious processions of Jacobins, calling them "hypocrites, liars, seducers of the people."[13] And in April 1560 the registers of the Parlement of Dijon recorded that "yesterday we heard from the officers of the mayor of this city of Dijon that for some time a

France, 1555–1563 (Geneva: Droz, 1956; 2nd edn. 2007); William Bouwsma, *John Calvin: A Sixteenth-Century Portrait* (Oxford and New York, NY: Oxford University Press, 1988); Randall C. Zachman, *Image and Word in the Theology of John Calvin* (Notre Dame, IN: University of Notre Dame Press, 2007); Randall C. Zachman, *John Calvin as Teacher, Pastor, and Theologian: The Shape of His Writings and Thought* (Grand Rapids, MI: Baker Academic, 2006); F. Bruce Gordon, *Calvin* (New Haven, CT: Yale University Press, 2009); and Anthony N. S. Lane, *A Reader's Guide to Calvin's Institutes* (Grand Rapids, MI: Baker Academic, 2009).

[9] Christopher Elwood, *The Body Broken: The Calvinist Doctrine of the Eucharist and the Symbolization of Power in Sixteenth-Century France* (Oxford: Oxford University Press, 1999), especially 21–32.

[10] See Amy Nelson Burnett, "The Social History of Communion and the Reformation of the Eucharist," *Past & Present* 211 (May 2011): 77–119. Also see Christian Grosse, *Les Rituels de la cène: La culte eucharistique réformé à Genève, XVIe-XVIIe siècles* (Geneva: Droz, 2008).

[11] Fromental, *La Réforme en Bourgogne*, 11.

[12] This seems the most realistic estimate of Dijon's Huguenot population, which I have calculated from the figures given by Jean Richard, "Les quêtes de l'église Notre-Dame et la diffusion du protestantisme à Dijon vers 1562," *Annales de Bourgogne* 32 (1960): 183–189.

[13] AMD, B195, fol. 139v, January 17, 1558; and B197, fol. 48r, August 11, 1559.

number of armed artisans have been assembling by night in various places throughout the city, and similarly that last Sunday during the sermon at church several women met and went throughout the city crying and singing the Psalms of David in a manner of derision and mockery of the preachers."[14] The mayor and city council did its utmost to deal with incidents such as these forcefully and publicly, believing that pre-emptive action was the best remedy against an escalation of violence, and they forbade all illicit assemblies of these "heretics," both in public and in private.[15] And their fears of violence were not entirely without foundation. When the Parlement of Dijon refused to register the Edict of Romorantin – an edict issued in May 1560 by the king's chancellor, Michel de l'Hôpital, which the local judges in Dijon's Parlement felt was too lenient in prosecuting heresy – the magistrates discovered that they themselves had become the targets of violence. On the night of July 19, "shameful" placards were posted all over the city: "Notice is hereby given that during the second week of July the court [of the Parlement] of Dijon refused to ratify the edicts sent to them by the king, but instead dispatched [an envoy] to the king in order to block them, which has been accomplished. Those on the court will be massacred, and the entire city of Dijon set afire."[16] The growing number adhering to the new faith had thus become much more than a nuisance by 1560. To many of the elites they now seemed to be a genuine threat to public order, and the mayor and city council duly repeated their prohibitions against all illicit assemblies of Protestants of any kind.

This atmosphere of religious tension and hostility escalated even further the following year. The Lenten season in the spring of 1561 was marred by reports that some artisans had been "singing the Psalms of David loudly and scandalously in French," after a Carmelite preacher had informed them after his sermon "that it was not a bad deed if anyone, after having praised God in church in the morning, should sing the Psalms in his house, shop, or in the fields." The mayor and *échevins* quickly put a stop to this, and they ordered the clergy at the Chapelle aux Riches, who had hired this preacher, to prevent him from preaching anymore. Moreover, they publicly declared "at the sound of the trumpet and in all the crossroads of the city that it was prohibited for all persons of whatever estate or quality to sing either publicly or in secret any psalms or other songs in French, on

---

[14] BMD, Fonds Saverot 1491, fol. 999.

[15] AMD, B198, fol. 138v, 15 June 1561, B199, fols. 36v–37r, July 15–16, 1561.

[16] AMD, B 198, fol. 30r, July 20, 1560.

pain of being declared and punished as a seditious rebel."[17] In addition the city council reported to the Parlement that several inhabitants of the city had journeyed to Geneva on the feast of Pentecost "to make their co-called supper," and that they had also heard that a baby was baptized in a private house by a minister who came from Geneva.[18] Moreover, fearing trouble and some kind of Protestant attempt to disrupt the annual Corpus Christi procession in June, the council authorized all Catholics who participated to arm themselves.[19] Although nothing happened on that occasion, those of the new religion in Dijon politicized the religious issue by mounting a serious campaign to elect one of its own as mayor of Dijon in the annual mayoral elections. Although he was eventually defeated, the candidacy of the Protestant Antoine Brocard, a royal councilor in Dijon's Chamber of Accounts (*Chambre des Comptes*), demonstrated how strong the movement had become by the summer of 1561.

Just the year before, the Protestant Brocard had previously attempted to become elected mayor, garnering a mere 31 votes out of a total of 234 votes cast (or 13.2 percent). He finished third to the winner, Jean Maillard, and the more militantly Catholic Bénigne Martin, a lawyer and former mayor who had previously been elected in 1557, 1558, and 1559 (see Table 4.1). But this was just a prelude to the election of June 1561.

By the summer of 1561 Protestant strength and boldness had increased, and a more serious effort was mounted to elect Brocard as mayor of Dijon. This election was more hotly contested and conducted in an atmosphere of religious and political hostility. The day before the election, in fact, the city council had banned all Protestant demonstrations entirely, hoping to curb the rising enthusiasm for Brocard's candidacy.[20] The result was a much larger vote for the Protestant candidate, more than three times greater than the previous year. The politicized nature of the religious division in the city, however, had resulted in an even greater Catholic reaction to the upsurge of Protestant electoral strength. Although Brocard did finish second in 1561, among a half dozen candidates receiving votes, he was soundly defeated by the militantly Catholic former mayor, Bénigne Martin, by 322 votes to 123.[21] And as Table 4.1 clearly shows, the

---

[17] AMD, B 198, fols. 113r–115v, March 31–April 1, 1561.
[18] BMD, Fonds Saverot 1491, fol. 1100–1101.   [19] AMD, B 198, fols. 133v–134r, June 3, 1561.
[20] Belle, *La Réforme à Dijon*, 40. Also see James R. Farr, "Popular Religious Solidarity in Sixteenth-Century Dijon," *French Historical Studies* 14 (1985): 199, n. 18.
[21] The figures are taken from AMD, B 199, fols. 1r–10r, June 21, 1561. A full list of Dijon's mayors from 1197 to 1837 as well as their terms of office is printed in Claude Courtépée and Edme Béguillet, *Description générale et particulière du duché de Bourgogne*, 5 vols. Avalon and Paris: Nabu Press, 3rd edn. 1967–2010), 2: 28–32. For a corrected list for the sixteenth century, see Mack P. Holt, "Popular

Table 4.1 *Dijon mayoral elections of 1560 and 1561*

Candidate	Votes cast		Vigneron votes	% of all candidate's total	Vignerons voting for candidate
	Total	%			
1560					
Jean Maillard	68	29.1	4	5.9	19.0
Bénigne Martin	60	25.6	11	18.3	52.4
Antoine Brocard	31	13.2	3	9.7	14.3
Others	75	32.1	3	4.0	14.3
Total	**234**	**100**	**21**	**9.0**	**100**
1561					
Bénigne Martin	322	64.9	188	58.4	92.6
Antoine Brocard	123	24.8	10	8.1	4.9
Others	51	10.3	5	9.8	2.5
Total	**496**	**100**	**203**	**40.9**	**100**

Source: AMD, B 198, fols. 1 r–7v, June 21, 1560; and B 199, fols. 1 r–10 r, June 21, 1561.

foundation of Martin's victory was the virtual block vote of Dijon's vignerons, who accounted for 58.4 percent of Martin's winning total. He certainly would not have defeated Brocard without their support. Compared to the year before when only 21 vignerons turned out to vote, in the 1561 election 203 vignerons showed up to declare their voices in this highly charged election, and of that number 188 (92.6 percent) voted for the Catholic Martin. Even more striking, when we compare these numbers to the numbers of vignerons on Dijon's tax rolls, it becomes clear just how politicized this cohort of vineyard workers had become by 1561. Out of 541 vignerons on the tax roll, 203 (37.5 percent) voted in the election of 1561. As they made up only about 20 percent of the total population, they clearly participated in far greater strength relative to their proportion of the population than any other social group, making up 40.9 percent of all those who voted in 1561. By contrast, the city's artisans made up nearly one-third of the total population of the city and a similar proportion of those who voted in 1560 (36.5 percent), but only 178 out of 910 artisans (19.6 percent) participated in this heated election.[22] Clearly Dijon's vignerons

Political Culture and Mayoral Elections in Sixteenth-Century Dijon," in Mack P. Holt, ed., *Society and Institutions in Early Modern France* (Athens, GA: University of Georgia Press, 1991), 98–116.
[22] Figures are taken for the tax roll of 1553, the nearest year to 1561 that is complete, in AMD, L 192–193. The figures for the artisans come from Farr, "Popular Religious Solidarity," 199–201.

reacted more strongly to Martin's anti-Protestant campaign than any other group among the electorate. But why was that the case?

We have already seen in Chapter 1 that Dijon's vignerons were politically active and had already become very involved in disputed mayor elections before the Reformation. Moreover, it has already been pointed out how closely the mayor and *échevins* regulated Dijon's wine industry. So, there is every reason to expect the city's vignerons to want to participate in politically charged elections such as the one in 1561. But why did nearly all of them vote for the militantly Catholic Martin? There appear to be three principal reasons behind the vignerons' collective confessional allegiance to the Catholic church: (1) their belief that their wine was intimately linked to their salvation through the foundation of masses for the dead, (2) their insistence that wine was also closely tied to their salvation through the grace imparted by the Eucharist, and (3) finally their notions of sociability, community, and commensality, which they found to be far more compatible with the practice of Catholicism than with that of Protestantism. Because I have already devoted so much space to the links between the vignerons' wine and their salvation as well as the foundation of masses for the dead in Chapter 2,[23] I shall spend the bulk of the space to follow analyzing the Eucharist and the vigneron's sense of sociability and commensality.

Ironically, it was the communal nature of the Eucharist itself that legitimated the withdrawal of the chalice from the laity in the twelfth century in the West, as the priest alone consumed the holy blood of Christ for the entire assembly of communicants.[24] The priest and laity eating from the same loaf and drinking from the same cup as members of one Christian community followed by the kiss of peace had social connotations that were as powerful as the theological connotations. The new dogma of the twelfth century that *per concomitantiam* Christ's blood was a part of his body and therefore entirely present in both species meant that the priest could partake of the chalice for the entire congregation. The withholding of the chalice and resulting emphasis on the host and its public demonstration, as well as the increased emphasis on the feast of Corpus Christi in the late Middle Ages, are well known and need not be recounted here.[25] The

[23] See Chapter 2.

[24] This process is described by Joseph Jungmann, *The Mass of the Roman Rite: Its Origins and Development*, trans. Francis A. Brunner, 2 vols. (New York, NY: Benziger Brothers, 1951–1955), 2: 382–386. See also John Bossy, "The Mass as a Social Institution, 1200–1700," *Past & Present* 100 (August 1983), 29–61.

[25] See Chapter 3.

newly invigorated powers of the host, however, were not won at the expense of the mysteries of the cup. Although her concern is primarily with women, Carolyn Walker Bynum has demonstrated that with the permanent withdrawal of the chalice, the laity's thirst for Christ's blood only intensified.[26] In any case, we need to remember that the new doctrine of concomitance did not remove wine from the Mass for the laity altogether. Although it was only consecrated in Bohemia, it continued to be served throughout most of Western Europe, and this unconsecrated but blessed wine continued to play an important role in the liturgy in Burgundy as elsewhere. According to John Bossy, it was "clearly something more solemn than the mouth-cleansing fluid the orthodox clergy felt obliged to pretend."[27]

The implications for the vigneron were therefore not necessarily a loss of prestige or the lessening of the bonds between the juice from their vines and Christ's blood. And in one specific sense, the withdrawal of the chalice from the laity paralleled and reinforced the emphasis on patriarchy at the vigneron's own table. As the verse of the unknown "bon vigneron" made clear, not only was the vigneron the master of his wife, but he denied her the chalice just like the priest. He alone drank his own "sacred" wine, "which makes the mute to speak, and not water, which is only worth putting in soup ... I leave that for my wife to drink ... Women, children, and many of the poor can easily spend their entire lives without wine and only water."[28] Seen in this light, it is easier to understand why the Protestant rite that embittered the Burgundian vignerons more than any other in the 1560s was the one that challenged the patriarchal and sacerdotal authority of the priest: the observance of the Lord's Supper. To them, the thought of heretics and even women swilling down their sacred wine was desecration. In Beaune on Easter Sunday 1561 a barn where a group of Protestants celebrated the Lord's Supper in both kinds was burned to the ground by an angry group of vignerons.[29] A few weeks later in Autun in southwest Burgundy a mob broke into another barn where Protestants had just celebrated the Lord's

---

[26] Carolyn Walker Bynum, *Holy Feast and Holy Fast: The Religious Significance of Food to Medieval Women* (Berkeley, CA: University of California Press, 1989), 56–59.

[27] John Bossy, *Christianity in the West, 1400–1800* (Oxford: Oxford University Press, 1985), 70.

[28] "Monologue du bon vigneron sortant de sa vigne, et retournant soupper en sa maison," in Charles Moiset, ed., "La poésie auxerroise au XVI e siècle," *Annuaire historique du département de l'Yonne* 21 (1857): 77–78. The "monologue du bon vigneron" was written in Auxerre in western Burgundy in the 1590s and published anonymously in 1607.

[29] [Theodore de Bèze, et al.], *Histoire ecclésiastique des églises reeformés au royaume de France*, eds. G. Baum and E. Cunitz, 3 vols. (Paris: Librairie Fischbacher, 1883–1889), 1: 864 and 3:489.

Supper on Ascension Day: "They broke up the seats and the minister's chair with the intention, as it has since become known, of setting the place on fire." Only the proximity of several houses and a nearby abbey prevented them from repeating the scene in Beaune.[30] As Natalie Davis has shown, purifying a polluted space with fire was just as much a Catholic ritual of violence as the desecration of relics and images of the Virgin was for Protestants.[31] Moreover, the new religion's practice of the Lord's Supper, even if most vignerons were probably unaware of its theological foundations, served as a talisman for their opposition to the new religion, as it called into question not only their relationship with God, but also their very labor that went into producing the wine that was consecrated at the Mass and turned into Christ's blood.[32]

But maybe the strongest and most visible links the Burgundian vignerons had to the traditional church were neither about their salvation nor maintaining the purity of the Eucharist, but built upon their conception of sociability and commensality. There was a clear contrast between the vignerons' and the Protestants' views concerning the social use of wine. In Burgundy wine served as an astringent to bind the community together as well as to God. Its communal role was thus one that emphasized society collectively by promoting sociability, commensality, and hospitality. "Eat good food and drink the best wine with your neighbour," proclaimed the "bon vigneron" of Auxerre.[33] The new Reformed religion, by stressing the individual's relationship with God and implying that every man was his own priest, confronted the traditional religion of most vignerons in a way that undermined the community of believers and their certainty that salvation was a collective exercise. After a brief experiment of placing French vernacular Bibles in all the taverns in Geneva, John Calvin adopted a different approach to discourage tipplers from drinking together, as the Genevan pastors' ordinances for the supervision of their churches attest: "There is to be no treating of one another to drinks, under penalty of three *sous* . . . There are to be no carousals, under penalty of ten *sous*."[34] Imposing

---

[30] Ibid., 3: 487–488.
[31] Natalie Zemon Davis, "The Rites of Violence: Religious Riot in Sixteenth-Century France," *Past & Present* 59 (1973): 51–91; and reprinted in her collection of essays, *Society and Culture in Early Modern France* (Stanford, CA: Stanford University Press, 1975), 152–187.
[32] Christopher Elwood, *The Body Broken: The Calvinist Doctrine of the Eucharist and the Symbolization of Power in Sixteenth-Century France* (Oxford and New York, NY: Oxford University Press, 1999).
[33] "Monologue du bon vigneron," ed. Moiset, 69.
[34] "Ordinances for the Supervision of the Churches dependent on the Seigneury of Geneva . . . [February 3, 1547]," in J. K. S. Reid, ed. and trans., *Calvin: Theological Treatises* (London and Philadelphia, PA: Westminster John Knox Press, 1954), 81.

a fine on a Christian for sharing a drink with a friend was a far cry from the vigneron's perception of wine as a social bond. This had nothing to do with how much one should drink or drunkenness, a subject over which both Catholic vignerons and Calvinists were in complete agreement. As the "bon vigneron" pointed out, "God gave it [i.e. wine] to them to use, but not to abuse."[35] Even the emphasis on sharing food and wine with neighbors was tempered by the cautionary advice "that a drunk and a glutton offend God equally."[36] Thus, the real differences Protestants and Catholics had with wine were not over temperance, on which they both agreed, but over sociability and commensality. Ultimately, the ties most vignerons maintained with the traditional church in Burgundy were based on the doctrine of grace provided by consuming wine in the Eucharist, as well as by the very different notion of sociability and commensality stressed by Calvin.

Throughout Western Europe, in fact, agricultural workers in general and vignerons in particular were among the least likely cohorts to be attracted to Protestantism, and most remained staunchly Catholic. Vignerons were almost completely absent from the Protestant communities in other French towns such as Amiens, Béziers, Bordeaux, Montpellier, Rouen, Toulouse, and Troyes.[37] In two of the largest wine-growing regions in all of France, Guyenne and Languedoc in the southwest of the kingdom, court records for heresy trials do not indicate that a single vigneron was ever brought before the court and charged with heresy. The records of the Parlement of Bordeaux in the first half of the sixteenth century, of the hundreds of accused Protestants whose occupations are known – largely clergy, merchants, royal officers, and artisans – not a single one was identified as a vigneron. The records of the Parlement of Toulouse show a similar pattern. Of the 424 accused heretics whose occupations were listed between 1500 and 1560, there were only two agricultural workers: a laborer and a shepherd. The large numbers of vignerons in these two wine-

---

[35] "Monoloque du bon vigneron," ed. Moiset, 78.   [36] Ibid.

[37] For Amiens, see David Rosenberg, "Social Experience and Religious Choice: A Case Study, the Protestant Weavers and Woolcombers of Amiens in the Sixteenth Century," unpublished Ph.D. dissertation, Yale University, 1978, 234–235, and Olivia Carpi, *Une république imaginaire: Amiens pendant les troubles de religion (1559–1597)* (Paris: Belin, 2005), 67–75; for Béziers and Montpellier, see Emmanuel Le Roy Ladurie, *Les paysans de Languedoc*, 2 vols. (Paris: Mouton), 1: 343; for Bordeaux, see Ernest Gaullieur, *Histoire de la Réformation à Bordeaux et dans le ressort du parlement de Guyenne* (Paris and Bordeaux: H. Champion, 1884), 240; for Rouen, see Philip Benedict, *Rouen during the Wars of Religion* (Cambridge: Cambridge University Press, 1981), 80–81; for Toulouse, see Joan Davies, "Persecution and Protestantism: Toulouse, 1562–1575," *The Historical Journal* 22 (1979): 31–51; and for Troyes, see A. N. Galpern, *The Religions of the People in Sixteenth-Century Champagne* (Cambridge, MA: Harvard University Press, 1976), 175–176.

growing provinces were conspicuous by their absence.[38] And in the rural
hinterlands surrounding the city of La Rochelle, where growing grapes for
wine was one of the foundations of the local economy for town and
country alike, there was not a single Calvinist church.[39] Moreover, there
is evidence that in other French towns, as in Dijon, it was the vignerons
who led the resistance against the new religion. In Gaillac in the south, for
example, it was a group of vignerons who attacked a family of Protestants
and threw them into the Tarn in 1562 when they were discovered eating
meat during Lent.[40] To be sure, there were certainly some vignerons in and
around some of the Protestant towns in southern France. But for the most
part, in France those in the wine industry remained loyal to the Catholic
Church. In the wine-growing regions of Europe outside of France, only in
the German Empire were there any significant numbers of vignerons who
became Protestant, especially in the Rhine valley. And it is well known that
the Peasant Wars of 1524–1525 broke out in the heart of the German-
speaking wine areas such as Alsace, the Rhineland, and Franconia, but their
grievances were socioeconomic rather than religious, and Luther soundly
condemned them.[41] Where some vignerons did convert to Protestantism,
such as in the areas around Heidelberg, it was as much to do with the
Count-Duke of the Palatinate's conversion to Lutheranism, and after 1555,
the requirement of the Peace of Augsburg that everyone in the region had
to conform to the religion of the prince. The same was true in the free city
of Augsburg after the city council adopted Lutheranism as the official
religion of the city in the 1530s, though those outside the city walls
remained Catholic.[42] Indeed, some of the biggest boosts to the wine
industry came from Catholic bishops. In Franconia, for example, the
bishop of Würzburg, Julius Echter von Mespelbrunn, founded the city's
Juliusspital in 1576 and endowed it with some of the regions finest vine-

---

[38] See Henri Patry, ed., *Les débuts de la Réforme protestante en Guyenne, 1523–1559: Arrêts du parlement* (Bordeaux: Féret et fils, 1912); Raymond A. Mentzer, *Heresy Proceedings in Languedoc, 1500–1560* (Philadelphia, PA: American Philosophical Society, 1984), 151–157, and the same author's "Heresy Suspects in Languedoc Prior to 1560: Observations on their Social and Occupational Status," *Bibliothèque d'humanisme et Renaissance* 39 (1977): 561–568.

[39] Kevin C. Robbins, *City on the Ocean Sea, La Rochelle, 1530–1650: Urban Society, Religion, and Politics on the French Atlantic Frontier* (Leiden and New York, NY: Brill, 1997), 40–41.

[40] Le Roy Ladure, *Les paysans de Languedoc*, 1: 344.

[41] Thomas Robisheaux, *Rural Society and the Search for Order in Early Modern Germany* (Cambridge: Cambridge University Press, 1989), 61–66; and Roy L. Vice, "Vineyards, Vinedressers, and the Peasants' War in Franconia," *Archiv für Reformationsgeschichte* 79 (1988) 138–157.

[42] For Augsburg, see B. Ann Tlusty, *Bacchus and Civic Order: The Culture of Drink in Early Modern Germany* (Charlottesville, VA: University of Virginia Press, 2001), 18–21.

yards.[43] And in the city of Besançon in the Franche-Comté, Protestantism made early inroads like in Dijon, but pressure from the city fathers began in earnest in mid-century and eventually rooted it out.[44] In summary, the hostility to the Reformation by Dijon's vignerons appears to be representative of those in the wine industry throughout France and most of Western Europe.

Thus, in 1561 the community of Protestants in Dijon was thus fighting against the opposition of the city's elites, who believed they were dangerous and prone to disorder, as well as the city's vignerons, who found their theology a threat to their sociability and livelihood in this world as well as their salvation in the next world. Nevertheless, they managed to get 123 heads of households to cast their voices for a Protestant candidate for mayor in June, and they began to organize more forcefully and systematically in the summer and autumn. By October there were organized meetings with ministers preaching sermons to large crowds in private homes. The councilors of the Hôtel de Ville were quick to investigate these "preachings (*prêches*)," as they were called, as they blatantly contravened the city council's proscription against all illicit assemblies. And on October 29, they investigated one of them in the home of a haberdasher named Nicolas Guyenot on the Rue des Forges. The *échevins* interrogated a young clerk named Claude Picard who was there to see how many of the people inside he could identify. Although he estimated that there were more than 500 hundred men, women, servants, and children inside, almost certainly an exaggeration, Picard could only identify 33 of them by name, nearly all artisans. He did recount that a Reformed preacher was there, "a man of small stature, having a short, black beard and dressed in black who preached to the people with a number of books before him," for more than an hour. "Speaking of the papists, he said that these poor abusive people only want to give us faggots in order to burn us, but we must pray for them."[45] The following day another "preaching" took place in the home of the lawyer Jacques de Presle in the same quarter of the city. This time the *échevins* interrogated a number of witnesses, including some of De Presle's neighbors, who told them that there were two or three hundred people present from all social conditions, including some "gentlemen

---

[43] Tom Scott, "German History," in Jancis Robinson, ed., *The Oxford Companion to Wine* (Oxford: Oxford University Press, 1994), 429–438.

[44] Kathryn A. Edwards, *Families and Frontiers: Re-Creating Communities and Boundaries in the Early Modern Burgundies* (Leiden and Boston, MA: Brill, 2002), 317–318; and Guy J. Michel, *La Franche-Comté et les Habsbourg, 1493–1678* (Wettolsheim: Mars et Mercure, 1978), 64–66.

[45] AMD, D 63 (liasse), October 29, 1561.

[*gentilshommes*]" and "strangers," that is, Protestants who were not resident in Dijon. The witnesses identified more than 60 Protestants present at this meeting, but again, the majority remained unidentified. But unlike the day before, this meeting at the home of Jacques de Presle incited a demonstration of students from the Catholic college nearby on the Rue des Champs. The students amassed outside the house and began shouting at the Protestants inside, though the *échevins* managed to break up the meeting before the situation could escalate further.[46] The following day, October 31, the eve of the feast of All Saints, a third consecutive Protestant "preaching" took place in the home of a cabinet-maker named Jacques de Varennes, directly across the street from the Hôtel de Ville on the Rue des Prisons where the mayor and councilors were meeting. This time things did become violent, as a group of angry Catholics began throwing rocks at the Protestants as they entered the house of Varennes. Hearing things getting out of hand, the mayor quickly ordered a syndic with armed guards to break up the illicit assembly from which both Protestants and Catholics were forcibly removed and ordered home. Belatedly, the mayor and council once again renewed the ban on all illicit assemblies in the city, which they believed "only tend to scandalize and stir up the people to sedition."[47]

Apparently, more than preaching was going on in the three assemblies of October 29–31, however, as when November 1 dawned, All Saints' Day, a large number of Protestants began gathering on the Rue des Forges, one of the streets where the most prosperous artisans in the city lived. Their numbers swelled, as they had called on Protestants from other nearby villages to join them. Because the mayor and council were either slow to act or, more likely, because they seemed unable to prevent the Protestant assemblies from taking place, a group of vignerons from the Rue St. Philibert and the Rue des Champs rang the tocsin of their parish church to call their fellow vignerons "to run against those of the Rue des Forges." More than a hundred vignerons duly turned up to counter the Protestant demonstration, many of them armed with their *serpes*, or pruning hooks. Many claimed that they were motivated by a rumor that the Protestants had stolen a silver image of the Virgin Mary from the nearby parish church of Notre Dame. Others claimed they heard that the Protestants assembling on the rue des Forges were armed and intended to take over the city by

---

[46] AMD, D 63 (liasse), October 30, 1561.
[47] AMD, D 63 (liasse), October 31, 1561; and AMD, B 199, fol. 80r, October 31, 1561. Also see BMD, Fonds Saverot 1491, fols. 1126–1127.

force, a claim that turned out to be false, but one that the mayor and city council were prepared to believe. Moreover, the vignerons began contacting their fellow vignerons from nearby villages and suburbs of Dijon, "because of the fear they had of these illicit assemblies." The resulting confrontation between the Protestant artisans and the Catholic vignerons on the Rue des Forges proved to be anticlimactic, as there was just a single casualty: a Catholic dyer. The city militia quickly dispersed the large crowd, and the same day the Parlement of Dijon issued an edict making it an offense "to all, of whatever estate, quality, or condition they were, to organize or to allow in their houses any illegal assembly, preaching, or the administration of the sacraments, or to lodge or allow to come into their houses any preachers not authorized by the bishop of this diocese or their ministers and vicars, on pain of death." The court also asked the mayor and councilors to round-up and arrest as many of the Protestants who took part as they could identify, and ultimately to banish all Protestants from the city of Dijon.[48] The mayor clearly recognized that he and the *échevins* on the council would be unable to complete this task successfully on their own. They wrote to Paris and demanded that the crown itself should clamp down on the Protestants. Their concern, they argued, was motived "as much by our faith and our Christian religion, afflicted and oppressed by these adversaries who wish to live unmolested in their fantasy, as by their enterprises against the authority and privileges of the city [of Dijon]."[49]

The city magistrates also sought the help of the lieutenant-general of the duchy of Burgundy, Gaspard de Saulx, seigneur de Tavanes, and pleaded with him to come to Dijon in person to safeguard the security of the city while they attempted to rid the community of Protestantism.[50] Tavanes was a career military officer who had served the kingdom in multiple wars and his loyalty to the crown had never been questioned. As a 16-year-old page on his first campaign he was captured along with King Francis I at Pavia in 1525, and he later served King Henry II both in the German Empire and in Italy. And he was rewarded for his service in 1556 with the post of lieutenant-general of the duchy, second in command to the royal governor, Claude de Lorraine, duke of Aumale, and commander of the king's arms in Burgundy whenever the governor himself was absent, which was most of the time. As an opponent and rival at the court of Francis, duke of Guise – Aumale's brother – Tavanes soon found himself excluded

---

[48] AMD, D 63 (liasse), November 1, 1561; and AMD, B 199, 81r–v, November 1–2, 1561.
[49] AMD, B 199, fol. 103v, December 9, 1561.
[50] AMD, B 199, fols. 90v and 108v, November 21 and December 19, 1561.

from affairs of state, however, as the Guises came to dominate the short reign of Francis II (1559–1560) and remained in the ascendancy during the early years of Charles IX's reign before he declared his majority in 1563.[51] Tavanes was thus exiled to his rural estate in Burgundy, after 1559, and the mayor and *échevins* were now urging him to come to the capital of the duchy to help them in their fight against Protestantism. As explained in the previous chapter, Tavanes had a townhouse in the parish of St. Michel, right at the end of the Rue Vannerie, so this was not an onerous request. And in the duke of Aumale's absence, Tavanes could govern with the full powers of the royal governor. Even so, his powers were limited to the military sphere; he had no jurisdiction at all in the areas of justice and finance. Indeed, apart from his commanding the king's arms and powder locked in the fortified Château, his real authority lay not so much in specific duties, but in the vast number of clients who served him through-out the province. And one of his closest and most loyal clients was Bénigne Martin, the mayor of Dijon since 1557, who was reelected in that hotly disputed election the previous June with Tavanes's full support. These two men, the mayor of the city and the lieutenant-general of the province, worked together to extirpate Protestantism from the community of Dijon, and they stepped up their efforts after the All Saints riot of November 1, 1561.[52]

Before this policy could be implemented, however, the queen mother and regent for the young Charles IX, Catherine de Medici, issued the Edict of St. Germain, otherwise known as the Edict of January 1562. This edict was a watershed, as it marked the crown's recognition of the Huguenots, as French Protestants were called, for the first time under the law. It was a very bitter pill for most French Catholics to swallow, and the reaction in Burgundy underscored how strong the opposition was. The edict not only recognized the right of Protestants to exist, but it allowed them to worship and preach openly, as long as they did so in the daytime, were peaceful, worshipped outside the walls of all cities and towns, and used no churches for their services.[53] The mayor Martin and the lieutenant-general Tavanes

---

[51] See the short biography of Tavanes published with his "Mémoires de très-noble et très-illustre Gaspard de Saulx, seigneur de Tavanes," in C. B. Petitot, ed., *Collection complète des mémoires relatifs à l'histoire de France depuis le règne de Philippe-Auguste jusqu'au commencement du dix-septième siècle*, I series, 52 vols., 23: 5–45.

[52] [Théodore de Bèze, et al.], *Histoire ecclésiastique des églises réformées*, 1: 862; Belle, *La Réforme à Dijon*, 52–77; and Robert R. Harding, *Anatomy of a Power Elite: The Provincial Governors of Early Modern France* (New Haven: Yale University Press, 1978), 58.

[53] The text of the edict is in E. and E. Haag, *La France protestante*, 10 vols. (Paris: Sandoz et Fischbacher, 2nd edn., 1877–1888), 10: 48–52. An excellent analysis of the edict is in N. M.

not only refused to recognize the edict, they outright opposed it. The same was true of the Parlement of Burgundy, who refused to register the edict as the queen mother required. The mayor and city council registered their opposition as soon as word of the edict reached Dijon.[54] Moreover, they sent a delegation to the court of the Parlement in March, composed of the mayor Bénigne Martin and five *échevins* plus the solicitor (*procureur*) of the Hôtel de Ville, to argue that the court should not register the Edict of January without some significant modifications. And they pleaded that such modifications were justified, and asked the king and queen mother

> to consider that this city of Dijon was significantly different from others in this respect, and they had diverse reasons why such publication could not be made here, reasons that did not apply to many other cities in the kingdom. Above all, this city was a frontier fortification and extremely close to another sovereign's territory. Moreover, it would be dangerous to permit the assemblies permitted by the Edict, whether within the city or in the suburbs, because to allow openly the preaching and other acts this new sect would carry out in the name of the Edict would only lead to sedition.[55]

No such modifications from the crown were ever issued, however, because earlier that month on March 1 some troops of Francis, duke of Guise – the brother of Burgundy's governor, the duke of Aumale – fired some shots at a group of Protestants worshipping in the parish church in the town of Vassy. The resulting "massacre," as the Huguenots would henceforth call it, marked the beginning of three generations of armed conflict over the issue of religion in France. For the mayor Martin, the lieutenant-general Tavanes, and the judges in the court of the Parlement of Dijon, the beginning of civil war allowed them to ignore the Edict of January and to continue unabated in their efforts to suppress the Reformation in Burgundy.

4.2 Civil War and Religious Cleansing

Because the military action of the first civil war (March 1562–March 1563) took place almost entirely in the Loire valley and in Guyenne in the southwest, the province of Burgundy was not directly affected. This did not mean, however, that those Protestants still in Dijon and elsewhere in

Sutherland, *The Huguenot Struggle for Recognition* (New Haven, CT: Yale University Press, 1980), 133–135 and 354–356.
[54] AMD, B 199, fol. 182r, February 26, 1562.
[55] See the deliberations of the Parlement of Dijon, March 23, 1562, printed in Belle, *La Réforme à Dijon*, 173–174 (quote on 174).

Burgundy were unaffected. In a long list of grievances addressed to Claude de Lorraine, duke of Aumale, royal governor in Burgundy, the mayor and city council pleaded that he should authorize the arrest and detention of all those Huguenots who had violated the terms of the Edict of January. Even though the mayor and lieutenant-general had no plans whatsoever to honor the rights of the Huguenots guaranteed in the Edict, they used any contraventions of it by the Protestants as a justification for their continued suppression. The document sent to the royal governor contained numerous references to those of the "so-called reformed religion (*la religion prétendue réformée*)" and how their behavior was contrary "to the honour of God, the service of His Majesty, the defence and protection of this city, [and] the peace and tranquillity of his good, loyal, and faithful subjects." The twelve specific complaints covered the entire realm of the regulation of the body social: the Huguenots' refusal to observe Catholic feast days, on which "the so-called reformers work and labor publicly and openly in their shops"; the selling of "censured and scandalous" books; tavern-keepers and hoteliers who served meat during Lent and other prohibited periods; the celebration of Protestant weddings and baptisms in the seasons prohibited by the Catholic church "to the great scandal of everyone"; the continued propagation of "secret pedagogies ... to seduce the poor and tender youth, who are incapable of resisting their odious words"; the "scandalous singing of the Psalms in public in a loud voice"; and even the Huguenot's opposition to the last mayoral election, in which the militant Catholic Bénigne Martin defeated a Protestant candidate for mayor in June 1561. This last complaint, the magistrates argued, was contrary to "all order of the policing of the city and contrary to the inhabitants' right to elect their own magistrates and officers, which had always been a sign of the most famous, ancient, and flourishing republics."[56]

The centerpiece of this list of grievances to the royal governor, however, was clearly the Huguenots' attacks against the Catholic Eucharist. "They parade openly in front of the Palais [de Justice] and generally everywhere in all public places selling libels, defamations, effigies and other figures of unworthiness and derision of the holy sacrament of the Mass." Moreover, many Protestants had openly blasphemed the sacrament, "daring impudently to call the holy sacrament *Jean Le Blanc* [John White, or John the Blank]."[57] Although this was the most explicitly theological of all the

—1561

[56] AMD, D63 (liasse), letter of city council to duke of Aumale [undated but clearly spring 1562].
[57] Ibid.

magistrates' complaints, it too was understood primarily because of its social implications. Calling the Host *Jean Le Blanc* on account of the color of the white wafer used in the Eucharist was an explicit profanation of the sacred. Like the Protestant taunts in Paris of "God of paste" that Natalie Davis has so convincingly described,[58] this epithet cut to the heart of the Catholic doctrine of transubstantiation. *Le Blanc* was a reference not only to the lack of color but also to the inefficacy of the Host. It was also an attack on the specific enfolding together of the body social, body politic, and body of Christ that Catholics believed the Eucharist represented. The magistrates informed the governor that they had already imprisoned those Huguenots who had blasphemed the holy sacrament by calling it *Jean Le Blanc*, and they urged him "to seize the initiative and uphold the king's will so that exemplary punishment can be done to eliminate and quell such audacious and seditious speech."[59] In short, the very definition of community in Dijon as defined by the Catholic city officials was perceived to be under attack by the Huguenots.

The repression of the Huguenots in Dijon continued in the spring and summer of 1562, as the first civil war broke out farther north. And the metaphor of cleansing the body social of the pollution of heresy the language evoked by Natalie Davis as well as by the letter to the governor of Burgundy, also seemed to be coming from the court in Paris. "Do everything that you can," Catherine de Medici wrote to Gaspard de Saulx, sieur de Tavanes, in June 1562, "to cleanse the entire region of Burgundy of this vermin of preachers and ministers who have introduced the plague [of heresy] there, as you have already begun to do."[60] The queen mother's use of the language of pollution and purification in her missive was very explicit.

At about the same time, Tavanes, who was unwilling to wait for the governor Aumale to act, issued an ordinance of his own on May 8, ordering all the Protestant preachers in Dijon to assemble at the Hôtel de Ville the following morning at seven o'clock to receive a safe conduct to leave Dijon and go wherever they wished. Those who refused to appear, he noted, "will be hanged and strangled without any other form of judicial process."[61] And the mayor of Dijon, Bénigne Martin, continued to pressure the duke of

---

[58] Natalie Z. Davis, "The Rites of Violence," in *Society and Culture in Early Modern France* (Stanford, CA: Stanford University Press, 1975), 157.

[59] AMD, D63 (liasse), letter of city council to duke of Aumale [undated but clearly spring 1562].

[60] Joseph Garnier, ed., *Correspondance de la mairie de Dijon extraite des archives de cette ville*, 3 vols. (Dijon, 1868–1870), 2: 22–23, Catherine de Medici to Tavanes, June 4, 1562. A copy of this letter is also in the city council deliberations of Dijon: AMD, B 199, fol. 277r, June 4, 1562.

[61] AMD, D 63 (liasse), May 8, 1562.

Aumale, the royal governor of Burgundy, about "the unlawful meetings [*conventicules*] and assemblies of people who oppose our faith and Christian religion, which is against the edicts of the king." He went on to urge the governor to inform the king that "these same black sheep [*dévoiéz*] continue daily in their assemblies in several houses, preaching there in their woeful and accustomed fashion in the middle of the day with their doors open."[62] Indeed, scores of Huguenots in Dijon were already being arrested in 1561–1562 for publicly singing the Psalms in French, which the city's Catholics found especially insulting.[63] Tavanes had issued repeated prohibitions "to all persons of whatever quality or condition whatsoever from singing or allowing to be sung hymns, canticles, or psalms in French, on pain of being punished as a seditious person."[64] Again, the beginning of the first civil war in the spring of 1562 meant that the edict of January never got registered in Dijon's Parlement, and both the mayor, Martin, and the lieutenant-general, Tavanes, could work in earnest "to cleanse" the city and province of the "vermin" as instructed by the queen mother. This resulted in a pattern that would be repeated with the outbreak of each successive civil war: arrests of Protestants, heavy fines or imprisonment, seizure of their property, expulsion from the city, and/or pressure to convert to Roman Catholicism.[65] In other words, the Burgundians strived to make sure that Huguenots were not just recognized as second-class citizens, but that they also understood that the Protestant definition of community was incompatible with that of Dijon's Catholics. Thus, when Tavanes asked the city council in Dijon to undertake a city-wide survey requiring all heads of household to make a profession of faith swearing "to live and die as a Catholic," the mayor and *échevins* were only too happy to comply. Moreover, when the lieutenant-general asked them to provide him with two hundred men to help him evict those who refused to take the oath, they sent him five hundred instead.[66]

When the edict of pacification ending the first civil war was signed at Amboise in March 1563, in theory the limited legal rights of the Huguenots of the Edict of January were restored. Once again the Parlement of Dijon refused to register the edict, and a special commission was dispatched to the court to protest the edict. At the head of this delegation was Jean Bégat, former *échevin* on Dijon's city council and now a presiding judge in the

[62] Garnier, ed., *Correspondance de la mairie de Dijon*, 2: 24.
[63] ADCO, B II 60/44, November 13, 1561, September 4, 1561 for just two of many examples.
[64] AMD, D 63 (liasse), April 18, 1561.   [65] Holt, "Wine, Community and Reformation," 69.
[66] AMD, B 199, fols. 270r–272r, June 6–7, 1562.

Parlement of Dijon. Bégat presented a remonstrance to the young king Charles IX in May 1563 outlining the Burgundians' complaints:

> Sire, since you are Christian and carry the title of Most Christian among all Christian kings . . . [and] you believe what the Roman church believes and know that all contrary doctrine is error . . . how can it be that you would suffer among your subjects a law so contrary and foreign that allows not only the public profession, but also the free and public exercise [of heresy], to the scandal and ruin of your own religion? . . . Religion, Sire, as Plato said, is the only sure bond of charity and peace, forging a similarity of morals and wills in one common measure.[67]

The Parlement of Dijon continued in its refusal to register the edict, and it was only under extreme duress and pressure from the young king and queen mother that on June 19, 1563 it finally registered the edict of pacification signed at Amboise, but only "upon the express command of the king and Queen Mother, made and reiterated several times, and only after the remonstrances made to His Majesty by the deputies of the estates of Burgundy also several times." But, defiantly, the judges also included the following language at the end of the document:

> The said court has prohibited and does continue to prohibit all subjects of His Majesty from participating in or allowing to take place any preaching or other practice of any other religion than the Christian, Catholic, and Roman religion in the entire jurisdiction of this court, seeing that the city of Lyon has now been restored to the true and complete obedience of His Majesty the King and back to the condition that it was before the wars.[68]

This language clearly negated the rights granted to the Protestants in the edict itself, and did not satisfy the king and queen mother at all. Ultimately, the edict was only registered in the form the king intended it when the young Charles IX appeared in person in Dijon in May 1564 on his royal tour of the provinces and forced its registration with a *lit de justice*.[69]

Thus, the pattern of a legal edict limiting Huguenots to second-class status and prohibiting them from worshipping inside the city or making

---

[67] The remonstrance is printed in *Mémoires de Condé, ou recueil pour servir a l'histoire de France*, 6 vols (The Hague and Paris : Jean Néaulme, 1743), 4, 356–412, quotations on 361 and 405. For more on this episode, see my "Burgundians into Frenchmen: Catholic Identity in Sixteenth-Century Burgundy," in Michael Wolfe, ed., *Changing Identities in Early Modern France* (Durham, NC: Duke University Press, 1997), 345–370.

[68] BMD, Fonds Saverot 1491, fols. 1390–1394, Deliberations of the Parlement of Dijon, June 19, 1563; also printed in Belle, *La Réforme à Dijon*, 183.

[69] BMD, Fonds Saverot, 1492, fols. 53–76, April 20–May 24, 1564, registers of the Parlement of Dijon.; a copy is in BNF, Fonds français 22302, fols. 1r–10r. For details see my "The King in Parlement: The Problem of the *Lit de justice* in Sixteenth-Century France," *The Historical Journal* 31 (1988): 507–523.

any public practice of their religion was breached by both Catholics and
Huguenots alike. Huguenots invariably refused to accept these restrictions
and, as the records show, they routinely sang the Psalms loudly and
publicly in French in their boutiques and homes, which Catholics perceived as a communal insult. At the same time, Dijon's city fathers refused
to enforce the edicts, attempting to remove all Huguenots from the city
altogether. In short, they instituted a policy of suppression of the "so-called
reformed religion," requiring all Huguenots either to go to Mass with their
Catholic neighbors or forfeit their property and right to live within the city
walls. Huguenots who were willing to live peacefully under the restrictions
of the peace edicts, that is, as second- class citizens, might be allowed to
stay, but their houses were searched for arms and munitions and all their
servants who were not Catholics were either imprisoned or forced to leave
the city. Moreover, they could not leave their houses at night, and they
were required to keep their boutiques closed on all Catholic feast days and
during all services in the parish churches.[70] The mayor and city council
were still insisting after the Edict of St. Germain of 1570 ending the third
civil war that the Huguenots in Dijon, who were "disturbers of the public
peace," were required to refrain from "singing Psalms, holding assemblies
in the city and in the suburbs, or doing anything else contrary to the said
edict."[71]

A closer look at an individual case demonstrates more clearly how the
suppression of Protestantism in Dijon actually worked. Nicolas Hurtault
was a cobbler who lived on the Rue des Forges, where so many of the city's
Protestants resided, along with his wife. In October 1562 the couple was
first suspected of heresy and interrogated and fined 50 *livres tournois* for
singing the Psalms of David in French.[72] It was not until a year later in
October 1563, however, that they were finally arrested and detained for
repeatedly "singing publicly in plain sight and in earshot of everyone the
Psalms of David in French."[73] Their trial took place in the mayoral court,
as the mayor and *échevins* were the court of first instance in the city. The
solicitor of the Hôtel de Ville had lined up five witnesses to testify against
the couple, and the first was a widow of fifty years old, Nicole Roze, widow
of the late Girard Picart, who lived in the same building as the Hurtaults on

---

[70] See AMD, B 204, fols. 71r (September 23, 1567), 94r (October 10, 1567); B 205 fols. 29v (July 2, 1568),
    58v (September 7, 1568), 106v (January 14, 1569), 129r (March 15, 1569), 132v–33v (March 24, 1569),
    and 139v (April 5, 1569).
[71] AMD, B207, ff. 147–152v (February 13, 1571), quotations on f. 151v.
[72] ADCO, B II 360/45, October 13, 1562.
[73] The entire case against the Hurtaults is in AMD, D 65 (liasse), October 2, 1563 to September 1568.

the Rue des Forges. She testified that "Hurtault and his wife with the rest of their family regularly sang . . . in their shop and in the street in plain sight and in earshot of everyone the Psalms of David in French, of which many passers-by and neighbors who heard this were scandalized for being residents in the same building." She claimed that she and other neighbors had remonstrated with the Hurtaults many times to stop, but this had no effect. "Even today," she continued, "his shop being open, he was singing the Psalms very loudly." Four additional witnesses, all women who were neighbors of the Hurtaults, repeated the same story, with two of the additional witnesses being women of high social standing: Isabeau de Mordault, wife of Jean de la Mothe, a presiding judge in the Chamber of Accounts, and Marguerite Chappelan, widow of former *échevin* Jean Chisseret. Hurtault and his wife were allowed to go home for the night, but ordered to appear when the trial reconvened the next day or they would be fined 50 *livres tournois* each. When only Hurtault's wife appeared when the trial reconvened, however, the mayor ordered the sergeant-at-arms of the city council to go to his house and shop and find him. When the sergeant reported back that he was not to be found, Hurtault's wife was imprisoned in the keep of the Maison du Roi, the former palace of the dukes of Burgundy, and fined 50 *livres*.

Hurtault at this point emerged and claimed that they cannot be imprisoned "for the simple fact of their religion." Moreover, he insisted that the crime they were charged with – singing the Psalms in French – was "a simple libel." Hurtault was then jailed alongside his wife, though he filed an appeal, which was not heard until November 4. The appeal was denied and the Hurtaults remained imprisoned for nearly five years. Despite numerous and frequent appeals to be released, they were not allowed to be reunited with their children until September 1568, and only then when they agreed to sign a certificate of abjuration, denouncing their Reformed faith and promising "to live Catholicly" in the Roman Catholic Church.[74] And the Hurtaults were far from alone as the scores and scores of requests to be released throughout the 1560s and early 1570s make very clear.[75] Even those Huguenots who obeyed the letter of the edicts of pacification after the first three civil wars and attempted to keep their religion private were subjected to public humiliation and insults. On January 1, 1564 the seigneur de Tavanes had to issue an order requesting all residents of the city of Dijon to stop

---

[74] AMD, D 65 (liasse), October 2, 1563 to September 1568.
[75] AMD, D 65 (liasse), October 2, 1563 to October 20, 1572.

"throwing stones, garbage or sewage against the houses, doors, and windows" of the Huguenots still residing in the city.[76] Once again, the linking together of heresy with pollution was explicit in the actions of those Catholics in Dijon who continued to fight to rid the community altogether of the presence of heresy. With the support and legitimation of the mayor, *échevins* on the city council, and the lieutenant-general of the province, the people of the city of Dijon felt legitimated in their efforts to cleanse the pollution of Protestantism from the body social.

4.3   Why No St. Bartholomew's Massacre in Dijon?

To be sure, the program of suppression certainly worked, as there was no St. Bartholomew's massacre in Dijon in 1572 as occurred in so many other French cities with significant Protestant minorities. Indeed, the evidence suggests that most of Dijon's Huguenots either fled the city altogether for places of refuge where they could practice their religion publicly – Geneva, for example – or they succumbed to the pressure to abjure their faith and convert to Catholicism. And those who did abjure were forced to sign certificates of abjuration recording their conversion for the municipality like the Hurtaults ultimately did in 1568.

A major factor in reducing the size of the Protestant community in Dijon between 1562 and 1572, as has already been explained, was the constant pressure on the Huguenots to either convert or leave the city. And the single most important weapon in this war against the Huguenots was probably the Confraternity of the Holy Ghost created by the lieutenant-general Tavanes in 1567. Neither condoned nor approved by either the crown or the church, this confraternity had as its sole purpose the eradication of Protestantism in the province of Burgundy, and it provided little more than a cover for shock troops for the church militant. The oath primarily required its members to give money, arms, and ultimately their lives to follow the leader of the confraternity, Tavanes, into action, and it made clear that they were defending their city as well as their faith:

> Because God, by his divine mercy and goodness, has provided a ready and certain means to men of goodwill to serve together with him, such that they are all made as the bones of his bones, the flesh of his flesh, and the limbs of his limbs, between the two of them [they compose] one same bread and one same body, Him being the vine, vine-shoots, and branches of the same by

[76] AMD, D 63 (liasse), January 1, 1563/64.

the high and wonderful sacrament of the altar, which is the spiritual and invisible weapon of all good and virtuous Catholics, by which they defend against the attacks and transgressions of the devil, of the world, and of the flesh. In this holy faith we have promised and do promise that each year on All Saints' Day, after having prepared for confession and being absolved of all our transgressions and sins, we shall present ourselves in church to receive the holy sacrament and communion, the precious body of our savior and redeemer Jesus Christ at the time of the Mass, in order to be fortified and strengthened with the same heart and will against the gates of Hell and the ruses and tricks of Satan and all his minions and every undertaking that the enemies of God's faith and church can make against the said city [of Dijon], and against us, our brothers, allies, and friends. We also promise to conduct and govern ourselves in this world as true and natural-born citizens and soldiers of the city of God and of his armies, and that after having strived to live a godly and steadfast life in his faith and law in the time it has pleased him to keep and preserve us here on earth, we shall at last be able to reach his holy kingdom to be placed and counted among the number of the blessed in his church triumphant.[77]

The members' oath thus paid homage to the sacrament of the Eucharist, the salvation of their souls, their opposition to Protestantism, their loyalty to the French king, and the city's dependence on viticulture in defining the community. And as the epigraph at the beginning of this book pointed out, the oath also resonated with the fifteenth chapter of the gospel of John: "I am the true vine and my Father is the vinegrower . . . I am the vine, you are the branches. Those who abide in me and I in them bear much fruit, because apart from me you can do nothing."[78] And there was no question that the members of the confraternity considered the Protestants to be dead and rotting branches that needed to be pruned.

What is striking is that similar confraternities were organized about the same time in other Burgundian towns at the command of Tavanes: Beaune, Chalon-sur-Saône, Tournus, and Mâcon. And like the one in Dijon, all these confraternities stressed the solidarity of the community of the faithful against the heresy of the Protestants. Whereas other confraternities divided and excluded its membership by occupation, craft group, or

---

[77] The oath is printed in Petittot, ed., *Mémoires de Tavanes*, 452–455; and Belle, *La Réforme à Dijon*, 215–219. A copy was inserted into the city council deliberations on January 7, 1571 signed by all the captains, lieutenants, ensigns, sergeants, etc. of each of the seven parishes, as well as a large number of other citizens: AMD, B 117, fols. 1205–1251, January 7, 1571: "Articles de société et fraternité jurez et affermez par plusieurs notables habitans de la ville de Dijon par maintenir la religion catholique, apostolique et romaine et conserver ceste ville de Dijon sous l'auctorité et souverainté du roy." Another copy is in AMD, B 9, cote 15 (liasse), September 7, 1571.

[78] John 15: 1–6.

specialized saints' cults, the Confraternities of the Holy Ghost promoted the solidarity of the entire social body. And although Robert Harding has demonstrated that most members who signed the oath of membership in Mâcon tended to be the more well-to-do and influential residents of the city, it is already clear that in the capital of Dijon the vignerons had already become militantly anti-Protestant and were ready to join their social betters in carrying out the confraternity's goals.[79] That the goals of the confraternity were being met is clear from the special tax roll compiled for a special tax on all Huguenots in the city of Dijon in February 1568 to help cover the costs of their incarceration. Less than a year after the confraternity's founding, Dijon's Protestant population had plummeted from 500–600 in 1562 to only 142 residents, and many of these were found to be either dead or they had abjured their faith and already returned to the Catholic fold.[80] Even so, the jailer in charge of the Protestants imprisoned in the Maison du Roi complained in May 1569 that he needed more than the six men the city council had allowed him to look after all the prisoners. With so many family members and friends of the prisoners bringing them food and clean clothing every day, he felt the security of the prison was in jeopardy without more men to assist him. The city council duly decided to levy another special tax to increase the jailer's budget.[81] But the overwhelming conclusion from the hundreds of certificates of abjuration that have survived from the period 1568 to 1572 is that Gaspard de Saulx, seigneur de Tavanes, the mayor and city council, the members of the Confraternity of the Holy Ghost, aided and abetted by the city's vignerons, had successfully managed to prune the vine of the Christian church to remove the withered branches of Protestantism and heresy.

Both the numbers and the contents of these certificates of abjuration are worth examining, because they go a long way toward explaining why the Protestant community in Dijon was no longer considered to be as threatening by August 1572 as it had seemed just a decade earlier. There is a good deal of formulaic sameness to these certificates, and they obviously reflect the perceptions of the city magistrates who required and collected them more than the views of those Huguenots who signed them. Nevertheless, they reveal a great deal. First of all, they tell us virtually nothing about religious conversion and abjuration in any meaningful way, because signing one was the only way any Protestant who was imprisoned or whose

---

[79] Robert R. Harding, "The Mobilization of Confraternities against the Reformation in France," *Sixteenth Century Journal* XI (1980): 85–107.

[80] AMD, D 63 (liasse), February 6, 1568. The list is also printed in Belle, *La Reforme à Dijon*, 201–203.

[81] AMD, B 174 bis, fols. 136r–137r, May 6, 1569.

property had been seized could liberate himself or his goods. This was not mandated by any of the edicts of pacification during the civil wars – and it was explicitly contrary to them – but it was the will of the local magistrates: the mayor and *échevins* on Dijon's city council along with the lieutenant-general Tavanes. Moreover, the chronology of these abjurations makes it very clear that whenever large numbers of Huguenots were imprisoned, large numbers of abjurations immediately followed. Of the surviving sample of certificates of abjuration – a total of 287 individuals – 76 of them (26 percent) were dated September 1568, immediately after the out-break of the third civil war ended the Peace of Longjumeau; 147 (51 percent) are dated between September 2 and October 31, 1572 following the St. Bartholomew's massacres in Paris and the imprisonment of all Huguenots in Dijon; and 34 (12 percent) were dated July and August 1585, following the Treaty of Nemours, when Henry III capitulated to the Catholic League. This accounts for 257 of the 287-person sample: 89 percent.[82] Thus, there is little question that these abjurations followed immediately after intensive efforts on the part of Catholic magistrates to incarcerate Burgundian protestants.

The certificates themselves are interesting in their own right, how-ever, for what they do tell us about Catholic perceptions of the Huguenots in their community and what abjuration and reuniting with the Catholic community actually meant. The certificates were drawn up by parish clergy selected by the city magistrates, but they had to be deposited in the town hall with the mayor and council before any prisoner or his property could be released. So, although there is a clerical signature on each document, it appears that the contents of the certificates reflect the sensibilities of the magistrates much more than those of the clergy. One of the most striking features about these certificates, for example, is that explicit references to doctrines, beliefs, and Roman Catholic theology generally are almost wholly absent. In only two certificates from the entire sample of 287 could I find any specific reference to doctrine. But what did the other 285 statements of abjuration say, then, if they did not refer to doctrines or theology?

---

[82] This includes 175 names on 40 different certificates, all with dates September 17–30, 1568 or September 2–October 31, 1572 in AMD, D 65 (liasse), and 102 names (not 93 as indicated on the wrapper) on certificates dated between 1560 and 1587 in AMD, D 66 (liasse). For a more detailed analysis of this evidence, see my essay, "Confessionalization beyond the Germanies: The Case of France," in John M. Headley, Hans J. Hillerbrand, and Anthony Papalas, eds., *Confessionalization in Europe, 1555–1700: Essays in Memory of Bodo Nischan* (Aldershot: Ashgate, 2004), 257–273.

The one phrase that occurred over and over again in virtually all the certificates is that each Huguenot promised to "*vivre catholicquement.*" What did "living Catholicly" mean for the magistrates of Dijon? It largely meant to live in peace with one's neighbors and in obedience to the king, that is, not to commit "scandalous acts." It also meant "to live and die" in the Roman Catholic church, and above all to do one's Easter duties by confessing one's sins and attending Mass. Typical was the metal-polisher Thibault de Rochefort, who denied all those who had testified that he was a Huguenot. "On the contrary," he attested, "he had always conducted himself modestly and Catholicly in the obedience of the Roman Catholic church. And since the beginning of these recent troubles he has always been ready and in arms under the charge of his captain [of the parish] to do service to the king and to the commonwealth whenever they were endangered." It was only "heinous enemies and liars" and those of "sinister opinions" who claimed he was now a Protestant, and "he would prefer to die than to be thought of as such." He concluded his statement, as so many others had also done, by promising "to live catholicly as he had done all his life," and by swearing that "he was perpetually committed to make humble and faithful service to His Majesty the king and to the commonwealth, and that he would always be ready to risk the last drop of his blood in order to serve the city of Dijon."[83]

Examples like this should not lead us to conclude, however, that all Huguenots either abjured, or that they became Nicodemites, conforming outwardly in their public behavior simply to gain their release from prison, though doubtless many did do exactly that. These 287 cases of public abjuration did not represent the entire Protestant community in Dijon. While the number of Huguenots in Dijon in 1562 has been estimated to be maybe as many as 500–600 persons (out of a population of about 15,000), many fled the city at the first sign of suppression by the magistrates. Significant numbers went directly to Geneva, in fact, which was far closer than either Lyon or Paris, French cities with sizable Huguenot congregations. There were also some who remained resolute to their faith and refused to abjure, at least for a time, such as Nicolas Hurtault and his wife. These were always a minority, as most either fled or abjured and then fled.

Thus, when news of the Paris massacres reached Burgundy on August 31, 1572, Léonor Chabot, count of Charny, who had succeeded his father-in-law Tavanes as lieutenant-general of the province in 1570, ordered all

[83] AMD, D65 (liasse), October 11, 1572.

Huguenots in Dijon to present themselves to the city magistrates at the Hôtel de Ville the following day. The Protestants were then herded into the keep of the Château – not the prison in the Maison du Roi – for their own safekeeping, though Chabot clearly believed "that those of the so-called reformed religion were disturbers of the public peace."[84] David El Kenz has recently demonstrated that it is a myth that Chabot and Pierre Jeannin, a young lawyer in the Parlement of Dijon, disobeyed the orders of the king in order to save the Huguenots' lives – a myth generated largely from Jeannin's memoirs written five decades later.[85] In writing his memoirs in 1622, Jeannin claimed that two days after "this bloody butchery in Paris," Charny received orders to massacre the Protestants in Dijon. And Jeannin says he strongly argued against this:

> In making this refusal I pointed to the law of the Emperor Theodosius, who, after having ordered in anger and too precipitously the death of a large number of Christians, was prevented from going to Mass by Saint Ambrose, who urged him to come to confession for penitence instead, and then to make complete satisfaction by creating a law by which all governors who presided over the administration of justice in the provinces would be prevented from carrying out any such extraordinary commands in the future, which are against the very order and form of justice, without waiting thirty days, during which time they [the governors] could then go back to the Emperor asking him for confirmation of the order in a good and proper form.[86]

To be sure, it is possible that a messenger arrived in Dijon claiming to have orders from Charles IX to carry out a massacre, which did happen in other cities, though no contemporary source actually mentions this. There is simply no evidence, however, contrary to several public monuments in Dijon today, that Jeannin ever uttered the words, "*Il faut obéir les rois lentement quand ils sont en colère*/One must obey kings with caution when they are angry." There was one Huguenot casualty in Dijon nevertheless, a sieur de Traves, who was murdered while in captivity and his body was thrown into a ditch. His crime was not only that he was a client of the Admiral de Coligny, the focal point of the Paris massacres that began on

---

[84] AMD, B 208, fols. 15v–17r, August 31–September 1, 1572.

[85] David El Kenz, "La Saint-Barthélemy à Dijon: Un non-événement?" *Annales de Bourgogne*, 74 (2002), 139–157.

[86] See Pierre Jeannin, "Discours apologétique fait par M. le président Jeannin, de sa conduicte durant les troubles de la Ligue, et depuis sous les règnes du feu roi Henry-le-Grand et du roi à present régnant, 1622," in M. Petitot, ed., *Collection des mémoires relatifs à l'histoire de France depuis l'avènement de Henri IV jusqu'à la paix de Paris conclue en 1763*, vol. 16, 2nd series (Paris: Foucault, 1822), 128–148 (quote from 130–131).

the night of August 24, but he refused to abjure his faith. The other 150 Huguenots imprisoned for nearly a month were all released "after having promised and sworn to live Catholicly."[87] Thus, the numbers of Protestants in Dijon were gradually reduced between 1562 and 1572, with many abjuring and converting to Catholicism, while others left the city never to return. By 1585 the zealous city fathers could find only 69 suspected Huguenots left in the city, and it seems likely that not all of those were actually practicing Protestants.[88]

What the example of Dijon suggests is that despite a very anti-Protestant culture of hostility toward the Huguenots, extending even to illegal imprisonment and seizure of their property, religious violence was not a foregone conclusion after the news of the massacres in the capital reached the city. What had motivated the city fathers from the beginning of the religious struggle was maintaining the unity of the Catholic community in practice and behavior, as well as maintaining the social and political order. Obviously, there were doctrinal implications to these goals, but preventing a breach in the community and maintaining order appear to have been higher on their list of priorities than doctrinal purity. In the end, they managed to achieve both without the violence of a St. Bartholomew's massacre, because their policy of attrition through abjuration had been working so well since 1562. The irony here is that the political policy in Dijon to ignore, or simply not to enforce, the various peace edicts of 1562, 1563, 1567, and 1570, all of which guaranteed the Huguenots some rights and legal protection under the law, ultimately led to the success in Dijon of reuniting the community around the Catholic majority. It was the crown's policy of limited toleration in the series of peace edicts, all designed to prevent violence and civil war, which ultimately ensured their continuation, as Penny Roberts has recently argued.[89] In the end it was Dijon, and towns like it all over France, that proved more successful than Paris and the dozen other sites of massacres in 1572 in avoiding violence and bloodshed on St. Bartholomew's Day. But why was that the case?

What I have tried to demonstrate here is that religious violence was neither inevitable nor irreversible once it began in sixteenth-century France. Natalie Davis's pollution model suggests that in communities where Protestants appeared dangerous and threatening – that is, where they practiced their religion openly and publicly in contravention of the

---

[87] AMD, B 208, fol. 23r, September 22, 1572.   [88] AMD, B 223, fols. 82v–83r, October 29, 1585.
[89] See Penny Roberts, "Peace, Ritual and Sexual Violence during the Religious Wars," in Graeme Murdock, Andrew Spicer, and Penny Roberts, eds., *Ritual and Violence: Natalie Zemon Davis and Early Modern France* (Oxford: Oxford University Press, 2012), 75–99.

edicts of pacification – violence could indeed break out. Where local magistrates suppressed the Huguenots and forced them through legal or extra-legal means to abjure their faith and re-join their Catholic neighbors in the Roman religion, violence was much less likely. In the one case, as in Dijon in 1561, the Huguenots were perceived as vermin to be cleansed and were thought to be very dangerous. Just a decade later, however, they were thought of more as irritants and "disturbers of the public peace." They were not only perceived as second-class citizens, but were seen to be a declining and less threatening cohort. With their numbers decreasing significantly after each successive civil war, the Protestant movement in Dijon had ceased to be a threat, and those few Huguenots remaining kept out of public view and were forced to accept their second-class status. This form of religious coexistence was still a kind of persecution, however, as Alexandra Walsham has recently reminded us: "toleration ... needs to be envisaged less as the polar opposite of persecution than as a species and subset of it."[90] So, not only did Dijon avoid a St. Bartholomew's massacre, when the capital of Paris and a dozen other provincial cities with significant Protestant minorities could not, but the city remained relatively calm and devoid of religious trouble until external events intervened, especially the death of the last Valois heir to the throne, Francis, duke of Anjou, in June 1584, placing a Protestant, Henry, king of Navarre, next in line to the royal succession. By that time not only had Léonar Chabot, count of Charny, replaced his father-in-law Tavanes as the lieutenant-general of Burgundy, but the royal governor, the duke of Aumale, was succeeded by his nephew in 1573, Charles of Lorraine, duke of Mayenne. Mayenne was the brother of Henry, duke of Guise, the principal opponent of King Henry III's religious policies of appeasing the Protestants in each successive edict of pacification. Moreover, Guise was the leader at court of a powerful and militant anti-Protestant faction who had opposed Henry of Navarre for more than a decade. His brother Mayenne was determined to do the same in his governorship in Burgundy, playing a much more hands-on role in Burgundian affairs than his uncle Aumale had ever done. When the Guises signed a pact with Philip II of Spain in late 1584 to provide assistance in preventing the Protestant Henry of Navarre from inheriting the French throne from the heirless Henry III, they also asked all good Catholics in France to join with them in a Catholic League of holy union. And the wars of the Catholic League in the 1580s and 1590s would bring the military

[90] Alexandra Walsham, "Toleration, Pluralism, and Coexistence: The Ambivalent Legacies of the Reformation," *Archiv für Reformationsgeschichte* 108 (2017): 183.

confrontation directly to Burgundy in a much more explicit way than in any of the earlier civil wars. They would also stretch Burgundian loyalty to the French crown, which had been strengthened and tested over and over again since 1477, to a breaking point. But the strong ties between Dijon's elites and its vignerons would remain intact throughout the religious wars.

CHAPTER 5

Origins of the Catholic League in Burgundy

When Francis of Valois, Duke of Anjou and the youngest of the four sons of King Henry II and Catherine de Medici, died in June 1584 leaving his childless older brother King Henry III without a direct male heir, the Parisian diarist Pierre de l'Estoile immediately noted that the Guise family "took great heart ... [since] it came at a very opportune time for them, facilitating and advancing the designs of their League, which from that moment began to grow stronger as France grew weaker."[1] Exactly what was this League that l'Estoile referred to? Initially it was simply a network of clients of members of the Guise family. The head of the family in 1584 was Henry, Duke of Guise, whose holdings included many lands in Lorraine, which lay outside France and was part of the Holy Roman Empire, but also significant lands in Normandy and in Champagne, where he was royal governor. His younger brother Charles of Lorraine, Duke of Mayenne, as we have already seen, was royal governor in Burgundy from 1573. Two first cousins, the Duke of Aumale, son of the former governor in Burgundy, and the Duke of Elbeuf, had significant holdings and strong client bases in Picardy and Normandy, respectively. And a distant cousin, the Duke of Mercoeur, was royal governor in Brittany and equally powerful in that province. So, the Guises wielded a great deal of influence in many parts of France. The principal goal of their "League," if it can be called that in 1584, and its only *raison d'être*, was simply to block the Huguenot Henry of Navarre, leader of the Bourbon family, from inheriting the French throne if the heirless Henry III were to die. According to the unwritten French constitution, Navarre was the legal heir, as he was descended directly through a cadet branch to King Louis IX, Saint Louis. But that same constitution required every king of France to be a loyal defender of the Roman Catholic Church in France, whose very coronation oath required

---

[1] Pierre de l'Estoile, *Journal pour le règne de Henri III (1574–1589)*, ed. Louis-Raymond Lefèvre (Paris: Gallimard, 1943), 357.

him to fight heresy wherever it appeared in his kingdom. And it was this aspect of the French constitution that the Guise family sought to privilege.

Although the pact signed at Joinville with Philip II of Spain in December 1584 promised both money and arms to support the Guises' effort to block Henry of Navarre from the throne, their so-called League only really began to gain momentum when they issued a manifesto in Reims in March 1585 to recruit further support. All its members were required to take an oath of loyalty to the Roman Catholic faith, to foreswear any recognition of Henry of Navarre as heir to the throne, and to support instead Navarre's aging uncle, the Catholic Charles, Cardinal of Bourbon, as the rightful heir. Furthermore, they agreed to take up arms for the cause: "We have all solemnly sworn and promised to use force and take up arms to the end that the holy church of God may be restored to its dignity and [reunited in] the true and holy Catholic religion."[2] The Guises having thrown down the gauntlet of Catholic resistance to the Huguenots in general and to Henry of Navarre in particular, King Henry III of France countered by trying to seize back the initiative from them. In July 1585 in the town of Nemours he issued an Edict of Reunion, which at one stroke took away all the Protestants' privileges and gains going back to the Edict of January 1562:

> Because we recognize and understand that if human foresight is uncertain and very weak in all things, it is especially so in the matter of religion. And in all cases wherever there has been controversy and division in a state over such matters, it has ended in complete despair and desolation, as the holy word of God has made clear. Thus, desiring to prevent and remedy this state of affairs, as a Most Christian King, concerned only for the welfare of his state and that of his subjects ... it is ordered from this day forward that no one will practice the new so-called reformed religion, but only that of our Roman Catholic and Apostolic religion ... And to better remedy the great evils and calamities that the toleration of a diversity of religious opinions has introduced into our kingdom, and to restore a more lasting peace and harmony among our subjects, we have ordered and do so order, on the same pain of punishment as mentioned above [i.e. arrest and banishment], that all our subjects will from this day forward live and worship according to the Roman Catholic and Apostolic religion. And those who are of the new religion will leave it and join themselves to the Roman Catholic and Apostolic religion and will make a public profession within six months of the publication of the present [edict].[3]

---

[2] Quoted in J. H. M. Salmon, *Society in Crisis: France in the Sixteenth Century* (London: Ernest Benn, 1975), 238.

[3] The edict was printed in Dijon by Jean Des Planches, and a copy is in AMD, D 63 (liasse), July 1585.

The edict also rewarded Henry, Duke of Guise, with several new governor-ships in the towns of Verdun, Toul, Saint-Dizier, and Châlons-sur-Marne. Thus, the Guise family was clearly in the ascendancy at court and through-out much of northern France. And after the Day of the Barricades in Paris on May 12, 1588, when the Duke of Guise marched into the capital and was received as a conquering hero as Henry III and his household fled to Chartres, the capital of France was firmly under the control of the militant Council of Sixteen, aided and abetted by Spanish troops, as well as Henry, Duke of Guise.[4] This chapter has two principal focal points: (1) what the League's emergence meant for Guise's brother and royal governor in Burgundy, the Duke of Mayenne, as well as his efforts to control politics in the province, and (2) how the economic disruptions of the wars of the League affected the relations between the elites and vignerons in Dijon.

5.1 Mayenne and His Clients

Having served as royal governor in Burgundy since 1573, Charles, Duke of Mayenne, had built up a number of clients and men loyal to him by the 1580s. Most were not directly on his payroll, but they had acquired positions of influence via his support in a variety of institutions in the province, from the Hôtel de Ville and Parlement as well as other sovereign courts to various venal offices in the *bailliage* administration and the Church. It would be very fair to say, in fact, that Mayenne had built up a large following loyal to him in all the major institutions in the province, even though he was never able to control policy or dominate the proceed-ings of most of them. Nevertheless, from 1587, when Mayenne first decided to live full time in the province, he had a loyal following of some of the most influential members of the elites in both Dijon and elsewhere in the

---

[4] For more on the militancy of the Catholic League in Paris as well as the role of the Council of Sixteen, see Robert Descimon, *Qui étaient les Seize: Mythes et réalités de la Ligue parisienne, 1585–1594* (Paris: Klincksieck, 1983); Elie Barnavi, *Le Parti du Dieu: Étude sociale et politique des chefs de la Ligue parisienne, 1585–1594* (Brussels and Louvain: Nauwelaerts, 1980); Robert Descimon and Elie Barnavi, *La Sainte Ligue, le juge et la potence: L'assassinat du president Brisson, 15 novembre 1591* (Paris: Hachette, 1985); Ann W. Ramsey, *Liturgy, Politics, and Salvation: The Catholic League in Paris and the Nature of Catholic Reform, 1540–1630* (Rochester, NY: University of Rochester Press, 1999); Denis Pallier, *Recherches sur l'imprimerie à Paris pendant la Ligue, 1585–1594* (Geneva: Librairie Droz, 1976); Denis Richet, "Sociocultural Aspects of Religious Conflicts in Paris in the Second Half of the Sixteenth Century," in Robert Forster and Orest Ranum, eds., *Religion, Ritual, and the Sacred: Selections from the Annales* (Baltimore: Johns Hopkins University Press, 1982), 182–212; and J. H. M. Salmon, "The Paris Sixteen, 1584–1594: The Social Analysis of a Revolutionary Movement," in his *Renaissance and Revolt: Essays in the Intellectual and Social History of Early Modern France* (Cambridge: Cambridge University Press, 1987), 235–266.

province of Burgundy. This *clientèle*, or affinity of supporters as some historians have preferred to call it, was built around several key supporters: Bernard des Barres, second of the six presiding judges (*présidents*) in the Parlement of Burgundy as well as a former mayor of Dijon (1573, 1574) and *échevin* (1569, 1570, 1571); Jean Fyot, seigneur de Chevanny, who was a judge (*conseiller*) in the Parlement of Burgundy; Perpetuo Berbisey, also a judge in the Parlement of Burgundy as well as a member of a family who provided a long line of mayors and *échevins* to the city of Dijon; Jacques La Verne, the current mayor of Dijon who had served in this role since June 1587; and maybe Mayenne's most important client, Pierre Jeannin, whom Mayenne had helped acquire, first, the position of barrister and then the office of third presiding judge in the Dijon Parlement. Not all of these men would stick by Mayenne until the end of his governorship, however. And Mayenne had no ties to Burgundy outside his *clientèle*. Neither the governor nor his wife were Burgundian by birth; neither did they own any land in the province. Moreover, Mayenne, despite being governor of the province for twenty-three years, never constructed a residence in the capital of Dijon, as the lieutenant-general Gaspard de Saulx-Tavanes had done on the rue Vannerie. Despite all this, Mayenne had clients in virtually every institution in the province, and this included the governor of the Château in Dijon, Jean de Boyault, sieur de Francheresse, who controlled all the king's arms, powder, and munitions in the fortress.[5]

Events at court in December 1588, however, transformed the political situation for Mayenne in Burgundy. King Henry III made the fateful decision to seek revenge against Henry, Duke of Guise, for being humiliated in the Day of Barricades the previous May. The king ordered the murder of both Guise and his brother – Louis of Lorraine, Cardinal of Guise – during the meeting of the Estates-General at Blois in December 1588. The murders were duly carried out on Christmas Eve and the news reached the city of Dijon just three days later.[6] The news was a bombshell in the Burgundian capital, and it generated a massive outcry against the king just as it did in Paris. Henry III had certainly hoped that the murders might restore his own authority and undermine the prestige and respect of the Guises and the Catholic League once and for all as his enemies, but the events at Blois had just the opposite effect. In Paris the Committee of

[5] For Mayenne's clients see Henri Drouot, *Mayenne et la Bourgogne: Étude sur la Ligue (1587–1596)*, 2 vols. (Dijon: Bernigaud et Privat, 1937), 1: 102–119 and 2: 89–91; as well as Sharon Kettering, *Patrons, Brokers, and Clients in Seventeenth-Century France* (New York: Oxford University Press, 1986), 147–150.
[6] AMD, B 226, fol. 128v, December 27, 1588.

Sixteen further tightened its control over the city and sent out letters to all those cities controlled by the League – including Dijon – that they had resolved to make war against Henry III, "and to have recourse to God, whom we hold as our true king."[7] Moreover, early the next year pamphlets began circulating in the French capital that were not only hostile to the king but in some cases actually clamored for regicide. The pamphlets of the Parisian curate and preacher Jean Boucher were particularly forceful in claiming that the death of the king was justified because of his murder of the Guises.[8] In Dijon, the hostility against the king was only slightly less vitriolic – there were no immediate calls for regicide – but Mayenne moved quickly to consolidate his power in the province as well as distance himself from the king, at whose pleasure he served as royal governor of the province. Indeed, two months before the murder of the Guises, Mayenne decided to nominate his own candidate for lieutenant-general of the province, Guillaume de Hautemer, baron de Fervaques and Count of Grancey. Immediately after the murders, however, Mayenne appointed Fervaques himself to the office.[9] Fervaques had been the first gentleman of the bedchamber of François, Duke of Anjou, in the 1580s and had traveled to the Netherlands with him, with an annual salary of 12,000 *livres tournois*.[10] But Mayenne was so anxious to appoint his own client as lieutenant-general in place of Henry III's own choice – Guillaume de Saulx, sieur de Tavanes, the son-in-law of the previous lieutenant-general, Léonor Chabot, Count of Charny, and the son of Charny's predecessor – that he was willing to overlook Fervaques's history of employing "the crude politics of deceit and treachery." Fervaques was also the first cousin of Chabot-Charny's widow, Françoise de la Baume. Of course, Mayenne did not have the authority to make a royal appointment, so in his announcement he conferred the authority of the office of lieutenant-general on Fervaques without the actual title.[11]

At Mayenne's request, the mayor and city council drew up an oath of loyalty to the Catholic Church as well as the League in Burgundy. On January 9, 1589, the city council drew up a list of names of those who had refused to take the oath or who were otherwise the source of "divisions"

[7] Joseph Garnier, ed., *Correspondance de la Mairie de Dijon extraite des archives de cette ville*, 3 vols. (Dijon: Rabutot, 1868–1870), 2: 128–130.

[8] See Frederic J. Baumgartner, *Radical Reactionaries: The Political Thought of the French Catholic League* (Geneva: Droz, 1976), 101–144.

[9] AMD, B 226, fol. 148r–v, January 17, 1589; and Drouot, *Mayenne et la Bourgogne*, 1: 198–199.

[10] Mack P. Holt, "Patterns of Clientèle and Economic Opportunity at Court: The Household of François, Duke of Anjou," *French Historical Studies* 13 (Spring 1984): 320.

[11] Drouot, *Mayenne et la Bourgogne*, 1: 199–200 and 240–241 (quote on 199–200).

within the city, a list of 72 names including some women and even one widow. They also included some of the most prominent members of the city's elites: members of the Requelene, Humbert, Richard, Brocard, Chisseret, and Gros families among others, including lawyers in the Parlement as well as judges in the Chamber of Accounts. They were ordered to be exiled from the city or face imprisonment.[12] Those who did not leave were eventually imprisoned in the convent of the Cordeliers and guarded by the friars.[13] Mayenne also publicly recognized the mayor of Dijon, Jacques La Verne, as his deputy in the city during his absence.[14] The following month Mayenne ordered that all houses in the city be searched for arms, grain, and wine, and that no foreigners were allowed to enter the city and that no one at all could exit the city without a signed passport from the mayor.[15] Finally, in March Mayenne drew up a new set of "Articles of Union" upon whose authority the League in Burgundy rested. According to the deliberations of the Hôtel de Ville, on March 22 between 3,000 and 4,000 heads of household came to the Hôtel de Ville "to swear upon the holy gospels the Articles of Union."[16] It was then presented to the Parlement of Dijon on March 23, where all the judges, barristers, and other lawyers stood and swore to uphold the articles:

> We swear and promise to God and the entire celestial court to live and die in the Roman Catholic and apostolic religion, to employer our lives and property for the conservation of it against all those who either overtly or by covert means are trying or will try to do anything to the prejudice of the said religion. We swear to maintain this city of Dijon in peace and tranquility, to oppose all those who make any trouble here and drive them away either by just or any other means, and to employ all our forces that we have to conserve the province [of Burgundy] and this city of Dijon in their entirety, to render them peaceful and to protect them from all evils and oppressions, together with all other cities, towns, and villages of this kingdom united for the benefit of the Roman Catholic and apostolic religion, and to make open warfare against all heretics and trouble-makers or their supporters ... We hold as heretics and destroyers of the public good all those who refuse to bind themselves or sign on to this present union, or who do anything whatsoever contrary to it, and we shall hunt them down everywhere. We also swear to render ourselves obedient to the command of Monseigneur, the Duke of Mayenne, governor in this province, and in his absence, Monsieur de Fervaques, count of Gramey, his lieutenant-general,

---

[12] AMD, B 226, fols.140r–141v, January 9, 1589; and AMD B 9, cote 21, January 14, 1589.
[13] AMD, B 226, fols. 181v, March 10, 1589.   [14] AMD, B 226, fols. 146v–147r, January 16, 1589.
[15] AMD, B 226, fols. 160v, 167v, 171v, and 174v, February 12–March 3, 1589.
[16] AMD, B 226, fols. 187r–189v, March 21–22, 1589.

from whom we shall never separate ourselves regardless of any order or commandment that might arrive whatsoever.[17]

Neither the king nor the king's authority was even mentioned, and Mayenne was now the *de facto* sovereign power in the province. Moreover, just days before, Mayenne had promised his lieutenant-general Guillaume de Fervaques from Paris, where he had been conferring with the Sixteen, that he would be sending him many more troops "in order to cleanse the province (*pour nettoyer la province*)" and "to cleanse the region of this vermin (*faire nettoyer le pais de ceste vermyne*)."[18] Unlike earlier in the religious wars, however, this was not to be primarily a cleansing of Protestants, of whom there were precious few still living in Burgundy due to the earlier efforts, but a cleansing of all enemies of the League, most of whom were Catholics. And in Burgundy, this primarily meant enemies of the Duke of Mayenne. But no one could have thought that one of the first such enemies would be the duke's own lieutenant-general, Guillaume sieur de Fervaques, who was imprisoned in the Château in Dijon just a few weeks later for refusing to swear to the oath of the Articles of Union, "declaring that in his particular case he was a very humble servant of the king, not having ever thought or believed that M[onsiuer] de Mayenne, governor of this province, and to which he had given his faith for the conservation of the same, wanted to separate himself from the king."[19] Moreover, Fervaques had been accepting bribes for royal agents to serve the king, both for himself and for his sons-in-law.[20] Mayenne thus had his own lieutenant-general locked up as a prisoner in the Chateau on April 23.[21] And he then preempted Henry III once again – the king he no longer recognized as legitimate – by naming his own replacement for Fervaques as lieutenant-general of Burgundy, Claude de Bauffremont, baron of Sennecey.[22] Alas, Sennecey would prove no more loyal than Fervaques.

Mayenne's hand was further strengthened when the calls for the death of Henry III by Jean Boucher and others in Paris finally yielded the desired result on August 1, 1589, when a 24-year-old Jacobin monk, Jacques Clément, stabbed Henry III to death while he was attending Mass at

---

[17] BMD, Fonds Saverot 1493, registers of the Parlement of Dijon, 270–272, March 23, 1589.

[18] Garnier, ed., *Correspondance de la Mairie de Dijon*, 2: 225, March 13, 1589, and 2: 287, April 9, 1589.

[19] Quoted in P. M. Baudouin, *Histoire du protestantisme et la Ligue en Bourgogne*, 2 vols. (Auxerre: Imprimerie Vosgien et Chambon, 1881–1884), 2: 372.

[20] Drouot, *Mayenne et la Bourgogne*, 1: 322–326 and 337–338.

[21] AMD, B 226, fol.210r, April 23, 1589.

[22] BMD, Fonds Saverot 1493, p. 299, November 20, 1589.

Saint-Cloud just outside Paris.[23] When the news "of the miraculous deliverance of the future of this state by the death of the king" reached Dijon on August 12, the judges in the Dijon Parlement noted that the Parlement of Paris had declared Henry of Navarre to be a heretic and thus barred from inheriting the throne and had already recognized the elderly Charles, Cardinal of Bourbon, as Henry III's successor. The Cardinal of Bourbon was Henry of Navarre's uncle, and clearly less directly in line to the succession than his nephew. Even though he renounced all such claims and declared his nephew the rightful heir to the throne, nevertheless, the Catholic League promoted him as King Charles X of France. And in Dijon the Parlement insisted in August 1589 that

> it is necessary to unite everyone under the obedience of the new king [the Cardinal of Bourbon], and concerning those who want to support the side of the King of Navarre, it is necessary to declare them to be proper heretics, and whatever else is said, we must consider them as such and punish them as heretics ... [Thus, the court of the Parlement of Dijon] prohibits anyone from recognizing Henry of Navarre as King [of France] or favoring him or aiding him in any manner whatsoever, directly or indirectly, on pain of being punished as a heretic and disturber of the public peace.[24]

Although it strengthened the hand of Mayenne, the absence of a recognized king put all the royal officers and especially the judges in the Parlement of Dijon into a quandary. Who would pay their salaries and who would protect their investments in their royal offices if there were no recognized king? Moreover, what were they supposed to do when Henry of Navarre assumed the title of Henry IV and ordered all his royal officers to leave Dijon and obey him rather than the Duke of Mayenne? To which part of the French constitution were they supposed to give priority? The part that said kings were only legitimate if they descended directly in bloodline from their predecessors, as the supporters of Henry IV now claimed? Or the part of the constitution that required kings of France to be good Catholics and use all their means to fight heresy, as the League and Mayenne maintained? Many members of the Parlement and the Chamber of Accounts were troubled by the Articles of Union, as it undermined the king's authority even if they were not overjoyed to have a king who was a heretic. And when Henry IV ordered all his royal officers not only not to

---

[23] For more on the events surrounding the assassination of Henry III, see the gripping account of Nicolas Le Roux, *1er août. Un régicide au nom de Dieu. L'Assassinat d'Henri III* (Paris: Gallimard, 2006).
[24] BMD, Fonds Saverot 1493, 284–286.

participate with the League in those cities it controlled but also to leave League-controlled cities such as Dijon in order to carry out their duties elsewhere, it forced them into a choice none of them wanted to make.[25] Should they leave Dijon to protect their royal offices and their careers, but risk losing their houses and property back home? Or should they stay to defend their families and homesteads but risk losing their offices and their livelihoods in joining with the League? These men knew that whatever they decided, it was a huge risk.

Above all, these divisions into rival camps of Leaguers and royalists seemed to underline two very different notions of what the elites' own roles were in the polity of the French monarchy. Those who sided with the League tended to see themselves as part of a community where their authority and legitimacy were tied to the local commune as first created in the Middle Ages, where their political power first emerged. They valued horizontal ties with other inhabitants and cohorts who occupied this same commune. As a result, they tended to fight fiercely to protect all local privileges and liberties, and they resisted just as fiercely all efforts by the state to diminish them, whether they came from the Duke of Burgundy before 1477 or from the King of France thereafter. Those elites who sided with the royalist camp in Flavigny, on the other hand, tended to share a very different set of values. They saw their future as more closely linked to the monarchical state than to the local commune. Moreover, they tended to perceive their identities as being much more closely connected with the aristocracy rather than with the urban bourgeoisie. As such, they cherished the more hierarchical values of the monarchical state than the horizontal ties and civic values of the medieval commune. While both groups were devoutly Catholic, the Leaguers continued to see religion as part of the binding agent of the local commune, including the traditional ties to Rome. The royalists, however, tended to view themselves as more Gallican Catholics than Roman Catholics, and they saw the monarchy in much the same way. They certainly believed the *Rex christianissimus* – the Most Christian King – ought to be a devout Christian, but more Gallican than Roman Catholic. The principal distinction between the two groups was largely about authority. Gallican Catholics were French Catholics, who viewed the king's political authority as more important than the Pope's, rather than Roman Catholics. Thus, the royalists could justify their support of the monarchical state despite the king's own personal religion, though they fervently hoped he would abjure his Protestantism

---

[25] Drouot, *Mayenne et la Bourgogne*, 1: 365–395.

and become a Catholic king. The Leaguers, on the other hand, viewed the monarchical state with deep suspicion and were unwilling to accept a king who was a heretic. Thus, Leaguers and royalists alike were both devoutly Catholic and were of the same social backgrounds and origins; what divided them ultimately was their sense of themselves and their vision of the French state in the future. In a real sense, the emergence of the Holy Catholic League in Paris, Dijon, and a host of other cities in 1589 was a real turning point in the evolution of the French polity. With the urban elites turning away from the commune to collaborate ever more closely with the king, we can see the early germination of the absolute monarchy of the seventeenth century. Robert Descimon was the first to make this argument over thirty years ago in a path-breaking book on the League in the capital of Paris, and he has continued to provide more evidence for it over the last three decades.[26] What I hope to show in the pages that follow is that a very similar division took place in Burgundy during the period of the League. I certainly do not want to overplay the breach as being irreparable or permanent, as it shall become clear that there were many moderates in both camps who continued to work for reconciliation. Moreover, several of those who left Dijon for Flavigny in 1589 ultimately changed their minds and returned, just as several of those elites who stayed behind to side with the League later departed to join their royalist colleagues in Flavigny. Nevertheless, the eventual defeat of the League in Burgundy, just as Robert Descimon described in Paris, ultimately underscored the recognition by both groups that collaborating with the king was the better way to maintain their authority and legitimacy. And this shift of the urban elites

---

[26] Descimon, *Qui étaient les Seize?* 294–300. Also see the following Descimon articles for more detailed evidence supporting this thesis: "L'échevinage parisien sous Henri IV (1594–1609): Autonomie urbaine, conflits politiques et exclusives sociales," in Neithard Bulst and Jean-Philippe Genet, eds., *La ville, la bourgeoisie et la genèse de l'état moderne (XIIe-XVIIIe siècle)* (Paris: C.N.R.S., 1988), 113–150; "Le corps de ville et les élections échevinales à Paris aux XVIe et XVIIe siècles: Codification coutumière et pratiques sociales," *Histoire, Économie, et Société* 13 (1994): 507–530; "The Birth of the Nobility of the Robe," in Michael Wolfe, ed., *Changing Identities in Early Modern France* (Durham, NC: Duke University Press, 1997), 95–123; "The 'Bourgeoisie Seconde': Social Differentiation in the Parisian Municipal Oligarchy in the Sixteenth Century, 1500–1610," *French History* 17 (2003): 388–424; and "Le catholicisme corporative des temps de la Ligue: Témoignages de testaments parisiens des XVIe et XVIIe siècles," in Jean-Pierre Bardet, Denis Crouzet, and Anne Molinié-Bertrand, eds., *Pierre Chaunu historien* (Paris: Presses de l'Université de Paris-Sorbonne, 2012), 169–188. Also very useful are two books: Robert Descimon and Fanny Cosandey, *L'Absolutisme en France: Historie et historiographie* (Paris: Le Seuil, 2002) and Robert Descimon and Elie Haddad, eds., *Épreuves de noblesse: Les expériences nobiliares de la haute robe parisienne (XVIe-XVIIIe siècles)* (Paris: Les Belles Lettres, 2010). Finally, see the excellent introduction titled "Robert Descimon and the Historian's Craft," in Barbara B. Diefendorf, ed., *Social Relations, Politics, and Power in Early Modern France: Robert Descimon and the Historian's Craft* (Kirksville, MO: Truman State University Press, 2016), 1–24.

toward the monarchical state would have serious consequences for their relations with the popular classes in Dijon, especially with the vignerons, after the Wars of Religion were over.

Although a more detailed analysis of the split of the judges, barristers, and lawyers of the Parlement and the Chamber of Accounts, as well as the rest of the royal officer corps, into two rival camps will be discussed in the next chapter, suffice it to say that in September 1589 a slow trickle of members of the sovereign courts began leaving Dijon and assembling in the town of Flavigny, the only significant town in the province of Burgundy not in the control of the League.[27] The exodus from Dijon was led by Bénigne Frémyot, the fourth president of the Parlement of Dijon, and over the next eighteen months a new royalist Parlement formed in Flavigny, consisting of two of the six presiding judges – Frémyot and Claude Bourgeois, the fifth president – and seventeen of the forty-three other judges (*conseillers*) in the court. A handful of other lawyers and notaries joined them. The first president, Denis Brûlart, the second president, Bernard des Barres, the third president, Pierre Jeannin, and the sixth president, Nicolas de Montholon, as well as the majority of the other judges stayed behind to support Mayenne and the League. These numbers were always in flux, however, as several members in each camp swapped sides during the conflict, as will be discussed later in this chapter. Moreover, there were several who left Dijon but never went to Flavigny, hoping to avoid making a choice. Nevertheless, from September 1589 until May 1595 when the city of Dijon surrendered to Henry IV, many of its most elite citizens were forced to divide themselves into two seemingly opposed camps: a royalist camp in Flavigny and a Leaguer camp in Dijon, with two sets of competing sovereign courts attempting to mete out justice to the province. The royal officers at Flavigny would eventually move to the town of Semur in Auxerrois in April 1592 for greater security,[28] but this great divide masked a great deal of common feeling and mutual obligation shared by the two cohorts. Indeed, the moderates in both camps would continue to try to work together to find a common solution throughout this entire period.

For his part, Mayenne managed to retain most of his important clients in Dijon in support of the League. Moreover, in the absence of a crowned king the duke set about trying to make Burgundy into a personal fiefdom, even though he owned no property there. The Council of State for the

[27] BMD, Fonds Saverot 1493, p. 291, September 5, 1589.
[28] BMD, Fonds Saverot 1493, 513–514, April 20, 1592.

League in Paris had already requested each urban cell of the League to create a similar Council of State. In Burgundy, this amounted to a group of elites, many of whom were Mayenne's clients. Thus, the duke hoped to use this Council to advise him and handle all politically sensitive matters. In many ways, Mayenne was acting like he had the authority of the Valois Dukes of Burgundy rather than that of a royal governor. This council consisted of some of his most loyal clients in both the political and ecclesiastical spheres, and Henri Drouot has referred to this group as "the most outspoken, ambitious and fanatical" of all the Leaguers in Burgundy.[29] In 1589 these men were the most militant members of the League in Burgundy, though several of them would moderate their views over the next six years. But like the Parlement and the Hôtel de Ville, having his clients in place on the Council of State in Burgundy did not always guarantee their complete loyalty to him. Moreover, they did not always speak with one voice, as various issues caused splits among their ranks. The origins of the Council in Burgundy are so vague because all the records of its meetings have been lost, or more likely destroyed. From the brief "extracts" of the registers of the Council that have survived, its principal members were the following:

(1)   Denis Brûlart, first president in the Parlement of Dijon
(2)   Esme de la Croix, abbot of Cîteaux
(3)   Girard Sayve, dean of the Sainte-Chapelle
(4)   André Bonnotte, abbot of Notre-Dame de la Buissière
(5)   Jean Fyot, seigneur de Chevannay, *conseiller* in the Parlement of Dijon
(6)   Perpetuo Berbisey, *conseiller* in the Parlement de Dijon
(7)   Pierre de Montmoien, *conseiller* and president in the Chamber of Accounts
(8)   Jean de Boyault, seigneur de Franchesse, captain and governor of the Château in Dijon
(9)   Guillaume Legouz, seigneur de Vellepesle, *conseiller* and *avocat du roi* in the Parlement of Dijon
(10) Pierre Michiel, former viscount-mayor of Dijon (died January 1590)
(11) Guillaume Rouhier, *échevin* and former viscount-mayor (1581–1587)
(12) Jacques La Verne, former and future viscount-mayor of Dijon
(13) Etienne Bernard, *échevin* and barrister in the Parlement of Dijon

---

[29] Henri Drouot, *Un épisode de la Ligue à Dijon: L'Affaire La Verne (1594) et notes sur la Ligue en Bourgogne* (Dijon: La Revue bourguignonne, 1910), 3: "adhérans les plus déclarés, ambitieux ou fanatiques."

(14)   Jacques Venot, *échevin* and barrister in the Parlement of Dijon
(15)   Edme de Chantepinot, royal barrister in the bailiwick court in Dijon
(16)   Philibert Jacob, former president in the Chamber of Accounts
(17)   Bernard des Barres, second president in the Parlement of Dijon
(18)   Jean Pignallet, captain of the walls of Dijon
(19)   Sieur de Petit-Ruffey, seigneur de Pouilly
(20)   Philibert Jaquot, president in the Chamber of Accounts
(21)   Guillaume Millière, *conseiller* in the Parlement of Dijon
(22)   Réne Fleutelot, *échevin* and solicitor in the Parlement, as well as future mayor[30]

In many ways the Council of State operated during the period of the League much like the Committee of Sixteen operated in the capital of Paris, as an extralegal body that came to supersede not only the mayor and city council but also the Parlement and other royal officers. In short, these were Mayenne's own specially chosen clients and they were his men; they dominated the political and religious institutions in the city and were expected to bring whatever institutional support was needed to support Mayenne and the League. They designated where troops would be deployed, they raised and borrowed money to fund them, and ultimately they attempted at Mayenne's bequest to coopt the authority of the city council, the Parlement, and the Chamber of Accounts.[31] For a while, at least, they were able to do so.

The Council of State began by ordering the mayor and city council to seize and sell all property confiscated from those men who had fled Dijon for Flavigny.[32] This was easier said than done, as most of those who had left Dijon left their wives and families in charge of their homes and property in Dijon. Despite significant opposition from these family members, the confiscation of property began in earnest, much like the confiscation of the property of the Huguenots in the 1560s and 1570s. On December 3, the Council seized the property of one of the judges in the Chamber of Accounts who was in Flavigny, the sieur de Crespy. His mother-in-law was living in his house in Dijon when the confiscation took place, and when she put up a fight the Council declared both she and her son-in-law to be "the enemies of the Holy League... [and] that all their goods will be confiscated, seized, and sold."[33] A few days later the Council did the same

---

[30]   This list comes from Drouot, *Mayenne et la Bourgogne*, 2: 43, and Drouot, *Un episode de la Ligue a Dijon: L'Affaire La Verne*, 3.
[31]   Drouot, *Mayenne et la Bourgogne*, 2: 41–64.   [32]   AMD, B 227, fol. 130r, October 9, 1589.
[33]   AMD, B 227, fol. 155v, December 3, 1589.

thing with the property of Jean-Baptiste Legoux, seigneur de la Berchère, a barrister in the Parlement who sided with the royalists in Flavigny.[34] Le Goux, no relation to the Leaguer Guillaume Legouz on the Council of State, was from a prominent family in Nuits.[35] And the following month Marguerite Frémyot, the daughter of the royalist fifth president of the Parlement, Bénigne Frémyot, begged the Council for the return of the wine that had been seized from her father's house. Instead of selling the wine as planned, the Council decided to distribute the wine to some of the religious orders in the city – one *feuillette* to the Jacobins, one *feuillette* to the Jesuits, and one *feuillette* to the Carmelites – "for their pains for having inspected and visited the wine cellars of the said heretics who were absent."[36] These scenes would be repeated over the next year as more and more royal officers left Dijon.

With the royalist Parlement in Flavigny and the Leaguer Parlement in Dijon both claiming to wield authority in executing royal justice in the province of Burgundy, and with many of the judges remaining in Dijon apparently still torn between the two courts, Mayenne sought to make the Hôtel de Ville in Dijon the foundation of his client network in the province. And he was largely dependent in this effort on two principal clients: Jacques La Verne, the city's mayor, and Etienne Bernard, a judge in the Leaguer Parlement in Dijon, but someone who also served as an *échevin* on the city council. La Verne, a lawyer by training, was first elected mayor of the city in June 1587, after having served as an *échevin* since 1578.[37] He was also one of the wealthiest members of the city council, and his family had funded their own richly decorated private chapel in the parish church of St. Michel, as we saw in Chapter 2 (see pp. 80–81 above). Bernard, also a lawyer, was first selected as an *échevin* in 1581,[38] and he and La Verne both served together on the city council throughout most of the 1580s, both representing the parish of St. Michel. Having been elected mayor in 1587 and reelected for a second term in June 1588, La Verne turned out to be much more independent than Mayenne had hoped. It was Jacques La

---

[34] AMD, B 227, fol. 162v, December 9, 1589.

[35] Abbé Bissey, "Précis historique sur les Legoux de la Berchère et en particulier sur Pierre Legoux, comte de Rochefort," *Société d'histoire, d'archéologie et de littérature de l'arrondissement de Beaune: Mémoires année 1886* (Beaune: Arthur Batault, 1887), 195–293. The Legouz family from Dijon normally spelled its name with a *z*, while the family from Nuits spelled Legoux with an *x*, though this was hardly consistent.

[36] AMD, B 227, fols. 186v–r, January 5, 1590. A *feuillette* was a small barrel of wine of approximately 114 liters; it was one-fourth of a *queue* (456 liters) and one-half of a *muid* (228 liters).

[37] For La Verne's first selection as an *échevin* in June 1578, see B 216, fol. 11r–v, June 20, 1578.

[38] AMD, B 219, fol. 8r, June 20, 1581.

Verne who had first exposed Fervaques's royalist sympathies and had him imprisoned in the Château in April 1589 before Mayenne had a chance to act. And in the 1589 elections Mayenne used the influence of his half-brother the Duke of Nemours to get a solicitor (*procureur*) named Pierre Michiel to run against La Verne. And Michiel duly won, a sign, Mayenne surely hoped, of the decline of La Verne's influence in the Hôtel de Ville.[39] Michiel lived for only six months, however, and the *échevins* decided to appoint their still popular former mayor, Jacques La Verne, in January 1590 to serve the remainder of Michiel's term.[40] And La Verne was also still popular with the electorate in Dijon, as he was reelected in June 1590 with more than 99 percent of the people's "voices."[41]

Just before the June elections of 1591 Mayenne wrote to La Verne and the *échevins* on the city council indicating that he wished to see Etienne Bernard elected mayor in the upcoming election, "as it is necessary and timely for the preservation of your city and the well-being of your province."[42] Jacques La Verne had no intention of standing down, however, and he did everything in his power to try to ensure his own reelection. Indeed, as explained in Chapter 1, the mayor traditionally turned over the symbol of power of mayoral authority – the painted gospel of St. John – to a keeper of the gospels (*garde des évangiles*) for the duration of the election, usually one of the current *échevins* selected by the *échevins* themselves (see p. 37). The mayor would then leave the city council during the elections, not to return unless he was either reelected or selected by the new mayor as one of the twenty *échevins*. This turning over the gospels to another and departing from the council was supposed to give the appearance of evenhandedness and fairness during the voting process, so as not to appear as if the outgoing mayor was trying to influence the choice of the people, either for his reelection or for the election of someone else. La Verne decided not to do this, however, making it clear to his colleagues that he wished to be elected himself as keeper of the gospels on June 14, 1591. The council split; fourteen voted for La Verne and ten voted for the *échevin* Jean Bourrelier (the twenty *échevins* and four ecclesiastical *échevins* all were allowed to vote). The ten *échevins* who voted against La Verne were furious at this innovation, and a small delegation of them, led by Etienne Bernard and René Fleutelot, went to the Parlement the same day to complain to the judges

---

[39] Drouot, *Mayenne et la Bourgogne*, 1: 423–428.
[40] AMD, B 227, fols. 192v–193v and 195r, January 10 and 11, 1590.
[41] AMD, B 228, fol. 22r–v, June 20, 1590.
[42] Garnier, ed., *Correspondance de la Mairie de Dijon*, 2: 387, May 23, 1591.

about this innovation. With all the chambers assembled, the king's own lawyer in the Parlement (*avocat du roi*), Guillaume Legouz, seigneur de Vellepesle, made it very clear that the election of the keeper of the gospels was to be overturned and a new keeper elected.[43] Thus, Jean Bourrelier was duly elected the keeper of the gospels, and Jacques La Verne was overwhelmingly reelected as mayor the following week, despite Mayenne's own personal support for Etienne Bernard.[44] An appeal of the result was filed in the Parlement the day after the election by Etienne Petit, sieur de Ruffey, who claimed there were rumors circulating in the city of various irregularities in the voting, but the Parlement upheld the result, and Jacques La Verne was duly elected for another year.

Mayenne's fears about La Verne's loyalties were quickly confirmed during this term as mayor, however, and it needs to be remembered that La Verne had been mayor of Dijon for all but six months since June 1587. On October 1, 1591, La Verne was walking in the street in front of his house in the Place St. Michel next to the parish church accompanied by Jean Fyot, a judge in the Parlement, and several others when they were confronted by Edme Chantepinot, one of the king's lawyers in the *bailliage* court of Dijon, who accused them both of leaving the city of Dijon vulnerable to the attacks of royalist troops in the area. Chantepinot was an ardent Leaguer, and the reports of soldiers in the area had been circulating since the beginning of the year.[45] Moreover, royalist troops under the command of the Marshal of Aumont had approached the walls of Dijon just a few days before on September 27, unsuccessfully attempting to seize several Leaguer strongholds.[46] La Verne had ordered that all the gates of the city be shut, but Chantepinot wished to exit to see how his parcel of vines outside the city walls was being affected, as this was the height of the grape harvest. The mayor refused him a passport to leave the city, and insults were exchanged. Chantepinot eventually struck the mayor, knocking him down, before the fight was quickly broken up.

The proud mayor was furious and ordered Chantepinot to be imprisoned immediately, and later the same day without any trial or formal legal process, La Verne ordered that his attacker be hanged. And the sentence was duly carried out by Pierre Fleuryet, the executioner of high justice in Dijon, not publicly in the normal place of execution, the Place Morimont,

[43] BMD, Fonds Saverot 1493, 370–372, June 14, 1591.
[44] AMD, B 229, fols.18v–28r, June 23, 1591.
[45] BMD, Fonds Saverot 1493, 359–360 and 369, January 29 and April 30, 1591.
[46] AMD, B 229, fols. 82r–83v, September 27, 1591.

but privately inside the courtyard of the Hôtel de Ville itself.[47] The Parlement was outraged, as all capital sentences were supposed to be automatically sent to the Parlement for appeal. But because there had been no sentence, or even a trial, there could be no such appeal. La Verne got away with this clearly unlawful and extraordinary act because he was so feared throughout the city, according to Henri Drouot, who referred to La Verne as "the dictator-mayor." Neither the judges in the Parlement nor the family of the murdered lawyer sought justice for the unfortunate Chantepinot. "This failure to press the issue was so characteristic: it revealed the fear inspired by the Leaguer mayor, or the power of the mayor that was so strongly established as the foundation of the party of the Holy Union, master of the hour."[48] Mayenne thus decided to make a much stronger effort to remove La Verne from office at the next mayoral election. Unfortunately for him, the fallout and the emotions from the incident on October 1, 1591, would continue to foment for another three years.

Mayenne at least succeeded in preventing Jacques La Verne from being reelected as mayor in June 1592, though barely, as the duke's preferred candidate, Etienne Bernard, was only elected with 558 out of 1,984 votes cast (28.1 percent), with Jacques La Verne coming second with 429 votes (21.6 percent).[49] There were more than a dozen candidates receiving votes, and Bernard's 28.1 percent of the total was the smallest in any mayoral election in Dijon since individual votes were first recorded in the city council's deliberations starting in 1545.[50] According to a local observer, Bénigne Pepin, a canon in the Sainte-Chapelle in Dijon, all the candidates canvassed for votes by offering money, food, and drink to anyone who would vote for them.[51] But at least Mayenne had managed to defeat Jacques La Verne, who was still popular in the city at large and even with some of the *échevins* on the council despite the extralegal execution of Chantepinot in 1591.

---

[47] The most complete assessment of these events and the surviving sources that describe them are in Henri Drouot, "Un crime dans la ville bloquée: Notes sur une situation et des mentalités de 1591," *Annales de Bourgogne* 21 (1949): 261–284. Also see Drouot, *Un episode de la Ligue a Dijon: L'Affaire La Verne*, 31–35; and Drouot, *Mayenne et la Bourgogne*, 1: 423–428.

[48] Drouot, "Un crime dans la ville bloquée," 265 and 275–276.

[49] AMD, B 230, fol. 1r–47v, June 23, 1592.

[50] Mack P. Holt, "Popular Political Culture and Mayoral Elections in Sixteenth-Century Dijon," in Mack P. Holt, ed., *Society and Institutions in Early Modern France* (Athens, GA: University of Georgia Press, 1991), 98–116, especially 102–103.

[51] Joseph Garnier, ed., *Journal de Gabriel Breunot conseiller du parlement de Dijon précédé du livre de souvenance de Pepin chanoine de la Sainte-Chapelle*, 3 vols. (Dijon: J.-E. Rabutot, 1864), 1: 83.

Very soon, however, a series of events served not only to thwart the duke's efforts to repress the activities of his client La Verne but also to provide evidence that popular support for the League might be beginning to wane. First, in Paris the radicals of the Committee of Sixteen began pushing for Mayenne and the League to recognize the daughter of King Philip II of Spain, the Infanta Isabella Clara Eugenia, as the legitimate monarch of France. The Infanta was the daughter of Philip II's second wife, Elisabeth of Valois, who was also the sister of Kings Francis II, Charles, IX, and Henry III. So, at least she was a direct descendent of the Valois dynasty, even if the Salic Law seemingly prevented the crown from passing to a woman or even through a female line. Because the Duke of Mayenne was equally reluctant to recognize a foreigner as monarch as a heretic, he decided to try to take the decision to select a Catholic king away from the radicals in Paris by calling for a meeting of the Estates-General in the capital in December 1592. This itself was a revolutionary move on Mayenne's part, as only the king was recognized as having the authority convoke the three estates of the realm to meet, and memories were still fresh of the last meeting of the Estates-General in Blois in 1588 that dissolved with the assassinations of Mayenne's two brothers, the Duke and Cardinal of Guise. Nevertheless, deputies from the League-controlled regions of the realm began arriving in Paris in January 1593, and one of these was Mayenne's client, Etienne Bernard, viscount-mayor of Dijon, who was representing the third estate. Another Mayenne client, Pierre Jeannin, a presiding judge in the Leaguer Parlement in Dijon, was also a deputy representing the third estate.

While Etienne Bernard was attempting to select a new Catholic monarch for the kingdom, Jeannin was involved in more delicate discussions with Catholic supporters of Henry IV – or Henry, King of Navarre, as the Leaguers continued to refer to him. In May 1593 Mayenne appointed Jeannin along with several bishops from the first estate and nobles from the second estate to meet with these Catholic royalists about the possibility of Henry abjuring his Protestantism and converting to Catholicism. Bernard reported back to the city council in Dijon that, while there were wild rumors flying around about these discussions, he was certain that the royalists were demanding that the Leaguer Estates-General recognize Henry as the legitimate King of France first and then invite him to become a Catholic.[52] Jeannin, who had been absent from Dijon almost the entire

---

[52] Garnier, ed., *Corrspondance de la Mairie de Dijon*, 2: 468–469, May 22, 1593.

time after the assassination of Henry III in 1589, yet who had maintained his ties with the League and had refrained from joining the royalists in the Parlement at Flavigny, was in fact a leader in these discussions. And if there were to be a rapprochement between the moderates of the League and their royalist counterparts, Jeannin was convinced that Henry would have to make the first move by abjuring his Calvinist faith before any of the Leaguers would recognize him as the legitimate King of France. The deputies of the Leaguer Estates-General, however, were being pressured by the Spanish ambassador present in Paris to abandon the heretic Henry of Navarre and support the candidacy of Philip II's daughter, the Infanta.[53]

Henry IV had already seized the initiative, however, and announced on May 17, 1593 that he would abjure his Calvinist faith and take Catholic instruction. He was instructed in the Catholic catechism by René de Beaune, the Archbishop of Bourges, and René Benoît, the vicar of the parish church of St. Eustache in Paris, one of the most ardently Catholic parishes in the capital throughout the civil wars. And on July 25, Henry IV formally converted and publicly attended mass at St. Denis, the burial site of past kings of France just north of Paris.[54] At one stroke, the king granted to Mayenne and the League the one goal they had been striving to achieve for nearly a decade: keeping the French monarchy Catholic. In this sense, Henry's abjuration and conversion was a victory for the League. The Sixteen, the Estates-General, and the majority of the Catholic clergy in Paris, not to mention Mayenne himself, were hardly rejoicing, however, as they all believed that Henry's conversion was nothing but a shameless act of political opportunism and not at all genuine.

Affairs in Dijon were also disrupted by events in Paris, as the mayor, Etienne Bernard, and the Duke of Mayenne remained in the capital through-out the summer of 1593 despite Dijon's annual mayoral elections in June. Because Dijon's elections required the candidates to be present in Dijon to hear the voices of the people declared in their presence on election day, Mayenne had attempted to get the city council to postpone the election until Bernard could return to Dijon.[55] With the former mayor Jacques La Verne dominating the council in Bernard's and Mayenne's absence, the *échevins* decided to go ahead and hold the election on its traditional date of June 21.[56]

[53] Ibid., 2: 470–471, May 22, 1593.
[54] For the circumstances surrounding the abjuration and conversion, see Michael Wolfe, *The Conversion of Henri IV: Politics, Power, and Religious Belief in Early Modern France* (Cambridge, MA: Harvard University Press, 1993), especially 115–188.
[55] AMD, B 230, fol. 279v, June 13, 1593.
[56] AMD, B 230, fols. 280r–281v, June 15 and 16, 1593.

And to no one's surprise, Jacques La Verne was chosen as the keeper of the gospels as well as elected for a fifth term as mayor, having previously been elected in 1587, 1588, 1590, and 1591. Out of 1,687 votes cast in the election in the Jacobin convent, La Verne garnered 1,084 votes (64.3 percent), while the only serious alternative, the more moderate *échevin* René Fleutelot, got 505 votes (29.9 percent). To be sure, 44 heads of household (2.6 percent) did end up casting their votes for Etienne Bernard despite the mayor's not being present as tradition required, but it was an overwhelming victory for La Verne and a sign that his popularity was hardly diminished despite his evil deeds of the past.[57]

Nevertheless, news of the king's conversion had filtered back to the Burgundian capital by late July. To be sure, there were some in the city who shared the opinion of Mayenne and the Sixteen in Paris that the king's conversion was nothing but hypocrisy, according to Gabriel Breunot, a judge in the Leaguer Parlement there.[58] But the city council and La Verne were hearing more and more reports that many in the city were prepared to accept the conversion of their new king and recognize him as legitimate. In fact, just one day after Henry IV announced his abjuration and re-conversion to the Catholic faith, one of the friars of the order of the Cordeliers had actually shouted "*Vive le roi!*" while preaching from the pulpit of his collegial church, causing quite a scandal. Indeed, over the next two years the Cordeliers would be among the Catholic clergy's most vocal critics of the League.[59] The council were alarmed to hear in early August "that there were several inhabitants of this city who said publicly and loudly that the King of Navarre had gone to mass, and that he is the king and no one else should be recognized as such."[60] At the end of the month they decided to banish a beggar named Jacques Gratepin from the city for claiming "that the King of Navarre was King [of France], and that he hoped for none other."[61] At the same time a royalist army led by Charles de Gontaut, Duke of Biron and Henry IV's marshal of France, had occupied 20 different villages in Burgundy by November, leading Fleutelot and the city council to write to Mayenne in alarm begging for troops to protect the city of Dijon from a royalist takeover.[62]

[57] AMD, B 231, fols. 1r–37r, June 21, 1593, for the votes cast in this election.
[58] Garnier, ed., *Journal de Gabriel Breunot*, 1: 359 and 364.
[59] Gregory Bereiter, "'Ils ne tendent pas à la defense de la Ligue': Discerner la opposition ecclésiastique de la Sainte Union," in Sylvie Daubresse and Bertrand Haan, eds., *La Ligue et ses frontiers: Engagements catholiques à distance du radicalisme à la fin des guerres de Religion* (Rennes: Presses Universitaires de Rennes, 2016), 169.
[60] AMD, B 231, fol. 70r, August 9, 1593.   [61] AMD, B 231, fol.82r-v, August 31, 1593.
[62] AMD, B 231, fol.103r, November 9, 1593.

Most alarmed of all were the city's vignerons, who had experienced significant attacks from brigands on both sides ever since the harvest of 1589.[63] They often needed special troops to protect them whenever they journeyed outside the city walls to tend their vines, and they also found that troops from both sides had often ravaged their vines. The wars of the League were certainly beginning to wear on the vignerons, and many of them were clearly disposed to accept Henry IV as their king now that he was a Catholic.[64] Moreover, the economic distress suffered by those who worked on the land had become especially difficult in the 1590s. This point will be addressed much more explicitly in the next section, but everywhere in the Burgundian countryside small property owners were being forced into share-cropping due to a series of poor harvests. As Pierre de Saint-Jacob has noted, "the greatest economic mutation in this century was from being a property owner no longer and becoming a renter, barn-dweller, share-cropper, or mercenary."[65] And the constant movement of troops across the countryside since 1589 only further exacerbated this distress. By 1594 Gabriel Breunot related that royalist troops had sought the support of the local vignerons by protecting them when they journeyed to and from their vines. In March and again in early May 1594 these vignerons could even be heard shouting "Long live the king! (*Vive le roi!*)" as they were escorted to and from their vines outside the city walls.[66] As Henri Drouot has noted, this was not a cry of revolt against the League so much as a cry of hope that the war would soon end.[67] Because the vignerons' economic distress had become so acute by the 1590s just as the wars of the League were coming to a climax, it is worth examining the Burgundian economy more closely to show how severely their material lives had been affected. And before examining the disruptions in the Burgundian economy at the end of the Wars of Religion, let us look at how the economy was supposed to work.

5.2   Justice in the Vines and the Moral Economy

At six o'clock in the morning every year in late summer sometime between early August and early September the mayor and city councilors of Dijon gathered in front of the portal of the parish church of St. Philibert

---

[63] AMD, B 227, fols. 105, 143, and 301, September 5–25, 1589; also see Henri Drouot, "Vin, vignes et vignerons de la côte dijonnaise pendant la Ligue," *Revue de Bourgogne* 1 (1911): 343–361, especially 348.

[64] Drouot, "Vin, vignes et vignerons," 351–360.

[65] Pierre de Saint-Jacob, "Mutations économiques et sociales dans les campagnes bourguinonnes à la fin du XVIe siècle," *Études rurales* 1 (1961): 35–49, quote on 47.

[66] AMD, B 231, fol. 144r-v, March 8, 1594; and Garnier, ed., *Journal de Gabriel Breunot*, 2: 111–112.

[67] Drouot, "Vin, vignes et vignerons," 360.

accompanied by the *juré* vignerons of the city. A trumpet would sound and then the *bans de vendange* – the dates when the annual grape harvest could commence – were solemnly announced to the assembled crowd by the mayor. Administering justice involved supervising the vignerons' visits to the vines in late summer to determine the ripeness of the vines, announcing the banns, appointing monitors called *vigniers* to guard the vines and watch for anyone trying to pick grapes before the specified date for harvesting to begin, as well as punishing those transgressors who were caught picking grapes before the specified date. To use the language of the *échevins* themselves, this part of their job was "carrying out justice (*exercice de justice*)" in the vineyards.[68] Punishment could take several forms: public shaming and humiliation, beating, or more commonly a steep fine, or some combination of these. One of the most extreme was a fine of 90 *livres*, an enormous sum, levied in 1538 against a monk from the priory of Larrey, who was fined for harvesting grapes from a vineyard before the banns allowed, and more seriously for using a soldier to threaten one of the *vigniers* guarding the vines.[69] It was much more common to fine an offender who was caught trying to pick grapes before the banns allowed it 100 *sous*, that is, 5 *livres* at the beginning of the sixteenth century, though this fine had escalated to 3 *écus* and 20 *sous*, or 10 *livres* by the end of the century.[70] In exceptional cases, the fine could jump to 10 écus, or 30 *livres*.[71]

Thus, justice in the vines was understood as essential for the well-being of the entire community. And this idea also bled over into another of the *échevins'* essential duties: to police the local economy. Indeed, the idea of "the general interest of everyone" underlay a more general perception of the premodern economy that was at the same time a fiction and a cherished ideal: the concept of a moral economy. Thanks to Edward Thompson, this idea has been more usually associated with eighteenth-century England than sixteenth-century France, but it can be applied to nearly all premodern economies. In its essence, men and women of all socioeconomic levels, but especially those of the popular classes, believed in and generally expected a moral economy to operate, in which the state guaranteed a

---

[68] AMD, B 236, fol. 273v-274r, September 11, 1599.   [69] ADCO, B II 360/32, August 31, 1538.
[70] AMD, I 148 (*liasse*), "Reglemens pour les vendanges," undated but clearly around 1520 for the fine of 5 *livres*, and AMD B 230, fol. 124v, September 22, 1592 for the fine of 10 *livres*. Just a few from among dozens of other examples that could be cited include AMD, B 165, fols.65–67r, September 1480; B 167, fols. 138r-v, September 12, 1498; B 168, fols. 14v-15r, August 1, 1500; and B 185, fols. 69v-71v, August 10, 1547.
[71] AMD, B 221, fol. 62r, September 2, 1583.

minimum level of subsistence for everyone, and where everyone could enjoy "traditional rights or customs" within this economic system.[72] To be sure, Thompson exaggerated the extent to which the authorities were "prisoners of the people," and his vision of the moral economy received extensive criticism from a variety of quarters when it was first published.[73] More recently, scholars have shown that in premodern economies both moral and market forces were equally strong and worked more interdependently rather than as opposing forces of feudalism and capitalism, respectively. Moreover, this recent scholarship has made it very clear that above all, the premodern economy in France was very heavily dependent on debt, as both investors and borrowers relied on debt to maintain their socioeconomic standing.[74] As we saw in Chapter 3, elite investors and vignerons alike relied on *rentes* for their financial security.

Nevertheless, the idea of a moral economy or a social contract was an operating principle and at least a theoretical goal, even if it rarely actually operated in practice as the theory might suggest. Moreover, the idea of a moral economy resonated acutely in the annual banns announced for the grape harvest in sixteenth-century Burgundy. Clearly the *échevins* were acting in a paternalistic manner to try to maintain the highest quality and quantity with every grape harvest, which translated into a higher standard of living for those who owned the vines and sold the wine. It benefitted the vignerons who worked in the vineyards and who made the wine only indirectly and less significantly. As for the consumers of wine, the moral economy of the wine harvest only benefitted them when the harvest yield was abundant – meaning more wine available at lower prices. In poor harvest years, however, when wine was scarce and prices were high, there was not a lot that the paternalist authorities could do but try to prevent hoarding by the wealthy and, if possible, import wine from elsewhere into the city. They threatened hoarders with fines, but this only worked very incompletely. Thus, a poor grape harvest, whether due to the weather or because of civil war, badly exposed the fiction of the moral economy. It was a wonderful concept in times of plenty, as the paternalism of the state

[72] E. P. Thompson, "The Moral Economy of the English Crowd in the Eighteenth Century," *Past & Present* 50 (1971): 76–136, especially 78–79.

[73] For a good summary of these critiques as well as Thompson's extensive responses to them, see "The Moral Economy Reviewed," in E. P. Thompson, ed., *Customs in Common* (London: Penguin Books, 1993), 259–351.

[74] See, for example, Laurence Fontaine, *The Moral Economy: Poverty, Credit, and Trust in Early Modern Europe* (Cambridge: Cambridge University Press, 2014); and Jeff Horn, *Economic Development in Early Modern France: The Privilege of Liberty, 1650–1820* (Cambridge: Cambridge University Press, 2015).

and the rights and customs of the people could coexist within an eco-nomic system that claimed to protect both. But if poor weather or marauding troops threatened even a single grape harvest, that stability was shattered until the next year's harvest might possibly make up for it. When endemic civil war and a series of poor grape harvests over several years arrived together, as was the case in Burgundy in the 1590s during the height of the war between the Leaguers and royalists, the fiction of the moral economy was brutally exposed. A close look at price series for wine as well as basic cereal grains and other foodstuffs makes this very clear.

5.3   Inflation and Economic Disruption in the 1590s

When considering wholesale prices in Dijon during the religious wars, it is important to understand that long-term inflation had produced rising prices of all goods throughout Western Europe in the sixteenth century. This inflation was especially acute for agricultural prices, so much so, in fact, that economic historians coined the term "price revolution" to describe it.[75] Its causes were complex. First, there was the arrival in Europe of a great deal of silver from the mines of the Spanish Empire in the New World, which flooded the European economy with more money. Second, European governments periodically debased their coinage by putting in less precious metal, thereby devaluing the coins that they minted. And third, the booming population growth Western Europe experienced in the sixteenth century, finally making up for the demo-graphic losses suffered two hundred years earlier as a result of the Black Death, far outstripped food production, with the inevitable result that food prices soared. Thus, the regular and steady rise of food prices from about 1520 to 1600 occurred independently from the harvest fluctuations and weather-related causes of normal price rises. And as already seen in Chapter 3, wages remained relatively stagnant, or over the longer term rose not nearly fast enough to keep pace with the inflation of prices throughout the sixteenth century. The result was a massive rise in the cost of living that was

---

[75] The classic statement is Earl J. Hamilton, *American Treasure and the Price Revolution in Spain* (Cambridge, MA: Harvard University Press, 1934). Also see Emmanuel Le Roy Ladurie and Michel Morineau, eds., *Histoire économique et sociale de la France, vol. 1: De 1450 à 1660* (Paris: Presses universitaires de la France, 1977), 941–978; Harry A. Miskimin, *The Economy of Later Renaissance Europe, 1460–1600* (Cambridge: Cambridge University Press, 1977), 23–52; and Frank C. Spooner, *The International Economy and Monetary Movements in France, 1493–1725* (Cambridge, MA: Harvard University Press, 1972).

detrimental to all but the very wealthy.[76] The nominal prices of cereal grains as well as wines more than doubled or even tripled from the start of the Wars of Religion in the early 1560s to the last civil war in the 1590s. This was true all over France, from the rural north of the kingdom to the region around the capital of Paris, all the way to the southernmost past of the kingdom in cities like Lyon and Toulouse as well as the rural hinterland of Languedoc.[77]

A number of contemporaries sought to explain this systemic inflation in France during the Wars of Religion, including Jacques Colas, Jehan Cherruyl de Malestroit, and Jean Bodin. All of them pointed to a massive influx of foreign coins – specifically Spanish silver coins, as a principal culprit – which appeared to be driving out French gold coins such as the *écu de soleil*. And the inflation was even greater in the money of account – the *livres* and *sous* that were used in the everyday accounting of money – than in the actual coins like the *écu* and the *franc*, a silver coin with the nominal value of a *livre*. As Jean Bodin explained, in order to return to price stability, the monarchy had to control the influx of foreign coinage, had to stabilize the ratio of values of silver and gold coins, and had to better control the costs and supply of minting them. Only the last two of these were realistically controllable, so the inflation continued, despite the reforms of 1577 undertaken by Henry III, which, among other things, temporarily fixed the value of the *écu de soleil* at three *livres tournois*.[78] Thus, the prices of foodstuffs and other staples in Dijon during the French religious wars were affected by more than just annual harvest fluctuations, as most of Western Europe experienced demographic growth as well as significant price inflation in the second half of the sixteenth century, when wages for most could not keep up with the rising prices.

[76] E. H. Phelps-Brown and Sheila Hopkins, "Wage Rates and Prices: Evidence for Price Pressure in the Sixteenth Century," *Economica* 24 (1957): 289–306; and Fernand Braudel and Franck C. Spooner, "Prices in Europe from 1450 to 1750," in E. E. Rich and Charles H. Wilson, eds., *The Cambridge Economic History of Europe*, vol. 4 (Cambridge: Cambridge University Press, 1967), 470–475.

[77] For northern France, see Pierre Goubert, *Beauvais et le Beauvasis de 1600 à 1730: Contribution de l'histoire sociale de la France du XVIIᵉ siècle* (Paris and The Hague: Mouton, 1966), 1: 364–461, which has a lot to say about sixteenth-century prices and wages despite the dates in the title. For the capital of Paris and the rural region around it, see Micheline Baulant and Jean Meuvret, eds., *Prix des céréales extraits de la Mercuriuale de Paris, 1520–1698*, 2 vols. (Paris: S.E.V.P.E.N., 1960), 1: 241–246; and Jean Jacquart, *La crise rurale en Île-de-France, 1550–1670* (Paris: Armand Colin, 1974), 761–778. For the city of Lyon, see Richard Gascon, *Grand commerce et vie urbaine au XVIᵉ siècle: Lyon et ses marchands*, 2 vols. (Paris: S.E.V.P.E.N., 1971), 2: 538–590. For the city of Toulouse, see Georges and Geneviève Frêche, eds., *Les prix des grains, des vins et des légumes à Toulouse, 1486–1868* (Paris: Presses universitaires de France, 1967). And for rural Languedoc, see Emmanuel Le Roy Ladurie, *Les paysans de Languedoc*, 2 vols. (Paris and The Hague, 1966), 1: 187–259.

[78] All of this is admirably summarized in Jotham Parsons, *Making Money in Sixteenth-Century France: Currency, Culture, and the State* (Ithaca, NY: Cornell University Press, 2016), 104–152.

Starting in 1568 the city council of Dijon recorded in its deliberations the prices of basic foodstuffs and wine sold at the *étape*, or local wholesale market, every autumn. The prices were recorded at the first market after St. Martin's Day, November 11, though the prices often did not get transcribed into the council's official deliberations until later. Titled "*Taux des gros fruits* (Prices of principal foodstuffs)," the *échevins* listed the wholesale prices for cereal grains (best wheat, good wheat, rye, barley, and oats), for different grades of wine (from Dijon's own vineyards including the extramural villages of Talant, Chenove, and Fontaine, as well as vineyards from villages farther south toward Nuits that the city administered), for dried legumes (broad-beans, peas, chickpeas, and lentils), seeds and oils (hempseed and rapeseed, as well as hempseed oil, rapeseed oil, and walnut oil), and tallow wax made from raw animal fat such as suet, used for making candles and soap.[79] The city council only started recording these prices systematically in 1568, so it is impossible to compare Dijon prices with those in other parts of France with surviving price records from earlier periods. Nevertheless, it is clear that there were significant fluctuations in the markets of all foodstuffs in the Burgundian capital.

Figures 5.1, 5.2, 5.3, and 5.4 demonstrate strikingly that in certain crisis years, the prices of wine and all foodstuffs skyrocketed significantly. The harvest years of 1572–1573, 1585–1587, 1592, and 1595–1596 were especially bad years for all foodstuffs as well as wine. For cereal grains a similar pattern of prices existed in both abundant harvest years and crisis years. The best quality of wheat was always the highest priced, followed by a lesser but still good quality wheat, followed by a mixture of wheat and rye, followed by rye, and then barley, with oats being the very cheapest of the cereal grains. The price hierarchy of these grains did not change at all even in the severest

---

[79] The "*Taux des gros fruits*" appears in the deliberations of the Hôtel- de Ville every year from 1568, usually in November or early December following the first market after the feast day of St. Martin, November 11, though occasionally the clerk forgot to record them in the deliberations until January or even February of the following year (such as the prices for 1570, 1571, 1587, 1589, 1590, and 1592). The data from Figures 5.1, 5.2, 5.3, and 5.4 were taken from AMD, B 205 (for the year 1568) and every register thereafter through B 233 (for the year 1595). Although the figures were recorded in various monetary units including money of account (*livres tournois*, *sous*, and *deniers*) as well as actual coins (*écus, francs, gros*, and *blancs*), I have translated all prices into *sous* for easier comparison. The various values of all currency units are given on p. xvi. One further complication is that measures for dry goods such as grain and legumes were normally given in a *quarteranche* or a *boisseau*. In much of France these were different quantities, with the *quarteranche* (sometimes spelled *cartranche*) about one-quarter larger than the boisseau. In Dijon, however, though cereal grains were always measured by the *quarteranche*, many dry goods such as legumes were as likely to be expressed in a *quarterache* in one year and in a *boisseau* in the next without any price fluctuation, suggesting that the two were often indistinguishable to contemporaries. Thus, I have treated them as the same in the figures given here.

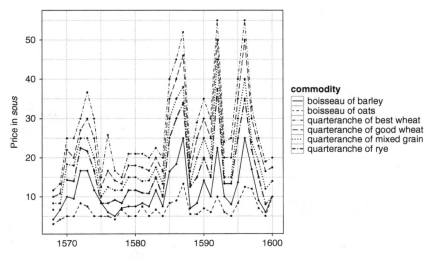

Figure 5.1 Wholesale Dijon grain prices, 1568–1600

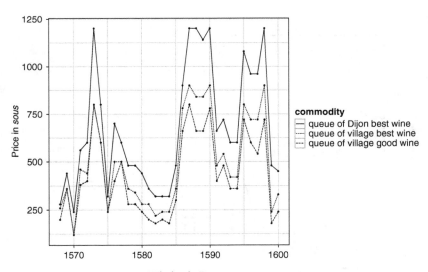

Figure 5.2 Wholesale Dijon wine prices, 1568–1600

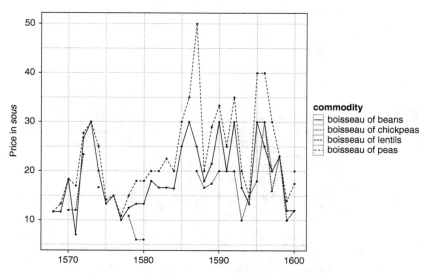

Figure 5.3 Wholesale Dijon legume prices, 1568–1600

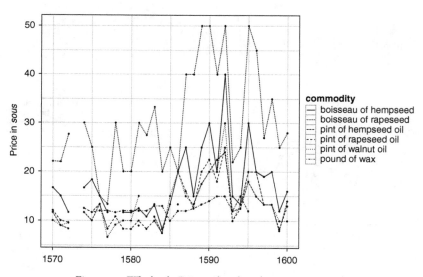

Figure 5.4 Wholesale Dijon oil and seed prices, 1570–1600

crisis years, as Figure 5.1 makes very clear. Wheat and rye prices were always significantly higher than barley and oats, because it was used to make the best bread. And the most sought-after bread of all was the all wheat *pain blanc* (white bread). The darker wholegrain *pain bis*, though more nutritious, was less popular for a variety of reasons, while bread made from a mixture of wheat and rye was less popular still. Rye bread, while popular in Germany, was seen only as a last resort in much of France, while bread made from barley or oats was so unpopular that bakers rarely even tried selling it. In sixteenth-century Dijon, everyone, including even the poor, preferred to eat the very best white bread if it was available. But it was inevitable that price fluctuations in the wholesale market for wheat would lead to fluctuations in the price of the 16 ounce loaf of *pain blanc* that everyone wanted to buy.

The 1580s serves as a good example during the Wars of Religion. Bread prices were relatively stable in the early 1580s, with a 16 oz. loaf of white bread costing between 6 and 8 *deniers*. But with the wholesale price of wheat more than doubling in 1585, 1586, and 1587, retail prices shot up considerably, as Table 5.1 shows. In fact, the retail price of a 16 oz. loaf of white bread more than tripled between October 1585 and July 1586, and these prices remained high for more than two years, not returning to the earlier levels until late 1588. But as hard as these fluctuations were on Dijon's consumers, they were equally hard on Dijon's bakers, who claimed regularly that they could not earn enough money to continue baking bread at the prices controlled by the city council, and they regularly demanded that the *échevins* raise the retail price of a 16 oz. loaf. Thus, periods of crisis were always marked by bakers being fined for selling underweight bread. In November 1585, for example, 13 different bakers were fined 30 *sous* for selling a loaf underweight by 3 ounces or less, 65 *sous* for selling a loaf underweight by more than 3 ounces, and 100 *sous* for selling a loaf of best quality white bread that had rye mixed in.[80] Indeed, some bakers in Dijon had already gone on strike and refused to bake any bread until the city council raised the prices. Some of these, such as Philibert Narvet, were imprisoned for refusing to bake and sell bread, which he claimed he was forced to do because he was losing money.[81] And if there was a genuine shortage of bread, bakers were fined even more harshly, such as Didier Lache, who was fined the sum of 20 *livres tournois*, or 400 *sous*, in July 1586 for selling a 16 ounce loaf of white bread that was 4 ounces underweight, more than six times the fine levied for the same offense a year earlier.[82]

[80] AMD, B 223, fol. 105v-106, November 27, 1585.   [81] AMD, B 223, fol. 86, October 31, 1585.
[82] AMD, B 224, fol. 60v, July 29, 1586.

Table 5.1 *Retail bread prices in Dijon for a best quality 16 ounce loaf of white bread (all prices in* deniers*)*

Date	Price	Source
24 March 1583	8 d.	AMD, B 220, fol. 106
30 August 1583	10 d.	AMD, B 221, fol. 61v
10 July 1584	9 d.	AMD, B 222, fol. 34
26 July 1584	8 d.	AMD, B 222, fol. 42v
19 February 1585	9 d.	AMD, B 223, fol. 105v
22 October 1585	8 d.	AMD, B 223, fol. 80
4 March 1586	18 d.	AMD, B 223, fol. 160
1 June 1586	26 d.	AMD, B 223, fol.201v
1 July 1586	24 d.	AMD, B 224, fol. 50v
14 August 1586	18 d.	AMD, B 224, fol. 74
30 June 1587	26 d.	AMD, B 225, fol. 26
11 August 1587	22 d.	AMD, B 225, fol. 70
17 September 1587	23 d.	AMD, B 225, fol. 93
16 October 1587	22 d.	AMD, B 225, fol. 120v
22 October 1587	21 d.	AMD, B 225, fol. 124v
22 March 1588	18 d.	AMD, B 225, fol. 197
1 April 1588	16 d.	AMD, B 225, fol. 199v
29 April 1588	10 d.	AMD, B 225, fol. 210
31 October 1588	8 d.	AMD, B 226, fol. 100v
7 February 1589	7 d.	AMD, B 226, fol. 157v

By October of that year, the shortage was so severe that the city council threatened "exemplary punishment (*punition exemplaire*)" for any baker who went on strike and refused to sell his normal quota of bread.[83] By the first of the new year, grain and wine shortages were so severe that the lieutenant-general of the province of Burgundy – Léonor Chabot, count of Charny – ordered the mayor and city council to conduct a door to door search of every house in Dijon "without any exception (*sans en exception aucune*)" to look for hoarders as well as to establish an inventory of all grain and wine stored inside the city walls.[84] And when the Duke of Mayenne informed the city in September of that year that the city's bakers would need to provide 2,000 loaves of bread to a company of Swiss soldiers serving in the king's army in the vicinity, it was clear that meeting the needs of Dijon's inhabitants was not always the highest priority.[85] Thus, the moral economy could not keep up the state's end of the social contract

[83] AMD, B 224, fol. 123v, October 17, 1586.   [84] AMD, B 224, fol.186, January 23, 1587.
[85] AMD, B 225, fols. 89–91v, 9 and September 15, 1587.

with consumers in times of extreme scarcity, and the situation was exacerbated by civil war.

A brief look at wages in the period of the civil wars shows a slight increase over time for some, but when prices fluctuated as much as this – monthly and even weekly – distress was inevitable. The most complete account of wages in the period are the records of the Carthusian monastery just outside the city walls, where the former Dukes of Burgundy were buried. The monks there hired a number of Dijon's artisans and other workers throughout the sixteenth and seventeenth centuries to perform various construction jobs, and their records show that in some trades wages did not increase at all, especially for journeyman artisans. For example, the monks paid journeyman carpenters a nominal daily wage of 3 s.4 d. from 1561 to 1610, journeyman plasterers earned 3 s. during the same period, journeyman masons 2 s.6 d., coppersmiths and chandlers 5 s., and tailors earned 4 s.6 d.[86] The wages of some master artisans did rise slightly between 1561 and 1610, but the sharp price rises in years such as 1586 and 1587 meant that wages could never keep up. For nearly all journeyman artisans, however, as well as for vignerons, whose wages we examined in Chapter 3, times were very tough in periods of war and poor harvests. James Farr is surely correct to note that in crisis years in Burgundy, even after giving up nonessentials such as meat and vegetables and after sending their children out as servants, "many wage-earning families clearly had a tough time making ends meet."[87] Once again, the moral economy was an economic system that justified complete state control of prices and wages in order to prevent starvation and food shortages suffered by the masses. But it worked only imperfectly at the best of times; and in the worst of times, such as the late 1580s and mid-1590s, its shortcomings were exposed most completely. Nevertheless, especially during these periods of extreme shortages, this imagined economy continued to function as a means of underscoring the duties and responsibilities of a paternalist state as well as the dependence and loyalties the people owed to that state. But if the state ever failed completely to provide for the basic needs of the people, or was perceived to have done so, then those loyalties could easily become more tenuous.

[86] See the excellent analysis of artisan wages and their buying power in Dijon by James R. Farr, *Hands of Honor: Artisans and Their World in Dijon, 1550–1650* (Ithaca, NY: Cornell University Press, 1988), 105–113. Farr's analysis is based on the actual wage figures from the Carthusian monastery in Dijon as published in Cyprian Monget, *La Chartreuse de Dijon d'après les documents des archives de Bourgogne*, 3 vols. (Montreuil-sur-Mer and Tournai: Imprimerie Notre-Dame des Près, 1898–1905), 418–419.

[87] Farr, *Hands of Honor*, 111.

5.4   Anatomy of Urban Life: Rue Vannerie

If we return to Rue Vannerie in the parish of St. Michel that we examined so closely in Chapter 3, we can gain an even closer look at how the material lives of Dijon's inhabitants fluctuated during the civil wars. One of the most noticeable changes is the significant escalation in the amount of taxes paid by Dijon's inhabitants as a result of the ongoing warfare, and Tables 5.2 and 5.3 demonstrate this escalation very clearly. Before the Wars of Religion broke out in 1562, most inhabitants of the Burgundian capital paid a mean tax of around 10 *sous*. The wealthiest inhabitants paid much more than this, of course, up to 40 *sous* in 1523 and up to 60 *sous* in 1552. But the mean tax amount for most inhabitants averaged around 10 *sous*, this at a time when the daily wage of a vigneron working as a day-laborer was 30–50 d. per day, the equivalent of between 3 and 4 *sous*.[88] Vignerons who lived on Rue Vannerie paid slightly less than that, but nevertheless, during the first half of the sixteenth century it would take a vigneron two days of labor in order to fulfill his fiscal duty to the state. Once the civil wars broke out in 1562, however, these amounts escalated sharply. In the 1570s, 1580s, and 1590s when the mean tax for vignerons on Rue Vannerie rose by more than five times the earlier levels in peak years such as 1589, a vigneron on a daily wage could have to work up to ten days just to pay his tax assessment. With wages rising only marginally or not at all in most years in the intervening period, paying taxes became a much harder proposition during the civil wars.

One noticeable change in the tax system was the new tax called the *taillon* introduced by King Henry II in 1549. Meaning "little *taille*," the *taillon* was intended to be an occasional supplement to the more common *taille*, or property tax, that French taxpayers were accustomed to paying. Created by royal ordinance, the *taillon* was designed to spare French towns and villages from the hardship of the forced billeting of soldiers on them. In other words, it was a tax to provide for military expenses of the royal army with as little material affliction as possible for the king's subjects.[89] But military expenses skyrocketed during the civil wars, and instead of an occasional supplement to the *taille*, the *taillon* became a permanent part of it with a dramatic increase in assessments for Dijon's inhabitants. The *taillon*

---

[88] These figures come from Claude Tournier, "Notes sur la culture de la vigne et les vignerons à Dijon," *Annales de Bourgogne* 24 (1952), 159.

[89] The ordinance was issued on November 12, 1549. See F. A. Isambert, et al., eds., *Recueil général des anciennes lois françaises, depuis l'an 420 jusqu'à la Révolution*, 29 vols. (Paris: Balin-Leprieur, 1821–1833), 13: 119–133.

was raised in stages throughout the civil wars, and Dijon's tax roles show that it did not begin to decrease until after peace was made with Henry IV in 1595. Moreover, it did not disappear once the wars had ended either, remaining a permanent part of the French tax system during the Old Regime. To be sure, the crown had always collected taxes for military expenses before the intro-duction of the *taillon* in 1549, as Dijon's tax rolls make very clear. But the *taillon* essentially replaced the *taille* as the primary tax on Burgundians during the civil wars, with ever-increasing amounts to be levied.[90]

Another change suggested by Tables 5.2 and 5.3 is the slow decline in the number of vigneron households within the parish as well as on Rue Vannerie over the course of the second half of the sixteenth century. The overall number of households headed by vignerons residing in the parish of St. Michel declined from 180 in 1523 – out of 480 total households, or 36.8 percent – to just 93 in 1599 – out of 544, or 17.1 percent. And the decline of vignerons living on Rue Vannerie was even more pronounced: from 38 out of 82, or 46.3 percent in 1523, to 21 out of 137, or 15.3 percent in 1599. This slow decline in numbers mirrored the reduction in the overall number of vignerons residing in the city of Dijon. As noted in Chapter 1, vignerons made up more than one-fourth of the total number of households in Dijon in 1500.[91] By mid-century, vignerons made up only 18.7 percent of the total number of households in the city: 541 out of 2,888 in the year 1553.[92] When the religious wars finally ended at the end of the sixteenth century, those numbers had declined even further. By 1599 there were only 478 house-holds headed by vignerons in the city out of 2,949, or 16.2 percent.[93] Much of this decline in numbers was due to the disruption of the civil wars, as the city as a whole actually increased in numbers throughout the sixteenth century. But even at the end of the century, vignerons still made up the single largest occupational cohort in the city.

The tax rolls of the city also reveal other less evident aspects of urban life. If we concentrate on just the wealthiest residents of Rue Vannerie who paid taxes, for example, the decline of vignerons over the second half of the sixteenth century has another dimension. As Table 5.4 shows, of the twelve wealthiest tax-payers on Rue Vannerie – and this does not include noble families such as the Tavanes, who were exempt from paying taxes – vignerons made up eight of twelve in 1552. By the end of the century,

---

[90] For more on the *taillon* and its effects, see Martin Wolfe, *The Fiscal System of Renaissance France* (New Haven, CT: Yale Univeristy Press, 1972), 305, and Jean-Jules Clamageran, *Histoire de l'impôt en France*, 3 vols. (Paris: Librairie de Guillaumin, 1867–1876), 2: 188.
[91] AMD, L 163.   [92] AMD, L 192–193.   [93] AMD, L 210.

Table 5.2 *Tax assessments in the parish of St. Michel, Dijon: 1523, 1552, 1576, and 1599 (all tax values are given in sous tournois)*

Year	Total Households	Mean Tax	Vigneron Households	Vigneron Mean Tax	Rue Vannerie Households	Vannerie Mean Tax	Vannerie Vignerons	Van. Vign. Mean Tax
1523	489	10.26	180	7.24	82	9.34	38	7.34
1552	614	9.48	164	7.78	90	7.37	34	7.85
1576	636	55.96	175	29.35	116	30.67	39	22.31
1599	544	56.45	93	39.25	137	45.69	21	34.77

Source: AMD, L 164, fols. 20–212 (1523); L 189, fols. 68–104 (1552); L 204, fols. 140–175 (1576); and L 210, fols. 270–289 (1599).

Table 5.3   *Tax assessments for Rue Vannerie (includes Rue Roulotte; all tax values are given in* sous tournois*)*

Year	Households	Mean Tax	Vignerons	Vigneron Mean Tax
1576	116	30.67	39	22.31
1582	134	30.99	44	25.98
1584	101	49.71	33	33.48
1589	126	64.28	33	56.97
1599	137	45.69	21	34.77

Source: AMD, L 204, fols. 140–175 (1576); L 206, fols. 197–203 (1582); L 207, fols. 204–209 (1584); L 209, fols. 118–122 (1589); and L 210, fols. 270–289 (1599).

Table 5.4   *Wealthiest households on Rue Vannerie ranked by tax assessment, 1552–1599*

1552

1. Michel Pechart, treasurer-general

2. Guillemin Bourrelier, clerk
3. Simon Heron, hotel keeper
4. Jean Malnourry, vigneron
5. Jean Daisey, vigneron

6. Jean Michelin, vigneron

7. Thibaut Nault, vigneron
8. Henri Beret, vigneron
9. Huguenin Maulard, vigneron
10. M. de Pilles (occupation not given)

11. Widow of Jacob Ragetier, vigneron
12. Vincent Navet, (vigneron)

1584

1. Jean Fleutelot, solicitor in Parlement

2. [Bénigne] Petit (king's solicitor in the bailiwick court)
3. Bernard Chasot, merchant

4. Jean Nault, vigneron (son of Vincent Nault)
5. (Jean) Pechart, treasurer-general

1576

1. Jean Fleutelot, solicitor in the Hôtel de Ville

2. Jacques Boyvault (occupation not given)
3. Bernard Chasot, merchant
4. Guillaume Choillot, *échevin* and lawyer
5. Vincent Nault, vigneron (son of Thibaut Nault)
6. Widow of Michel Pechart, treasurer-general
7. Claude Disier, vigneron
8. Claude Jomard, sergeant royal
9. Etienne Cothier, stationer
10. Widow of Barthélemy Gagne, judge in Parlement
11. Pierre Belin, joiner
12. Jean Arviset, solicitor in Parlement

1599

1. Guillaume Des Gans, (lawyer in the Parlement)
2. Guillaumette Morelet, (daughter of lawyer in Ch. Comptes)
3. Jean De Vaulx, lawyer (son of former judge in Parlement)
4. Nicolas Dubuisson, (lawyer in the bailiwick court)
5. Widow of Nicolas Fraude

Table 5.4 (*cont.*)

1584	1599
6. Benigne Turlot, vigneron	6. Guillaume Clerc, vigneron (son-in-law of Vincent Nault)
7. Claude Jomard, sergeant royal	7. Jean Brechillet (solicitor in the Parlement)
8. Nicolas de Houy, painter	8. Jean Nault, vigneron (son of Vincent Nault)
9. Pierre De Lisle, shoemaker	9. Philibert Carrey, sergeant royal
10. Jean Arviset, solicitor in Parlement	10. Claude Martin, (lawyer in Parlement)
11. Claude Disier, vigneron	11. Antoine Logerot, sergeant royal
12. Jean Piquelin, (vigneron)	12. Claude Channot (occupation not given)

Source: AMD, L 189 (1552), L 204 (1576), L 207 (1589), and L 210 (1599).

however, there were only two vignerons remaining among the twelve wealthiest taxpayers on Rue Vannerie: Jean Nault, son of Vincent Nault and descended from Thibault Nault, on the rolls in 1552 (see Chapter 3), and Guillaume Clerc, son-in-law of Vincent Nault. The Nault family was one of the most prosperous and well-connected vigneron families in the entire parish; when Jean Nault's son Nicolas was born in 1601, the god-father of the child was Nicolas Gagne, a lawyer in the Parlement whose father and uncle were also judges in the Parlement.[94] Nevertheless, the continued prosperity of the Nault family apart, during the Wars of Religion not only were vignerons declining in real numbers in the parish of St. Michel and in the city as a whole, but most were also declining in wealth relative to their neighbors. What stands out clearly is that men of the law and officers in the royal courts had come to dominate the wealthiest houses on Rue Vannerie by the end of the civil wars, marking a significant change from the domination of the vignerons in 1552.

Moreover, the wealthiest householders on Rue Vannerie were hardly a static group. To be sure, nobles such as the Tavanes and Le Compasseur families, who anchored either end of Rue Vannerie and who inhabited the largest and most sumptuous houses on the street, were constants in their townhouses at the north and southern ends of Rue Vannerie, respectively. But among those who were not exempt from taxes, the very wealthiest families changed frequently over the course of the civil wars. Only the

[94] AMD, B 495, fol. 131, October 31, 1601.

Table 5.5 *Votes cast from Rue Vannerie
in the mayoral election of 1592*

Jacques La Verne	18
Claude Moisson	11
Etienne Bernard	9
Others (4)	14

Source: AMD, B 230, fols. 20–21, June 20, 1592.

Nault family appears on all four lists of Table 5.4, and the Pechart family appeared on three of the four. And between 1576 and 1584 – only a span of eight years – seven of the twelve wealthiest families had changed during that interval; only the Nault, Chasot, Pechart, Jomard, and Arviset families were still among the twelve wealthiest families on the street eight years later. Thus, fluctuations of relative wealth were a common occurrence during this period and reflected the larger uncertainty and instability of economic fortunes during the civil wars.

And finally, before leaving Rue Vannerie it might be worth exploring how politically active residents of the street were within the parish. We saw in Chapter 3 that the residents of the parish of St. Michel, and the vignerons of this parish in particular, were among the most militant supporters of the Catholic mayor, Béngne Martin, in the mayoral elections of the early 1560s when a Protestant candidate was running for mayor. Most of the election rolls do not list those who gave their voices at municipal elections by street, only by parish. The rolls of the mayoral election on 1592, however, do list voters by street, and there were 52 heads of household on Rue Vannerie who voted in the mayoral election that year, as follows.

Jacques La Verne and Etienne Bernard were both residents of St. Michel parish. As discussed earlier in this chapter (see pp. 180–183), La Verne was first elected mayor in 1587 and was reelected in three out of the next four years. In the 1592 election, however, he was defeated by the client of the Duke of Mayenne, Etienne Bernard, in the largest voter turnout of the sixteenth century, with 1,984 heads of household participating in the citywide election.[95] La Verne remained the most popular

---

[95] Mack P. Holt, "Popular Political Culture and Mayoral Elections in Sixteenth-Century Dijon," in Holt, ed., *Society and Institutions in Early Modern France* (Athens, GA: University of Georgia Press, 1991), 103–104.

candidate among the voters on Rue Vannerie, however, and was even reelected in June 1593 before being removed, arrested, tried, and ultimately executed as a traitor shortly thereafter.

The inhabitants of the city of Dijon as well as most Burgundians outside the city suffered serious economic distress throughout the Wars of Religion, with outbreaks of plague and famine, and shortage of foodstuffs and wine common occurrences. The period of the wars of the League in the 1590s, however, was a time of truly exceptional hardship. It was an era of wide-ranging economic destitution throughout Western Europe, in fact, though the Wars of Religion in France exacerbated the distress for French men and women even further.[96] And in Burgundy in particular the encroachment of the province by invading troops in 1587 and again in 1595 was reflected in the spectacular price fluctuations of most cereal grains and principal foodstuffs discussed earlier in the chapter. We have also seen how by 1595 Dijon's vignerons helped persuade the city to rally behind a rapprochement with King Henry IV in order to bring the warfare and its accompanying economic disruptions to a halt. Thus, economic crisis was the backdrop to the wars of the League in the 1590s. Even if the strong ties between Dijon's elites and the vignerons forged earlier in the century remained intact, the real question was whether the new king Henry IV would be able to win over the loyalties of both after such a long period of civil war.

What is also clear as the Wars of Religion in Burgundy wound down in the 1590s is that politics, religion, and material culture remained as firmly enfolded together as they had been at the outset of the civil wars when Protestantism seemed such a serious threat to Catholics' salvation as well as to their wine harvests. Moreover, it was clear that their salvation still depended ultimately on "the true vine." When Guillaume Rouhier – a former mayor four times in the 1580s, a senior member of the League's Council of State in Burgundy, and a barrister in the Parlement of Dijon – was chosen to give a Lenten prayer in March 1593 in the Sainte Chapelle, he evoked this image in his prayer. Rouhier addressed his Latin prayer "to our Lord Jesus Christ, the Son of God: Christ, the father of the eternal word, the cherished vine, the

---

[96] See Philip Benedict, "Civil War and Natural Disaster in Northern France," and Mark Greengrass, "The Later Wars of Religion in the French Midi," both in Peter Clarke, ed., *The European Crisis of the 1590s* (London: George Allen and Unwin, 1985), 84–105 and 106–134.

savior of all mankind."[97] And just four months later in July the king publicly abjured his Calvinist faith and converted to Catholicism, thereby returning to the true vine of the Church. With this one public act, Henry IV brought about the beginning of the end of the Holy Catholic League.

[97] AMD, B 230, fols. 247v–250, quote on fol. 250.

CHAPTER 6

The Collapse of the League in Burgundy

By May 1594 Henry IV had driven the Spanish troops out of the capital of Paris and had been warmly welcomed by the city's inhabitants during Easter week. It certainly appeared that the popular support the League had enjoyed for so long was beginning to wane. On May 19 in Dijon the Jesuit preacher Father Christophe preached a sermon in the Saint-Chapelle excoriating all those who recognized Henry IV as their legitimate king as traitors. He singled out the city's vignerons in particular, whom he accused of being always drunk and willing to sell their votes in the annual elections for drink or for money. They confronted him afterwards and claimed "that they are worthy men, not wicked (*que ils sont gens de bien, non méchans*)." And the following Sunday Père Christophe repeated the same charges, after which a wife of one of the vignerons "said loudly that Père Christophe had lied about them, that the vignerons were worthy men (*gens de bien*)."[1] It was already becoming clear, however, that many vignerons and other inhabitants of Dijon were willing to consider making peace with the king in order to end the fighting that had been going on for more than five years. It was at this point that the confrontation between the Duke of Mayenne and Jacques La Verne finally came to a head.

In the annual election of Dijon's mayor and selection of its twenty *échevins* in June 1594, the Duke of Mayenne had used his remaining influence to elect one of his clients as mayor, a *procureur* named René Fleutelot, who had actually come second to La Verne the previous June. To be sure, Mayenne had backed Etienne Bernard, another *procureur* in the Parlement of Dijon, for mayor in previous years, but the duke came to see in June 1594 that a new candidate was required. The French church as well as the capital of Paris had already accepted the king's abjuration, and

---

[1] Joseph Garnier, ed., *Journal de Gabriel Breunot conseiller au Parlement de Dijon, précédé du livre de souvenance de Pepein, chanoine de la Sainte-Chapelle de cette ville*, 3 vols. (Dijon: J.-E. Rabutot, 1864), 2: 128 and 132.

with many local remnants of the League outside the capital still seriously considering the claims of the Spanish Infanta, Mayenne was increasingly distressed that the only choice left open to him was apparently either a Spanish-dominated monarchy or the acceptance of a newly converted Henry IV, neither of which he was inclined to choose. When his client Etienne Bernard opted to support Philip II's daughter at the Estates-General in Paris, however, Mayenne threw his support in the 1594 mayoral elections behind another of his clients, the more moderate René Fleutelot, who was duly elected mayor on June 21, 1594.[2] Fleutelot won handily with 1,190 votes out of 1,922 votes cast (61.9 percent), with La Verne getting 502 votes (26.1 percent), and a handful of other candidates receiving 230 votes (12.0 percent).[3] Just days after his defeat in the election of 1594, now out of office and not even retained as an *échevin* by Fleutelot, a personal slight for a former mayor of the city, Jacques La Verne sought to be admitted as a judge in the Leaguer Parlement of Dijon. But the former mayor was also rejected by the Parlement, with Nicolas de Montholon, one of the presiding judges, speaking out against seating La Verne in the court with "two or three words of great weight (*deux ou trois mots de grand poids*)." Normally, becoming a judge in the Parlement was only possible by purchasing the office from the crown or through inheritance, but as the League had still not formally accepted Henry IV as their king, the usual rules might be relaxed. But the court ultimately rejected La Verne's application for membership on other grounds, "as he had without even the appearance of a trial ordered the late Chantepinot to be strangled and hanged and then immediately buried by the executioner and his wife in a pit they had dug in the cemetery of the parish of St. Michel right next to the house of the said La Verne." Many others spoke out against La Verne, including a number of relatives of the late Chantepinot.[4]

Spurned by Mayenne, the new mayor, the new city council, and the Leaguer Parlement, La Verne approached the royalist Parlement in Semur with a plan to turn over the city of Dijon to royalist troops in Burgundy. The ardent Leaguer and former loyal client of Mayenne devised a plan that those still loyal to Mayenne saw as treachery. Drouot notes that many of the city's elites were involved, including many of the moderates who were now leaning toward making a deal with Henry IV. These included several

---

[2] Henri Drouot, *Mayenne et la Bourgogne: Étude sur la Ligue (1587–1596)*, 2 vols. (Dijon: Bernigaud et Privat, 1937), 2: 347–352.

[3] AMD, B 232, fols. 1r–38v, June 21, 1594. The figures here do not tally exactly with those given by Drouot, *Mayenne et la Bourgogne*, 2: 349, as Drouot has undercounted the votes.

[4] BMD, Fonds Saverot 1493, 457–459, quote on 457.

judges in the Parlement: Claude Bretagne; Jean Fyot the younger, not to be confused with his cousin Jean Fyot the elder, a member of the Leaguer Council of State; Pierre Quarré; and Jean Gagne. And according to Drouot, these judges were the organizers of the plot, not La Verne.[5] Even La Verne himself claimed that Fyot and Gagne had pushed him to contact the royalist Parlement.[6] The plot to turn over the city to the king was foiled, however, on August 21, 1594 before it could be carried out. The Council of State formally investigated and discovered that there were hundreds of people involved one way or another in what everyone was now calling "the La Verne affair." The Council of State split into two factions. A militant group who wanted revenge against La Verne and his conspirators was composed of Jean de Boyault, sieur de Franchesse, the captain of the Château, as well as three judges in the Parlement, Bernard des Barres, Guillaume Legouz, and Perpetuo Berbisey. These men were militants who were consistently opposed to any peace with Henry IV, and they were among Mayenne's most loyal clients. There was also a more moderate faction, who were less concerned with revenge against La Verne than in simply finding out what happened: former mayor Etienne Bernard, current mayor René Fleutelot, first presiding judge in the Parlement Denis Brûlart, judge in the Parlement Jean Fyot the elder, and Mayenne himself.[7] Ultimately, the Council condemned La Verne as well as Claude Gault, a captain of the city militia who was designated as the one to open the gates of the city to royalist troops, to be hanged. The other ringleaders were either imprisoned or managed to escape the city.[8] Jacques La Verne and Claude Gault were duly hanged on August 29, and those who had escaped were hanged in effigy alongside them. The widows of both La Verne and Gault were forbidden from holding any funerals for their husbands, either publicly in their parish church of St. Michel or privately, nor could the church ring any bells on their behalf. All of the coats-of-arms of La Verne that had been placed on city property during his five terms as mayor were to be effaced, and La Verne's son, Chrêtien La Verne, was even relieved of his office as captain of the parish of St. Michel.[9] Although the La Verne affair marked a final victory for Mayenne over his recalcitrant client, its real significance, as Henri Drouot has pointed out, was that "even in the heart

[5] Henri Drouot, *Un episode de la Ligue à Dijon: L'affaire La Verne (1594) et notes sur la Ligue en Bourgogne* (Dijon: La Revue bourguignonne, 1910), 37–41.
[6] AMD, B 232, fol. 91v, August 22, 1594.
[7] Drouot, *Un episode de la Ligue à Dijon: L'affaire La Verne*, 70–73.
[8] Ibid., 77–100; and AMD B232, fols. 107v–109v, September 22, 1594.
[9] AMD, B 232, fols. 130v–133v, November 3 and 4, 1594.

of Burgundy, the chief place of Mayenne's fief, the royalist party had become strong enough to dare to mount a coup [against the League]."[10] The League moderates as well as many of Dijon's inhabitants were ready to make peace.

Henry IV finally made direct overtures to the Hôtel de Ville in September 1594, appealing to the mayor and *échevins'* loyalty to the crown of France over any loyalty to Philip II of Spain, and Fleutelot and a majority of the chamber soon were leaning strongly toward reconciliation.[11] While Mayenne decided to hold off on making peace with the king until Henry had been formally absolved by the Pope, Fleutelot and his moderate allies in the Hôtel de Ville had no reservations about a formal submission to the king once the surrounding towns of Beaune, Autun, and Auxerre fell to the royal army in early Spring 1595. When the final submission came in late May, the Hôtel de Ville and the presidents of the Parlement in Dijon presented their terms to the king: Henry would recognize all their traditional liberties and privileges, the city could keep its Jesuit college, all those appointed by Mayenne could keep their offices, all back taxes owed to the crown since the death of Henry III would be extinguished, and the exclusive exercise of the Catholic religion throughout the jurisdiction of the Parlement of Dijon would be enforced.[12] Henry IV only agreed to the first and last of these, however. And though the city had surrendered to the king, the Château, still loyal to Mayenne, did not, with cannon fire onto the city killing some residents even after the arrival of Henry IV.

The king immediately requested that in return for guaranteeing all the city's privileges, liberties, and franchises, he wanted the mayor of Dijon, the moderate Leaguer, member of the Council of State, and client of Mayenne, René Fleutelot, to be reelected in the upcoming mayoral election scheduled for June 21, 1595.[13] This was hardly an imposition on the city, much less an attempt to bribe the loyalty of Fleutelot and the Hôtel de Ville, but a reward for a moderate Leaguer who had agreed to submit to the authority of the king and helped to negotiate the truce between the city and the crown. Moreover, the king did not interfere in the election itself, which proceeded in its traditional manner, with Fleutelot being reelected nearly unanimously as mayor, with 632 out of 634 votes cast.[14] The king only

---

[10] Drouot, *Un episode de la Ligue à Dijon: L'affaire La Verne*, 130.

[11] J. Berger de Xivrey and J. Guadet, eds., *Recueil des lettres missives de Henri IV*, 9 vols. (Paris: Imprimerie nationale, 1843–1856), 4: 213, Henry IV to Chambre de Ville of Dijon, September 15, 1594.

[12] AMD, B 232, fols. 67r–74v, May 24, 1595.   [13] AMD, B 232, fols. 295r–96v, June 16, 1595.

[14] AMD, B233, fols. 1r–10v, June 21, 1595.

imposed his will on the city in a couple of discrete but important ways. First, instead of the newly elected mayor choosing the twenty *échevins* to serve with him in the Hôtel de Ville for the coming year according to traditional custom, the king allowed Fleutelot to choose ten, and then he chose the remaining ten from a list of 61 names that Fleutelot had submitted to him. The king insisted that he was not interfering in the city's traditional privileges, and that this innovation was "for this one time only and without any consequence or prejudice for the ancient privileges of this city or its elections in the future."[15] The other royal imposition was that Henry personally selected the captains of the municipal militia (*milice bourgeoise*) from each parish, a selection traditionally made by the newly elected mayor and newly appointed *échevins*. Marshal Biron, the leader of the royal army and Henry's representative in Dijon, explained this to the mayor and *échevins*:

> Gentlemen, please believe that I do not desire anything so much as seeing you maintained in your franchises and privileges, and I would sooner see their augmentation than their reduction. Concerning the role of the captains [of the militia] and others of your city that have been chosen for you on the part of the King, this has been done as an example for the cities of Paris, Rouen, Troyes and all those other towns which were brought under his obedience, where His Majesty made changes that seemed good to him. This is no way derogates your privileges, as it is for one time only. His Majesty is going to Dijon and you will be able to speak to him about this, and he will tell you his wishes himself.[16]

What Henry was clearly doing was making sure that the security and obedience of the city was in the hands of men he could trust, almost entirely composed of those moderate Leaguers who had explicitly supported the recent settlement.

When Henry marched into Dijon on June 4, 1595, his actions as Gallican King of France were far more important and effective than any profession of faith in convincing his Burgundian subjects that his abjuration and conversion were both genuine and permanent. As in Paris the year before, when Henry entered the Burgundian capital, he publicly attended mass, kissed the cross, and swore an oath to maintain the Roman Catholic and apostolic religion. Again, how did his Catholic subjects react to these pious gestures of his new faith? According to the deliberations of the Hôtel de

---

[15] AMD, B 233, fol. 21r, June 21, 1595.
[16] Joseph Garnier, ed., *Correspondance de la mairie de Dijon extraite des archives de cette ville*, 3 vols. (Dijon: J.-E. Rabutot, 1868), 3: 2–3, Biron to the Chambre de ville of Dijon, July 10, 1595.

Ville, they received him very warmly and many tried to touch him as he rode past on horseback:

> There were many inhabitants in arms on both sides of the street, with their tambours sounding and crying in full voice: "Long live the King!" They approached him, embraced and kissed his leg ... And all the people were so overjoyed and happy to see His Majesty in order to embrace him that the streets were completely covered with people, and the windows were packed with others crying, "Long live the King!" So many men, women and children felt truly happy that they could get close enough to His Majesty to embrace him and kiss his leg.[17]

These over the top popular reactions to Henry were also recorded by other witnesses, including the *parlementaire* Gabriel Breunot, whose journal corroborates the account of the Hôtel de Ville.[18] Henry rounded off a very full day of celebration by traveling out to the Charterhouse of Champmol after dinner. This chapel and mausoleum was constructed by Duke Philippe le Hardi in the 1390s as a Burgundian mausoleum like St. Denis was for French kings, and it contained the remains of the four Valois dukes of Burgundy in the intricately carved tombs of Claus Sluter. There the king prayed for more than half an hour, paying homage to these Burgundian heroes as well as to his new religion.[19] Henry was also paying homage to the province's past as well as to the *foy de Bourgogne* represented by the Valois dukes of Burgundy. Thus, Henry's public actions as well as his professions of faith were clearly designed to convince his Catholic subjects in Dijon of the sincerity of his religious transformation.

But the king's explicit and public practice of his new religion in Dijon was hardly over. The city was unable to hold its traditional Corpus Christi Day procession two weeks earlier on May 25, because the royal army of Marshal Biron had surrounded the city and was close to breaching its walls. All public attention that day was focused on the intense negotiations going on between Biron and the city's elites, and a public assembly was even called to read aloud the latest terms of negotiation.[20] The king took advantage of the situation, however, and to make up for the missed Corpus Christi Day festivities, he ordered that a special religious procession with the consecrated Host take place

---

[17] AMD, B 232, fols. 283r–84v, June 4, 1595.
[18] BMD, Ms. 1070, fols. 313–22; and Garnier, ed., *Journal de Gabriel Breunot*, 2: 548–549.
[19] BMD, Ms. 1070, fol. 318.
[20] AMD, B 232, fols. 267r–74r, May 24–25, 1595; Garnier, ed., *Journal de Gabriel Breunot*, 2: 525–529.

on July 1 and that he would grace it with his royal presence. He used this public occasion to make clear his religious reconciliation with his Catholic subjects in Dijon. The route went from the Sainte Chapelle, where mass was heard, to the high altar of the church of Notre-Dame, which was one station, to the high altar of the church of St. Michel, which was another station, then back to the Ste. Chapelle via the cemetery of St. Médard. The procession was led by the secular clergy of the parishes and members of the various religious orders in Dijon carrying crosses, candles, and images. They were followed by the Host itself, carried by two prelates from the Ste. Chapelle under a canopy carried by four *échevins*. Immediately after the Host came the king's party: guards, members of the king's household, followed by the king himself dressed in a black taffeta cape and wearing around his neck the collier of the Order of the Golden Fleece founded by the Valois dukes of Burgundy. Immediately behind the king, however, came Jean de Saulx, sieur de Tavanes, and the knights of the order of the Holy Ghost carrying a large cross. This confraternity was founded by Tavanes's father nearly thirty years before to provide shock troops to defend Burgundy from Protestantism, and they and the younger Tavanes had been among the most militant supporters of the League in Dijon. Ironically, Tavanes's brother Guillaume had long been a royalist supporter of Henry, and the two brothers found themselves on opposite sides during the wars of the League. That Henry IV wanted to be seen marching with the Leaguer brother immediately behind the consecrated Host, however, is about as explicit a sign as he could make to his Catholic subjects that his abjuration and conversion were genuine, and that he was ready to reconcile with his former enemies.[21] It was time to restore the traditional notion of one faith, one king, and one law, which necessarily required the enfolding together once again the body politic, the body social, and the body of Christ. This, at least, was the ideal, and despite the continued holdout of the Duke of Mayenne, the king's reconciliation with his subjects in the province of Burgundy was an initial success. Indeed, by 1595 all but one League city had surrendered to Henry in similar fashion, with Marseille in the south holding out until July 1596.[22] Thus, the scene in Dijon was repeated all over the kingdom where the League had once held sway.

---

[21] AMD, B 233, fols. 32v–34v, July 1, 1595.
[22] Wolfgang Kaiser, *Marseille au temps des troubles: Morphologie sociale et luttes de factions, 1559–1596* (Paris: EHESS, 1991), 347.

6.1 A *bourgeoisie seconde?*

As explained in the previous chapter, the Catholic League opposed the authority of Henry of Navarre, whom the League's members refused to accept as King Henry IV, and they continued to refer to him only as the King of Navarre. The League was a loosely connected network of urban cells and aristocratic affinities, both groups aided and abetted by many members of the regular and secular clergy. While nominally under the leadership of the Guise family – led by Henry, duke of Guise, until his assassination in December 1588 and then by his brother Charles, duke of Mayenne – the League was always more of a local or regional than a national power. In certain places, such as the capital of Paris and the cities of Amiens, Dijon, Marseilles, Rouen, and Toulouse, its authority and influence were widespread. In most cities and towns in the realm as well as most rural areas, however, with the exception of those controlled by agents of the Guise or other nobles loyal to the League, its influence was virtually nonexistent. One persistent question historians have always asked concerning the League is why certain towns joined the League revolt against the crown while others did not. And even within the cities that eventually sided with the League, why did some individuals choose to support the League while others fled to side with Henry of Navarre, even before he abjured his Calvinist religion? In short, what was the attraction of the League, and why did some support it while others did not? Because the League was a series of local or regional associations, however, historians have only been able to study the League in any detail at the local level. This has meant that how they approach the question of what attracted members to the League has produced a wide variety of answers and explanations, ranging from the political, the socioeconomic, the religious, to the sociocultural.[23]

---

[23] Jean-Marie Constant, *La Ligue* (Paris: Fayard, 1995) is a recent attempt at synthesis, but despite its merits, it is still clear that the only way to study the League in depth is at the local level. This literature is now becoming extensive, especially for the capital of Paris, outlined in Chapter 5, Note 4. There are also many important provincial studies, with a good place to start being the admirable recent collection of essays: Serget Brunet, ed., *La Sainte Union des catholiques de France et la fin des guerre de Religion (1585–1629)* (Paris: Classiques Garnier, 2016). For Rouen and Normandy see Philip Benedict, *Rouen during the Wars of Religion* (Cambridge: Cambridge University Press, 1981) and Stuart Carroll, *Noble Power during the French Wars of Religion: The Guise Affinity and the Catholic Cause in Normandy* (Cambridge: Cambridge University Press, 1998). For Marseilles see Kaiser, *Marseille au temps des troubles.* For Limoges see Michel Cassan, *Le temps des guerres de religion: Le cas du Limousin, vers 1530-vers 1630* (Paris: Publisud, 1996). For Troyes see Penny Roberts, *A City in Conflict: Troyes during the French Wars of Religion* (Manchester: Manchester University Press, 1996). For Grenoble see Stéphane Gal, *Grenoble au temps de la Ligue: Étude politique, sociale et religieuse d'une cité en crise, vers 1562-vers 1598* (Grenoble: Presses Universitaires de Grenoble, 2000).

Henri Drouot argued in 1937, in what is arguably the best and most comprehensive provincial study of the Catholic League ever written, that motivation to join the League in Burgundy was fomented in large part by social tensions that derived from within the articulated hierarchy of six-teenth-century society. Highly fluid and ambiguous social boundaries earlier in the sixteenth century had allowed many wealthy sons of mer-chants as well as some younger sons of nobles to gain political access through the study of the law to the Parlement and *bailliage* courts and the noble status that went with it. Suddenly, these boundaries closed down during the Wars of Religion. This was partly the result of the rising price of judicial offices, which began escalating rapidly in the 1570s and 1580s, placing them beyond the means of many applicants. And even for many who could afford to purchase these royal offices, *conseillers* and *présidents* in the Parlement of Burgundy had already begun resigning their offices in favor of their sons and sons-in-law, resulting in fewer royal offices becom-ing available at any price. The overall result, according to Drouot, was serious social tension between those who had managed to reach the summit in Parlement and those who were shut out. "These *robins* who had upset the old social order during the preceding century already had become by 1587 a conservative body. They wanted to maintain the regime that had favored their ascent as well as the peace that could guarantee their future. They also tended to isolate themselves as a social class on the summit they had climbed and to draw up the ladder behind them."[24] And who was left behind? According to Drouot, there were large numbers of barristers (*avocats*), solicitors (*procureurs*), doctors of law, notaries, and recorders (*greffiers*) whose social advancement into the upper echelon of the legal elite had come to a halt, "These overflowing corporations of lawyers, this surplus of legal chicaners (*chicanous*) with their hunger for the high life, formed one of the principal elements of provincial society, and one which above all others it is necessary to turn to explain the composition of the

---

For Poitiers, see Hilary J. Bernstein, *Between Crown and Community: Politics and Civic Culture in Sixteenth-Century Poitiers* (Ithaca, NY: Cornell University Press, 2004). For Champagne, See Mark W. Konnert, *Local Politics in the French Wars of Religion: The Towns of Champagne, the Duc de Guise, and the Catholic League, 1560–1595* (Aldershot: Ashgate, 2006). For Nantes, see Elizabeth C. Tingle, *Authority and Society in Nantes during the French Wars of Religion, 1559–1598* (Manchester: University of Manchester Press, 2006). For Amiens, see Olivia Carpi, *Une République imaginaire: Amiens pendant les troubles de religion, 1559–1597* (Paris: Belin, 2005). For Brittany, see Hervé Le Goff, *La Ligue en Bretagne: Guerre civile et conflit international, 1588–1598* (Rennes: Presses Universitaires de Rennes, 2006). For Toulouse see Mark Greengrass, "The Sainte Union in the Provinces: The Case of Toulouse," *Sixteenth Century Journal* 14 (1983): 469–496. And for Burgundy see Drouot, *Mayenne et la Bourgogne.*

[24] Drouot, *Mayenne et la Bourgogne*, 1: 48–53, quote on 48.

groups that attained political prominence under the League."[25] And it was Drouot who coined the term *bourgeoisie seconde* to describe these "legal chicaners," focusing on their competition with and jealousy of the *bourgeoisie première* in the Parlement.[26] Throughout his two large volumes Drouot referred again and again to the "two bourgeoisies" or the "rival bourgeoisies" as a way of underscoring his point about social competition being at the foundation of the League.[27] Shut out from further social advancement, these lawyers found in the Catholic League a means of opposing the royal officers in the Parlement. They used Dijon's Hôtel de Ville as the base from which they operated, as it proved to be a natural outlet for their hostility toward the judges in Parlement and other royal officers. "The social war of the [two] bourgeoisies," Drouot concluded, "between the ambitious lawyers and the well-off officers, disguised its complexity beneath the surface and has for the most part escaped the gaze of historians."[28] And what role, if any, did religion play in the formation of the League in Burgundy? Following the academic fashion of his time, Drouot firmly believed that "religion might dress up these antagonisms in its own colors, or even exacerbate them with some fanaticism, but it was these class hatreds that most clearly served as the basis of local conflicts during the period of the League."[29]

My purpose here is not to try to undermine Drouot's thesis by claiming he ignored the factor of religion, though that is exactly what he did. What interests me more is how he used the term *bourgeoisie seconde* to refer to the lesser ranks of the legal profession, and how this might relate to the group's social and political outlook during the League. And while Drouot's book is thoroughly researched with a wealth of documentation from some of the most copious archives in France on the period of the League, he really made no effort at all to prove his thesis with any archival evidence or other empirical analysis. He simply presented the argument of social competition as the principal reason for the formation of the League in Burgundy and accepted it as if it needed no further evidence or elucidation. Thus, what is needed is a close look at what he calls the "two bourgeoisies" in a more systematic way: the *échevins* on the city council in Dijon who made

---

[25] Ibid., 1: 50.
[26] Ibid., 1: 51, for the use of the term *bourgeoisie seconde*. The term *bourgeoisie première* was first used by Robert Descimon, "La Ligue à Paris (1585–1594): Une révision," *Annales: E.S.C.* 37 (January–February 1982): 72–111, to refer to *conseillers* and *présidents* in Parlement. I have used the term here in the same way that Descimon does.
[27] See Drouot, *Mayenne et la Bourgogne*, 1: 33–55, 138, 154, 160–162, 340, 411; and 2: 405–409, 413–414, and 465–466.
[28] Ibid., 1: 340.   [29] Ibid., 1: 33.

up the heart of Drouot's *bourgeoisie seconde*, to see how much their social composition did change over time, as well as the *conseillers* and *présidents* in the Parlement who made up the *bourgeoisie première*. What fits uncomfortably with Drouot's thesis is that this latter group divided, with many of them breaking with the king to remain in Dijon and throwing in their lot with Mayenne and the Hôtel de Ville. What were the interests that linked this highest element of the bourgeoisie with their social inferiors? And why did Drouot virtually ignore the many bourgeois merchants who continued to dominate Dijon's city council up to and including the period of the League? From this examination, it would certainly appear that the reasons for joining the League in Burgundy had very little to do with the kind of social tensions Drouot described. Moreover, it seems more likely that these were personal and political choices that were made neither hastily nor without a lot of soul-searching. And as suggested earlier, these choices also reflected a difference in outlooks between a preference for a future based on the horizontal ties with the local community, or a future based more on hierarchical ties with the monarchy. For that reason alone, it should come as no surprise that those Dijonnais who supported the League closely resembled their royalist counterparts who left the city in terms of their social status, their political views, as well their religious commitment.

There is no doubt that some of the premises on which Drouot based his argument are demonstrably true. For example, if we look at the social origins of the *échevins* who were co-opted to serve on the city council in Dijon from the early sixteenth century to the mid-seventeenth century, a clear pattern emerges. From the 1520 s on the majority of the *échevins*, composed primarily of merchants and wealthy bourgeois, began to be leavened with the presence of a few *avocats, procureurs*, and doctors of law. Drouot's argument is that by the time of the Wars of Religion, this *bourgeoisie seconde* actually composed the largest single social cohort on the council, as they began to be shut out of the Parlement and other sovereign courts in Dijon and made the Hôtel de Ville their locus of power. In 1560, for example, of those *échevins* whose social origins are listed in the city council deliberations, nine out of twelve, or three-fourths, were either *avocats* or *procureurs*. Of the entire council of twenty *échevins*, they made up nearly half.[30] Because the social origins of so many *échevins* are not listed in the documents, however, these figures are somewhat ephemeral. Doubtless most of the *écuyers*, royal officers, and lawyers who could argue cases before the court of Parlement had their social origins

---

[30] AMD, B 198, fols. 10r–11v.

mentioned in the city council records. And a perusal of the tax rolls in Dijon confirms that virtually all of those for whom no social origins are listed were members of the bourgeoisie. But this is just one year. If Drouot's thesis is to be sustained, there needs to be evidence of a long-term trend in the Hôtel de Ville, with the lawyers and notaries of Drouot's *bourgeoisie seconde* replacing the merchants and other bourgeois who traditionally had dominated the city council. Because Drouot himself made no such analysis, what do the documents actually show over the long term?

The numbers in Table 6.1 provide a rough overview of the social make-up of the Hôtel de Ville in Dijon from 1577 to 1610.[31] I have chosen to focus on these years as they provide a good run-up to the signal event that triggered the League's takeover in so many cities in France – the assassinations of the duke and cardinal of Guise at Blois by Henry III in December 1588 – and they also include a fifteen-year period following the collapse of the League.

If we look at these figures, it must first be pointed out that Dijon's system of selecting, or really co-opting, the deputies on the city council each year was a complex affair. First, a mayor was elected each June by the heads of household of the city. He was required to select six *échevins* to retain on the council from the previous year, then those six plus the mayor selected the remaining fourteen *échevins*. There was thus a lot of repetition, as many members served on the council for years at a time, being co-opted by their peers each year. Thus, the total of 680 who served on the council from 1577 to 1610 were obviously not 680 different men, but a group of around 300 men from about a hundred families. I have chosen to present the data in terms of the total number of positions of *échevin* rather than individual men, because this should better exaggerate Drouot's social thesis. And it is clear from the totals that the majority of those who served on the city council in these years consisted of wealthy merchants and other bourgeois – 302 out of 680 (44.4 percent) – and barristers and solicitors – 252 out of 680 (37.1 percent). In order to approximate Drouot's categories, however, we must add the notaries and recorders to the barristers and solicitors to get his *bourgeoise seconde*. Clearly, the royal officers were part of the *bourgeoisie première*, but what do we do with the fourth category:

---

[31] These figures are compiled from AMD, B 213–248 (deliberations of the Hôtel de Ville) and L 203–218 (rolls for the *taille* and *taillon*). The tax rolls enabled me to identify the social status of most *échevins* whose occupations were not mentioned in the city council records. Of the 680 positions of *échevin* between 1577 and 1610, I was able to identify the social status of 656 (96.5 percent).

Table 6.1 *Social make-up of the Hôtel de Ville in Dijon, 1577–1610*

Year	Ecuyers	Présidents conseillers	Officiers	Bourgeois	Avocats procureurs	Notaries recorders	Unknown	Total
1577	3	0	1	7	6	0	3	20
1578	2	0	2	8	8	0	0	20
1579	3	0	1	9	5	0	2	20
1580	1	0	2	6	8	0	3	20
1581	1	0	0	10	8	1	0	20
1582	0	0	1	8	9	1	1	20
1583	1	0	3	8	8	0	0	20
1584	0	0	1	10	9	0	0	20
1585	0	0	1	7	7	1	4	20
1586	0	0	2	9	7	2	0	20
1587	0	0	1	10	9	0	0	20
1588	0	0	1	8	7	2	2	20
1589	0	0	1	7	8	3	1	20
1590	0	0	0	11	8	1	0	20
1591	0	0	2	10	8	0	0	20
1592	0	0	2	7	9	1	1	20
1593	0	0	1	11	7	1	0	20
1594	0	0	2	11	6	1	0	20
1595	0	0	1	10	8	1	0	20
1596	0	0	3	10	6	1	0	20
1597	0	0	2	10	8	0	0	20
1598	0	0	3	11	5	0	1	20
1599	0	0	1	10	8	1	0	20

Year								Total
1600	0	0	0	10	8	1	1	20
1601	0	0	2	7	9	0	2	20
1602	0	0	3	8	9	0	0	20
1603	0	0	3	10	7	0	0	20
1604	0	0	2	11	6	1	0	20
1605	0	0	5	6	7	2	0	20
1606	2	0	3	7	7	1	1	20
1607	0	0	5	7	6	1	1	20
1608	0	0	3	7	9	0	1	20
1609	0	0	4	10	6	0	0	20
1610	0	0	3	11	6	0	0	20
TOTAL	13	0	67	302	252	22	24	680

Sources: AMD, B 213–248 and L 203–218.

wealthy merchants, other bourgeois, and professionals such as doctors of medicine (labeled as Bourgeois in Table 6.1)? In his study of the League in Paris, John Salmon argued for grouping them with the *bourgeoisie première* rather than with the lawyers, notaries, and recorders on account of the prestige they enjoyed at the Hôtel de Ville.[32] No doubt many in this category were equally well-respected in Dijon's Hôtel de Ville. And though these categories make for a very simplistic way of looking at the social divisions of the Hôtel de Ville, it is nevertheless true that for the most part the wealth and status of the *écuyers*, royal officers like the *trésoriers, élus*, and lieutenants were much closer to the magistrates of the Parlement than to the lawyers and functionaries who made up Drouot's *bourgeoisie seconde*. Denis Richet and Robert Descimon, however, have argued persuasively that wealthy merchants really ought to be grouped together with the lawyers and solicitors rather than with the royal officers, that is, as part of the *bourgeoisie seconde*.[33] Drouot was so focused on the lawyers, solicitors, and notaries in the legal system that he never explicitly addressed the many merchants who served on the city council. His claim was that by the time of the League, merchants had been replaced by the *bourgeoisie seconde* of the legal profession, a claim he offered no evidence for. When, then, did the "legal chicaners" of the *bourgeoisie seconde* come to dominate the city council in Dijon?

If we break down the data a different way and group the figures chronologically, we get a clearer picture of what was happening during the years of the League. Table 6.2 separates out the years of the League by selecting those elections between the assassination of the Guises in December 1588 and the fall of Dijon to Henry IV in May 1595. (Table 6.2 only includes those *échevins* whose social origins are known, 656 out of 680, or 96.5 percent.)

The long-term trends are now more apparent, and despite Drouot's contention that those trained in the law came to dominate the city council by the time of the League, in fact, their numbers increased only marginally during the years of the League compared to the period 1577–1588, and they even declined in the years 1595–1610. From 1575 to 1588 *écuyers*, royal

[32] J. H. M. Salmon, "The Paris Sixteen, 1584–1594: The Social Analysis of a Revolutionary Movement," in his *Renaissance and Revolt: Essays in the Intellectual and Social History of Early Modern France* (Cambridge: Cambridge University Press, 1987), 243, n.39.

[33] Denis Richet, "Sociocultural Aspects of Religious Conflicts in Paris in the Second Half of the Sixteenth Century," in Robert Forster and Orest Ranum, eds., *Religion, Ritual, and the Sacred: Selections from the Annales* (Baltimore, MD: Johns Hopkins University Press, 1982), 201; and Robert Descimon, "The '*Bourgeoisie Seconde*': Social Differentiation in the Parisian Municipal Oligarchy in the Sixteenth Century, 1500–1610," *French History* 17 (2003): 388–424.

Table 6.2 *Social make-up of the League in Dijon*

Social category	1575–1588		1589–1594		1595–1610	
	No.	%	No.	%	No.	%
1. *Écuyers*	11	4.9	0	—	2	0.6
2. Magistrates (*conseillers, présidents*)	0	—	0	—	0	—
3. Royal officers	16	7.1	8	6.8	43	13.7
4. Bourgeois, merchants, professionals	100	44.5	57	48.3	145	46.3
5. *Avocats* and *procureurs*	91	40.4	46	39.0	115	36.8
6. Notaries and *greffiers*	7	3.1	7	5.9	8	2.6
TOTAL	225	100.0	118	100.0	313	100.0

Sources: AMD, B 213–248 and L 203–218.

officers, merchants, and other bourgeois made up 127 of the *échevins* on the council whose social origins are known (56.4 percent), while lawyers, notaries, and recorders made up only 98 of the total (43.6 percent). During the years of the League (1598–1594) the numbers of the *bourgeoise première* and the merchants declined just slightly (65 out of 118, or 55.1 percent), while those from the legal profession rose marginally (53 out of 118, or 44.9 percent). Those very slight gains during the League were soon reversed, however, in the fifteen years after 1595, when the numbers of the royal officers and merchants increased to 190 out of 313 *échevins* whose social status is known (60.7 percent), while those "legal chicaners" from the *bourgeoisie seconde* decreased to only 123 out of 313 (39.3 percent). While Table 6.1 does indicate that there were a few individual years in which those from the legal profession outnumbered their social superiors on the city council, the overall trends moved in the opposite direction, with merchants and wealthy bourgeois dominating the city council throughout and even increasing that domination in the period immediately after the Wars of Religion. Thus, Drouot's thesis that lawyers and other legal functionaries came to dominate the city council in Dijon and offered their support to the Catholic League rather than Henry of Navarre because they were unable to rise higher up the social ladder appears to be suspect. The fact is that these men of the law never came to dominate the city council in Dijon during the League, and they would not do so until the seventeenth century. By the late 1630s the records of the Hôtel de Ville show that lawyers and notaries began to outnumber their merchant colleagues on a regular basis, though even as late as the 1650s the men of the law still only made up about

45 percent of the total number of *échevins*, though this was still significant progress over their numbers immediately after the Wars of Religion.[34]

The real winners, however, were not so much the men of the law as the other royal officers in Dijon, a trend that is apparent in Table 6.2. The percentage of royal officers who served on the city council more than doubled from 6.8 percent of the total during the League to 13.7 percent of the *échevins* who served in the years 1595–1610. And if we look at the position of mayor (*vicomte-mayeur*) of Dijon – and the mayor was the one who had the most influence on the selection of the *échevins*, after all – lawyers and notaries were well represented in the seventeenth century, but they hardly dominated the city council. As Michael Breen has shown, while the men of the law began to be elected as mayor of Dijon with far greater frequency in the seventeenth century than during the Wars of Religion, once again it was royal officers who came to be elected as mayor of the city with even greater frequency. Between 1595 and 1670 a total of 38 men were elected mayor of Dijon, with most serving more than one term: 19 were royal officers (50 percent), 13 were lawyers or legal functionaries (34.2 percent), while just 4 were wealthy bourgeois or merchants (10.5 percent).[35] Thus, even though Drouot's "legal chicaners" would come to play a much more influential role on the city council in the seventeenth century than during the religious wars, even then the lawyers would be competing with royal officers rather than merchants and bourgeois for domination of the council. It seems the men of the law never really managed to shake the *bourgeoisie première*, though by 1660 it would appear that the socioeconomic gap that had existed between them had narrowed considerably. Though it is not my purpose to explore this here, one could even argue that by the second half of the seventeenth century the men of the law had risen to the *bourgeoisie première* while the merchants and other bourgeois seem to have fallen to the *bourgeoisie seconde*. Thus, my argument here really supports Descimon's overall view of things in Paris where merchants came to be replaced in influence by royal officers. Thus, in my view Drouot's use of the term *bourgeoisie seconde* is both too limited and too broad: too limited in that he ignored the fact that merchants still made up the largest cohort in the Hôtel de Ville in Dijon during the League, not his "legal chicaners," and too broad because

---

[34] See AMD, B 268 to 299 for the deliberations of the Hôtel de Ville for the years 1630–1660. This is also confirmed by Michael Breen, *Law, City, and King: Legal Culture, Municipal Politics, and State Formation in Early Modern Dijon* (Rochester, NY: University of Rochester Press, 2007), especially 61–64.

[35] Figures derived from the table in Breen, *Law, City, and King*, 64.

he also includes notaries and *greffiers* whose social status was clearly below that of most merchants and lawyers.

This does not necessarily mean, however, that the lawyers' and notaries' social status and their rivalry with the magistrates of the Parlement and other officers were irrelevant to their support for the League in the 1580s and 1590s. There is no question that there was an institutional rivalry between the Hôtel de Ville and the Parlement in Dijon that had existed ever since the creation of the sovereign court in the late fifteenth century. There is also little doubt that the *échevins* on the city council saw themselves as protectors of the city's privileges and independence from the crown's ever-reaching grasp. While in some ways this perception was self-constructed and overlooked the many occasions during the religious wars in which the Parlement joined and even led the *échevins* in resisting royal policy, it is nevertheless true that one of the principal foundations of the mentality within the Hôtel de Ville was a firm belief in the urban independence Dijon enjoyed from its charter as a medieval commune, whose privileges were recognized and accepted by all previous dukes of Burgundy and kings of France.[36] Thus, as Robert Descimon has shown for the Sixteen in Paris, there is no question that the *échevins* in the Hôtel de Ville in Dijon during the period of the League saw themselves as saviors and protectors of a traditional urban independence under threat from the crown.[37] But how does this mentality relate to the social or class tensions envisaged by Drouot?

We can get a much better sense of what motivated the Leaguers in Dijon if we take a brief look at the Parlement of Dijon, especially those *présidents* and *conseillers* who made up the *bourgeoisie première*, and how they split apart when a royalist Parlement was formed in Flavigny in early 1589. By the end of 1589, one year after the murder of the duke and cardinal of Guise at Blois, two of the six *présidents* and 17 of the 43 *conseillers* of the Parlement had left behind their families and property in Dijon and set up a royalist Parlement in Flavigny. And more than a dozen *avocats, procureurs*, and notaries also joined them there.[38] A clear majority of both groups, however – the *bourgeoisie première* and the *bourgeoisie seconde* – remained

---

[36] See, for example, Charles Bertucat, *La juridiction municipale de Dijon: Son étendue* (Dijon: J. Nourry, 1911), 75–95, and Joseph Garnier and Ernest Champeaux, *Chartes de communes et d'affranchissements en Bourgogne* (Dijon: V. Darrantière et Paul Jobard, 1918), 317–330.

[37] For Descimon's argument, see Chapter 5.

[38] For the names of these individuals, see Louis Gros, *Le Parlement et la Ligue en Bourgogne* (Dijon and Paris: Damidot and H. Champion, 1910), 32–41, as well as the records of the royalist Parlement in Flavigny in BMD, Fonds Saverot 1493, 512–514.

behind in Dijon to support the League. It seems most unlikely that there were any social divisions like the one's Drouot describes at work here, as both Leaguer *parlementaires* and royalist *parlementaires* were of equal social status. Moreover, the Dijon tax rolls make it very clear that members of both groups were among the wealthiest citizens in the city.[39] What is clear, however, is that decisions to leave Dijon for the royalist Parlement in Flavigny were made neither in haste nor without a great deal of soul searching. As Michel De Waele has demonstrated for the Paris Parlement, nearly all the judges felt themselves pulled by two equally compelling forces.[40] As Dijonnais and as Catholics, they felt a natural urge to stay in Dijon and defend their families, their homes, their neighbors, and their religion from both war and heresy. As royal officers, however, they also felt an allegiance to the king and to follow his supporters to Flavigny in order to maintain royal justice.

To be sure, a few in both camps found the decision an easy one. The murder of the Guises at Blois was seen as a sign by some of a betrayal of the king's own responsibilities. The Guises, after all, had been royal governors of Burgundy since the early sixteenth century, and many Guise clients were littered throughout the legal and fiscal courts in Dijon. So, some found it relatively easy to support the League. Most, however, found it a much more difficult decision, as they recognized that losing their offices and even their careers was a possibility if they formally opposed Henry III in early 1589 or Henry IV after August 1589. As the fifth *président* of the Parlement, Claude Bourgeois, wrote to his wife in June 1589 after deciding to join the royalists, "I have been extremely pressured to go [to Flavigny]. They [the *parlementaires* at Flavigny] have ordered me in two *arrêts* to go there or risk losing my estate, and to tell you that I have received a letter from the king which expressly commands me to go there."[41] On the other side, the city council issued special tax assessments against those judges who left Dijon for Flavigny in order to cover the costs of the war, and also seized many of their homes and imprisoned their wives, demanding forced loans to liberate them.[42] The highest ranking royalist in the Parlement at Flavigny, fourth *président* Bénigne Frémyot, noted that his

---

[39] See AMD, L 476, for the tax roll for 1589.

[40] Michel De Waele, "De Paris à Tours: La crise d'identité des magistrats parisiens de 1589 à 1594," *Revue historique* 299 (1999): 549–577.

[41] AMD, B 457, fol. 59, Claude Bourgeois to his wife, June 25, 1589, written from Semur.

[42] Annette Finley-Croswhite describes what happened to the wives left behind in Dijon in her article, "Engendering the Wars of Religion: Female Agency during the Catholic League in Dijon," *French Historical Studies* 20 (Spring 1997): 127–154.

enemies promised to send him the head of his son in a sack if he did not quit Flavigny and return to Dijon and join the League.[43] The fact is that most judges in both groups were devout Catholics who cared deeply for their religion, just as most also perceived themselves as loyal servants of the crown. The fact that several judges who originally decided to remain in Dijon ultimately left for Flavigny, such as the judge Claude Bretagne discussed earlier, and some who originally went to Flavigny also returned to Dijon, only underscores the ambiguity in the magistrates' decisions. Moreover, there were a significant number of judges in the Parlement as well as other royal officers in the sovereign courts who sought to maintain a neutral status. Some, such as the judge Gabriel Breunot and the lawyer Antoine Petit, left Dijon but went to the neutral town of Auxonne in 1589 rather than to Flavigny, hoping not to have to make a choice between the rival factions, though the former eventually returned to Dijon a short time later rather than cast his lot with the royalists in Flavigny.[44] And about thirty officers of the sovereign courts and the Bureau of Finances left Dijon as well the same year "to live in exile with honor," they claimed, rather than submit to the League in Dijon or to risk arrest by the royalists in Flavigny.[45]

The tendency until recently of most historical writing about the League, as Robert Descimon first pointed out, has been to demonize the Leaguers as violent and extremist militants under the thumb of Spain, and to sanctify the royalists as modernist *politiques* who were fighting to preserve the future of France. Even in Paris where "the Sixteen" represented the most radical group of those loyal to the League, Descimon has demonstrated "that one could be a member of the 'Sixteen' without being a 'terrorist'."[46] Thus, not only is the traditional view of the League an inaccurate caricature, it also unfairly draws a sharp distinction between Leaguers and royalists that really was much more ambiguous at the time. Drouot himself is guilty of this tendency, as his sympathies are clearly displayed on his sleeve in the way he describes some of the principal actors. He refers to the moderate Leaguers who remained in Dijon, men like the first *président* of the Parlement of Dijon, Denis Brûlart, as "cowardly servants of the king" (*serviteurs du roi pusillanimes*), in other words, as

---

[43] Garnier, ed., *Correspondance de la mairie de Dijon*, 2: 212, Frémyot to Fervacques, March 5, 1589.

[44] AMD, B 227, fol. 26v and 114v. For Breunot's escape to Auxonne and about face and return to Dijon, see Drouot, *Mayenne et la Bourgogne*, 1: 285.

[45] For these defections, see Henri Drouot, "Flavigny contre Dijon: Notes sur le schisme dijonnais de 1589," *Mémoires de l'Académie de Dijon* (1922), 47–120; as well as Drouot, *Mayenne et la Bourgogne*, 1: 285–343 (quote on 343).

[46] Robert Descimon, *Qui étaient les Seize?: Mythes et réalités de la Ligue parisienne, 1585–1594* (Paris: Klincksieck, 1983), 219.

sheep in wolf's clothing who did not have the courage to follow the other royalists to Flavigny.[47] A contemporary of Drouot, Louis Gros, echoed these same sentiments in his history of the Parlement and the League in Burgundy published in 1910. Gros claimed that "a movement of anger and rage" permeated the moderates in the Leaguer Parlement, which was exacerbated by the "jealousy they felt toward their more courageous colleagues" who had come out publicly for the king.[48] By referring to the *bourgeoisie seconde* as "legal chicaners" and the Leaguer *parlementaires* as cowards, Drouot not only tipped off his own prejudices about the League, but he also perpetuated the long-held notion that there was a great divide, even an ideological gulf, separating Leaguers from royalists. The reality was more complicated.

First of all, many families split apart during the League, and family members continued to remain in contact despite prohibitions by the city council and attempted to help each other despite their political differences. Claude Bretagne, a *conseiller* who had served in Parlement since 1555, longer than any other member, is an especially interesting case. He received his doctor of law degree at Toulouse in 1547, joining the Parlement of Dijon in June 1555 as a *conseiller*. He married Denise Barjot, who came from a Huguenot family in Franche-Comté, the following year. He was one of the few members of Parlement who had been willing to register the edict of pacification in 1563 ending the first civil war, and when he eventually sided with the League after 1588, many considered him to be "a Huguenot disguised as a Catholic."[49] Bretagne remained in Dijon as a Leaguer, while his son Jules Bretagne and nephew Isaac Bretagne, both *conseillers*, joined the royalist Parlement in Flavigny. And Claude's daughter, also named Claude after her father, was married to a *conseiller* in the royalist Parlement, Jacques Bossuet (grandfather of Jacques-Bénigne Bossuet).[50] All of them were moderates in their respective assemblies. Claude Bretagne was deemed too moderate a Leaguer, in fact, and in 1594 he was compelled to flee the city after the La Verne affair, aided by the wife of Pierre Jeannin, another moderate and third *président* of the Leaguer Parlement in Dijon.[51] Indeed, the Bretagne family was one

---

[47] Drouot, *Mayenne et la Bourgogne*, 1: 224. Drouot later calls Brûlart "le timide premier président," ibid., 1: 234.

[48] Gros, *Le Parlement et la Ligue en Bourgogne*, 45.

[49] Xavier Le Person, *"Pratiques" et "pratiquers": La vie politique à la fin du règne de Henri III, 1584–1589* (Geneva; Droz, 2002), 467.

[50] BMD, Fonds Saverot 1493, 517–518, May 26, 1592; as well as Gros, *Le Parlement et la Ligue en Bourgogne*, 32, n.5 and 166.

[51] Garnier, ed., *Journal de Gabriel Breunot*, 2: 399–400.

of the most striking examples of how easily families could become divided during the League. Although Claude Bretagne was a moderate Catholic, the family had many ties to Protestantism, including Jacques Bretagne, an *échevin* from Autun, who was the leader of the Protestant deputies at the Estates-General of 1561 at Pontoise.[52]

These divisions stand out sharply in this family portrait of the Bretagne family, commissioned by Bretagne's widow, Denise Barjot, shortly after her husband's death in 1604 (see Figure 6.1). This was originally an altarpiece with a central panel, which was a depiction of the nativity of Christ and the adoration of the shepherds. This central panel was later destroyed during the French Revolution, so all that remains are the two side panels depicting the Bretagne family members. The work was painted by the Dutch artist Nicolas De Hoey, who had been living in Dijon since the religious wars.[53] This was the same artist who painted the private chapel of the La Verne family in the parish church of St. Michel. In the left panel, Claude Bretagne is shown kneeling with his hands folded in the middle of the first row wearing his scarlet robe as a parlementary judge (*conseiller*). He is flanked by his two oldest sons; Guy Bretagne on his right in the black robe was the oldest son and a barrister (*avocat*) in the Parlement of Dijon, who remained with his father in Dijon with the League, while the second son on his left, Jules Bretagne in the scarlet robe, also a judge in the Parlement like his father, left Dijon and joined the royalist Parlement in Flavigny. After the wars of religion were over, Jules converted to Protestantism and left Burgundy altogether. Standing behind the father and the two oldest sons were the third and fourth sons, Antoine Bretagne, later admitted as a judge in the Parlement in 1597 by Henry IV, and Claude Bretagne, named after his father, who actually succeeded his father as a judge when the former retired, and later became the first presiding judge (*premier président*) in the Parlement of Metz. Both are wearing the scarlet parlementary robes of judges. Standing next to Antoine and Claude Bretagne are two sons-in-law who married two of the daughters of Claude Bretagne and his wife Denyse Barjot: Philibert Lenet, who was a presiding judge in the Chamber of Accounts in Dijon and married Marthe Bretagne, and

[52] Noel Valois, "Les états de Pontoise (août 1561)," *Revue d'histoire de l'Église de France* 116 (1943), 237–256, especially 251.
[53] For more about this painting, see Marguerite Guillaume, *La peinture en Bourgogne au XVIe siècle* (Dijon: Musée des Beaux-Arts de Dijon, 1990), 157–160; as well as G. Blondeau, "Claude Bretagne, conseiller au Parlement. De Bourgogne: Son portrait et ceux de sa famille au musée de Dijon," *Annales de Bourgogne* 5 (1933): 101–129.

(a)   (b)

Figure 6.1 Painting of the family of Claude Bretagne on two panels of an altarpiece,
1604. © Musée des Beaux-Arts de Dijon, photograph by François Jay

Jacques Bossuet, also a judge in the parlement of Dijon, who married
Claudine Bretagne, and was also the grandfather of the more famous
Jacques-Bénigne Bossuet, bishop of Meaux and celebrated preacher at the
court of Louis XIV in the seventeenth century. Both Lenet and Bossuet
left Dijon to join the royalists at Flavigny. At the far right of this panel are
two small blond children dressed in grey, who died very young.
The right-hand panel depicts Bretagne's wife Denyse Barjot and their
four daughters: Marthe and Claudine, whose husbands are on the facing

panel, as well as Jeanne and Denise, who both married barristers in the Parlement of Dijon, Isaac Fournier and François Boyvault, respectively.[54] Many other families were also divided. The fourth *président* of the Parlement, Bénigne Frémyot, who also joined the royalists in Flavigny, had a brother, Jean Frémyot, who was both a cleric and an *échevin* back in Dijon.[55] Some of the most extensive family links were those of Jean Fyot, a royalist *parlementaire* in Flavigny, and his wife Gasparde de Montholon. Fyot himself had a cousin, Pierette Fyot, who was married to Bernard Des Barres, the second *président* of the Leaguer Parlement in Dijon. His wife's cousin, Nicolas de Montholon, was the sixth *président* of the Leaguer Parlement in Dijon. His wife, Gasparde de Montholon, who also had a sister married to the fifth *président* in the royalist Parlement, Claude Bourgeois, was required to stay in Dijon as a form of hostage, like all family members of those royalist *parlementaires* in Flavigny. She eventually escaped by donning a disguise and ultimately joined her husband in Flavigny, with both royalists and supporters of the League within her family aiding her escape. Thus, there was obviously a lot of communication and familial interaction among the Fyots and Montholons, divided as they were between both groups.[56] There is no question that the political disputes that divided this family did not prevent, much less destroy, the social interaction that family life required. To be sure, being separated by distance and forced to interact in secret was more than a minor nuisance. Nevertheless, however much the split between the Leaguers and the royalists in Dijon may have divided the body politic, it proved to be much less of a threat to the body social.

A number of noble families were also divided between Leaguers and royalists just like the *parlementaire* families. Perhaps the most notable was the Tavanes family. The two sons of Gaspard de Saulx, sieur de Tavanes, who was lieutenant-general of Burgundy and marshal of France in the early religious wars, were Jean de Saulx, viscount of Tavanes, who supported the League and was a client of Mayenne, while his older brother, Guillaume de Saulx, count of Tavanes, supported Henry IV from 1589.[57] Like the Tavanes, the Bauffremont family had divided loyalties during the

---

[54] See Georges Blondeau, "Les Bretagne au Parlement du Metz," *Mémoires de l'Académie nationale de Metz* 16 (1933): 275–288.

[55] Gros, *Le Parlement et la Ligue en Bourgogne*, p. 30, n.1.

[56] AMD, B 9, "Articles faicts concernants les parents et alliances de Fyot et De Montholon"; and Garnier, ed., *Journal de Gabriel Breunot*, I, 88. Also, see Finley-Croswhite, "Engendering the Wars of Religion," *passim.*

[57] Arlette Jouanna, Jacqueline Boucher, Dominique Biloghi, and Guy Le Thiec, eds., *Histoire et dictionnaire des guerres de religion* (Paris: Robert Laffont, 1998), 1281–1282.

League. Claude de Bauffrement, baron of Sennecey, supported the League, while his brother Georges supported the royalist cause, and their sister Françoise was married to Louis de l'Hôpital, marquis of Vitry, another loyal supporter of the king.[58] It is worth pointing out that nearly all of these families, including the Bretagne and Tavanes families, deliberately kept an important male member in both camps in order to guard their interests, a point that the mother of the two Tavanes brothers – Françoise de Baume, widow of Gaspard de Saulx-Tavanes – made clear.[59] One way to do this was through a marriage alliance.

The most explicit family alliance was the marriage that took place in November 1593 between Nicolas Brûlart, the son of Leaguer first *président* Denis Brûlart, and the daughter of the aforementioned royalist fifth *président* Claude Bourgeois. Both men were moderates in their respective Parlements, and coming on the heels of Henry IV's abjuration earlier that year, even contemporaries remarked on the marriage as a sign of rapprochement. While not everyone in Dijon necessarily welcomed the marriage according to Gabriel Breunot, a *conseiller* in the Leaguer Parlement, it was nevertheless clear that socialization between Leaguers and royalists continued throughout the years of the League.[60] And this was not the only link between the Leaguer Brûlart and the royalist Bourgeois families. Denis Brûlart's younger brother, Nicolas Brûlart, was both a *conseiller* in the Leaguer Parlement in Dijon and a master of requests. He was married, however, to Marie Bourgeois, sister of the royalist *président* Claude Bourgeois.[61] Moreover, Denis Brûlart's daughter Marguerite had already married, in 1592, Jean-Baptiste Legoux, seigneur de la Berchère, a royal officer who had fled to Flavigny in the autumn of 1589.[62] Other well-known families that were divided across party lines included the brothers Jean and François Blondeau, of which the first was a *conseiller* in the Leaguer Parlement in Dijon and the second a *conseiller* in the royalist Parlement in Flavigny. The same was true of the Quarré brothers; Jean Quarré was a *conseiller* in the Dijon Parlement, while his brother Pierre Quarré was a *conseiller* in Flavigny. Also, royalist fourth

---

[58] Ibid., 702–703. Also see the forthcoming book on three generations of the Bauffremont family by James B. Collins.

[59] Garnier, ed., *Correspondance de la mairie de Dijon*, 2: 159–161, Françoise de Baume to Fervaques, February 10, 1589.

[60] Garnier, ed., *Journal de Gabriel Breunot*, 1: 386 and 402–403.

[61] See the baptismal records for the birth of this couple's daughter Marguerite in August 1594: AMD, B 490, fol. 86r, parish of St. Jean, August 21, 1594.

[62] See the baptismal records for the birth of their son Bénigne Le Goux in December 19, 1599: AMD, B 490, fol. 226v, December 19, 1599.

président of the Parlement Bénigne Frémyot was married to Marguerite Berbissey, sister of one the most militant *conseillers* in the Leaguer Parlement, Perpetuo Berbissey. Other families that also experienced familial divisions between the Leaguer and the royalist Parlements included the Bouhier, Saumaise, Odebert, and Poligny families.[63]

If there was any social division at work that divided the *parlementaires* in Dijon, however, it was age and experience rather than class. The royalist *conseillers* and *présidents* who left Dijon for Flavigny in 1589 had on average 10.9 years of experience in Parlement. The Leaguer *parlementaires* who stayed behind in Dijon, however, had on average 16.9 years' experience.[64] Thus those judges who opted ultimately to support the League were generally older and more experienced than their royalist counterparts. While this differential in experience was not as pronounced as in some other Parlements – in Rouen, for example, the Leaguer *parlementaires* averaged 18 years of experience while their royalist counterparts averaged only 4 years of experience – there was nevertheless a visible distinction of age and experience between the two cohorts. This should not be taken as a universal measure of support for the League everywhere in France, since the situation was very different in Paris, where judges in the Leaguer Parlement in Paris had served for an average of 10 years, while their royalist counterparts in Tours had served an average of fourteen years. The same was true in Brittany, where the senior judges of the Parlement and the Chamber of Accounts supported the king while their younger colleagues supported the Duke of Mercoeur and the League.[65] Nevertheless, in Burgundy the older and more experienced judges remained in Dijon to support the League rather than fleeing to form a royalist Parlement in Flavigny.

Finally, an examination of the reconciliation between the Leaguers and royalists in 1595 when Dijon finally submitted to Henry IV is very instructive and has much to tell us about the differences that divided the city during the years of the League. The king's own policy toward the League after its capitulation to him is a case in point. Far from punishing or removing its members from office after the city of Dijon surrendered to his

---

[63] Gros, *Le Parlement et la Ligue en Bourgogne, passim,* but especially the table on 165–171.

[64] These figures are compiled from the registers of Parlement, which indicate when each man first took office. See BMD, Fonds Saverot 1491, fols. 1280–1283, to 1493, fols. 292–293, November 12, 1562 to November 13, 1589.

[65] Figures for Rouen and Paris come from Philip Benedict, *Rouen during the Wars of Religion,* 185–186. For Brittany, see James B. Collins, *Classes, Estates, and Order in Early Modern Brittany* (Cambridge: Cambridge University Press, 1994), 129–130.

army in May 1595, Henry IV rewarded many of them, particularly those moderates who had helped negotiate the surrender. The most obvious examples include Denis Brûlart, whom Henry retained as first *président* of the reunited Parlement in Dijon.[66] According to Courtépée and Béguillet, Henry did reprimand Brûlart when the city surrendered to him in 1595 for not having the courage to join the royalist Parlement in Flavigny, the only first *président* of any Parlement in France to side with the League.[67] He could have easily opted to promote the fourth président, Bénigne Fremiot, the highest ranking judge among the royalists, who had presided over the royalist Parlement in Flavigny, but he did not, because Brûlart had been so supportive of a settlement with the king and had actually helped negotiate the city's surrender. A second example is René Fleutelot, the mayor of Dijon. He had been elected by the League in June 1594 and had already nearly completed a term as mayor when the city surrendered to him in May 1595. Henry insisted that Fleutelot be retained for another term, however, and urged his reelection one month later.[68] Again, Fleutelot had been a Leaguer moderate who had supported the reconciliation with the king. Finally, the best example of a leaguer being rewarded by Henry IV was the third *président* of the Parlement in Dijon, Pierre Jeannin. Ironically, Jeannin had been absent from Dijon throughout most of the period of the League. At first trying to maintain his neutrality, he ultimately decided not to join his royalist colleagues in Flavigny, which, combined with his declarations of loyalty to the League, kept him in their good graces. Jeannin was really playing a double game, however, since much of the time he was away from Dijon he was actually with Henry of Navarre, attempting to convince him to abjure his Protestantism. Once Navarre did abjure in 1593 and was soon crowned as Henry IV, Jeannin continued to try to work out a settlement so that the League in Burgundy could surrender to the king with their dignity intact. Jeannin was not only allowed to keep his position in the Parlement of Dijon; he was also rewarded with the office of second *président* in the Parlement of Paris, as well as admitted to the king's own privy council. In later years he became a personal confident of Henry IV, who trusted Jeannin so much that he was dispatched on numerous diplomatic missions for the kingdom of France.

---

[66] For a good analysis of Henry IV's treatment of League towns in general, see Annette Finley-Croswhite, *Henry IV and the Towns: The Pursuit of Legitimacy in French Urban Society, 1589–1610* (Cambridge: Cambridge University Press, 1999), especially 23–87.

[67] Claude Courtépée and Edme Béguillet, *Description générale et particulière du duché de Bourgogne*, 5 vols. (Avallon and Paris: F. E. R. N., 3rd edn. 1967–2010), 2: 355.

[68] AMD, B232, fols. 295r–96v, June 16, 1595.

Jeannin was awarded 15,000 *écus* by the king, in theory for expenses he had incurred during the wars, and had his estates augmented with several new additions. In short, this son of a tanner from Autun and former member of the League became one of the most significant counselors of state under Henry IV.[69]

What this all shows is that the split between Leaguers and royalists in Dijon was neither the greedy social-climbing struggle that Drouot claimed it was, nor even the stark ideological and religious confrontation that many liberal historians of the nineteenth century made it out to be. While this is certainly the way that many of the more militant participants on both sides branded it – with royalists depicting the Leaguers as servants of the Pope and of Philip II, and Leaguers depicting royalists as godless and without religion for putting expediency over their faith – the situation in Dijon shows that a large group of moderates on both sides actually had quite a lot in common and strived to maintain various means of interaction and communication between the two groups. It is also clear that families that were divided during the League with members in both groups tended to make up the leadership of these moderate factions. Despite Drouot's claim that there were numerous social pressures that pushed the many lawyers and notaries in Dijon toward the League, it seems more likely that other factors, not the least being Mayenne's extensive patronage ties among the *échevins*, lawyers, and notaries in Dijon, were more significant in forming the initial coalition that became the League in Burgundy.

6.2 Henry IV and the Duke of Mayenne

That Henry IV quickly and successfully managed to dissolve and eradicate the political and religious tensions at the end of the Wars of Religion – reconciling royalists with Leaguers and Huguenots with Catholics – has long been part of the traditional narrative of French history. As a heady mix of myth, propaganda, and history, this narrative of *le bon roi* Henry IV was constructed in his own lifetime, as the memoirs of the duke of Sully fully attest. In fact, the first complete biography of Henry, published in 1641 by Bishop Hardouin de Péréfixe, adopted this depiction of Henry as a miracle worker, who restored a depleted and devastated France within a few short years:

---

[69] For the rewards of Jeannin, see Drouot, *Mayenne et la Bourgogne*, 2: 445–448. For evidence of Jeannin's efforts at attempting to persuade Navarre to abjure his Calvinist religion and convert to Catholicism, see Garnier, ed., *Correspondance de la Mairie de Dijon*, 2: 459–460 and 468–469, Etienne Bernard to the city council, May 12 and 22, 1593.

Following the example of the king, the bourgeois repaired their houses that the wars had destroyed. The nobles, having lost their armies, and not having anything but a stick in their hands, turned to looking after their goods and increasing their revenues. All of the people were hard at work. And it is a miracle to see this kingdom, which only five or six years earlier had been a pit of venomous snakes, full of thieves, robbers, rascals, and brigands, having been purged of all these evils by this great king and transformed into a hive of busy and innocent bees, who were trying so hard to prove their industry by storing up wax and honey.

Thus, *Henri le Grand*, the great miracle worker, converted a pit of venomous snakes into a peaceful hive of busy worker bees in just a few short years.[70]

The first questions to ask are whether this magical transformation, or some more realistic version of it, really happened. And if it did, how did Henry do it? Hardouin de Péréfixe never mentioned anything about religion, or anything about institutions such as the various Hôtels de Ville and the Parlements that had opposed the king so tenaciously during the wars of the League. Did the king succeed at reconciliation with a politics of bribery – purchasing the loyalty of his enemies with royal favors and perquisites, as so many older accounts have long maintained? "Henry IV never refused the price of submission," according to Jean-Hippolyte Mariéjol at the beginning of the twentieth century.[71] And another historian wrote at mid-century that Henry "was quite cynical in his readiness to buy off the self-seeking, recalcitrant Catholic leaders still arrayed against him."[72] These historians were only relying on contemporary sources, however. Sully, for just one example, lamented in his memoirs that Henry had to pay a total ransom to his former enemies of more than 32,000,000 *livres* in order to make peace.[73] Even more blunt was the English ambassador George Carew, who noted sarcastically that "those who hazarded their lives and fortunes for setting the crown on his head, he neither rewardeth nor payeth; those who were of the league against him, he hath bought to be his friends and given them preferments."[74] To be sure,

---

[70] Paul-Philippe Hardouin de Péréfixe de Baumont, *Histoire du roy Henry-le-Grand* (Amsterdam, 1661), quoted in Danièle Thomas, *Henry IV: Images d'un roi entre mythe et réalité* (Bizanos: Héraclès, 1996), 163.

[71] J.-H. Mariéjol, *La Réforme et la Ligue: L'Edit de Nantes, 1559–1598*, vol. 6, part 1 of *L'Histoire de France des origins à la Révolution*, ed. Ernest Lavisse (Paris: Hachette, 1904), 429.

[72] J. E. Neale, *The Age of Catherine de Medici* (London: Harper Torchbooks, 1978, orig. ed. 1943), 101.

[73] Mariéjol, *La Réforme et la Ligue*, 429, n. 15.

[74] Quoted by Richard Bonney, *Political Change in France Under Richelieu and Mazarin, 1624–1661* (Oxford: Oxford University Press, 1978), 85.

Henry did not pay out these vast sums all at once, but in installments, and many were still being paid even after Henry's death in 1610. This was a strategy to insure that his new clients remained loyal by making them dependent on these annual royal payments.

What was the case with the Duke of Mayenne, however, Burgundy's royal governor? As we have already seen, the Burgundian capital was one of the foremost centers of opposition against Henry, with both the Hôtel de Ville and the Parlement of Dijon united in their refusal to recognize his legitimacy and royal authority officially until May 1595. Moreover, the royal governor of Burgundy and aristocratic leader of the League, the Duke of Mayenne, had many of his clients in both institutions. And Mayenne himself still refused to recognize the new king even after May 1595, as the Pope had not given Henry his own blessing of absolution. But the mayor and *échevins*, along with the judges and lawyers in the Parlement, obviously put aside their differences and recognized Henry as their legitimate monarch in May 1595. And it certainly seems that the new king had also won over the hearts and minds of the population of Dijon simply by promising an end to civil war. If there were still any who doubted the sincerity of his abjuration and conversion to Catholicism, Henry tried to allay their fears by his personal participation in the Corpus Christi day procession in Dijon later that summer. But reconciliation with Mayenne was still an issue.

When the tide began to turn in Burgundy in the early spring of 1595 toward recognizing Henry IV as King of France, Charles, duke of Mayenne, decided not to follow the majority of his clients in Dijon's Hôtel de Ville and Parlement in Dijon, most of whom followed the examples of mayor René Fleutelot and first president of the Parlement, Denis Brûlart, by recognizing the king's authority. Mayenne decided to hold out for full absolution by the Pope before he would publicly recognize Henry as sovereign. It was a calamitous decision, as it cost him the governorship of Burgundy as a result. After Mayenne and his troops were unable to stop the advance of the royal army in early 1595, Henry appointed Charles de Gontaut, baron de Biron, and the leader of his royal army in Burgundy, as Mayenne's replacement on April 20.[75] Thus, the governorship that had been held by the Guise family since 1543 was now lost due to Mayenne's intransigence. Mayenne sought refuge in various Burgundian towns, including Beaune and Chalon, and he even fled east

---

[75] Robert R. Harding, *Anatomy of a Power Elite: The Provincial Governors of Early Modern France* (New Haven, CT: Yale University Press, 1978), 221. The change in the governorship was registered by the Parlement in July. See Garnier, ed., *Journal de Gabriel Breunot*, 3: 8–9.

into the Franche-Comté, but the public tide had already turned and the leader of the League found himself unwelcome as a holdout against the king.[76] With his powerbase now completely reduced to a few loyal supporters and nearly all his former clients now having recognized the king, Mayenne found himself standing alone in Burgundy, the leader of a League that no longer existed. He used Clement VIII's absolution as a fig leaf to cover his political nakedness and formally signed a treaty with Henry in September to lay down his arms and accept the inevitable.[77] The final terms of the deal were not fully hammered out until January 1596; and Mayenne clearly received nothing like what he asked for: six fortified towns with troops to garrison them paid for by the king, the right to retain the governorship of Burgundy in his family in perpetuity, and the right to nominate all bishops and other ecclesiastical benefices in Burgundy. Although he suffered significantly for his belated submission with the loss of his governorship and the income and clientage that went along with it, Mayenne nevertheless received more generous terms than he might have expected. Although he lost the governorship of Burgundy, a new governorship was created for him in the Ile-de-France – minus Paris, Soissons, St. Denis, and Melun – allowing him to retain the appearance of authority and dignity without the powerbase. Second, the king agreed to write off Mayenne's debts totaling 350,000 écus, and relieved him of all other financial obligations that may have accumulated during the civil wars. The elimination of Mayenne's debts was clearly a major expense for Henry, and he did the same with several other aristocratic leaders of the League. It was crucial, however, to the king's enterprise of wiping out all memories of division and rebellion in the kingdom, a concept that was inherent in all of the previous edicts of pacification throughout the Wars of Religion, and an idea that would also be the foundation of the Edict of Nantes a few years later in 1598.[78] If all memories of the confessional and political divisions of the civil wars could be erased, then no one could be blamed for being the cause of these divisions. This was a grand gesture at remaking the national memory by requiring a national forgetting of the past. War debts, even those generated in fighting against royal authority,

---

[76] Drouot, *Mayenne et la Bourgogne*, 2: 391–422.

[77] Ibid., 2: 455–458. On the significance of the pope's absolution in winning over French Catholic support, see N. M. Sutherland, *Henry IV of France and the Politics of Religion, 1572–1596*, 2 vols. (Bristol: Elm Bank, 2002).

[78] Mack P. Holt, "The Memory of All Things Past: The Provisions of the Edict of Nantes," in Richard L. Goodbar, ed., *The Edict of Nantes: Five Essays and a New Translation* (Bloomington, MN: National Huguenot Society, 1998), 28–32.

were best served by being erased along with the national memory. Finally, all warrants for Mayenne's arrest were annulled, and he was formally absolved from any involvement in or blame for the assassination of Henry III. As for his remaining supporters, they were allowed to retain all offices they had acquired from Mayenne during the period of the League as long as they swore their loyalty to the crown.[79]

Just as with the councilors in the Hôtel de Ville and the judges in the Leaguer Parlement who made peace with the king, Mayenne cannot be said to have been bribed by the king for his submission. He lost perhaps more than any other member of the League in Burgundy, both in terms of income and political influence, as a result of his tardy submission to the crown, and nothing he received in the final negotiations could make up for that. So, while some contemporaries may have claimed, as did Pierre de l'Estoile, that Henry felt his former enemies had sold out rather than freely rendered their loyalty to him – "*pas rendu, vendu*" was the way l'Estoile put it – Henry generally only rewarded those Leaguers who unconditionally accepted his authority first.[80] As for Mayenne, he proved his loyalty to the crown by becoming personally involved in trying to win over the remaining aristocratic Leaguers still holding out against Henry, especially his cousin, the duke of Mercoeur in Brittany. Mayenne later also refused efforts by some militant Catholic clerics who tried to enlist his aid in an effort to overthrow the Edict of Nantes when it was published in 1598. If not an actual client of the king, Mayenne certainly made himself into a loyal servant of the king.

How best to summarize, then, Henry IV's politics of reconciliation with the League in Dijon? First, all of the king's negotiations with his former enemies seem to have been undertaken with one goal in mind: placing men he could trust in positions of power and authority in the offices and institutions that mattered in terms of maintaining order and preserving royal authority. Henry was much less concerned whether the men he appointed had been royalists or Leaguers prior to the submission of the city in June 1595, than whether they had fully supported this resolution and had worked to make it happen. In short, he sought to turn Mayenne's clients of the League into his own royal clients. Those who opposed the

---

[79] The original manuscript of the treaty is in the Archives départementales de la Côte-d'Or, B 12085, fols. 105–111. It is summarized nicely by Drouot, *Mayenne et la Ligue*, 2: 458–462. Also, see Garnier, ed., *Journal de Gabriel Breunot*, 2: 577 and 3: 8–9.

[80] Pierre de l'Estoile, *Journal de l'Estoile pour le règne de Henri IV*, eds. L.-R. Lefèvre and André Martin, 3 vols. (Paris: Gallimard, 1948–1960), 1: 393; quoted in Mark Greengrass, *France in the Age of Henri IV: The Struggle for Stability* (London: Longman, 1984), 59.

submission to the king outright, or even belatedly accepted it as in the case of Mayenne, suffered for their recalcitrance. Henry's choices for those he kept in power were clearly practical rather than ideological, and this was just as true for royalists and Leaguers as it was for Huguenots and Catholics. His greatest achievement as king was in bringing about a ceasefire and ending the civil wars. While it can easily be argued that his politics of reconciliation was only partially successful – the Huguenots, for example, were never fully reconciled or integrated into the French state that emerged after the civil wars – Henry did end the anarchy and rebellion that had reigned in much of France for so long. That he followed a series of kings, all sons of Henry II and Catherine de Medici, who were spectacularly unsuccessful at doing this, was all the more to his credit. While claiming that Henry IV single-handedly turned a pit of venomous snakes into a hive of innocent bees, as Hardouin de Péréfixe did shortly after Henry's death, is pure hyperbole, it is nevertheless true that Henry managed to secure the peace, however imperfect and however impermanent, after nearly 40 years of civil war. Thus, the myth of *le bon roi Henri* may be an exaggeration, but many of his contemporaries believed the king fully earned his legacy. Thus, Henry's politics of reconciliation were neither a politics of bribery nor a politics of absolutism; they were primarily a politics of clientage.

And what is the final judgment of the League in Burgundy? One recent historian of the League in Paris, Denis Pallier, has remarked that the moralism of the Leagers in the capital tended "to make the Leaguers penitents at the same time as militants."[81] Philip Benedict adopted this same phrase to describe the Leaguers in Rouen in Normandy, "penitents as well as militants."[82] Although there were doubtless some militants and penitents in the League in Burgundy, what I have tried to stress in this chapter is that there were a number of men who were devout Catholics without being penitents, and moderates rather than militant Leaguers. I would even put the Duke of Mayenne in this group, though he held out longer than most Leaguer moderates. Nevertheless, it seems to me that the success of the League in Burgundy – and helping to persuade Henry IV to abjure his Calvinist religion and become a Catholic was paramount in that success – was a result of men who were both devout in their faith and who wanted to serve a Catholic king, but who were largely neither penitents nor

---

[81] Pallier, *Recherches sur l'imprimerie à Paris pendant la Ligue*, 173: "*Le moralisme ... tend à faire des liguers des penitents en même temps que des militants.*"

[82] Benedict, *Rouen during the Wars of Religion*, 190–192.

militants. Above all they sought to protect the traditional liberties, rights, and privileges they had enjoyed from the crown before the civil wars and that they had enjoyed from the Dukes of Burgundy before that. They swore their loyalty to Henry IV after having submitted to him, believing that he would uphold those traditional rights.[83]

At the same time, the popular classes in Burgundy generally and the vignerons in particular were equally loyal to the new king. Once Henry IV had converted to Catholicism, they, like their social superiors in the League, saw little reason to continue to hold out. To be sure, as fully explained in the previous chapter, the vignerons had economic motives to want to accept their new king and end the fighting altogether. Thus, in 1595 the popular classes saw their new king as a savior, who was expected to bring about a return to economic stability and even prosperity. Like the mayor, *échevins*, and judges in the Parlement of Dijon, the city's vignerons were ready to turn the page and begin a new chapter. All of them desperately sought to put the religious wars behind them.

[83] The texts of the oaths sworn by the officers of each parish and the individual inhabitants of city are in Henri Drouot, "Le serment de fidélité des Dijonnais à Henri IV (1595)," *Mémoires de l'Académie des sciences, arts et belles lettres de Dijon* (1924): 269–274.

PART III

From Foy de Bourgogne *to Absolute Monarchy*
(1595 to 1630)

CHAPTER 7

The Contraction of Popular Politics and Catholic Reform

Most narratives of France after the civil wars of the second half of the sixteenth century have stressed the growth of royal power and efforts by first King Henry IV (1589–1610) and then his son King Louis XIII (1610–1643) to strengthen and centralize royal authority throughout the realm by various means: by weakening the power of local magnates and aristocrats, by interfering in local elections to control the independence of city councils, by inhibiting the autonomy of the sovereign courts such as the Parlement of Paris as well as the seven provincial Parlements, and by reining in the system of tax collection procedures in the various *pays d'état* such as Burgundy, whose provincial estates assessed and collected royal taxation rather than the crown's own tax assessors. The end result, according to these narratives, was the emergence of a stronger and more efficient system of government, giving the French crown the ability to prevent outbreaks of rebellion and disobedience such as were the norm during the civil wars from ever happening again. In short, more than three decades of civil war spurred Henry IV and Louis XIII to lay the foundations of absolute monarchy.[1]

While there is obviously some truth to these narratives, other scholars have modified or at least significantly revised them in a number of ways. First of all, as Fanny Cosandey and Robert Descimon have reminded us, historians have too often failed to distinguish between the theory and practice of absolute monarchy. In their view "absolutism" is "an entirely

---

[1] For various versions of this narrative see, among many others that could be cited, the following: Roland Mousnier, *The Assassination of Henry IV: The Tyrannicide Problem and the Consolidation of the French Absolute Monarchy in the Early Seventeenth Century*, trans. Joan Spencer (London: Faber and Faber, 1973); J. H. M. Salmon, *Society in Crisis: France in the Sixteenth Century* (London: Ernest Benn, 1975); Richard Bonney, *Political Change in France under Richelieu and Mazarin, 1624–1661* (Oxford: Oxford University Press, 1978); J. Russell Major, *From Renaissance Monarchy to Absolute Monarchy: French Kings, Nobles, and Estates* (Baltimore, MD: Johns Hopkins University Press, 1994); and John J. Hurt, *Louis XIV and the Parlements: The Assertion of Royal Authority* (Manchester: Manchester University Press, 2004).

theoretical indicator first and foremost, an indicator of applied theory."[2] In other words, even when historians have sought to move beyond theory and examine the practice of absolute monarchy, they have too often done so primarily by applying the theory of absolute monarchy. In effect, if the theory of absolute monarchy is typically royalist propaganda, historians need to critique the theory before applying it to practice. In addition, a more specific critique of the traditional narrative has come from scholars who have done exactly that, with the result that Henry IV, Louis XIII, and ultimately Louis XIV did not so much emasculate and weaken local magnates, city councils, sovereign courts, and provincial estates as they negotiated and collaborated with them in their own mutual interests. As William Beik put it so succinctly, absolutism "was the result, not of repression, but of a more successful defense of ruling class interests, through collaboration and improved direction."[3] This is clearly a long way from the royalist propaganda of an ever stronger and more centralized monarchy.

What I propose in this chapter and the next is to examine the process of negotiation with the crown in a slightly different way. Rather than focusing exclusively on the outcomes and results of collaboration and negotiation, we gain a better understanding of how absolute monarchy worked in practice if we analyze the very processes of the negotiations themselves. Indeed, by doing so I shall argue that we gain a very different understanding of the outcomes and results. This will allow us to better understand not just why modern-day historians have been misled by the royalist propaganda of absolutism, but also how those living in early seventeenth-century Burgundy came to be enticed by it as well. So, the emphasis here will be on the process of negotiations rather than simply outcomes. To be sure, the outcomes certainly mattered to all parties concerned, but looking at the process of negotiation helps us to see that in many cases short-term outcomes were often deceptive. Sometimes what

---

[2] Fanny Cosandey and Robert Descimon, *L'absolutisme en France: Histoire et historiographie* (Paris: Seuil, 2002), 26.

[3] William Beik, *Absolutism and Society in Seventeenth-Century France: State Power and Provincial Aristocracy in Languedoc* (Cambridge: Cambridge University Press, 1985), 31. For other versions of this revisionist narrative, see James B. Collins, *Classes, Estates, and Order in Early Modern Brittany* (Cambridge: Cambridge University Press, 1994); James B. Collins, *The State in Early Modern France* (Cambridge: Cambridge University Press, 2nd edn. 2009); James B. Collins, *La Monarchie républicaine: État et société dans la France moderne* (Paris: Odile Jacob, 2016); Julian Swann, *Provincial Power and Absolute Monarchy: The Estates General of Burgundy, 1661–1790* (Cambridge: Cambridge University Press, 2003); and Jérôme Loiseau, *"Elle fera ce que l'on voudra": La noblesse aux états de Bourgogne et la monarchie d'Henri IV à Louis XIV, 1602–1715* (Besançon: Presses universitaires de Franche-Comté, 2014).

appeared initially to be royal repression turned out to be a process of collaboration, while at other times what appeared to be noninterference and cooperation in the longer run proved to be more absolutist and interventionist. And Henry IV's relationship with Dijon's municipal magistrates in the Hôtel de Ville, especially in the way he sought to intervene in the annual municipal elections for mayor, is a prime example. And another is Henry's negotiations with the city over the implementation of the decrees of the Council of Trent as well as how to enact Catholic reform more generally.

7.1   Transformation of the Hôtel de Ville

Intervening in municipal elections was one way that Henry IV believed that he could guarantee the loyalty of those Leaguer cities that had fought against him so fiercely after the assassination of Henry III in 1589. Indeed, in cities such as Bordeaux, Lyon, Troyes, Amiens, Nantes, Poitiers, La Rochelle, Limoges, and Marseille, the new king had no hesitation in intervening in municipal affairs when necessary in order to prevent his former enemies from selecting their own mayors and *échevins* in their accustomed manner. In some cases, he even reduced the number of *échevins* a town was allowed to have. In most of them, according to Bernard Chevalier, he demanded that cities send him three names from which he would personally select the next mayor.[4] Indeed, in nearly all cases he sought to insert royalist supporters of the crown whom he could trust to replace recalcitrant Leaguers in city councils all over France.[5] Until

---

[4] Bernard Chevalier, *Les bonnes villes de France du XIVème au XVIème siecles* (Paris: Aubier, 1982), 204–205.

[5] For towns generally see Annette Finley-Croswhite, *Henry IV and the Towns: The Pursuit of Legitimacy in French Urban Society* (Cambridge: Cambridge University Press, 1999), 65–96 and 126–138; for Lyon see Yann Lignereux, *Lyon et le roi: De la bonne ville à l'absolutisme municipal, 1594–1654* (Seyssel: Champs Vallon, 2003), 548, and Raymond F. Kierstead, *Pomponne de Bellièvre: A Study of the King's Men in the Age of Henry IV* (Evanston, IL: Northwestern University Press, 1968), 76–89; for Troyes, see Penny Roberts, *A City in Conflict: Troyes during the French Wars of Religion* (Manchester: Manchester University Press, 1996), 15; for Amiens, see Olivia Carpi, *Une République imaginaire: Amiens pendent les troubles de religion, 1559–1597* (St. Etienne: Belin, 2005), 202–222; for Nantes, see Elizabeth C. Tingle, *Authority and Society in Nantes during the French Wars of Religion, 1559–98* (Manchester: Manchester University Press, 2006), 198–202; for Poitiers, see Hilary J. Bernstein, *Between Crown and Community: Politics and Civic Culture in Sixteenth-Century Poitiers* (Princeton, NJ: Princeton University Press, 2004), 28–37; for la Rochelle, see Kevin C. Robbins, *City on the Ocean Sea, La Rochelle, 1530–1650: Urban Society, Religion, and Politics on the French Atlantic Frontier* (Leiden: Brill, 1997), 30–37; for Limoges, see Michel Cassan, *Le temps des guerres de religion: Le cas du Limousin, vers 1530-vers 1630* (Paris: Publisud, 1996), 298–299; and for Marseille see Wolfgang Kaiser, *Marseille au temps des troubles (1559–1596): Morphologie sociale et luttes de factions* (Paris: EHESS, 1991), 346–350.

recently, historians have traditionally interpreted these actions as part of Henry's absolutist policies of destroying municipal privileges and weakening urban elites in favor of a more centralized royal authority. As John Salmon wrote in 1975, at the end of the religious wars "the crown had a clear policy of reducing municipal independence."[6]

Paris was a special case, as the court had generally resided there since the beginning of the Wars of Religion, and the king's own royal officers in the Parlement, the other sovereign courts, and the Chancellery already had many explicit powers of police and administration over the capital that did not exist in other towns. Moreover, the king had tried to intervene in Parisian elections even before the beginning of the civil wars when Henry II substituted his own choice for *prévôt des marchands* (the equivalent of the mayor in Paris) in 1557 in place of the candidate who received the most votes. In general, however, Henry IV's immediate predecessors tended to work within the electoral framework established by local elites and tended to accept their choices of *prévôt des marchands* and *échevins*.[7] And Henry IV followed this path in the capital after the civil wars as well. As Robert Descimon has shown, Henry's interventions in appointing municipal leaders were usually fairly benign. He tended to appoint candidates to the position of *prévôt des marchands* who had already been elected as *échevins* and almost always the candidate with the highest number of votes.[8] And this was the pattern he chose to follow in Dijon as well.[9]

The new king Henry IV got a chance to intervene in municipal politics very quickly after his reconciliation with the League in Burgundy in May–June 1595, as René Fleutelot, the newly reelected mayor died suddenly and unexpectedly just a few months later in September 1595. The newly reunited Parlement of Dijon, wanting to insert itself into municipal affairs after the tumultuous years of the League, wanted one of their own to succeed the deceased Fleutelot as interim mayor, Bénigne Frémyot, the fourth president (presiding judge) in the Parlement of Dijon and the leader of the royalist Parlement that had met in Flavigny and then Semur until the two opposing Parlements in Burgundy could be reunited.

---

[6] J. H. M. Salmon, *Society in Crisis: France in the Sixteenth Century* (London: Ernest Benn, 1975), 301.

[7] Barbara B. Diefendorf, *Paris City Councillors in the Sixteenth Century: The Politics of Patrimony* (Princeton, NJ: Princeton University Press, 1983), 20–22.

[8] Robert Descimon, "L'échevinage parisien sous Henri IV (1594–1610): Autonomie urbaine, conflits politiques et exclusives socials," in N. Bulst and J.-Ph .Genet, eds., *La Ville, la bourgeoisie et la genèse de l'état moderne, XIIe-XVIIIe siècles* (Paris: Editions du CNRS, 1988), 113–150.

[9] An older study of Dijon argues that Henry IV was very interventionist in the mayoral elections, and thus runs counter to my argument here: F. Bourcier, "Le régime municipal à Dijon sous Henri IV," *Revue d'histoire moderne* 10 (1935): 97–120.

And Henry IV readily agreed to support Frémyot, a royalist judge who had been loyal to the king throughout the wars of the League.[10] In addition, his religious credentials were above reproach, as he had a brother who was an ecclesiastical *échevin* in Dijon's Hôtel de Ville, while his daughter, Jeanne de Chantal, would help found the Order of the Visitation for women just a few years later (see later in this chapter). The *échevins* on the city council had other ideas, however, and they resented the interference of the Parlement and the king, claiming that only they could select the interim mayor, until the next popular election when the choice would be up to the people again.[11] The *échevins* ultimately conceded and accepted Frémyot as the interim mayor on account of the support of Henry IV, who made Frémyot a member of the king's Council of State. Moreover, Henry recommended that Frémyot be reelected for a full term of his own in June 1596, and he was duly elected by the people for such a term.[12]

It has to be said, however, that Henry's inclination was not to interfere in the municipal elections in Dijon unless he was forced to do so. In fact, after the election of Bénigne Frémyot in 1596, Henry did not even nominate his choice for mayor for the next several years and allowed his Dijonnais subjects to select their own mayor according to their traditional election rituals. The judges in the Parlement of Dijon, however, continued to try to influence the choice of mayor in the city after Frémyot's term ended in June 1597. Their reason was that the elections were still being disrupted by various commotions and potentially disruptive political demonstrations with various candidates proffering wine for votes.[13] They wanted changes in the format of the election, with only those who had paid a substantial *taille* in the preceding year to be able to vote, which would have prevented most vignerons and artisans from participating.[14] One of the *échevins*, Bernard Coussin, a former Leaguer moderate, was named keeper of the gospels for the June 1598 election and became the figurehead for opposition to the Parlement by the city council. The Chamber of Accounts, as was traditionally the case, presented Coussin as "the candidate

[10] AMD, B 233, fols. 120v–126v, September 13–16, 1595.

[11] Joseph Garnier, ed., *Journal de Gabriel Breunot, conseiller de Parlement de Dijon, précédé du livre de souvenance de Pepin, chanoine de la Sainte-Chapelle de cette ville*, 3 vols. (Dijon: J.-E. Rabutot, 1864), 3: 25–30.

[12] Joseph Garnier, ed., *Correspondance de la mairie de Dijon extradite des archives de cette ville*, 3 vols. (Dijon: J.-E. Rabutot, 1868–70), 3: 7–8, Henry IV to the Chambre de ville de Dijon, June 12, 1596.

[13] See my own article, "Political Culture and Mayoral Elections in Sixteenth-Century Dijon," in Mack P. Holt, ed., *Society and Institutions in Early Modern France* (Athens, GA: University of Georgia Press, 1991), 98–116.

[14] Garnier, *Journal de Gabriel Breunot*, 3: 116–118.

of the king" at the election on June 20. And Coussin was elected over-whelmingly as mayor himself by 1,240 out of 1,710 votes cast (72.5 percent).[15] Having failed to change the election format, the Parlement decided to act unilaterally the following year and announced that in future the new mayor would be chosen by lot from among the three highest vote-getters. Mayor Coussin mobilized the opposition once again, and this time he made an appeal to the royal governor of Burgundy, Charles de Gontaut, duke of Biron, as well as to Pierre Jeannin, former presiding judge of the Parlement of Burgundy under the League, who had recently been promoted to a presiding judgeship in the Parlement of Paris. Once again, the city council prevailed, and the judges of the Parlement of Dijon were forced to accept *lettres de jussion* from the king ordering that the annual elections for mayor should take place "in the traditional format on the usual days, places, and times without any changes, alterations, or innovations of any kind. And in order to remove the possibility of abusing or mistreating the said election we expressly forbid all persons of whatever quality or condition they are from corrupting, canvassing, or influencing directly or indirectly with money or any other illicit means whatsoever the voices and votes of the people."[16] This kind of popular canvassing – usually with wine being offered by the candidates – had been going on for decades, as has been shown in previous chapters. The mayoral election of 1599 had been postponed in June, in fact, because Henry IV requested that the city send him the names of the three highest vote-getters so that he could personally choose the mayor from among them, as he had done in other cities since 1595. The king's justification was because of all the "intrigues and plots (*brigues et monopoles*)" affecting the elections caused by the canvassing with wine.[17] The magistrates balked at the suggestion, and the election was postponed until September, when the king finally backed down and agreed to hold the election in the usual format.

---

[15] Ibid., 103; AMD, B 236, fols. 5r–41v, June 20, 1598; and Michael P. Breen, Law, *City, and King: Legal Culture, Municipal Politics, and State Formation in Early Modern Dijon* (Rochester, NY: University of Rochester Press, 2007), 72–79, for a thorough discussion of Parlement's attempts to intervene in Dijon's mayoral elections from 1595 to 1611.

[16] AMD, B 236, fols. 217r–219v May 13–14, 1599, fol. 246r, July 7, 1599, fol.252r–v, July 29, 1599, and AMD, B 12, côte 36, September 6, 1599: "*en la forme ancienne aux jours, lieu et temps accoutumés sans y rien changer, alterer ou innover; deffondons toutes fois tres expressement pour oter les moyens d'abus ou malversations au fait de lad[ite] election et creation a toutes personnes de quelque qualité et condition qu'elles soient, de corrompre, briguer ne praticquer directement ou indirectement par argent ou autres moyens illicites quelconques les voix et suffrages du peuple.*" Also, see Breen, *Law, City, and King*, 74–75.

[17] AMD, B 236, fols. 233v–293r, June–October 1599; and BMD, Ms. 1493, 747–748, June 15, 1599.

Henry IV did not give up, however, and he eventually issued an edict in June 1608 requiring the city council to send him the names of the three highest vote-getters of that year's election. His justification was that he wanted "to prevent the disturbances and insurrections that have taken place during the elections in the major cities everywhere throughout the kingdom and especially in Dijon (*empêcher les perturbations et les séditions qui avaient lieu pendant les élections dans les grandes villes partout dans le royaume et notamment à Dijon*)." The king did promise, however, that having chosen the new mayor from among the three candidates with the most votes, "the said candidate will be received and installed in his office in the accustomed manner (*le dit [candidat] sera reçu et installé [dans son office] comme à l'accoutumée*)." To the Dijon magistrates this was the whole point: The king's proposal was not "in the accustomed manner."[18] When nearly a year later the mayor and *échevins* had still not agreed to this innovation, Henry issued letters patent dated May 30, 1609 and a *lettre de jussion* dated May 31 requiring the mayor to send him the names of the three candidates with the most votes in the forthcoming election so that he could name the next mayor.[19] As before, however, the king did in fact select the candidate with the highest total that year, Etienne Humbert, a royal tax controller. Thus the king had negotiated a new system of selecting the mayor of Dijon with the city's political elites, a system that kept in place the traditional rituals and format of the elections, though giving the king the final choice in selecting who would actually be invested with the office. To be sure, this negotiation lasted more than a decade and only came to an end with the king's *lettre de jussion* in May of 1609, requiring the obedience of the city to his demand to be able to choose the new mayor from among the three highest vote-getters. Because Henry duly selected the candidate with the most votes, however, his reputation as a just king who did not interfere in Dijon's electoral process remained intact, despite the fact that he put in place a system that his successors could – and did – use to bypass candidates with the most votes in the annual elections.

Henry IV was assassinated by François Ravaillac on May 14, 1610, just a month before the mayoral elections in Dijon that year. Just a fortnight later Henry's young son – now King Louis XIII – sent the mayor and *échevins* a letter urging them to remember the *lettre de jussion* his father had sent them in 1609, ordering them to send him the names of the three

---

[18] AMD, B 11, cote 41, June 1608.
[19] AMD, B 11, cote 41, May 31, 1609; B 246, fols. 264v–266v, June 18, 1609; and BMD, Ms. 1494, 234–235, June 19–20, 1609.

highest vote-getters in the upcoming election.[20] The election took place on June 20 without incident, with a total of 1,290 male heads of household casting their voices in the election. The three candidates with the most votes were as follows: Edme Joly, a lawyer and judge in the Parlement of Dijon, with 412 votes; Nicolas Humbert, brother of the previous mayor and also a lawyer and judge in the Parlement, with 393 votes; and Guy Nicolas, a royal secretary and a sitting *échevin*. The Baron de Lux, the king's lieutenant-general in Burgundy, announced that these three names would thus be sent to the young king Louis XIII as previously requested.[21] To be sure, most in Dijon duly expected that the young king, or possibly his regent Marie de Medici, would duly nominate Joly to be the mayor. But the king did not oblige, naming Nicolas Humbert, the second highest vote-getter as the new mayor on July 6, 1610.[22] Although Humbert was eventually sworn in as the new mayor, this precedent of royal intervention and alteration of the traditional manner of electing Dijon's mayor became a major issue in the city's relationship with the new king.

Even the new mayor Humbert, as well as the *échevins* and a large number of notables in the city, was troubled by what he saw as royal interference in the city's traditional right to choose its own mayor. In February 1611 the mayor and *échevins* sent a strongly worded letter to the king that all previous kings of France, including the king's own father Henry IV, had recognized the city's right "on the accustomed day and hour and at the accustomed place" to proceed to the election of their mayor in the accustomed manner. They noted that these privileges had been given to the commune of Dijon in 1237 by Duke Hugues of Burgundy, and every Duke of Burgundy and King of France ever since, including the king's own father, had upheld them. They urged the king, his mother the regent, and the royal council to do the same.[23] The king and regent prevaricated, however, and replied that they needed to consult with the king's newly appointed royal governor of the province of Burgundy, Roger de Saint-Lary, seigneur de Bellegarde.[24] The king ordered the election of June 1611 to be postponed, initially until August 31, 1611, but eventually until June 2012, with the mayor and *échevins* serving for another year. Moreover, Louis XIII – or more likely, Marie de Medici – eventually agreed with Bellegarde to restore the traditional format of the elections

[20] Garnier, *Correspondance de la mairie de Dijon*, 3: 113–114, May 31, 1610.
[21] AMD, B 248, fols. 1–25v, June 21, 1610.   [22] AMD, B 248, fols. 44r–v, July 6, 1610.
[23] AMD, B 248, fols. 199v–202v, February 23, 1611.
[24] Garnier, *Correspondance de la mairie de Dijon*, 3: 118–119, Louis XIII and Marie de Medici to the mayor and échevins, May 18, 1611.

with one significant exception: starting with the next election in June 1612 only those who had paid a minimum of 40 *sous* in each of the two annual *taille* assessments for each of the three previous years were eligible to cast their voices in the election, thus eliminating the poorer vignerons and artisans from participating at all.[25] At the turn of the seventeenth century the mean tax paid by the vignerons in the parish of St. Michel was just under 40 *sous*, so just more than half of all vignerons in the parish would henceforth be excluded from participating in the elections.[26] This also reduced the overall number of voters in the annual elections, thereby terminating the idealized fiction of elections functioning as a ritual of binding the community together as a whole. Vote totals in the 1630s and 1640s occasionally reached 1275 voters, though most years were much less.[27] And though these numbers compare favorably to most years in the sixteenth and early seventeenth centuries, the fact that roughly 40 percent of the entire electorate was now permanently excluded from participating in the elections was a serious blow for the poorest vignerons.

The postponement, and ultimately cancellation, of the 1611 election, along with the new voter requirements, further exacerbated the growing tensions between crown and city. Dijon's notables ultimately saw Henry IV's interventions in Dijon's elections as minimal, traditional, and hardly the sharp end of an absolutist agenda aimed at destroying municipal privilege. To be sure, he did initiate a process that would allow royal intervention in the future, and this innovation alone could be considered an intrusion on local and municipal independence. But Henry chose to wield his authority lightly and unobtrusively in the city. It was a sharp contrast with the city's view of Louis XIII. Indeed, Henry IV was always remembered as a popular king in Dijon who ended the civil wars. Even though it was he who negotiated the policies of intervention used by his son Louis XIII, he was always remembered as having preserved Dijon's traditional privileges and liberties, including the right to hold their own elections, without royal interference. In the eyes of Dijon's citizens, it was Louis XIII who was perceived as the architect of absolutism, as he over-turned the custom of allowing the candidate with a plurality of votes to become mayor in 1610, and he limited the suffrage in the city to the wealthier and more prosperous inhabitants. To be sure, the new require-ments under Louis XIII did reduce the need to canvass for votes with food and wine, though it did not stop it entirely. To Dijon's disenfranchised

---

[25] AMD, B 248, fols. 256r–258r, June 10, 1611, fols. 299v–301v, August 27, 1611.   [26] See Figure 5.2.
[27] Breen, *Law, City, and King,* 79 and 246, n. 44.

vignerons and artisans, however, Louis XIII was perceived as the very opposite of his father, *le bon roi* Henry IV. It hardly mattered that Louis XIII, in fact, did not intervene in the mayoral elections between 1612 and 1630. Indeed, apart from the election of 1610 – which was an aberration given the recent assassination of Henry IV as well as the regency of Marie de Medici – Louis XIII's relationship to mayoral elections in Dijon was about as benign as that of his father, at least up to 1630, when events in Dijon forced the king's hand (see Chapter 8). But what mattered more were popular perceptions of the two kings in the city. Henry IV was forever viewed as a champion and protector of local liberties and privileges, while his son Louis XIII would forever be viewed as an absolutist and interventionist who wanted to undermine those same local privileges and liberties. The events of 1629 and 1630 would exacerbate that contrast.

A very different way of understanding the Hôtel de Ville in the period following the Wars of Religion is to shift away from the rituals of elections and look at the elites who were elected, and how most elite families attempted to forge ties with other elites both in the Hôtel de Ville and in the Parlement and other sovereign courts in the city. But first of all, which Dijon families dominated the municipal elections in the sixteenth and early seventeenth centuries? One way to get a quick overview of the families who made up the membership of the Hôtel de Ville in the period is to look at who served on the council in selected years over the course of this period. In some ways, this is even more revealing than looking at the make-up of the Hôtel de Ville in specific years, because there was always a required carryover of a minimum of six members from one year to the next. The city's charter required that, after his election in June every year, the mayor was required to select six members from the previous year's Hôtel de Ville to serve in the upcoming year, providing some continuity and stability from year to year even if a new mayor was elected. The newly elected mayor and these six *anciens échevins* would then select the remaining fourteen *échevins*, to make up the full component of twenty *échevins*. So, this was truly a self-perpetuating oligarchy, all the more so as most mayors who were elected had previously served on the council as an *échevin*. Thus, looking at the membership of the Hôtel de Ville at periodic intervals gives us a more accurate sense of turnover as well as continuity. The Berbisey family is a good example. In 1477 when the last Valois Duke of Burgundy, Charles the Bold, was killed, the mayor of Dijon was Etienne Berbisey, who had a law degree and was appointed a *conseiller au Roi* upon declaring the city's loyalty to King Louis XI. The Berbisey family would have members of its family serving in the Hôtel de Ville for the next one hundred and fifty years. For example, Etienne's grandson Thomas Berbisey was an *échevin* for much of the first two decades of the sixteenth century. He was already an influential member of the council by 1510 and was still serving in 1520. By 1540 Claude Berbisey, Thomas's son, was an *échevin*. In 1553 Claude's brother Guillaume Berbisey was elected mayor, reelected in 1554, and then served as an *échevin* very year thereafter until 1562. A nephew, Jean Berbisey, was selected *échevin* in 1567 and 1570, and his son, also named Jean, was selected in 1591and 1592. By this time there were also numerous other Berbiseys serving in the Parlement as judges (*conseillers*) and lawyers. Perpetuo Berbisey, for example, was first elected as an *échevin*, and then he became a prominent judge in the Parlement during the period of the League, ultimately becoming a presiding judge in the Parlement of Dijon in 1600, where he served until his death in 1611. And the experience of the Berbisey family was by no means atypical.[28]

A list of the families who dominated the Hôtel de Ville over the course of the sixteenth and early seventeenth centuries appears in Table 7.1. Every family that had at least two members appointed as *échevin* between 1550 and 1630 is included.

What is striking is how many families managed to keep at least one member appointed to the city council on a regular basis between 1550 and 1630. For example, the Requelene family had ten different members serve a total of 46 times during this 80-year period, easily the most often represented family in the entire cohort. Other families – such as the Bourrelier, the Coussin, the Fleutelot, the Jacquiet, the Malpoy, and the Marc families – were represented almost as regularly. Still others – such as the Berbisey, the Bouhier, the Chisseret, the Joly, the La Verne, the Martin, and the Petit families – were very well represented for certain decades, though they did not have the continual presence on the city council for the entire period as other families did. In some cases, there are obviously generational gaps, such as exhibited by the Chisseret, Euvrard, Le Compasseur, and Tisserand families, who had several family members over several generations serve the city. In others – such as the Goudran, La Verne, Mailliard, and Martin families – it was just one family member who served for a long period of service in the Hôtel de Ville that made up the majority of the family's contribution. But it would also be a mistake to look at our *échevin* families as simply independent corporate units all competing against one another in a mad political scramble for

---

[28] For details of the Berbisey family, see Jules d' Arbaumont, *Armorialde la Chambre des comptes de Dijon* (Dijon: Lamarche, 1881), 159–162.

Table 7.1 Échevin families in Dijon, 1550–1630 (Numbers in parentheses refer to the total number of family members who served as mayor or échevin during this period. Numbers in each column refer to the number of times a family member served as mayor or échevin in each decade. Only families with at least two members are listed in the table.)

Name	1550s	1560s	1570s	1580s	1590s	1600s	1610s	1620s
ARVISENET (2)					2	2	4	
BERBISEY (5)	8	3		1	2	3	4	
BERNARD (2)				8	4			1
BILLOCART (5)			1	2	2	2	1	
BOISSELIER (3)			4	3	1		1	3
BOSSUET (3)		1					2	2
BOUHIER (4)	1	6	1	5	8	1	3	1
BOURRELIER (3)	2	5	1	3		1	3	
BRECHILLET (2)				1		1		3
CARRELET (3)	2			2	4	5	8	2
CHISSERET (6)		3	7	7	5	6		
COUSSIN (2)	2	4	2	6	3	2		
DAVID (2)					2		1	
DES BARRES (2)	1	3	4			1	3	3
EUVRARD (5)		4	3			1	3	1
FLEUTELOT (7)	1	3	8	7	7		1	1
FRASANS (3)					3	5	2	4
FYOT (2)	1	1						
GELLIOT (2)								2
GOUDRAN (2)	10					1	1	
HUMBERT (3)	1					2	4	6

	1	2	3	4	5	6	7
JACHIET (4)	3		3	2	7		2
JACQUIN (2)		1		1			
JACQUINOT (2)				1	9	3	
JOLY (4)		5	2	5	5	2	3
LA VERNE (6)	7	5	4	10	6		1
LE COMPASSEUR (3)	2	3					6
LENET (2)					2		3
MAILLARD (2)	8	10	4				
MAIRE (2)						7	
MALPOY (7)		1	3	3	1	1	1
MARC (5)		4	3	3	2	6	5
MARTIN (2)	8	10	4	4	2	1	
PETIT (5)					2	1	6
PIGNALLET (3)		2	5	6	3		
PREVOST (2)		4	2	5	1		
PROCESS (2)			8	3			
QUILLARDET (4)	1					3	1
REQUELENE (10)	4	3	6	5	9	9	6
ROUHIER (3)	3	2		6	4		4
SAINTONGE (3)		1					2
TISSERAND (3)		8	6				3
VENDERESSE (3)	1	1	1	1	1		3

Source: AMD, B188 to B268.

wealth and influence. To be sure, politics in Dijon was competitive, as the analysis of Dijon's elections in previous chapters has already suggested. Nevertheless, these families had many mutually dependent ties and links with one another that created vast networks of families who were linked together socially through marriage and godparentage.

What follows is taken from a sampling from the baptismal records of the *État civil* in Dijon, which only begin in 1578 in some parishes, though not until 1595 in others, and not until 1603 in one. Nevertheless, I have tried to locate all examples of marriage and godparentage for the forty-three *échevin* families listed in Table 7.1 between the years 1578 and 1610. Baptismal records highlight the expansion of kinship ties through godparentage in ways that notarial records do not, and because, ultimately, social relations were at the heart of premodern politics,[29] these records can shed light on politics in the Hôtel de Ville. Moreover, baptismal records are relatively rare for the sixteenth and early seventeenth centuries. What emerges are four principal networks of family social ties linking many of the *échevin* families together in the sixteenth and seventeenth centuries: (1) a Berbisey–Des Barres network, (2) a Bourrelier–Fleutelot–Requelene network, (3) a Bernard–Chisseret–Martin network, and (4) a Humbert–Jachiet–Joly network, all of which are shown in Table 7.2. In addition, many of the other families are linked peripherally to these four main networks. Moreover, many of these families formed ties to more than one of these four principal networks, forming bridges between the principal networks. A short summary reveals a lot about how these social networks actually shaped politics within the Hôtel de Ville.

Let me take just one of these networks to illustrate how social interaction came to play a role in the politics of the sixteenth and early seventeenth centuries. The Berbisey–Des Barres network was forged between two of Dijon's most important families. The Berbisey, as has already been discussed, were important in Dijon under the reign of the Valois dukes of Burgundy. Etienne I Berbisey was a merchant who became licensed in law and was elected as Dijon's vicomte-mayeur in 1437. His son Etienne II Berbisey was also licensed in law and was a councilor to Duke Charles the Bold. He served as an *échevin* from 1453 onwards and was elected *vicomte-mayeur* himself for nine straight years from 1475 to 1484. His son Thomas I Berbisey was appointed *greffier* in the new Parlement of Dijon in 1480 and was also a secretary to King Louis XI, and he served as an *échevin*

---

[29] See Barbara B. Diefendorf, ed., *Social Relations, Politics, and Power, in Early Modern France: Robert Descimon and the Historian's Craft* (Kirksville, MO: Truman State University Press, 2016), especially Diefendorf's introduction, 1–24.

Table 7.2 *Family networks in the Hôtel de Ville, 1578–1610*

I.	**Berbisey–Des Barres**	
	Other linked families:	Des Frasans
		Goudran
		La Verne
		Mailliard
		Rouhier
II.	**Bourrelier–Fleutelot–Requelene**	
	Other linked families:	Bouhier
		Coussin
		Goudran
		Joly
		Le Compasseur
		Mailliard
		Petit
		Tisserand
III.	**Bernard–Chisseret–Martin**	
	Other linked families:	Le Compasseur
		Requelene
IV.	**Humbert–Jachiet–Joly**	
	Other linked families:	Bernard
		Bossuet
		Bouhier
		Brechillet
		Lenet
		Mailliard
		Petit

Source: AMD, État civil: B 482, 490–491, 494–495, 504, and 506

throughout most of the first two decades of the sixteenth century. His son Guillaume Berbisey, a lieutenant in the bailliage court in Dijon, was also elected *vicomte-mayeur* in 1553, while Guillaume's son Perpetuo Berbisey was from 1575 a *conseiller* in the Parlement, and from 1599 a president in the Parlement.[30] The Des Barres family was not as prominent in the Hôtel de Ville as the Berbisey, even though Jean des Barres was an *échevin* for three years in the early 1560s and Bernard des Barres was elected *vicomte-mayeur* in both 1573 and 1574. It was in the Parlement where the Des Barres had the most influence, as two generations held the office of president in the Parlement in the late sixteenth century, including the former mayor Bernard des Barres. Indeed, it was the marriage of Bernard's daughter,

---

[30] For the Berbisey family, again see d'Arbaumont, *Armorialde*, 159–162.

Anne, to Perpetuo Berbisey in 1584 that provided the critical liaison between the two families. In addition, Perpetuo's sister, Marthe Berbisey, soon married his wife's brother, Charles des Barres, who was a treasurer-general in Burgundy, providing a second marital link between the two families. The baptismal records show that members of the two families served as godparents for each other's children on eight different occasions between 1600 and 1610.[31] And members of these two families also served as godparents for other families in the same period: the Des Frasans, Goudran, La Verne, Mailliard, and Rouhier, linking these other *échevin* families to the network.

As is already clear, however, the Berbisey–Des Barres network was also heavily linked to other families outside the Hôtel de Ville, especially to parlementary families. This is hardly surprising given that both Perpetuo Berbisey and Bernard Des Barres held the office of president in the Parlement of Dijon. But the families also forged marriage links to some of the other principal families who held positions of influence in the Parlement. For example, Jean Berbisey, Perpetuo's cousin and a *conseiller* in the Parlement, married Anne Catherine, daughter of Guy Catherine, another *conseiller* in the Parlement.[32] When Anne gave birth to a daughter (also named Anne) on May 10, 1610, the godfather was a *conseiller* in the Chamber of Accounts, while the godmother was the wife of a lawyer in the Parlement.[33] And the Berbisey and Des Frasans also served as godparents for other prominent parlementary families, including the Bégat, Casotte, Catherine, Frémyot, Fyot, Gagne, Le Goux, Quarré, and Thomas families. Thus, the Berbisey–Des Barres network was just as firmly tied to the families of the *bourgeoisie première* from the Parlement of Dijon as it was tied to the families of the *bourgeoisie seconde* families in the Hôtel de Ville. And while there is no question that there were often serious political tensions between the Hôtel de Ville and the Parlement throughout the sixteenth century and especially during the period of the League, many families had strong and social ties to both bodies. Indeed, it would be very difficult to define the entire extended Berbisey–Des Barres network as belonging either to the *bourgeoisie première* or to the *bourgeoisie seconde*. While in the mid-sixteenth century the network was more deeply rooted in the Hôtel de Ville than in the Parlement, this began to change by the end of the century. Indeed, by the early seventeenth century both the Berbisey and the Des Barres were socially integrated into the families of the political

[31] AMD, État civil: B482, fols. 22r, 27v, 32v, 53v, 109r, 182v, 201v, and B 490, fol. 236v.
[32] d'Arbremont, *Armorial*, 159–162.   [33] AMD, État civil: B 490, fol. 209r.

elites of the city, both from within the Parlement as well as other sovereign courts and royal officers. Moreover, the experience of the Berbisey–Des Barres families shows that marriage was often the safest and sometimes the only route to political advancement to the very highest political positions such as the presidents in the Parlement. Given the inflation in the price of offices in the late sixteenth century, as well as the tendency of high office-holders to try to pass on their offices to their heirs, Perpetuo Berbisey's marriage in 1584 to Anne des Barres, daughter of Bernard des Barres, was fortuitous. When Bernard des Barres died in 1599, his presidency in the Parlement was left to his son-in-law, Perpetuo Berbisey, who was a *conseiller* but had little hope of ever rising to one of the presidencies in the chamber except through his marriage to a daughter of a president.[34]

To move from the social to the political realm, it goes without saying that the various families of these *échevin* networks tried to work together within the Hôtel de Ville. Moreover, these networks tended to support the same candidates for mayor in the annual elections each June. Not only did the Berbisey and the Des Barres support each other when a member of one family was running for mayor, but they also usually voted for the same candidate in other years. Interestingly, the two families only overlapped in the Hôtel de Ville in the 1550s, 1560s, and 1570s. And while there are no surviving baptismal or marriage records from this period to reinforce this impression, it would appear from the voting patterns in the mayoral elections that the two families had already forged a political alliance before the double marriage in the 1580s of Perpetuo Berbisey and his sister Marthe to Anne and Charles des Barres. It is also clear that the Berbisey–Des Barres network tended to stick together and supported the League in Dijon during the 1590s. Not only did the second president of the Parlement of Dijon, Bernard des Barres, and his son-in-law, Perpetuo Berbisey, *conseiller* in Parlement, both stay in Dijon to support the League rather than flee to Flavigny to join the royalist Parlement, so did the members of the other parlementary families they were aligned with: Catherine, Fyot, Gagne, Quarré, and Thomas.[35] It is certainly true that the politics of the League managed to divide some families, pitting father against son or brother against brother, as we saw with the Bretagne family in Chapter 5. Nevertheless, it is equally true that the political and social alliances forged within the Hôtel de Ville in Dijon before the League could survive that troubled period, even if the League offered opportunities to forge new alliances.

---

[34] d'Arbremont, *Armorial*, 159–162.   [35] BMD, Fonds Saverot 1493, p. 433.

I have focused in detail here only on the Berbisey–Des Barres network to the exclusion of the other three alliances listed in Table 7.2. All three suggest very similar patterns, however, with perhaps the only difference being that the other three networks enjoyed less exalted links with the Parlement and other royal officers. Most of the parlementary ties forged by the members of the Bourrelier–Fleutelot–Requelene network, the Bernard–Chisseret–Martin network, and the Humbert–Jacquiet–Joly network, for example, were made with barristers (*avocats*) and solicitors (*procureurs*) in the Parlement rather than with ordinary judges (*conseillers*) and presiding judges (*presidents*). Still, these other family networks that originated in the Hôtel de Ville had extensive ties with members from the sovereign courts as well as other royal officers. How all this fits into the larger argument being made in this chapter that the Hôtel de Ville was undergoing various transformations in the period following the Wars of Religion is that these networks demonstrate two separate but related shifts that were taking place over the long term. First, it is clear that the Hôtel de Ville itself was changing from a body dominated by wealthy merchants and other members of the bourgeoisie – as it was in the first half of the sixteenth century – to a body becoming more and more controlled by men trained in the law. While I argued in Chapter 6 that the Hôtel de Ville had not become completely dominated by men with legal training by the time of the wars of the League in the 1590s, as Henri Drouot had argued, the transformation from a commercial to a legal elite was clearly well underway. And it was completed in the first half of the seventeenth century, as Michael Breen has convincingly shown.[36] Second, it is equally clear that as relations between the Hôtel de Ville and the Parlement were becoming more strained due to the court's interference in the municipal elections, the very families who dominated the city council during and after the Wars of Religion were also advancing to the Parlement once they left the city council as well as placing other family members at the court in some function: barristers, solicitors, ushers, and even judges.

One final way that the Hôtel de Ville was changing in the decades following the end of the civil wars was that the ecclesiastical *échevins*, who had sat on the council going back to the reign of the Valois dukes of Burgundy, were suddenly dismissed in 1626 and did not return. Traditionally, the canon of the Sainte Chapelle, the prior or sub-prior from the abbey of St. Bénigne, the canon and provost of the collegial church of St. Etienne, the canon of the Chapelle aux Riches, and usually

---

[36] Breen, *Law, City, and King*, especially 58–67.

one or two chaplains representing the secular clergy of the seven parish churches in the city, who served on a rotating basis, made up the ecclesiastical *échevins*. These men were named in the deliberations of the Hôtel de Ville every June alongside the newly selected *échevins* immediately after each mayoral election. Moreover, they were listed among those *échevins* attending every single meeting of the city council throughout the year in the written deliberations. Their principal functions were to lead prayers and celebrate mass whenever called upon at council meetings, as well as to organize the various religious processions outlined in Chapter 2. Occasionally, their roles took on a more explicitly political function, such as during the Wars of Religion when scores of Dijon's Protestants recanted and abjured their religion to return to the fold of the Catholic Church. It was the ecclesiastical *échevins* who recorded their confessions of faith and abjuration (see above, pp. 160–162). But for the most part, their roles were as much symbolic as political. Of course, trying to separate religion and politics is fruitless for this period, as much of this book has argued. Moreover, the same families who contributed many of the mayors and *échevins* throughout the period also contributed many of the ecclesiastical *échevins* as well. But other than being listed as attending, they were rarely referred to in the written deliberations.

Ironically, the issue that led to the demise of the ecclesiastical *échevins* was an internal dispute over whether ecclesiastical *échevins* could take priority over the other twenty *échevins* during a religious procession. The dispute was over who had the right to sit on the right side of the altar and who would sit on the left side when the procession entered a church, and this was much more than a simple dispute of social hierarchy. On the feast day of St. James and St. Christopher in July 1625 a dispute arose when the procession concluded at the abbey church of St. Etienne. This was the annual procession inside the city walls on the eve of the feast day of St. Anne. In that year when the religious procession terminated at the abbey church of St. Etienne, the dean of St. Etienne, a Monsieur Moisson, "took his place among the raised seats on the left-hand side approaching the high altar, instead of leaving those seats free to be occupied by [the gentlemen of] the Chambre [de Ville], and those on the right side for the ecclesiastics, just as it has been carried out from time immemorial ... which could bring prejudice to the honor and to the authority of the magistracy."[37] Moisson claimed as dean that this was where he always sat in this church, which was almost certainly true. But

[37] AMD, B 263, fols. 65v–66r, July 25, 1625.

this dispute over who would sit where eventually turned into a legal case, with the mayor and *échevins* appealing to the Parlement of Dijon for a ruling. In March the following year, the mayor De Frasans asked that the ecclesiastical *échevins* be barred altogether from the Hôtel de Ville until the judges could sort out and eventually settle the dispute. The judges not only agreed and ruled against the ecclesiastics in favor of the mayor but they also declared that the ecclesiastical *échevins* should hereafter be barred permanently from the meetings of the Hôtel de Ville.[38] Thus, in less than a year from the original dispute in July 1625, the membership of the primary governing, administrative, and policing body in the city was changed permanently, not by royal fiat or pressure from the crown, but over a simple and very common local dispute over who had priority in church. This was yet a further nail in the coffin of the fiction that the mayor and *échevins* governed a city in which the community's elites, whether lay or clerical, were all bound in harmony with Dijon's inhabitants in order to safeguard the common welfare of all and the public good. Indeed, with about half of male heads of household barred from participating in annual elections after 1611, it is easy to understand why many of them, largely vignerons and artisans, might feel that both the king and the local magistrates were now siding together to restrict their voice in the political affairs of the city.

7.2   Politics and the People

The heads of households in Dijon who were excluded from voting due to the new tax requirements introduced in 1611 clearly considered voting in mayoral elections every year a vital part of their participation in the politics of the city, as is evidenced by the significant number of voters who showed up to give their voices even though they did not meet the new tax requirement. Though the election of 1612 was the first in which a voter had to have paid at least 40 *sous* in taxes in every assessment for the *taille* or *taillon* during the previous three years, there had always been some restrictions on who could vote. For example, one had to be a male head of household. Female heads of household, even wealthy widows of Dijon's elites, could not vote. Moreover, outsiders of any kind were not even admitted to the Jacobin convent on election day, nor were any servants, beggars, students, women, children, or anyone who was armed, on penalty of

---

[38] AMD, B 263, fols. 214v–15v, March 10, 1626.

arbitrary fine or even imprisonment.³⁹ Even some eligible voters were sometimes disqualified or their votes were dismissed in nearly every election. In 1598, for example, the vote of a vigneron named Nicolas Drouhin was not counted, because he said that "Claude Regnaudot gave him a present of some wine and one *sou* to vote for Monsieur Moisson, master of requests." That same year Nicolas Mariotte "said that he had something to drink, but did not know in which house, to vote for Poffier."⁴⁰ Canvassing in this manner had been commonplace for decades, as described in Chapter 1, and the election of 1602 was a case in point. A total of 24 votes were dismissed for various offenses from St. Michel parish and St. Philibert parish, the parishes containing the majority of vignerons in the city. Indeed, only one other vote outside these two parishes recorded a tainted vote, so obviously these were the two parishes targeted for canvassing by the mayoral candidates or their supporters. Léonard Forrot said "that he had been given a pint of wine on behalf of [the candidate Michel] Bichot," who was elected mayor that year.⁴¹ Similarly, Claude Furette "said that he had drunk on behalf of Bichot."⁴² And Jacques Tridon also "said that he had drunk [some wine] to give his vote to Bichot."⁴³ And Claude Petit noted "that he had drunk on behalf of Monsieur Bichot, but that Etienne Coret made him drink."⁴⁴ But the supporters of Michel Bichot were not the only ones handing out wine to canvass for votes. A number of votes on behalf of Bichot's principal challenger, Nicolas Gobin, were also disqualified.⁴⁵ And several voters willingly admitted that they had been offered and accepted wine or money, but they could not remember which candidate had provided it. Guillaume Caillivet, for example, "said that he had been given some money, but that he did not know from whom."⁴⁶ Claude Le Maigre "said that he had drunk with his neighbors, but did not know where it came from."⁴⁷ Chrêtien Maitrot "said that he had drunk and eaten but did not know on behalf of whom."⁴⁸ Claude Le Follet "said that he had drunk two or three glasses of wine, but said he did not know from whom it came."⁴⁹ And finally one very honest voter named Claude

³⁹ For just a few of many examples that could be cited, see AMD, B 225, fol. 2r, June 20, 1587, and B 230, fols. 2r–3v, June 20, 1592.
⁴⁰ AMD, B 236, fol. 22r, June 20, 1598.   ⁴¹ AMD, B 240, fol. 11v, June 21, 1602.
⁴² AMD, B 240, fol. 12v, June 21, 1602.   ⁴³ AMD, B 240, fol. 13r, June 21, 1602.
⁴⁴ AMD, B 240, fol. 25r, June 21, 1602.   ⁴⁵ AMD, B 240, fols. 13r and 23v, June 21, 1602.
⁴⁶ AMD, B 240, fol. 12r, June 21, 1602.   ⁴⁷ AMD, B 240, fol. 13v, June 21, 1602.
⁴⁸ AMD, B 240, fol. 13v, June 21, 1602.   ⁴⁹ AMD, B 240, fol. 13v, June 21, 1602.

Laudriote told the *échevins* "that he had been solicited to give his vote on behalf of Gobin, nevertheless he gave it to Monsieur Bichot." In this last instance, Laudriote's vote was counted.[50] At the same time, in nearly every election voters turned up who could not name any of the candidates, so they were escorted out of the convent without ever casting a vote. For just one example of the many that could be cited, in 1607 Jacob Caron was dismissed from the convent "for not knowing anyone to name."[51]

What do all these examples mean? Should we just assume as the elites of the city did that the vignerons and artisans who turned up at elections every year in large numbers did so primarily to quaff some free wine? Should we accept at face value that the neighborhoods of the vignerons and artisans were targeted for canvassing because they were the easiest to bribe with food and wine? The judges in Parlement, not to mention the king and queen regent, obviously thought so, which explains why the tax restriction was placed on the electorate for the elections of 1612 and thereafter. The result was an immediate drop in the numbers of those voting. In the two decades between 1591 and 1610, the average number of those who showed up at the Jacobin convent to vote on election day each year was 1,486. In the election of 1612 only 772 qualified voters cast their voices in the mayoral election, declining by nearly half compared to those who turned out the previous two decades.[52] Moreover, in this same election an additional 192 voters turned up who were not allowed to vote, because when their names were checked against the tax rolls, it was determined that they had not paid a minimum of 40 *sous* in each tax levy the previous three years.[53] Even though there had been widespread publicity about the new voter requirements, 192 heads of household – overwhelmingly vignerons and artisans – either did not remember what they had paid, or they expected to be admitted to cast their vote anyway.

I would argue, however, that the judges in Parlement and even most *échevins* in the Hôtel de Ville, who castigated the behavior of the masses for only participating in the election to get some free wine, or who arrived unable to name any of the candidates running for office, or who turned up at 6:00 in the morning to vote even though they were ineligible, were overlooking a primary motivation of the masses: that is, to participate and take part in one of the principal political events of the city. The event itself

[50] AMD, B 240, fol. 19v, June 21, 1602.
[51] AMD, B 245, fol. 21r, June 20, 1607. Also see AMD, B 250, fol. 4v, June 20, 1612.
[52] Voting totals for each year are given in Holt, "Popular Political Culture," 103.
[53] AMD, B 250, fols. 1r–22r, June 20, 1612.

was a political ritual of the commune to elect a worthy individual to serve as mayor for the next year. To take part in this process necessarily bestowed honor on all those who participated. For vignerons and artisans the elections were one of the few opportunities where they could demonstrate their worthiness as citizens, where their voices really were the equals of their social betters. In the Jacobin convent they could assemble and stand together with lawyers, merchants, and noblemen of the city in common accord. And while the honor of participating in these elections in no way garnered them any significant influence in the body politic, it earned them considerable esteem in the body social. In their own neighborhoods and on their own streets, participating in the election translated into worthiness in the community. Obviously, there were clearly issues of importance in certain elections – religion in the early 1560s, for example, as shown above in Chapter 5 – but to participate and validate one's own membership in the community mattered as much as any campaign issue or even the result. And that some voters went to the polling place even though they were unable to name any candidates only underscores the premium placed on participation in the event at the expense of the result. To be sure, the magistrates were concerned about the widespread drunkenness and disorderliness that resulted from the canvassing of votes among the lower orders by the leading candidates, which did dominate many of the elections before 1612. But surely this concern ought to be seen in the context of the feast day of St. John the Baptist and accompanying festivities rather than as an intrusion into some nonexistent democratic process. Thus, the elections served as an outlet of political expression for the masses, who were exclaiming and validating their own worth in the community.

Another way that the vignerons tried to validate their worth in the community as well as substantiate their relationship with the city's elites was their interaction with a series of plays put on and performed by the Mère Folle, a group of around two hundred young elite males, primarily lawyers, notaries, or other legal officials, as well as some wealthy merchants. They were paid by the city to provide entertainments and amusements for various festive occasions such as Carnival, royal entries, royal births, and especially the twelve days between Christmas (December 25) and Epiphany (January 6).[54] The theatrical troupe of the Mère Folle was called the Infanterie Dijonnaise, and it put on various

---

[54] References to periodic payments from the city to the Mère Folle and the Infanterie Dijonnaise are scattered throughout the deliberations of the Hôtel de Ville. For just a few examples from this period, see AMD, B 239, fol. 163v, September 16, 1601; B 252, fol. 171r–v, January 13, 1615; and B 253, fol. 73v, July 24, 1615.

plays and farces written by and performed by its members. Some scholars believe that the origins of the Mère Folle lay with the late medieval Feast of Fools and performances of plays in Dijon in the thirteenth, fourteenth, and fifteenth centuries. In other words, it was believed that the Mère Folle had medieval origins in the twelfth or thirteenth century, was composed of priests or sons of priests, and that in the intervening years the society had become secularized. It was also believed that the Mother in the Mère Folle was the Virgin Mary, because of the organization's association with the Sainte Chapelle in Dijon under the Valois dukes, which had a painting of the "Dormition of the Virgin" as its altarpiece. But recent literature, especially the work of Juliette Valcke, has proved these ideas to be incorrect. Not only were the origins of the Mère Folle much more recent – the charter had originally been granted by Philip the Good, Duke of Burgundy, on December 27, 1454 – but the festive society had from its origins been an entirely lay organization. Thus, Mère Folle, or Mother Folly, is almost certainly a derivative from the Dame Folly of humanist critics like Erasmus rather than a reference to the Virgin Mary.[55]

The plays performed by the masked and costumed actors of the Mère Folle – all males – were largely comedic satires in which Mère Folle herself, a male actor dressed as a woman, carried on conversations and debates with various other characters, including a character named Bon Temps (Good Times), and several Roman gods and goddesses, with others playing the role of fools, the latter always dressed as vignerons. The most striking thing about these plays is that they were almost always performed in two

[55] For all these views, see Jean-Baptiste Lucotte Du Tilliot, ed., *Mémoires pour servir à l'histoire de la fête des fous qui se faisait autrefois dans plusieurs églises* (Lausanne and Geneva: Marc-Michel Bousquet, 1741); Joachim Durandeau, *Histoire de la Mère Folle laïque de Dijon* (Dijon: Réveil Bourguignon, 1911); Luc Verhaeghe, "Vers composés pour les enfants de la Mère-Folle de Dijon vers la fin du XVIe siècle," Mémoire de licence, University of Ghent, 1969, 26–33; Natalie Zemon Davis, "The Reasons of Misrule," in her *Society and Culture in Early Modern France* (Stanford, CA: Stanford University Press, 1975), 97–123; James R. Farr, *Hands of Honor: Artisans and Their World in Dijon, 1550–1650* (Ithaca, NY: Cornell University Press, 1988), 214–219; Juliette Valcke, "La société joyeuse de la Mère Folle de Dijon: Histoire (xve-xviie s.) et édition du répertoire," 3 vols., Ph.D. thesis Université de Montréal, 1997, 1: 31–99; J. Valcke, "La satire sociale dans le repertoire de la Mère Folle de Dijon," in Konrad Eisenbichler and Wim Hüsken, eds., *Carnival and the Carnivalesque: The Fool, the Reformer, the Wildman, and Others in Early Modern Theatre* (Amsterdam: Rodolphi, 1999), 147–163; J. Valcke, "Théâtre et spectacle chez la Mère Folle de Dijon (XVe-XVIe s.)," in Marie-France Wagner and Claire Le Brun-Gouanvic, eds., *Les arts du spectacle dans la ville (1404–1721)* (Paris: Champion, 2001), 61–80; Sara Beam, *Laughing Matters: Farce and the Making of Absolutism in France* (Ithaca, NY: Cornell University Press, 2007), 188–196; J. Valcke, *Théâtre de la Mère Folle de Dijon XVIe-XVIIe siècles* (Orléans: Paradigme, 2012), a condensed version of her Ph.D. thesis; and J. Valcke, "De l'intermède comique à la leçon de morale: polyvalence des dialogues des vignerons dans le théâtre de la Mère Folle de Dijon," in Corrine Denoyelle, ed., *Le dialogue en question* (Orléans: Paradigm, 2013), 269–282.

languages: with Mother Folly and the gods and goddesses nearly always speaking in French, and the fools and other vignerons usually speaking in the local Burgundian patois. Hence, these plays are one of the best examples we have of high and low culture being enfolded together with elite lawyers, royal officers, and wealthy merchants performing in roles of vignerons, while the actual vignerons of the city made up a large part of the audience. If nothing else, it is yet another example of elites and the popular classes meeting together and engaging in common activities – just as they prayed together in church and encountered each other daily and routinely in their neighborhoods and streets such as the Rue Vannerie. Many of the texts of these plays were also published in Dijon, and after his appointment in 1608 as the city council's official printer, most were printed by Claude Guyot.[56] Thus, many of the city's elites may have been more familiar with the plays as printed texts, while the city's vignerons would likely have been more familiar with the performances of these plays. But again, the most striking thing was that part of the dialogue was in Burgundian patois, the very fact of which had multiple meanings for the vignerons actually watching these performances.[57]

Juliette Valcke has transcribed and analyzed the texts of sixteen of these plays that were written and performed between 1576 and 1650 and have survived in manuscript.[58] She has found a total of 27 plays that have survived in manuscript or in published form, written and performed between 1576 and 1650, with 21 of the 27 being products of the period after 1600.[59] As she has noted at the beginning of her history of the Mère Folle, "from the fifteenth to the seventeenth century, the joyous society of the Mère Folle displayed its ostentation in the streets of Dijon ... If moral control and political blame represented the two principal reasons for the existence of the Mère Folle, it was equally occupied with official functions and organized parades or entertainments on feast days such as May Day, as well as during the festivities marking the entry of an important person into the city, an illustrious birth, or any other event of national importance."[60] Thus, "by its

---

[56] For more on Guyot, see Sara Beam, *Laughing Matters*, 190–192. And for Guyot's appointment as *imprimeur de la ville*, see AMD, B 246, fol. 77, July 29, 1608.

[57] Valcke, "La société joyeuse de la Mère Folle de Dijon," 100–210; Valcke, "De l'intermède comique à la leçon de morale," 269–282; and Valcke, *Théâtre de la Mère Folle*, 69–73.

[58] The texts of the 16 plays are reproduced with copious notes of commentary and explanation of the Burgundian patois in Valcke, "La société joyeuse de la Mère Folle de Dijon," 2: 212–509 and 3: 511–685. The published version of her dissertation – Valcke, *Théâtre de la Mère Folle* – includes the texts of only six of these 16 plays. Thus, I shall be citing the plays from the unpublished version.

[59] Valcke, *Théâtre de la Mère Folle*, 229–230.

[60] Valcke, "La société joyeuse de la Mère Folle de Dijon," 31.

parades and satirical performances, this company made itself the censor of its citizens as well as criticizing whatever it considered abusive on the part of the authorities."[61] If we look at recurring themes in the plays as a corpus, these two functions clearly stand out: censoring immoral behavior of Dijon's citizens as well as criticizing abuse by the state and other authorities. One theme that stands out sharply in all the plays is social inversion: men dressed as women, wealthy elites dressed and speaking like vignerons, fools speaking words of wisdom, etc. It is this social inversion, in fact, that not only created the comedic foundation of the plays, but also allowed the actors to get away with criticisms of behavior and authority that might ordinarily warrant reprimand or even punishment.[62] Normally associated exclusively with Carnival, the Mère Folle extended this type of social comment disguised as comedy to other parts of the ritual calendar as well as to mark special events of importance in the city. So, comedy and social inversion were as much a mask for social and political criticism as they were occasions for public entertainment.

Criticizing the corruption of government as well as the court, however, was a principal focus for many of the plays, such as "Le Reveil de Bontemps," written and performed during Carnival 1623. The king was mentioned early on as "Conquering Louis [*Vanqueur Louis*]," a reference to Louis XIII's defeat of the Huguenots in Montpellier in October 1622, with great esteem. But Bontemps did not take long to criticize some of Louis's courtiers: "I have seen some harpies at court, with the aid of a young vulture, make their way by sucking the blood from your purses," a reference to too many wars and too many taxes to support an overly luxurious court.[63] The play carefully refrained from criticizing the king directly but, like "Asnerie," it was not hesitant to call out those who served the king for corruption and dereliction of duty.

A second theme of this entire body of plays is the role of the vignerons, as just noted, as a monitor of the city's moral compass. To be sure, on occasion some vignerons were themselves ridiculed for drunkenly and unruly behavior, but for the most part they served as the servants of Mère Folle, as guardians of the social and moral order. In "La Comédie des Mécontents," written and performed in the 1580s, for example, the play opened with several servants, a miller, an artisan, a vigneron, and some fools all in discussion about their lives. Their accounts quickly

---

[61] Ibid.
[62] See especially Natalie Zemon Davis, "Women on Top," in *Society and Culture in Early Modern France*, 124–151.
[63] "Le Reveil de Bontemps," in Valcke, "La société joyeuse de la Mère Folle de Dijon," 561.

revealed, however, that servants were trying to act and dress above their station, that millers were thieves and of dubious honesty, that artisans were charging too much for their services, that apothecaries were mean and stingy, and that nurses were behaving like prostitutes. Monsieur Bontemps, who had been listening to this conversation, then interjected that only the vigneron was without fault, and he rewarded him with wine: "I will fill your barrels and your butts with wine."[64] And when the others complained to Bontemps, the vigneron replied to him: "By my faith, they are very wrong, you speak the truth, sir."[65] In a different play written in 1620, "La Comédie du Ris," the vignerons played a different kind of monitoring role. The title is a play on words of the French word *ris*, which means laughter as well as rice, the rice used at weddings to shower the bride and groom. This play opened with a fool announcing the forth-coming wedding of Bontemps and a new wife, his former spouse being deceased, who wanted to be married during Lent. But the vignerons insisted that this could not happen, since only those from Geneva – i.e. Calvinists – got married during Lent, as the Catholic clergy did not marry anyone during the Lenten season because of the prohibition of all flesh including sex. Thus, the vignerons suggested Mardi Gras instead, the last day of Carnival, when all shops would be shut and everyone would be cooking, drinking, and celebrating anyway. The fool agreed.[66] The wedding was just a foil, however, for the main role of the vignerons, which was to criticize the selfish and corrupt behavior of just about every-body in the city. Instead of throwing rice – *ris* – on the wedding couple, the vignerons and the fool throw laughter onto many of their fellow citizens, especially the women: wives of merchants who wore luxurious hats inside their boutiques, those women who dressed themselves above their social station in clothes made of golden thread or silk, or certain women who would only wear petticoats made of silk.[67] In short, the fool and the vignerons threw rice/laughter onto anyone who they believed behaved badly.

A third theme of these plays is the veneer of humanism that permeated all of them. Not only was there frequent mention of Roman gods and goddesses, but the format of so many of the plays was a classical legal

[64] "La Comédie des Mécontents," in Valcke, "La société joyeuse de la Mère Folle de Dijon," 421, line 191.

[65] Ibid., 428, line 246.

[66] "La Comédie du Ris," in Valcke, "La société joyeuse de la Mère Folle de Dijon," 485–491, lines 1–82.

[67] "La Comédie du Ris," in Valcke, "La société joyeuse de la Mère Folle de Dijon," 492–501, lines 99–192.

tribunal as if those being mocked were standing in a physical court being judged by vignerons and fools. This is no accident, of course, as the authors of most of these plays were lawyers in the Parlement of Dijon. And humanism was the foundation of their legal training and education in France.[68] Although all the plays were written and published anonymously, it is clear that Pierre Malpoy, Edmund Bréchillet, and Bénigne Pérard, for example, wrote many of the plays in the first three decades of the seventeenth century.[69] Members of both families had served for a number of years as *échevins* on Dijon's city council in the late 1580s and throughout the 1590s.[70] And Etienne Bréchillet himself was first selected as *échevin* in 1626 and served for three consecutive terms, as well as later in the 1630s and 1640s.[71] By the 1620s both Malpoy and Bréchillet had been admitted as *avocats à la cour*, that is, as lawyers who had the right to argue cases before the judges in the Parlement of Dijon. But they were more than garden variety lawyers at the Parlement. Bréchillet and Malpoy took on leadership roles within the court and for the city, as they were charged with designing and planning for the royal entries of King Louis XIII in 1629 and Louis de Bourbon, Prince of Condé, in 1632, respectively.[72] It thus comes as no surprise that talented lawyers such as these would be charged with writing entertainments for the Mère Folle. But what specific political messages did these plays contain? Michael Breen is surely right to say that the purpose of the plays was "to translate the urban elite's philosophy into the terms of the city's lower classes."[73] But what exactly was that philosophy? Certainly, every magistrate desired to maintain the social and political order, and making fun of corruption and immoral behavior was clearly designed to do that. Sara Beam has gone further and argued that the plays of the Mère Folle, like so many others performed by elite groups in municipalities all over France, were a means for urban officials "to participate in the censorship of political and religious criticism in order to cement their own positions of power in the emerging state." In other words, being guardians

---

[68] Breen, *Law, City, and King,* 42–44; George Huppert, *Public Schools in Renaissance France* (Urbana and Chicago, IL: University of Illinois Press, 1984); and William Bouwsma, "Lawyers and Early Modern Culture," *The American Historical Review* 78 (1973): 303–327.

[69] Beam, *Laughing Matters,* 189; and Valcke, *Théâtre de la Mère Folle,* 229–230.

[70] AMD, B 226, fol. 12r–v, June 21, 1588.

[71] AMD, B 264, fols. 23r–24v, June 23, 1626; B 265, fols. 49v–51v, July 10, 1627; and B 266, fols. 22r–23r, June 23, 1628; and Breen, *Law, City, and King,* 59.

[72] Breen, *Law, City, and King,* 59–61 and 167–172; and Michel P. Breen, "Addressing *La Ville des Dieux*: Entry Ceremonies and Urban Audiences in Early Modern Dijon," *The Journal of Social History* 38 (2004): 341–364.

[73] Breen, *Law, City, and King,* 60.

of civility, "a code of manners that at once distinguishes the elite form the rabble and demands subservience to the prince, was useful for ambitious urban officials who sought to profit from the consolidation of power." In short, Beam argues, the Mère Folle's enfolding together of the dialogues among fools and vignerons with more respectful neoclassical themes was nothing less than "the discourse of absolutism."[74]

This is all very convincing, at least concerning the motives of the elites and the messages they were attempting to convey to their audiences. For the other elites in the city, not to mention all the royal officers and other officials who resided there, this may indeed be the message they took away. But what were the messages being received by the vignerons, artisans, and other members of the popular classes who watched these plays in the streets? Though there is evidence that the mayor and city council were trying to find an indoor site for the Mère Folle to perform its plays,[75] this was largely to allow the gentlemen of the city council to see the plays without having to stand and mingle with the popular classes in the street where the plays were normally performed. There is very little, if any, evidence, however, that the discourse of absolutism is the message the vignerons took away from these performances. Indeed, we have very little evidence at all about reactions to the actual performances, and those few we do have were all composed by elites. Perhaps the most well-known and most cited reaction is that of the canon of the Sainte-Chapelle, Bénigne Pepin, who was more interested in the procession preceding the play than the performance itself, about which all he wrote was that "it was one of the most beautiful masquerades that one could put on."[76] In fact, we have no direct evidence at all concerning the reactions of the vignerons and artisans to these masquerades. It certainly must have been amusing to them to see the city's elites pretending to dress and speak like them in their own patois. And it is equally likely that many of the neoclassical allusions may not have been picked up at all. But how can we be sure that the vignerons did not also come away from these performances with very different messages: that it was not just permissible for vignerons to criticize royal officials publicly, but that it was their duty to do so, and that it was also their duty as vignerons to be the guardians of proper political, social, and moral order in the city? In other words, we should at least consider the possibility that what the vignerons took away from these performances may have been the

---

[74] Beam, *Laughing Matters*, 10, 246, and 193.
[75] For example, see AMD, B 253, fol. 73v, July 24, 1615.
[76] Garnier, ed., *Journal de Gabriel Breunot*, 1: 26–27.

very opposite of the discourse of absolutism. Once again, there is no direct evidence to support this claim, but some of their actions afterward, especially in the popular uprising known as Lanturelu in February 1630, suggest that this may have been the case, and I shall analyze those events more closely in Chapter 8.

As the popular classes of Dijon found themselves removed from the direct election of their mayors after 1611, they had fewer and fewer means of participating directly in the negotiation over how power was wielded by the elites, or even in the general ordering and welfare of the community. Nevertheless, as just suggested, Dijon's vignerons and artisans continued to see themselves as the guardians of the political, social, and moral order of the community, and on occasion they sometimes believed they had to act on their own authority to maintain this order when their superiors failed to do so. One such episode was the attempted execution of an unmarried 21-year-old woman named Hélène Gillet, who was accused of having suffocated her new-born baby immediately after giving birth in May 1625.[77] She was the daughter of a noble from Bourg-en-Bresse, and she had been seduced by a curate from a neighboring village. She managed to conceal her pregnancy, but according to one Charles Fevret, "in the imbecility of her age, in the infirmity of her sex, in the horror of her punishment and in the apprehension of death," she had killed her infant.[78] She was soon discovered, however, and eventually taken to trial in the Dijon Parlement, where she was sentenced to death in the Grand Chambre. The execution was scheduled to take place in the Place du Morimont, the traditional place for executions in Dijon, on May 12, and the executioner assigned to execute the sentence was a man named Simon Grandjean. Gillet's noble status spared her from being hanged, so she was sentenced to be beheaded instead. But Grandjean, for whatever reason, was not up to the task. Grandjean's wife had cut Gillet's hair and pulled back her collar to bare her neck, but the first blow of his sword struck Gillet in the left jaw. A second attempt was equally unsuccessful, striking Gillet in the right shoulder, greatly stirring up the inhabitants of the city assembled

---

[77] AMD, B 262, fols. 196r–97r, May 13, 1625; *Discours faict au Parlement de Dijon, sur la presentation des lettres d'abolition obtenües par Hélène Gillet, condamnée à mort poir avoir celé sa grossesse et son fruict. Comme aussi les lettres d'abolition en forme de chartes et arrest de verifications d'icelles* (Paris: Henry Sara, 1625) reprinted in Edouard Fournier, ed., *Variétés historique et littéraires*, 10 vols. (Paris: P. Jannet, 1855–1863), 1: 35–47; Elisabeth-François de la Cuisine, *Le Parlement de Bourgogne depuis son origine jusqu'à sa chute*, 3 vols. (Dijon: Rabutot and Paris: A. Durand, 1864), 2: 308–312; and James R. Farr, *Authority and Sexuality in Early Modern Burgundy, 1550–1730* (New York, NY: Oxford University Press, 1995), 128.

[78] Fournier, ed., *Variétés historique et littéraires*, 1: 38.

to view the execution. They began to throw stones at the executioner, who retreated to the chapel beneath the scaffold. At the same time the executioner's wife, seeking to save his honor and prevent further humiliation, rushed to the scaffold and proceeded to kick Gillet in the stomach, then tried to choke her with the cord around her neck, and finally stabbed her with the scissors she had used to cut Gillet's hair. One thrust of the scissors passed between Gillet's throat and jugular vein, a second was beneath the lower lip and sliced Gillet's tongue, a third passed between two ribs and went just beneath her heart, a fourth was in her side, and two were in the head. Grandjean's wife then dragged Gillet down from the scaffold by the rope still around her neck until she – Madame Grandjean – was felled by stones. The angry mob by this time had broken down the door of the chapel where the frightened executioner had been hiding and proceeded to throw stones and hurl abuse at him and his wife. Miraculously, Hélène Gillet survived this gruesome ordeal and she was rushed to a nearby surgeon.[79]

So, what are we to make of this astonishing and extremely bizarre event, which the deliberations of the Hôtel de Ville referred to as "one of the strangest cases we have heard spoken of in a long time?" The municipal authorities were very quick to call it "a great scandal" and "sedition," caused not by the incompetence of the executioner, but by the reaction of the people to these unfortunate events. The city council saw these events as a blow not just against the injustice of a failed execution, but as a strike against their own authority. "Such sedition focuses attention on the authority of the magistrate, which ought not to be permitted . . . and it seems that this would be an attempt against the authority of the Parlement." They noted that the solicitor-general of the Parlement has given the city council the responsibility "to oversee and undertake proceedings against those guilty of such sedition, so that it will serve as an example to maintain the people in the resect and obedience which is owed to the magistrates, and to prevent another even greater revolt, which would doubtless occur with impunity, as there is nothing more dangerous in a city than to let everyone be dominated by their own fantasies and to give authority to the people, which they abuse too licentiously, as so many examples bear witness."[80]

"Order was political and social but also moral."[81] That the people might have a morality of their own and were trying to make sure that justice was

---

[79] Fournier, ed., *Variétés historique et littéraires*, 1: 43–45.
[80] AMD, B 262, fl. 196r–97r, May 13, 1625.
[81] James B. Collins, *Classes, Estates, and Order in Early Modern Brittany* (Cambridge: Cambridge University Press, 1994), 249.

carried out properly did not cross the magistrates' minds.[82] To be sure, the people had attempted to execute the executioner and his wife, and the Hôtel de Ville was rightly concerned that they could not let this act go unpunished. But Louis XIII intervened, and before a second attempt at carrying out the sentence against the poor Gillet could be arranged, he pardoned her, claiming she only acted to kill her baby because of "bad counsel" and out of a desire to spare her family from shame.[83] As a result, no one was ever arrested for the attacks on Grandjean and his wife. Moreover, Gillet herself, once she recovered from her wounds, was convinced that God had saved her by a divine miracle. So, she entered a convent in her native Bourg-en-Bresse to live out the remainder of her life.[84] To be sure, this entire event was unusual and extremely out of the ordinary experience of anyone. But it is striking that when a botched execution occurred – and this was not what was so extraordinary – the people took it upon themselves to execute justice in their own manner. As Natalie Davis underscored so vividly, in acts of popular violence the people often took on the role of magistrates if they perceived their own officials were not carrying out their expected function.[85] And this is precisely what worried the local magistrates so much. But the people had few such opportunities to execute justice in this fashion, and they rarely seized it even when they did. The events of February 1630, which will be recounted in Chapter 8, offered yet another opportunity for the people to execute their own justice in the absence of what they perceived as magisterial action. But before analyzing those events, we first need to examine the religious changes that were taking place at this same time, resulting from the impact of the Council of Trent as well as lay-inspired reforms of French Catholicism after the end of the Wars of Religion.

7.3   Catholic Reform in Burgundy

The defeat of the Catholic League after the abjuration and conversion of King Henry IV at the end of the Wars of Religion has often been cited as the genesis of Catholic reform and revival in France, as former Leaguers turned their energies toward religious renewal in the early seventeenth century. As Denis Richet noted more than 40 years ago, "it was during the

---

[82] A point also made by William Beik, *Urban Protest in Seventeenth-Century France: The Culture of Retribution* (Cambridge: Cambridge University Press, 1997), 252–253.

[83] The king's pardon letter is printed in Fournier, ed., *Variétés historique et littéraires*, 1: 39–42.

[84] La Cuisine, *Le Parlement de Bourgogne*, 2: 311–312.

[85] Natalie Zemon Davis, "Rites of Violence," in *Society and Culture in Early Modern France*, 161–164.

period of the League that what would later be called the *dévot* party was formed . . . [and] where the Catholic Reformation first took root."[86] Richet was writing about the city of Paris and the experience of the League in the capital, and in many ways his assessment rings true: In Paris, Catholic reform was a by-product of the defeated League. But as Joseph Bergin has more recently argued, this was not generally true of most French towns, where the antagonisms between Leaguers and royalists were not permanent and where these Catholic factions soon reunited after the king's abjuration of Protestantism.[87] This was certainly true in Burgundy, where Catholic reform emerged equally from the efforts of both Leaguers and royalists alike.

The twin poles of Catholic reform in France, like elsewhere in the Catholic world, were the Council of Trent (1545–1563) and the foundation of new orders of religious men and women. Trent confirmed the doctrinal differences with Protestantism, while at the same time it introduced many reforms in the institutional church. The other goal of Trent was to reform the behaviors of Catholic laity in order to create a more godly society. The new religious orders founded in the sixteenth and early seventeenth centuries were a means of aiding this quest. And even though the French crown – meaning both monarchs as well as Parlements – refused to officially sanction the decrees of the Council of Trent because it was seen as an institution of papal power and influence, Catholic reforms that were the product of the Council nevertheless took root in the kingdom, often strongly supported by the king, the Gallican church, as well as the laity. Henry IV and Louis XIII, for example, played a significant role in reform by refusing to appoint minors, foreigners, and unqualified candidates to the episcopacy, and by insisting on residency for all bishops.[88]

The reasons for the monarchy's rejection of the decrees of the Council of Trent were numerous. Even though Henry IV promised as early as 1595 to accept and implement the Tridentine decrees, he went to his grave never having done so. Moreover, the issue remained a political thorn in the side of his successor, Louis XIII, especially during his regency under the tutelage of Henry's widow, Marie de Medici. The principal reason Trent

---

[86] Denis Richet, "Aspects socio-culturels des conflits religieux à Paris dans la seconde moitié du XVIe siècle," in Richet, *De la Réforme à la Révolution: Études sur la France moderne* (Paris: Aubier, 1991), 36 and 40. This essay was originally published in *Annales* in 1972.

[87] Joseph Bergin, *The Politics of Religion in Early Modern France* (New Haven, CT: Yale University Press, 2014), 87.

[88] Joseph Bergin, *The Making of the French Episcopate, 1589–1661* (New Haven, CT, and London: Yale University Press, 1996), 186–188, 299–301, and 390–392.

was never accepted in France, at least by the political classes, was the belief that the decrees impinged upon the traditional "Gallican liberties" of the French church, both real and imagined ever since the Pragmatic Sanction of Bourges of 1438. It was a political institution – the Parlement of Paris – that saw itself as the self-imposed guardian of these liberties, and since the Pragmatic Sanction the judges realized that they needed to defend the church from the French crown as well as from Rome.[89] But after the Wars of Religion it was primarily the Pope in Rome who was perceived to be the biggest threat to the Gallican church, especially after the Council of Trent explicitly increased his authority and influence. At the Estates-General of 1614, for example, the Third Estate attempted to get the crown under the guardianship of the regent, Marie de Medici, to agree to a new funda-mental law of the realm, declaring that "no power on earth whatever, spiritual or temporal" had any authority over the French monarchy.[90] The bishops of the First Estate ultimately convinced Marie de Medici to oppose the proposed law, and she prevailed upon the deputies of the Third Estate to drop it from their list of grievances. What the clergy could not do, however, was persuade either the deputies of the Second (Nobility) or Third Estates to formally accept the decrees of the Council of Trent.[91]

Thus, the general historical view has traditionally been that France rejected the decrees of the Council of Trent and that its role in the Council was one of nonparticipation and complete absence, at least until the final sessions of 1562–1563 when Charles, Cardinal of Lorraine and Archbishop of Reims, led a French delegation to the council.[92] But this was hardly the case. In the memorable phrase of Alain Talon, France's role in the council was more than "an empty chair (*la chaise vide*)."[93] In fact, there was a French delegation at the opening sessions in Trent from 1545 to 1547 – three ambassadors, three bishops, and eight theologians – as well as at the sessions that met in Bologna from 1547 to 1549 – two ambassadors, twelve bishops and six theologians. Indeed, the only session of the entire Council in which the French chair was empty was the brief period from September 1551 to April 1552.[94] Above all, it is clear that the

---

[89] See especially the excellent book by Tyler Lange, *The First French Reformation: Church Reform and the Origins of the Old Regime* (Cambridge: Cambridge University Press, 2014).
[90] The text is taken from the translation by J. Michael Hayden, *France and the Estates General of 1614* (Cambridge: Cambridge University Press, 1974), 131.
[91] Bergin, *The Politics of Religion*, 83–85.
[92] See, for example, Jean Delumeau, *Le catholicisme entre Luther et Voltaire* (Paris: Presses universitaires de France, 1971), 73–75.
[93] Alain Tallon, *La France et le Concile de Trent (1518–1563)* (Rome: École française de Rome, 1997), 1.
[94] Tallon, *La France et le Concile*, 5 and 838–839.

Cardinal of Lorraine was a principal supporter of the many reforms that emerged from the Council in 1562–1563.[95]

The Council announced a double agenda at its very first session in December 1545: "the extirpation of heresies . . . [and] the reform of the clergy and Christian people."[96] And while the Council never succeeded in its first goal, the bulk of the Council's work in implementing the second goal rested on the reform of the episcopacy, without which a reform of the parish clergy and the laity would be impossible. To put it most bluntly, in far too many cases the office of bishop had become more a source of revenue and income – a benefice – as well as an honor and reward for political patronage, with the pastoral and apostolic duties and responsibilities of the office all but forgotten. Many bishops never set foot in their diocese, a problem compounded by some bishops holding multiple bishoprics.[97] For just one egregious example, Jean de Lorraine, the uncle of the Cardinal of Lorraine, held three archbishoprics and nine bishoprics. Moreover, he had a reputation as an unrepentant womanizer who had sired illegitimate children.[98] But in France the greatest problem was absenteeism. In 1559, of the 101 incumbent bishops in France, only 19 resided in their dioceses on a regular basis; roughly 80 percent were nonresidents. And nonresidency increased even above 80 percent in the last decade of the Wars of Religion.[99] Thus, as Henry Outram Evennett put it nearly a century ago, "the strengthening of the episcopate in every respect, as the nodal point of every aspect of reform, may be regarded as a cornerstone of the counter-reformation Church."[100]

The problem in Dijon was not so much that it had a nonresident or immoral bishop, but that it had no bishop at all. Of the eight towns that housed the sovereign courts of the Parlements and Chambers of Accounts at the end of the Wars of Religion – Paris, Rouen, Rennes, Dijon, Bordeaux, Toulouse, Aix, and Grenoble – Dijon alone had no bishopric. While there was a bishop as well as a glorious medieval cathedral in the

---

[95] John W. O'Malley, *Trent: What Happened at the Council* (Cambridge, MA: Harvard University Press, 2013), 198–202, and Tallon, *La France et le Concile*, 777–785.
[96] H. J. Schroeder, ed. and trans., *The Canons and Decrees of the Council of Trent* (Rockford, IL: Tan Books, 1978), 11.
[97] H. Outram Evennett, *The Spirit of the Counter-Reformation* (Notre Dame, IN: University of Notre Dame Press, 1970), 96–99.
[98] O'Malley, *Trent*, 16, and Frederic J. Baumgartner, *Change and Continuity in the French Episcopate: The Bishops and the Wars of Religion, 1547–1610* (Durham, NC: Duke University Press, 1986), 119–120.
[99] Baumgartner, *Change and Continuity*, 110–111.
[100] Evennett, *Spirit of the Counter-Reformation*, 97.

Burgundian town of Autun, the Burgundian capital of Dijon had no bishop or cathedral. Indeed, the city along with most of northern Burgundy was within the very large diocese of Langres to the northeast. Even before the League came to power in Burgundy, however, there had been significant support from local elites to press Rome to create a new see in Dijon. A combination of urban pride and provincial independence meant that these efforts only intensified during the period of the domination by the League.[101] Moreover, after his accession to the crown, Henry IV added his own support to these efforts, with the royal council formally petitioning Rome in July 1597 to create a new episcopal see in Dijon.[102] This further cemented the bond of the king with his Burgundian subjects, even though Dijon would not get its own bishop until 1730. And Henry never even got to nominate a new bishop of Langres, as its incumbent, Charles Pérusse d'Escars, held the see throughout Henry's reign. The king wanted, but did not pressure, D'Escars to resign, as he had a bright young protégé he wanted to appoint to the see in Langres, Sebastien Zamet, a financier whose Italian family had emigrated to France from Piedmont. Zamet was an ardent Leaguer who turned toward Henry IV when he led a League delegation to the king in 1593 seeking his abjuration. Zamet soon became a close confident of Henry and an important royal financier, however, and he is another prime example of Henry rewarding former Leaguers who accepted his authority. D'Escars would not resign, however, so Zamet was unable to occupy the bishopric until after Henry's death, when he was nominated by Marie de Medici in 1614 upon the death of D'Escars. And he would remain the bishop-duke of Langres until his death in 1655.[103] But Sebastien Zamet proved to be exactly the kind of reforming bishop that the Council of Trent had in mind, unlike his predecessor.

Charles d'Escars was as much a courtier as a bishop. He was first appointed to the bishopric of Poitiers in 1560, and then he was elevated to the larger diocese of Langres in 1569, where he served until his death. But he spent more time at court than in his diocese, where he rarely resided, being inaugurated as a *chevalier* of the order of the Holy Spirit by Henry III in 1578 and later assisting at the coronation of the young Louis XIII in 1610.

---

[101] See, for example, AMD, B 227, fols. 171v–72r, December 18, 1589, during the visit to Dijon of the papal legate, Cardinal Cajetan.

[102] Noel Valois, ed., *Inventaire des arrêts du conseil d'état (règne de Henri IV)*, 2 vols. (Paris: Imprimerie Nationale, 1866–1893), 1: 251, no. 3789, July 3, 1597. Also, see Joseph Garnier, ed., *Correspondance de la mairie de Dijon extraite des archives de cette ville*, 3 vols. (Dijon: Rabutot, 1868–1870), 3: 12, Biron to the Chambre de ville de Dijon, May 16, 1597.

[103] Joseph Bergin, *The Making of the French Episcopate, 1589–1661* (New Haven, CT: Yale University Press, 1996), 719.

His income from all his benefices totaled 30,000 *livres* per year, making him the wealthiest cleric in all of Burgundy. Although his opposition to heresy was acute, his interest in the reform of either church or society was lukewarm at best.[104]

Zamet, on the other hand, was almost the epitome of a post-Tridentine bishop. Unlike his predecessor, he took very seriously the Tridentine requirement that bishops reside in their dioceses as well as maintain regular visitations of all his parishes to insure both clerical competence and conscientiousness. Moreover, he held regular synods, meetings of local parish priests throughout the diocese, such as the ones in Dijon in 1617. As a close confident of Cardinal Richelieu, who was himself a bishop and had established a successful career in the Church before he entered politics, Zamet was linked to the most powerful Catholics and bishops in the kingdom. It is true that as a nobleman, a duke, and *pair* of France, he was just as much implicated in French politics as was d'Escars. Moreover, his family's banking activities not only continued to fund political activities of the crown, but they made Zamet even wealthier than his predecessor. The difference, however, was that Zamet took his episcopal responsibilities seriously, never trying or needing to profit financially from his ecclesiastical benefices. His background was also very different from that of d'Escars. Zamet was educated at the Jesuit Collège de la Flèche, established by Henry IV in 1604, and in 1609 he entered the Sorbonne in Paris to study theology, where he came under the influence of Pierre Bérulle, one of the leading figures of Catholic reform in France. Moreover, Zamet was also the nephew of another major figure in French Catholic reform, Père Joseph, who was his mother's brother. Thus, Zamet was already a champion of Catholic reform as well as a supporter of the Tridentine decrees when he was appointed bishop of Langres in 1614.[105]

The long tenure of Zamet as bishop of Langres was marked by efforts to reform existing clerical orders as well as support for the new reformist

---

[104] Henri Drouot, *Mayenne et la Bourgogne: Étude sur la Ligue (1587–1596)*, 2 vols. (Dijon: Bernigaud et Privat, 1937), 1: 63; and Jean-Baptiste-Joseph Mathieu, *Abrégé chronologique de l'histoire des évêques de Langres* (Langres: Laurent et Fils, 1844), 202–209.

[105] The best source on Zamet's career is still Louis-Narcisse Prunel, *Sébastien Zamet (1588–1655), Évêque-Duc de Langres, Pair de France: sa vie et ses oeuvres, les origins du jansénisme* (Paris: Alphonse Picard, 1912). But for brief accounts in English, see James R. Farr, *Authority and Sexuality in Early Modern Burgundy (1550–1730)* (New York, NY: Oxford University Press, 1995), 53–55; Linda Lierheimer, "Gender, Resistance, and the Limits of Episcopal Authority: Sébastien Zamet's Relationship with Nuns, 1615–1655," in Jennifer Maria DeSilva, ed., *Episcopal Reform and Politics in Early Modern Europe* (Kirksville, MO: Truman State University Press, 2012), 147–172; and Bergin, *Making of the French Episcopate*, 419–420 and 719.

orders in his diocese, especially those created for women, as well as endeavors to reform lay society generally through moral and social discipline. The bishop's focus on women's orders was constant throughout his tenure, though he faced regular resistance from the nuns themselves. This was partly because the Council of Trent required convents to be under the jurisdiction of a bishop, or a male monastic in the case of the female offshoots of the Benedictines and Cistercians, and most were unused to the episcopal oversight that Zamet sought. Trent also required that all female orders be cloistered.[106] It was also true that many nuns resisted reform altogether, with little desire to follow the rules and ascetic lifestyle required of the order. Starting in 1621, for example, Zamet tried over the next two decades to reform the female Benedictine abbey of Puits d'Orbe. The abbess, who was appointed in 1601, was a woman from a prominent Dijon family, Rose Bourgeois, who was the daughter of Claude Bourgeois, a presiding judge in the Parlement of Dijon during the Wars of Religion, one of two presiding judges who had left the city to sit with the royalist Parlement in Flavigny and then Semur during the time of the League. And given that her appointment was more political than spiritual, the abbess was not inclined to follow the monastic rule, allowing the nuns to have their own possessions and apartments, as well as to leave the abbey whenever they liked to visit friends and family. Thus, this was an obvious target for the reforming bishop of Langres, who spared no effort to bring it under Tridentine compliance. But the abbess resisted his efforts for more than two decades, and ultimately Zamet had to leave it to the Parlement of Dijon to intervene and force compliance.[107] Other similar examples include the attempt to combine the female Cistercian abbeys of Nôtre-Dame de Tart in Burgundy and Port-Royale outside Paris to form a new female order entirely of Zamet's own creation, the Institute of the Holy Sacrament. This too failed, though not because of any resistance of the two abbesses – Jeanne de la Tournelle, abbess of Tart, and Angélique Arnauld, abbess of Port Royale – both of whom were firmly behind Zamet's plan. The real resistance was from the Cistercian order, whose founding monastery of Cîteaux was only a few kilometers outside Dijon. The abbot of Cîteaux was naturally reluctant to turn over jurisdiction of two of his principal female abbeys to episcopal control by the bishop of Langres. Reform did occur in these abbeys, and the abbey at Tart eventually moved

---

[106] For the Tridentine reform of nunneries and convents, see Schroeder, ed. and trans., *Canons and Decrees*, 217–226.
[107] Lierheimer, "Gender, Resistance, and Limits of Episcopal Authority," 154–160.

to the city of Dijon in 1623 as a result. But by 1635 Zamet's dream of the Institute of the Holy Sacrament had dissolved.[108]

On the whole, however, and despite these instances of resistance, Zamet was a strong supporter of the female orders, of which there were many in Dijon. Indeed, a variety of new female orders emerged in Dijon just after the end of the religious wars. The order of Ursulines was established in Dijon as an uncloistered order for women in 1605 by Françoise de Xaintonge, daughter of Jean de Xaintonge, a judge (*conseiller*) in the Parlement of Dijon who had supported the League during the Wars of Religion. The Ursuline order, founded in Italy in 1535, was created to educate and teach young girls, and the congregation established in Dijon was designed to serve the same purpose. A decade after its establishment, however, the new foundation soon ran short of operating funds, and a wealthy widow, Catherine de Montholon, came to the rescue. Montholon was a member of a prominent robe family in Dijon who had married a Parisian lawyer in the Parlement of Paris, and, now widowed, she returned to Dijon to support the new female order.[109] She offered Xaintonge 16,000 *livres tournois* to finance the new Ursuline congregation in 1615, upon condition that the order become cloistered, as the Council of Trent had required half a century earlier. Although Xaintonge opposed the enclosure of the order, the financial support proved too tempting to turn down, and the Ursuline nuns duly took formal vows of religion in 1619. But the arrangement proved so successful that together with the full-fledged support of Bishop Zamet, the Ursulines expanded rapidly to 37 ancillary houses within the bishop's diocese by 1650.[110]

In addition to the foundation of the Ursulines in 1605, there were a lot of other new male and female congregations founded in Dijon just after the religious wars. The Capuchins were a male order first established in 1602 by Joachim Damas, having been founded in Italy in 1529. They were an offshoot of the Franciscans who wanted to return to the stricter ways of the order's founder.[111] A female order of Discalced (or barefoot) Carmelites, a female offshoot of the male Carmelite order, was established

---

[108] Ibid., 165–170.
[109] Jean-François Senault, *La Vie de Madame Catherine de Montholon, veuve de Monsieur de Sanzelles, maistre des requestes, et fondatrice des Ursulines de Dijon* (Paris: Pierre Le Petit, 1653). Montholon was the cousin of Gasparde de Montholon, mentioned in Chapter 5, the wife of one of the royalist presiding judges, Jean Fyot, during the period of the League.
[110] Lierheimer, "Gender, Resistance, and Limits of Episcopal Authority," 160–165; and Farr, *Authority and Sexuality*, 54.
[111] Henri Chabeuf, *Dijon: Monuments et souvenirs* (Dijon: Damidot, 1894), 266.

in Dijon in 1605.[112] The male congregation of the Oratory was originally founded by Filippo Neri in Italy in 1575, and Pierre de Bérulle established the first French congregation in Paris in 1611. A congregation in Dijon was established in 1621 in a chapel on the Rue St. Jean.[113] And a female congregation of Jacobines, an offshoot of the male Dominican order in Dijon, was established in 1615.[114] All these new religious houses of friars and nuns added to the already prominent role played by the numerous parish churches, abbeys, and chapels already located in the Burgundian capital. But the most significant of all these new foundations in the city in terms of its impact was a new female order co-founded by Francis de Sales and another wealthy widow, Jeanne Frémyot, baroness of Chantal, daughter of the Fifth President of the Parlement of Dijon. This was the Order of the Visitation.

In August 1603 Dijon's viscount-mayor, Jean de Frasans, urged the city council to invite the bishop of Geneva, François de Sales, to come to Dijon to preach a series of Advent sermons later that year as well as a series of Lenten sermons the following spring, because, as the mayor noted, De Sales was "a person of great doctrine and theology."[115] De Sales responded very quickly that he was already committed to preaching the Advent sermons in Annécy, where the bishop resided, but that he would be delighted to come to Dijon to preach the Lenten sermons there in spring 1604.[116] He arrived on February 27, 1604 and remained in the city until April 26, a total of 56 days.[117] At the end of De Sales's visit, the Hôtel de Ville reimbursed Frémyot for all his expenses in accommodating the bishop during his stay with the sum of 280 *livres*.[118] While in Dijon, De Sales stayed at the home of Bénigne Frémyot, a presiding judge in the Parlement of Dijon who led the royalist court at Flavigny and Semur during the period of the League, as well as former mayor of Dijon in 1596–1597. Frémyot's son André was the abbot of St. Etienne in Dijon and, since 1603, also the archbishop of Bourges. His daughter Jeanne was a recent widow, having married Christophe de Rabutin, baron of Chantal. With her husband having been killed in a hunting accident just a few years before, the young baroness de Chantal was left to raise four very young children on her own.[119] She was immediately taken with her father's

---

[112] Ibid., 285–286.   [113] Ibid., 266.   [114] Ibid., 287.   [115] AMD, B 241, fol. 91r, August 12, 1603.
[116] Joseph Garnier, ed., *Correspondance de la mairie de Dijon extradite des archives de cette ville*, 3 vols. (Dijon: J.-E. Rabutot, 1868–1870), 3: 82–83, De Sales to the Hôtel de Ville, August 22, 1603.
[117] AMD, B 241, fols. 221r and 247r–v.   [118] AMD, B 241, 261v.
[119] Although there are several recent biographies, the most complete study of the life of Jeanne is still *Sainte Jeanne-Françoise Frémyot de Chantal, sa vie et ses oeuvres*, 8 vols., ed. by the Sisters of the Order

house-guest, François de Sales, and went along to hear his Lenten sermons that spring, which were delivered in the Sainte Chapelle, the private chapel of the Dukes of Burgundy until 1477 and used ever since as a place for special sermons and services in the city. De Sales made explicit overtures to many widows of elite families while in Dijon, not just to Jeanne Frémyot, urging them to consider joining a female order. But his closest relationship was undoubtedly that with Jeanne Frémyot. As Ruth Manning has described it, their relationship was so close that it bordered on the improper and could easily be called "a spiritual marriage."[120]

The spiritual friendship between De Sales and Jeanne that began in the Frémyot home in Dijon in the spring of 1604 blossomed into a lifelong relationship that eventually resulted in the foundation of a new order for women, the Order of the Visitation, in 1610. Plans were begun three years earlier in 1607, however, when De Sales and Jeanne discussed how they might form a community of widows into a community of the devout. The first congregation of Visitandines, as the nuns were called, was established in 1610 in Annecy, where the bishopric of Geneva had become established ever since an earlier bishop had been forced out of Geneva by the Reformation a century earlier. And while most histories of the Visitation indicate that De Sales himself was the real founder of the order, and Jeanne just an inspiration, we now know that she played just as great a role as her mentor in the order's founding.[121] The order was designed to be an apostolic – that is, uncloistered – community, with the nuns taking on significant duties of performing acts of charity, visiting the poor, and educating young girls in the devout life. A constitution for the order was drawn up in 1613 and further Visitandine communities were established in Lyon in 1615, Moulins in 1616, Grenoble and Bourges in 1618, Paris in 1619, Nevers in 1621, and finally in Dijon itself in 1622.[122]

The order remained noncloistered for six years, when with the expansion to Lyon in 1616 the Archbishop-Cardinal of Lyon, Denis-Simon de

---

of the Visitation of Annecy (Paris: Plon, 1874–1879). Also see Jeanne's correspondence with François de Sales and many others in Jeanne-Françoise Frémyot de Chantal, *Correspondance*, 6 vols., ed. Marie-Patricia Burns (Paris: Cerf, 1986–1996). A small portion of this correspondence is translated into English in Wendy M. Wright and Joseph F. Power, eds., *Francis de Sales, Jane de Chantal: Letters of Spiritual Direction*, trans. Péronne Marie Thibert (New York, NY: Paulist Press, 1988).

[120] Ruth Manning, "A Confessor and His Spiritual Child: François de Sales, Jeanne de Chantal, and the Foundation of the Order of the Visitation," in Ruth Harris and Lyndal Roper, eds., *The Art of Survival: Gender and History in Europe, 1450–2000* (Oxford: Oxford University Press, 2006), 101–117 (quote on 109).

[121] See ibid., especially 106–107.

[122] Françoise Kermina, *Jeanne de Chantal, 1572–1641* (Paris: Perrin, 2000), 319.

Marquemont, insisted that the order must become cloistered or face resistance from the French church. His insistence was partly due to the Council of Trent's requirement for all female religious orders to be enclosed, but also because noncloistered nuns did not have to renounce their worldly goods and give up all rights of property inheritance. In short, a Visitandine could easily leave the community at any time and even re-marry, creating potential havoc for her family. De Sales and Jeanne eventually agreed, albeit reluctantly, to conform to the required enclosure under the Augustinian rule, the least restrictive, which would still allow them to accept widows and girls of poor health.[123] Thus, from 1616 the order of the Visitation had to give up visiting the poor and the needy as well as teaching young girls outside the convent. Nevertheless, their striking success in the early years prior to enclosure from 1610 to 1616 established a benchmark as well as an example for future apostolic – noncloistered – congregations of women. In this sense, the Visitandines were the forerun-ners of the Daughters of the Cross and the Daughters of Charity, who in 1633 finally won the right to exist as a noncloistered female order. Even though the Order of the Visitation was destined to remain an enclosed order, it can be said that the work of a widow in Dijon and the Archbishop of Geneva managed to supersede the authority of bishops and even the Council of Trent.[124]

The most significant male order of the Catholic Reformation was undoubtedly the Society of Jesus, founded by the Spaniard Ignatius de Loyola in 1530 and officially recognized by Pope Paul III a decade later. In 1587 a Jesuit college was founded in Dijon – the Collège de Godrans – and it was strongly supported by the mayor and *échevins* in the Hôtel de Ville. Indeed, the college received regular financial support from the municipal elites, such as the donation of 100 *écus* given to the Jesuits in 1589.[125] Thus, it was hardly a surprise when the Jesuits publicly supported the League in Dijon. And even less surprising was that the expulsion of the Jesuits from France altogether in 1595 was poorly received in

---

[123] Manning, "A Confessor and His Spiritual Child," 116. Also, see Elizabeth Rapley, *The Dévotes: Women and Church in Seventeenth-Century France* (Montreal: McGill University Press, 1990), 39–40.

[124] See especially Ruth Manning, "Breaking the Rules: The Emergence of the Active Female Apostolate in Seventeenth-Century France," unpublished Ph.D. thesis, University of Oxford, 2006) and Barbara B. Diefendorf, *From Penitence to Charity: Pious Women and the Catholic Reformation in Paris* (New York, NY: Oxford University Press, 2004).

[125] AMD, B 227, fol. 71v, August 8, 1589: "*considerant la peyne et le labeur auquel incessement ilz semployent tant aux predica[tio]ns quilz font po[ur] maintenir et edifier le people au salut de leurs ames, mantention et conservacion de la sainte religion Catholique, apostolique et Romaine.*"

Dijon.[126] The expulsion was largely a judicial decision made by the Parlements rather than a policy of King Henry IV's own making, though he did not interfere with it. And when the Jesuit college in Dijon secretly reopened in 1597, Henry chastised the city fathers for explicitly disobeying him.[127] Yet as Eric Nelson has recently shown, Henry was as responsible as anyone for rehabilitating the Jesuits and bringing about their recall. Though the judges of the Parlement of Paris continued to insist that the Jesuits be excluded from their jurisdiction, Henry issued a royal edict in September 1603 formally reopening the Jesuit college in Dijon as well as several others elsewhere, and recognized the Society of Jesus's right to be part of the French church at least in the south and west of the kingdom.[128] And while the Jesuits would maintain a constant and visible presence in Dijon thereafter, especially in educating the sons of elites in the city, it was the new female orders that made the more visible mark. The efforts of elite women like Jeanne Frémyot and Rose Bourgeois to help the poor and the popular classes generally was yet another example of ties being made and remade between Dijon's elites and popular classes, even if the Council of Trent's requirement of cloistering all female orders threatened to dissolve them.

Besides the reform of the episcopacy and the introduction of new religious orders, one final aspect of Catholic reform was the imperative to enforce the Edict of Nantes throughout the kingdom, above all, to restore the Catholic mass in towns the Huguenots had controlled for decades. These issues, combined with some intransigent resistance by a few Huguenot noblemen, especially in southern and western France, resulted in a series of military campaigns by King Louis XIII in the 1620s that threatened to renew the violence of the second half of the sixteenth century. Short military campaigns in the summers of 1620, 1621, and 1622 resulted in the surrender of Pau in Béarn, St. Jean d'Angély in Poitou, and Montauban and Montpellier in Languedoc. Finally, an even longer siege of more than a year of the Atlantic port city of La Rochelle, perhaps the Huguenots' largest and most significant fortified town remaining in France, eventually produced a surrender to the king on October 28, 1628. And though none of these events directly touched the province of Burgundy, indirectly the crown's need for more tax revenues to undertake

---

[126] J. Gazin-Goussel, "Un contre-coup de la Ligue en Bourgogne: L'expulsion et le retour des Jésuites de Dijon," *Revue de l'histoire de l'Eglise de France* 1 (1910): 515–526.

[127] Garnier, ed., *Correspondance de la mairie de Dijon*, 3: 27–29, September 13, 1599.

[128] Eric Nelson, *The Jesuits and the Monarchy: Catholic Reform and Political Authority in France, 1590–1615* (Aldershot: Ashgate, 2005), 57–96, especially p. 77.

these campaigns as well as the king's expectation to be treated as a conquering military hero certainly did. All these issues came to a head just three months later when Louis XIII decided to make his first visit to the city of Dijon. His "joyous entry" into the city would prove to be anything but joyous, however.

CHAPTER 8

The Crown, the Magistrates, and the People
The Lanturelu Riot of 1630

It took slightly more than a week for the news of the surrender of La Rochelle on October 28, 1628 and the king's subsequent entry into the city on November 1 to reach the city of Dijon. The mayor and *échevins* of the Hôtel de Ville ordered a *Te Deum* to be sung in the Sainte-Chapelle and began organizing a massive celebration in the city for Tuesday, November 21 replete with "joyous bonfires," reputed to be "the most beautiful that were ever seen in the city," as well as the firing of the cannons from the Château. In the square just outside the Sainte-Chapelle each of the *échevins* carried a torch to help light the bonfires. There they encountered "a great multitude of people." In the middle of the square there was also a freestanding four-sided stage, with "a woman with wild eyes" and a statue of a young Hercules.[1] This staged series of effigies was designed by one of the *échevins*, Pierre Guillaume, and another *échevin*, Etienne Brechillet, the author of some of the Mère Folle plays discussed in the previous chapter, organized the entire display. And the meaning of the staged display was pretty clear: The wild-eyed woman represented the recalcitrant rebels of La Rochelle, and the young Hercules was King Louis XIII reining them in.[2]

Of course, this was all part of a narrative of royalist, even absolutist, propaganda. The good citizens of La Rochelle did not see themselves as rebels against the authority of the king, but as defenders of their faith and urban independence. This did not stop the king from punishing the city as rebellious traitors, however: The city walls were to be razed; the office of mayor, *échevins*, and the city's militia were all to be abolished; all civic privileges were to be revoked; the city was fined an annual levy of the *taille* of 4,000 *livres*; and Catholic worship and institutions were to be

---

[1] AMD, B 265, fols. 141r–148v, November 11–21, 1628, quote on fol. 148r–v.
[2] Michael P. Breen, "Addressing *La Ville des Dieux*: Entry Ceremonies and Urban Audiences in Seventeenth-Century Dijon," *The Journal of Social History* 38 (2004): 348.

immediately reestablished throughout the city.[3] Whether Dijon's own *échevins*, especially Guillaume and Bréchillet, were fully aware of the terms of La Rochelle's surrender when they organized the display of bonfires and staged propaganda on November 21, they would certainly have been aware of the consequences any city in the kingdom was likely to suffer if there was overt and explicit disobedience of the king's will. It was one thing for these good Catholic magistrates to invoke royal authority and justice in the punishment of Protestant rebels in a city far away; it would be quite another, however, if that same royal authority and justice came under attack in Dijon itself.

8.1   The "Joyous Entry" of Louis XIII, January 1629

Barely six weeks after the bonfires and celebrations of the king's victory at La Rochelle were celebrated in Dijon on November 21, the city council received a missive from one of their own *échevins* who had been sent to the court in Paris on city business, Bénigne Euvrard. He informed his colleagues that the king was planning to travel to Dauphiné in southeastern France and wanted to stop in Dijon and several other Burgundian towns *en route*. The king and his retinue planned to leave Paris on January 15 and would arrive in Dijon by the end of the month.[4] Though they only had a few weeks to prepare, the city's elites saw an opportunity to turn this into a formal royal entry, that is, a much more significant ceremonial ritual than an ordinary royal visit. This special royal entry usually marked the king's first visit to a city after becoming king, and it was traditionally called a *Joyeuse entrée*, because the highlight of the ceremony was the king standing before the high altar of the abbey of St. Bénigne, the city's largest church, and, with his hand on the gospel of St. John, swearing an oath to uphold the city's traditional privileges, liberties, and franchises. This was the reciprocal arrangement of mutual loyalty and respect after the mayor had sworn the city's allegiance to the king. The last such "joyous entry" had occurred on June 4, 1595, when Louis XIII's father, Henry IV, swore such an oath after the city surrendered to him after his abjuration of Protestantism (see Chapter 6). That was a rushed affair, however, coming

---

[3] Kevin C. Robbins, *City on the Ocean Sea, La Rochelle, 1530–1650: Urban Society, Religion, and Politics on the French Atlantic Frontier* (Leiden: Brill, 1997), 355; and David Parker, *La Rochelle and the French Monarchy: Conflict and Order in Seventeenth-Century France* (London: Royal Historical Society, 1980), 17.

[4] Joseph Garnier, ed., *Correspondance de la mairie de Dijon extradite des archives de cette ville*, 3 vols. (Dijon: Rabutot, 1868–1870), 3: 185–186, Euvrard to the mayor and *échevins*, January 3, 1629.

immediately after a military siege, without any of the pomp or great expense expected of such entries. Thus, the mayor, Etienne Humbert, and the *échevins* asked Etienne Bréchillet to design five triumphal arches through which the king would march, and hire pipers and drummers from other nearby towns. And they also quickly borrowed 8,000 *livres* to pay for the expenses of such an entry.[5] The mayor also ordered that all able-bodied males between the ages of 18 and 60 turn out to muster with their arms with the captains of each parish's civic militia in order to welcome the king, on pain of a 50 *livres* fine. When the captains complained that too many men were refusing to do so, the fine was increased to 400 *livres*.[6] The city's elites wanted to make it very clear that this was a major visit by the king and everyone was expected to participate.

Louis XIII himself upset these plans, however, just two days before his expected arrival, when he announced that due to the absence of the Chancellor of France and Keeper of the Seals, Michel de Marillac, as well as all the king's secretaries of state, who normally recorded the king's oath swearing to uphold the city's liberties and privilege but were not traveling with the royal party, he would be unable to make such an oath. Although this seemed a mere technicality to the king, the city fathers of Dijon saw it rather differently. Two *échevins* were dispatched to meet him before he entered the city, asking him to reconsider, as the city would provide anyone the king chose from the city to record the oath. But Louis nevertheless refused.[7] And early on the morning of January 31 Cardinal Richelieu was dispatched to the mayor with the official news.[8] Thus, when "King Louis XIII nicknamed the Just and the Victorious" finally made his entry into the city about three o'clock in the afternoon of January 31, he duly went to the abbey church of St. Bénigne, received mass, and then heard the mayor and *échevins* on behalf of the entire city swear their loyalty to him. But he gave no such reciprocal oath to maintain the city and its citizens in all their traditional privileges, liberties, and franchises, though he did promise to do so once Chancellor Marillac could authenticate the act. Though they were extremely disappointed, the city magistrates put on a brave face and recorded in their official deliberations that when the king left the church to go to his lodgings on horseback, "all the people witnessing an

---

[5] AMD, B 266, fols. 191–192v, January 14–15, 1629; Garnier, ed., *Correspondance de la mairie*, 3: 196–203, January 22–27, 1629; and Breen, "Addressing *La Ville des Dieux*," 348.

[6] AMD, B 266, fols. 205r and 211v–212r, January 21 and 27, 1629.

[7] Garnier, ed., *Correspondance de la mairie*, 3: 200–202, Guillaume and Blanot to the mayor and *échevins*, January 27, 1629.

[8] AMD, B266, fol. 216r–v, January 31, 1629.

incomparable joy and happiness, crying in high voice 'Long live the king!', it was true that France had never had a more merciful or debonair prince."[9] The official deliberations obscured the fact, however, that the king's refusal to confirm the city's traditional liberties and privileges rankled both the elites and the popular classes.

The procession of Louis XIII from the abbey church of St. Bénigne to his lodgings in the *Palais des Ducs*, the palace of the former dukes of Burgundy, brought the king face to face with the triumphal arches designed and erected by Etienne Bréchillet. The smallest of them was 29 feet high, not counting the figures mounted on top, and 29 feet wide, and each contained a Latin inscription followed by a verse in French.[10] Etienne Bréchillet's triumphal arches represented the king as Neptune, Apollo, Hercules, and Caesar Augustus, and they underscored "the sanctity of kings" with divine vengeance for anyone who dared oppose the royalty and authority of a King of France.[11] What possible slight or lack of deference could Louis XIII have perceived from such a ceremonial display at his "Joyous entry" into Dijon? The problem was certainly not all the classical allusions and motifs that a humanist-trained lawyer such as Bréchillet would have naturally chosen to express the city's political messages of loyalty and obedience to the king. From Louis XIII's perspective, the problem was the way Bréchillet used these classical motifs to express a political understanding of the monarchy that he felt was completely out of date. As James B. Collins has emphasized repeatedly over the last decade or so, there was an evolving theory of monarchy that began around 1580 and was pretty much complete by 1630. During that period some jurists and royal propagandists began to use language that shifted emphasis away from a republican commonwealth, that is, a compact between the king and his subjects all in the name of protecting the public good – *le bien public* – and replaced it with language of a monarchical state centered much more on what was good for the king and his state, which he came to identify as his own property.[12] Commonly used terms such as the Latin *res publica* – which was translated in early modern English as commonwealth rather

[9] AMD, B 266, fols. 216v–219, January 31, 1629, quote on 219.
[10] AMD, B 266, fol. 219v, January 31, 1629.
[11] AMD, B 266, fols. 219v–226v, January 31, 1629. Etienne Bréchillet, the *échevin* who designed and oversaw the construction of the five triumphal arches, later published a description of them, based largely on the account in the city council deliberations quoted earlier: [Etienne Bréchillet], *Dessein des Arcz triomphaux, érigez à l'honneur du Roy, à son entrée en la ville de Dijon, le dernier de janvier mil six cens vingt-neuf* (Dijon: Guyot, 1629).
[12] Herbert H. Rowan, *The King's State: Proprietary Dynasticism in Early Modern France* (New Brunswick, NJ: Rutgers University Press, 1980).

than republic – and *le bien public* gave way and were replaced by *l'État*, the state. In short, as Collins notes, in France "the state slew the republic."[13] As I have argued previously, relations between cities or regions and monarchs were always negotiations, and the process of negotiating was just as important as the outcomes. Louis XIII's entry into Dijon in January 1629 demonstrates that the city and the king were negotiating using two entirely different political languages, which represented the city's older perception of France as a commonwealth based on *le bien public* and the crown's new understanding of France as a monarchical state, where the good of the king and his state were what mattered most. Thus, Etienne Bréchillet and Louis XIII both thought they were acting in the best interest of the kingdom, but they were speaking different political languages, and mutual misunderstanding was always the likely result.

Bréchillet's very first triumphal arch was a prime example. It was the only one that depicted the city of Dijon, and Bréchillet chose the figure of Cybelle, "Mother of the Gods," to represent the city. The king was a mere man mounted on horseback, while the city of Dijon was a goddess and mother of all the gods. Bréchillet certainly did not attempt to make the king feel less divine, much less subservient to the city, but this was the message that came across.[14] Moreover, this arch represented the traditional view of France as a commonwealth, where local leaders and the monarch worked together as partners for the common good, not equal partners, to be sure, but partners nevertheless, where each had a significant role to play. In a commonwealth, the king was *le chef*, or, as the Romans put it, first among equals (*primus inter pares*), indicating that the king was the principal and most important figure in the realm, but that the elites of the realm were also vital to the preservation of order and functioning of the state. Nobles and aristocrats voiced these claims from the beginning of the Wars of Religion and argued that it was their duty to protect and defend the state, even against the king if necessary.[15] And not just nobles but also the legal elites of the Parlements, Chambers of Account, and other sovereign courts espoused

---

[13] James B. Collins, *The State in Early Modern France*, 2nd edn. (Cambridge: Cambridge University Press, 2009), xxiii. Also see the same author's "De la république française à l'état français: Duplessis-Mornay et la transformation de la citoyenneté en France," in Hugues Daussy and Veronique Ferrer, eds., *Servir Dieu, le roi et l'état: Philippe Duplessis-Mornay (1549–1623)*, Albineana 18 (Niort: Cahiers d'Aubigné, 2006), 325–339; and most recently his *La Monarchie républicaine: État et société dans la France moderne* (Paris: Odile Jacob, 2016), especially 19–21.

[14] Breen, *Law, City, and King*, 168.

[15] See Arlette Jouanna, *Le devoir de révolte: La noblesse française et la gestation de l'État moderne, 1559–1661* (Paris: Fayard, 1989).

similar sentiments.[16] And now Étienne Bréchillet was making similar claims on behalf of the mayor and *échevins* of the city of Dijon. This was hardly the model Louis XIII wanted to see, a monarchical state where all his subjects had a duty to serve the king for the benefit of his state rather than for the common good.

A second slight perceived by the king that day was the gift the city presented to him, a cross of diamonds suspended from a gold chain that the Hôtel de Ville commissioned from the goldsmith Jean Papillon at a cost of 1,000 *livres tournois*.[17] The king was "very displeased (un desplaisir du tout)" with both the nature of the gift and the inscription engraved on it: "Conquest and Justice (*Victorii et Justo*)." He wanted and expected a gift alluding to his recent victory over La Rochelle as well as reversing the inscription to read "Justice and Conquest," thereby underscoring that any conquest within his own kingdom was just. Thus, a new gift was hurriedly commissioned, in the form of a gilded sculpture of the king on horseback "covered in a large number of diamonds, and a goddess at his feet wearing the ducal crown on her head representing the city of Dijon," presenting two palms to the king representing Justice and Conquest. The figures were mounted on a gold base sitting atop four gold books, with sixteen large diamonds decorating the base. This time the city spent 920 *écus* and 28 *sous*, equal to 2,761 *livres* and 8 *sous*, roughly three times the cost of the original gift.[18] Bréchillet himself was dispatched to go after the king when the new gift was ready to present it to him, as well as to plead for the king to give formal recognition of the city's privileges.[19] The mayor and *échevins* had badly miscalculated what would please the king, however. Their original gift, a diamond cross, underscored the sacrality of the monarchy as well as linking the royal gift to the *foy de Bourgogne*, the traditional understanding of the reciprocal relationship between the city and the Dukes of Burgundy as well as with the Kings of France. Thus, the *foy de Bourgogne* was seen as a cornerstone and foundation of the idea of France as a commonwealth. In both rejecting the city's gift and refusing to confirm the city's traditional liberties and privileges when he was at the altar in the abbey of St. Bénigne earlier that day, Louis XIII was perceived to be explicitly rejecting the

---

[16] See Marie Houllemare, *Politiques de la parole: Le Parlement de Paris au XVIᵉ siècle* (Geneva: Librairie Droz, 2011); and Sylvie Daubresse, *Le Parlement de Paris ou la voix de raison (1559–1589)* (Geneva: Librairie Droz, 2005).

[17] AMD, B 266, fol. 227, January 31, 1629.

[18] AMD, 266, fol.230r–231v, February 2 and 3, 1629; and Garnier, ed., *Correspondance de la mairie de Dijon*, 3: 210, February 2, 1629.

[19] Breen, *Law, City, and King*, 60.

traditional polity for a new one based on a monarchical state. The city dispatched deputies to the Chancellor Marillac and to the court in the coming months pleading for the king to confirm their privileges, all to no avail.[20] Most inhabitants of the city were alarmed, and to them the king's actions contrasted sharply with those of his father, Henry IV, at his "joyous entry" back in June 1595. Not only did Henry gladly confirm the city's traditional liberties, but afterward he made a public trek outside the city walls to the Chartreuse monastery to pray at the tombs of the Valois dukes of Burgundy.[21] Indeed, French kings had always confirmed a city's privileges and liberties, either outside the city walls before entering in the late Middle Ages and inside the walls after entering by the mid-sixteenth century, but Louis XIII refused to do so at all.[22]

From the king's perspective, of course, his refusal to confirm the city's privileges was a mere technicality caused by the absence of the Chancellor and secretaries of state to record such an oath. Indeed, he did finally confirm the city's privileges in royal letters patent six months later.[23] Moreover, Louis's rejection of the city's gift was for him just a personal preference rather than an explicit rejection of the past. But his actions fed into a growing narrative that his father Henry IV had clearly recognized and accepted the city's privileges and considered Dijon's leaders as partners in the running of the state, while Louis did not. Henry had always accepted the candidates elected as mayor by the city's electorate, while his son intervened and did not always accept the city's first choice. This was not an entirely justified narrative, of course, as was shown in Chapter 7. It was Henry IV who was the innovator and who negotiated the right to intervene in the city's mayoral elections, even though he chose not to do so. Louis XIII and his regent, Marie de Medici, merely acted within the innovations that Henry IV had put in place. But the public perception in Dijon was very different: Henry IV respected both the *foy de Bourgogne* and the role played by the city in the commonwealth of France, while Louis XIII clearly did not. The king's "Joyous entry" into the city on January 31, 1629 only reinforced this perception. Events over the next year would permanently fix this narrative in Burgundian memory and history.

---

[20] AMD, B 266, fols. 262v–263r and 269v, March 6 and 13, 1629.   [21] See Chapter 6.

[22] Neil Murphy, *Ceremonial Entries, Municipal Liberties and the Negotiation of Power in Valois France, 1328–1589* (Leiden and Boston, MA: Brill, 2016).

[23] AMD, B 267, fol. 55r, July 10, 1629.

8.2   A Popular Uprising in Dijon, February–March 1630

Just over a year after Louis XIII's "Joyous entry" into Dijon the city exploded in a night of unprecedented violence perpetrated by a number of vignerons and artisans against some of the leading elites of Dijon, mainly several judges in the Parlement as well as in the Chamber of Accounts. Several townhouses of these judges were singled out, broken into, and ransacked, with luxurious furniture, clothing, and libraries of books brought out into the street and ceremoniously burned in bonfires. The rioters danced and celebrated around these bonfires as they drank the wine from the wine-cellars of their chosen victims, one of whom was the First President of the Parlement of Dijon. The city fathers were very slow in calling out the civic militia to quell the rioting, with the result that seven townhouses of the wealthiest elites in the city were plundered and their contents destroyed before order could be restored. What in the world was going on? Nothing like this had ever happened during the Wars of Religion, and it is strange that some of the most respected men in the city should be victimized in this way. While it might be tempting to write this off as a typical incident of social and economic distress – both grain and wine prices had escalated higher in in the last two years than they had been since the scarcity of the wars of the League in the 1590s – or to explain it as simply a carryover of excess from the Carnival celebrations that ended only days before, the truth was much more complex. Although both socio-economic issues and carnivalesque elements were clearly visible in the actions of the rioters, it seems pretty clear that specific policies of Louis XIII and his efforts to implement them in the province of Burgundy were the triggers that set off the rioting. Moreover, as the following discussion will demonstrate, the vignerons who led the Lanturelu riot in Dijon in February 1630 – Lanturelu was a popular song that was sung by the rioters as they marched from one judge's townhouse to another – were expressing their own collective political opposition to the king's policies, while at the same time exploiting the divisions among the *échevin*s, judges in the royal courts, and other royal officers over these same policies.

The royal policies that divided Dijon's elites yet seemed to unite most of the popular classes were twofold. The first, with more long-term signifi-cance, was an ongoing effort by the king to replace the provincial estates in France's *pays d'état*, such as Burgundy, who represented the interests of the province, with royally appointed tax officials who worked for the crown. In other words, this was yet another effort to transform France into a more monarchical state and make it a more absolute monarchy in practice as well as in theory. The various *pays d'état* were largely formerly independent provinces around the periphery of the kingdom that had been incorporated into the French crown relatively recently in the fifteenth and early sixteenth centuries, such as Burgundy in 1477 after the death of the last Valois duke of Burgundy, Charles the Bold. Artois, Brittany, Languedoc, Provence, and Dauphiné, for example, were among the handful of other provinces that retained a degree of self-governance, especially in the area of tax assessment and collection, which the king had granted to them at the time of their incorporation into the French kingdom.[24] Indeed, this was one of the specific privileges that Burgundy enjoyed that Louis XIII had failed to confirm orally at the time of his royal entry the year before. But now, instigated by his keeper of the seals, Michel de Marillac, Louis XIII was determined to transform some of the *pays d'état* like Burgundy into *pays d'élections*, so called because the royal tax officials who would replace the deputies of the provincial estates were known as *élus*. Just as with the royal interference in Dijon's mayoral elections, however, it was Henry IV rather than his son Louis XIII who first implemented the policy of replacing provincial estates with royal *élus* to gain control of tax collection. In April 1604 Henry persuaded the Parlement of Bordeaux to register an edict creating *élections* in the province of Guyenne, despite local opposition from the provincial estates.[25] But as with the mayoral elections, it was Louis XIII who was saddled with the blame for this policy in the late 1620s. To be sure, his father had introduced the *élections* into only one *pays d'état* in 1604, while Louis XIII attempted to repeat his father's success in multiple *pays d'états* in 1628–1630. As Donald Bailey has noted, neither Louis nor Marillac had a systematic plan to reform all the *pays d'états* into *pays d'élections*. They were simply responding to fiscal shortages in a time of war and rebellion. Nevertheless, "in the pressure to get things done, reform happens."[26] And the opposition to this policy was clearly visible in Burgundy, especially among the *échevins* of Dijon's Hôtel de Ville as well as among the majority of the city's vignerons.

The second policy that aroused strong opposition in Burgundy was the crown's decision to consider increasing the *octroi*, the entry tax on all wine

[24] See J. Russell Major, *Representative Government in Early Modern France* (New Haven, CT: Yale University Press, 1980), 58–96 and 519–567.

[25] J. Russell Major, "Henry IV and Guyenne: A Study Concerning the Origins of Royal Absolutism," *French Historical Studies* 4 (1966): 363–383; and Major, *Representative Government in Early Modern France*, 279–289.

[26] Donald A. Bailey, ed., *Histoire de la vie de Michel de Marillac (1560–1632): Garde des sceaux de France sous Louis XIII* (Quebec: Presses de l'Université de Laval, 2007), xlvi.

from outside Dijon's own vineyards brought into the city to be sold by nonresidents. As explained in Chapter 3, the *octroi* was first established in 1428 by Duke Philip the Good at the rate of 20 *sous* per *queue* of wine, and it had been renewed by every King of France since Louis XI in 1477. Though the rate was often lowered in times of severe shortage, it never rose above 20 *sous* per *queue* for the next two centuries. Indeed, Louis XIII himself had confirmed this rate in a patent letter to the city earlier in his reign, where he noted that "from time immemorial it has been conceded to them in perpetuity 20 sous on each queue of wine entering or being brought into the said city from any region or territory other than the growths and inherited vineyards of the city."[27] Thus, when rumors circulated in February 1630 that the king was considering raising the rate, opposition was immediate. Interestingly, the Chamber of Accounts in Dijon had tried to raise the rate once before in 1574 during the religious wars by just one *sou* per queue, but the public outcry by the city's vignerons was so assertive – ten of them were arrested for protesting too forcefully – that the effort was dropped.[28] Now in 1630 rumors began circulating of increased *aides*, the colloquial name for any increase or new tax on wine.[29]

The introduction of new *pays d'élections* and new taxes on wine were perceived as more than just royal intrusions into local liberties and privileges, though they were definitely that. What rankled even more was that the grain and wine harvests since the end of the Wars of Religion had been uneven, with the result that prices of all foodstuffs as well as wine had been fluctuating wildly over the previous decade. Figures 8.1, 8.2, and 8.3 make clear that although harvests of cereal grains, legumes, and cooking oil improved immediately after the end of the civil war, with prices dropping to more affordable levels, the 1620 s brought some new fluctuations. Indeed, in the period 1628–1630 with a series of poor harvests and scarcity of foodstuffs, prices rose to even higher levels than during the Wars of Religion.[30] Wine prices fluctuated even more wildly, as a poor harvest in

---

[27] For the period up to the start of the Wars of Religion, see Claude Tournier, "Le vin à Dijon de 1430 à 1560: Ravitaillement et commerce," *Annales de Bourgogne* 22 (1950): 7–32 and 161–186. For the second half of the sixteenth century, see Henri Drouot, "Vin, vignes et vignerons de la côte dijonnaise pendant la Ligue," *Revue de Bourgogne* 1 (1911): 343–361. And for Louis XIII's patent letter, see BMD, Ms. 1012, p. 127, July 1617.

[28] AMD, B212, fol. 55r–v, August 2, 1574.

[29] For a discussion on *aides*, see Guy Cabourdin and Georges Viart, eds., *Lexique historique de la France d'Ancien Régime* (Paris: Armand Colin, 2nd edn. 1981), 12.

[30] As explained in Chapter 5, these figures come from the "*Taux des gros fruits*" in the deliberations of the Hôtel de Ville every year from 1568, usually in November or early December following the first wholesale market after the feast day of St. Martin, November 11, though occasionally the clerk forgot

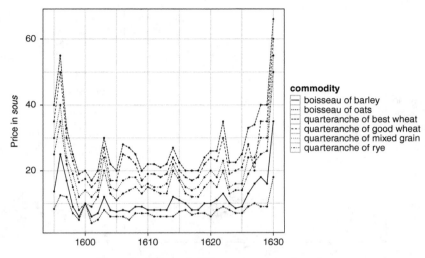

Figure 8.1 Wholesale Dijon grain prices, 1595–1630

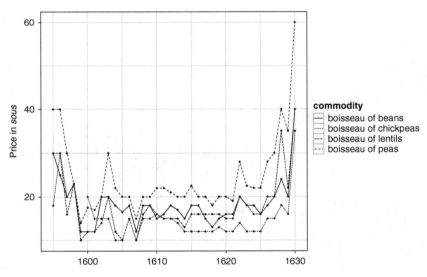

Figure 8.2 Wholesale Dijon legume prices, 1595–1630

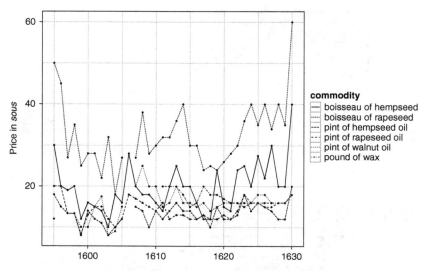

Figure 8.3 Wholesale Dijon oil and seed prices, 1595–1630

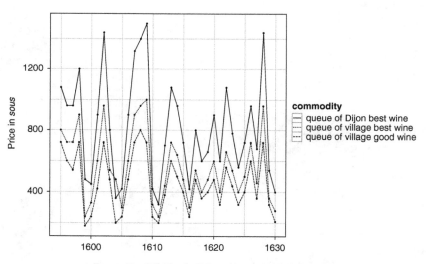

Figure 8.4 Wholesale Dijon wine prices, 1595–1630

1602 followed by a succession of poor grape harvests in 1607, 1698, and 1609, brought prices to an even higher level than during the 1590s, reaching 1,500 *sous* per barrel. Then dramatic and almost annual sharp fluctuations saw prices of a barrel of Dijon's best quality wine vary from a low of 300 *sous* per barrel to a high of 1,080 *sous* per barrel between 1610 and 1627. Then, in 1628 the price went up to 1440 *sous* per barrel, before dropping down to 400 *sous* per barrel in 1630. But vignerons did not benefit very much from the years of high prices because there was so little wine to sell in the years of poor wine harvests. And in years of abundant harvests, wine prices fell precipitously. For those vignerons who did not own any vines and depended entirely on wages paid for their labor, wages remained virtually flat in the period 1595–1630 for virtually all journeymen and day laborers.[31]

Another measure of vignerons' declining economic fortunes in 1630 is to look at the sales of land, especially vineyard land. Xavière Patouillet has taken a sampling of 10 out of 28 notaries in Dijon in the year 1630, and she has noted that a total of 175 land sales were recorded during that year, of which 93 (53.1 percent) involved parcels of vines. Only 31 of the purchasers were vignerons (17.7 percent), while 99 of the sellers were vignerons (57 percent) in these sales. Indeed, many vignerons had to sell vines to cover their debts in 1630, a case in point being the vigneron Jean Gobin, who sold a parcel of vines in Chenôve, a *demi-journal*, or roughly 1,712 square meters, to the merchant Isaac Jacob for the sum of 159 *livres* 18 *sous*, with payment spread over three years.[32] Neither the price fluctuations of cereal grains, wine, and other goods in the 1620s, nor growing vigneron indebtedness, with some forced to sell off some of their vineyards, can be viewed as a structural or underlying cause of the Lanturelu riots in February 1630.

to record them in the deliberations until January or even February of the following year. The data from Figures 8.1, 8.2, 8.3, and 8.4 were taken from AMD, B 233 (for the year 1595) and every register thereafter through B 268 (for the year 1630). Although the figures were recorded in various monetary units including money of account (*livres tournois*, *sous*, and *deniers*) as well as actual coins (*écus*, *francs*, *gros*, and *blancs*), I have translated all prices into *sous* for easier comparison. The various values of all currency units are given in Chapter 5. One further complication is that measures for dry goods such as grain and legumes were normally given in a *quarteranche* or a *boisseau*. In much of France these were different quantities, with the *quarteranche* (sometimes spelled *cartranche*) about one-quarter larger than the boisseau. In Dijon, however, though cereal grains were always measured by the *quarteranche*, many dry goods such as legumes were as likely to be expressed in a *quarteranche* in one year and in a *boisseau* in the next without any price fluctuation, suggesting that the two were often indistinguishable to contemporaries. Thus, I have treated them as the same in the figures given here.

[31] James R. Farr, *Hands of Honor: Artisans and Their World in Dijon, 1550–1650* (Ithaca, NY: Cornell University Press, 1988), 105–109.

[32] Xavière Patouillet, "L'Émeute des Lanturelus à Dijon en 1630," Mémoire de maîtrise, Université de Dijon, 1971, 58–60.

Similar or even worse economic conditions had existed in the past without anything close to the violence and destruction of property of the most elite families in the city in 1630. But these deteriorating economic conditions for the poorer vignerons do provide a context for why they were so concerned about rumors of the establishment of new *élections* for assessing tax levies in Burgundy and above all the rumored new taxes on wine brought into Dijon.

The establishment of the new *élections* was more than a rumor, as the king issued an Edict of Élection on June 10, 1629 abolishing the Estates of Burgundy and establishing 10 *élections* in the province to replace the Estates, each with a royal officer called an *élu* to administer and supervise tax assessment and collection. But the edict had to be registered in the Chamber of Accounts (*Chambre des comptes*) before it could go into effect.[33] The Chamber of Accounts had a checkered history in the Burgundian capital, as Louis XIII had recently removed it from Dijon in 1627 and ordered the judges to assemble in the town of Autun, 90 km away. The reason was that in October of that year one of the judges on the Chamber of Accounts had threatened a judge in the Parlement with a pistol over a dispute in jurisdiction between the two sovereign courts. Both bodies sought the support of the king in the dispute, and Louis sided with the Parlement, ordering the Chamber of Accounts out of the city.[34] Most of the judges in the exiled Chamber continued to reside in Dijon for most of the year, however, where they lived with their families in some of the most sumptuous townhouses in the city. Indeed, because of this they managed to convince the king to allow them to meet in Beaune by early 1630, which was much closer to Dijon, only 44 km away. And this was the situation at the end of the Carnival celebrations in February 1630. The Chamber of Accounts was meeting in Beaune and ready to register the Edict of Élections, while the judges in the Parlement were largely supportive of them, albeit with some opposition. The mayor and *échevins* in the Hôtel de Ville were clearly opposed, and they had already expressed their opposition a few weeks earlier by sending a delegation to Paris "to obtain the revocation of the edict establishing the *élections* in the said province [of Burgundy]" directly from the king himself. They even offered to give the king a donation of 1.8 million *livres* if he would withdraw his plan to implement the *élection*. This attempt to negotiate with the crown with what amounted to a bribe was rejected outright.[35] When this failed,

[33] Farr, *Hands of Honor*, 207.   [34] AMD, B 265, fols. 115v–120r, October 8 and 12, 1627.
[35] AMD, B 267, fol. 145r–v, January 29–30, 1630; AMD, B 462, no. 262; and J. Russell Major, *From Renaissance Monarchy to Absolute Monarchy: French Kings, Nobles, and Estates* (Baltimore, MD: Johns Hopkins University Press, 1994), 257.

the mayor sent another delegation to the Chamber of Accounts in Beaune on February 12 to argue against registering the Edict, "that if this happened, it would reduce to nothing the liberty of the Estates, the privileges of the said province, and it would lead to the ruin and desolation of the same, against the intentions of His Majesty, which at his coronation he had confirmed the said privileges, and by his justice and natural goodness he has never desired anything but the well-being and relief of his subjects."[36]

And one week later, on February 19, the mayor and *échevins* learned that "on the subject of the edict establishing the *élection*s, some rumors were circulating among the common people," and there was talk of possible violence if the edict was enacted. The magistrates decided they had better inform the captains, lieutenants, and ensigns of the parish militias that they were "to hold firm and safeguard with great care each part of the city, to insure that it remains in the respect and obedience which is owed to His Majesty, and that no popular disturbance breaks out under any pretext whatsoever anywhere in the city."[37] Moreover, a few days later the council received a stern warning letter from the royal governor in Burgundy, Roger de St. Lary, Duke of Bellegarde, who was in Paris attempting to plead with the king to withdraw the edict creating the *élection*s.

> For several days a rumor has been circulating here that great efforts are already underway in your city to oppose the edict of *élection*s with violence, that which your enemies, in an effort to harm you, are calling nothing less than a revolt. But I beg you to make the all the people understand from me that this would only bring complete ruin to your city and would serve as an example for all of France.[38]

Violence was even threatened against the judges in the Parlement, when on the morning of February 26 a handwritten note was found attached to the main door of the court, written in the familiar and insulting *tu* form: "You, who are the chief of the *élection*s, you and your household beware (*Toy, qui es chef delection, prends garde a toy et a ta maison*)."[39] And a day later, February 27, rumors circulated throughout Dijon that the Chamber of Accounts meeting in Beaune was scheduled to register the Edict of Élections and raise the tax on wine the very next day.[40]

That very night after dark on February 27 the long anticipated popular opposition to the establishment of the *élection*s and the new taxes on wine

---

[36] AMD, B 267, fol. 152r, February 12, 1630.   [37] AMD, B 267, fol. 154r–v, February 19, 1630.
[38] Garnier, ed., *Correspondance de la mairie de Dijon*, 3: 227, February 18, 1630. The city council did not receive this letter, however, until February 23: AMD, B 267, fol. 155v, February 23, 1630.
[39] AMD, B 267, fol. 156r, February 26, 1630.   [40] AMD, I 117, February 27, 1630.

erupted in violence.[41] About seven o'clock in the evening a group of 30 to 40 vignerons "armed only with 7 or 8 halberds [spears with axe-heads on them] and some spears, without any firearms (*armez seulement de sept ou huit hallebardes et de pieux sans aucunes armes a feu*)" gathered in front of the townhouse of Nicolas Gagne on the Rue Vannerie. Gagne was Treasurer-General of France for the generality of Burgundy and Bresse and a councilor of the king, and the royal official in charge of securing the registration of the Edict of Élections in the Chamber of Accounts. According to Fleutelot's account, the vignerons began throwing rocks at the door and windows of Gagne's townhouse, but they did not break in and eventually dispersed, assembling behind the nearby parish church of St. Michel. About nine o'clock they began marching through the streets with a drum "to excite the people," and then around midnight they began marching on the walls of the city to announce to those living in the outlying parts that they would carry out their measures the following day. The rest of the night was quiet, though they did go to the mayor's house and demand he give them the keys to the city gates, which he duly refused.[42]

About seven o'clock the next morning, February 28, a group of 40 to 50 vignerons "without any arms other than some halberds and batons" forced open the door of the parish church of St. Michel and sounded the tocsin, an alarm bell, announcing that the real activities of their demonstration

---

[41] The following narrative is based on a variety of primary sources: (1) the deliberations of the Hôtel de Ville of Dijon in AMD, B 267; (2) a mostly first-hand or eyewitness account written by François Fleutelot, sieur de Beneuvre, a master in the Chamber of Accounts and thus a supporter of the *élections*, in BMD, Ms. 2098, fol. 903–908, and this is the most detailed of all the eyewitness accounts; (3) an eyewitness account written by an anonymous bourgeois in Dijon, "Journal de la sedition dite Lanturelu," in BMD, Ms. 2098, fols. 908–914; (4) an eyewitness account written by Barthélemy Morisot in BMD, Ms. 1642, fols. 1–4; (5) another eyewitness account written by a Monsieur Sullot, a local official in Dijon, printed in *Lanturelu: Pièces contenant la relation d'une sedition arrivé à Dijon le 28 fèvrier 1630* (Dijon: Darantière, 1884), 29–32; (6) a collection of materials collected by the mayor and *échevins* concerning the riots, including among other things, the owners of the houses razed and inventories of property destroyed and their net replacement values in AMD, I 117; and (7) several other manuscript sources in the BMD. The best recent secondary accounts are in Farr, *Hands of Honor*, 201–210; William Beik, *Urban Protest in Seventeenth-Century France: The Culture of Retribution* (Cambridge: Cambridge University Press, 1997), 126–133; Patouillet, "L'Émeute des Lanturelus," 1–89; my own article, "Culture populaire et culture politique au XVIIe siècle: L'émeute de Lanturelu à Dijon en fèvrier 1630," *Histoire, économie et société* 16 (1997): 597–616, an English translation of which appeared as "Popular and Elite Politics in Seventeenth-Century Dijon," *Historical Reflections/Réflexions historiques* 27 (Summer 2001): 325–345; and Christine Lamarre, "Les Lanturelus de Dijon en 1630: le peuple en rébellion?" in Philippe Guignet, ed., *Le peuple des villes dans l'Europe du Nord-Ouest (fin du moyen âge-1945)*, vol. 1 (Villeneuve d'Ascq: Centre de recherché sur l'histoire de l'Europe du Nord-Ouest, 2003), 29–41.

[42] BMD, Ms. 2098, fols. 903–904.

were about to begin. The rioters then returned to the townhouse of Nicolas Gagne where they had thrown rocks the night before, and they found two horses and a coachman hiding in the back and only the elderly and very sick mother of Gagne inside house. They were all led out and were not harmed. Instead, the rioters broke apart the treasurer's coach, to which they then set fire. They made "a great fire in the street" by adding all the furniture and household items they could carry, including tapestries, beds, dishes, linens, armchairs, and gold and silver items. Indeed, they burned everything that was in the house apart from some grain and salt that they took away with them, as well as some wine found in the cellar, of which they drank as much as they could on the spot. And according to Fleutelot, "more than a thousand people saw them do all this, as if it had been some commission ordered by the king, without intervening in any way."[43] Even if this figure was an exaggeration, it seems clear that the residents of this neighborhood in the parish of Sr. Michel were sympathetic to the rioters' goals.

According to Fleutelot, the rioters then split into two groups, with one moving down the street to the house of Chretien Martin, a lawyer in Dijon, and the other to the townhouse of Jean Le Grand, First President, or presiding judge, in the Chamber of Accounts. The rioters then set fire to the contents of both houses just as they had done at the townhouse of Nicolas Gagne. The only inhabitants mentioned were the children of the Le Grand household, "whom they guided outside without doing them any harm." They also discovered a cache of silver coins at Le Grand's house estimated to be 10,000 *livres*. From there the rioters quickly moved on to the townhouse of Antoine Joly, clerk and registrar of the Parlement of Dijon, where they set fire to the entire house, and "more than 3000 people witnessed this furious performance, not doing anything but laughing, with some even applauding." From there the rioters moved on to the townhouse of Jean De Villemeureux, another official in the Chamber of Accounts, where similar deeds were carried out. The group then moved on to the townhouse of Jean-Baptiste Legoux de la Berchère, the First President in the Parlement of Dijon, and thus the most powerful judicial official in the entire province of Burgundy. There they encountered two officials from the Parlement standing outside, who talked the rioters out of attacking Legoux's luxurious townhouse. The band then descended on the nearby home of Jean Richard, one of the *élus* appointed to replace the Estates of Burgundy once the Edict of *Élections* was formally registered. They found

[43] BMD, Ms. 2098, fols. 904–905.

him outside his house surrounded by his seven children. He got down on his knees and begged for mercy, exclaiming that he would not benefit personally from the new *élections*, and that he was only following orders from the king. "One of the rioters said in his patois that since he [Richard] was occupying his house, it was certain that he was innocent, that otherwise he would have risked it." The rioters then returned to the sumptuous townhouse of First President Legoux, who was hiding in the Château along with his family for safety, and they proceeded to sack and burn it instead. There was some resistance, and Fleutelot noted that three or four of the rioters were killed. They rounded off their morning of violence and destruction by going to the townhouse of Etienne de Loisie, another presiding judge in the Chamber of Accounts, where they burned everything, and several more rioters were killed there as well.[44]

Fleutelot noted that the sacking of elite houses only came to an end when the judges of the Parlement, believing "that the rioters would indifferently attack all the houses [in the city] in order to pillage them," armed the bourgeois militia, went to the house of President De Loisie, and began firing on the rioters, killing 10 or 12, taking half a dozen prisoners, with the rest fleeing for their lives, and barricading themselves in a cul-de-sac in St. Philibert parish.[45] These prisoners were soon released, however, as the magistrates feared that further violence would break out if they continued to hold them.[46] It was not until the next day, March 1, however, that the violence came to an end. That was when Jacques de Chabot, Marquis of Mirabeau, the king's lieutenant-general in Burgundy and the officer in charge in the absence of the royal governor, arrived in Dijon, and began a systematic effort to try to round up the perpetrators. His troops fired on a group of vignerons in the Place St. Michel, killing 14 of them, with the rest fleeing. He also dispersed those vignerons barricaded in St. Philibert parish, killing several more.[47] But because most had already fled the city by then, hiding in the nearby villages in homes of fellow vignerons, efforts to round up the remaining rioters proved to be a near-impossible task. A week later the mayor and *échevins* did a house to house search to try to find any remaining rioters in the city. In the event, they managed to arrest only two scapegoats, a furrier named Jean Launois and a vigneron named Pierre Mutin, who were tried and convicted at the Parlement and then hanged, with their corpses drawn and quartered and displayed at the four gates of the city.[48] Thus, in

---

[44] BMD, Ms. 2098, fols. 905–906.   [45] BMD, Ms. 2098, fol. 906.
[46] AMD, B 267, fol. 161r, March 1, 1630.   [47] BMD, Ms. 1642, fol. iv.
[48] BMD, I 117, March 20, 1630.

the space of about six hours on the morning of February 28, a total of seven townhouses of the richest and most powerful men in Burgundy had been sacked and their contents taken outside and set afire. All told perhaps a total of 25 to 30 rioters lost their lives. If Fleutelot and the other sources are to be believed, hundreds, even thousands, of Dijon's citizens came out to witness these events. Not only did they make no effort to stop the rioters, they even cheered them on. Indeed, Fleutelot suggests the entire city was sympathetic to the rioters.

> In the middle of a city to allow a hundred or more unarmed rogues [*coquins*] to set fire to seven houses watched by 20,000 people who could have stopped them if they had wanted to, but who laughed and applauded at all their excesses, they [the rioters] would not have dared to commit them if they had not been assured of their support and assistance . . . The entire city is guilty and cannot be excused.[49]

This was certainly the king's own reaction as well. He blamed the mayor and *échevins* above all, as he wrote to them on March 4, because they had acted "so negligently and with so little courage in this encounter." He told them that "this troop of mutineers" would be severely punished, along with any members of the city council if they had any part in this rebellion. Louis XIII concluded by stating that he intended to punish the city by depriving it of all its traditional privileges, tearing down its walls, and taking down its clock towers and gates as an example to others.[50]

So, who organized the riot and who was its leader during the night and early morning of February 27–28? And as the king suspected, was there any collusion, or even tacit support, by the mayor and city council or from within the Parlement of Dijon? A number of sources – though interestingly not the most detailed eyewitness account written by Fleutelot – claimed the leader was a vigneron named Anatoire Changenet, who lived in the parish of St. Philibert. He had acted in the role as king of the recently ended Carnival in the city, and as a result, many of the sources referred to him by his Carnival name of King Machas (*le roi Machas*).[51] Changenet was a moderately successful vigneron in St. Philibert parish, paying a *taille* of 20 *sous* in November 1629, which would place him about midway or in the 50th percentile for tax in his parish that year.[52] But Changenet was neither killed nor imprisoned, and he disappeared from the city's tax rolls, and

[49] BMD, Ms. 2098, fol. 908.
[50] Garnier, ed., *Correspondance de la mairie de Dijon*, 3: 228–229.
[51] See, for example, BMD, Ms. 1642, fols. 1r–v (Morisot); and *Lanturelu: Pièces inédites*, 29 (Sullot).
[52] AMD, L 229, fol. 172 v, November 1629. This was the most recent tax assessment taken before the Lanturelu riot of February 28, 1630.

presumably from the city for good, after the riot. Thus, it is impossible to know his exact role, though none of the sources suggest any other leader. What we do know is that this was a carefully planned and orchestrated attack on specific individuals in the city, "all suspected of being the authors and supporters of the *élections* and wine taxes that the King wanted to establish in this region and duchy of Burgundy, against the rights and privileges of the said province."[53] Thus, the vignerons did not attack these houses at random – or "indifferently" as Fleutelot's account implied – but they chose the townhouses of those officials who they felt were most responsible for implementing the king's tax reforms. And how were the vignerons so well informed that they could identify the local ringleaders for implementing the *élections*? As already suggested in earlier chapters, vignerons had lots of ties to and opportunities to mingle with Dijon's elites through godparentage, elections, and the plays put on by the Mère Folle outlined in Chapter 7. But was there actual collusion between some of the elites and the vignerons?

Certainly, Louis XIII's suggestion that there might have been some kind of collusion was based on the inaction and delay of the local magistrates in not intervening sooner to stop the violence on February 28. The deliberations of the city council written after the violence ended on that day rather self-servingly claim that they tried to stop intervene but were unable to quell the violence. Moreover, they claimed that the rioters were heavily armed, which none of the other sources confirm.[54] Fleutelot's account suggested that some judges of the Parlement also tried to intervene and eventually succeed by arming the bourgeois militia, albeit only after seven townhouses were sacked and the contents burned. But the militia was under the command of the mayor, Bénigne Euvrard, not the Parlement, so this sounds suspect. What Fleutelot's account did indicate, however, was that there were some judges in the Parlement who were opposed to introducing the *élections* and actually supported the riot:

> Several members of Parlement contributed more than a little to incite this sedition, and even favored it. Monsieur Bretagne said to some [of the rioters] passing by his house that he was their servant, and that if they wanted to enter his house, they would be very welcome there, that it was the gentlemen of the Chamber of Accounts who were the cause of the *élections*, and that it was necessary to take it up with them.[55]

---

[53] *Lanturelu: Piéces inédites*, 30.   [54] AMD, B 267, fols. 157r–160v, February 28, 1630.
[55] BMD, Ms. 2098, fol.907.

So, while there is clear evidence of sympathy for the rioters' goals of protesting the *élections* both within the Hôtel de Ville and in the Parlement, there is no smoking gun that proves they aided them in other than delaying the suppression of the riot, as considerable as that benefit was. Nevertheless, the rioters' actions were sophisticated and they clearly had knowledge of who the chief supporters of the hated *élections* were. Because the majority were poor and perhaps less connected to the elites than the more prosperous vignerons, they must have had help or at least advice from some elites in the organization of the riot. William Beik is no doubt right that the riot was probably planned by the elites, who encouraged its outbreak, and then delayed in repressing it until it became a political necessity.[56]

How did the rioters justify and legitimate their actions of such wanton and destructive violence? As biased against the rioters as all the eyewitness accounts were, having been written by elites generally sympathetic to the creation of the *élections*, the sources do suggest that the vignerons tried to legitimate their actions by custom, tradition, and historical memory. The various accounts mention two powerful political symbols: a portrait of King Louis XIII as well as a tapestry bearing the image of King Henry IV, both liberated from the houses that were sacked. And both these images seem to have resonated with the popular historical memory of both kings in Dijon, especially with their memories of the two kings' "Joyous entries" into their city. Fleutelot, Morisot, and one of the anonymous accounts all mentioned the portrait of Louis XIII being paraded through the streets during the rioting along with cries of "Long Live the emperor!"[57] This was an echo from 1477 – the so-called *foy de Bourgogne* – when Burgundy was reincorporated into the crown of France after the death of the last Valois duke of Burgundy, Charles the Bold. Occasionally, such cries were heard in Burgundy whenever there was opposition to some royal policy. It did not mean that there was any sedition at work against the king, but it was simply a common expression of opposition to the crown's policies in Burgundy. Thus, it is difficult to classify the Lanturelu riot as a revolt against the king.[58] Burning of a portrait of Louis XIII in public, however, was a far more serious offense. Some historians have suggested that this may be apocryphal, given how extreme such an expression of political opposition was and that it could be considered a crime of treason against

---

[56] Beik, *Urban Protest in Seventeenth-Century France*, 133.
[57] BMD, Ms. 2098, fol. 908 (Fleutelot); BMD, Ms. 1642, fol. IV (Morisot); and BMD, Ms. 1642, fol. Ir (anonymous).
[58] A point also made by Lamarre, "Les Lanturelus de Dijon."

ie king, or *lèse majesté*.[59] Yet three different sources noted it, and perhaps ne only way to justify this kind of opposition to a King of France was to invoke the name of another King of France, that of Henry IV. And this the rioters also did.

The account written by Monsieur Sullot described a tapestry with the image of Henry IV being carried triumphantly through the streets to shouts of "Here is the great father; here is the good king, our good king; here is the father of the poor people. Long live this good king, whose image we safeguard and keep from being spoiled or damaged, as we kiss it and carry it to the altar." Sullot went on to note that the vignerons carried the image of Henry IV into the parish churches of St. Michel and St. Nicolas, where many people kissed it with tears in their eyes, "remembering the unspeakable loss that both France and Christianity has suffered with the deplorable death of this great prince, who, after God, was truly the blessing of the world, the miracle of all miracles, the true delight of his people, and the greatest and best king that had ever been throughout all the centuries or ever will be in the future."[60] Here was the vision of a king ingrained in the historical memory of Dijon, indeed, harkening back to his "Joyous entry" into the city in June 1595 ending the Wars of Religion in the city, where he was embraced as a savior and worthy successor to the Dukes of Burgundy, by whose tombs he visited and prayed after he swore to uphold all the city's liberties and privileges. The royal entry of Louis XIII in January 1629, on the other hand, was very different. Not only did he not publicly swear to uphold the city's liberties and privileges – a fact remarked upon by one of the sources of the Lanturelu riot – but he also refused to accept the special gift given to him by the city as not being worthy of such a great king.[61] Thus, the actions of the rioters in Dijon in 1630 reverberated with these contrasting images of Henry IV and Louis XIII, both based on images ingrained in their historical memory. They paraded the image of the sacral monarch Henry IV into the parish churches, where they kissed and worshipped it. The image of the absolute monarch Louis XIII they burned and jeered with the pro-Habsburg slogan that had echoed in Dijon ever since 1477 when any opposition to the king arose. So, the vignerons of 1630 legitimated their actions by defending their past, their God, and their notion of the traditional monarchy against what they saw as Louis's pernicious innovations. This use of historical memory to legitimate their

---

[59] Beik, *Urban Protest in Seventeenth-Century France*, 126.   [60] *Lanturelu: Pieces inédites*, 31–32.
[61] Morisot's account of the riot began with Louis XIII's refusal to confirm Dijon's liberties and privileges at his entry in January 1629 in BMD, Ms. 1642, fol. iv.

actions necessarily de-legitimated the more usual keepers of order in the city: the mayor, *échevins*, and judges in the Parlement. And the burning of Louis XIII's portrait clearly de-legitimated the king himself.

So, how could the rioters justify their actions, which explicitly de-legitimated the authority of mayor, Parlement, and the king? They did so by appealing to the authority of what they considered to be a more legitimate king, Henry IV, in whose memory and upon whose authority they were acting. The real irony, of course, is that Henry IV was the innovator who set in motion the means for intervening in Dijon's mayoral elections, not his son. And it was Henry IV who first created the hated *élections* in 1604 in another province, Guyenne, not his son in 1630. But Dijon's historical memory had a very different image of Henry. To the city's inhabitants of all social classes he was forever the sacral monarch who promised to protect the very privileges and liberties his son, Louis XIII, now threatened. And in a sense, their view of Henry IV was fair. Yes, he did establish the principle of royal interference in local elections if he so chose, but he still respected the forms of justice and order established in Dijon and realized that not interfering only increased his power there. Louis XIII having taken away the votes and voices from most of the vignerons with his electoral innovations in 1612, the vignerons viewed their actions in 1630 as the only way remaining in which they could express their political voices and interests, which they believed were being ignored. Obviously, the king and many of the city's elites rejected this view.

8.3 Royal Justice and the Contraction of Urban Privileges

If the owners' inventories of the property they lost during the Lanturelu riot are anywhere near accurate, and even if they are somewhat exaggerated, the destruction of property was truly staggering. It was not just the total amounts of damages claimed that is astonishing, but the various luxury goods that the significantly poorer rioters looted and burned are equally striking. In total, the owners of the seven ransacked houses claimed to have lost more than 400,000 *livres* worth of personal property, with each owner seeking between 13,000 and 90,000 *livres* of reimbursements from the city for damages. Table 8.1 gives an indication of the kinds of property being claimed, though not nearly all the property destroyed is listed here.[62]

---

[62] Inventories for six of the seven houses submitted to the city council for reimbursement are in AMD, I 117, March 8–11, April 10, and May 9, 1631. The inventory for the house of President Legoux de la Berchère, the most luxurious of all seven sacked homes, has not survived. And the inventory for Jean de Villemereux itemized destroyed property but gave no figures for the value of these items.

Table 8.1 *Property destroyed in the Lanturelu riot, 1630*

Townhouse of Nicolas Gagne, Treasurer-General of the King in Burgundy

> Tapestries, crystal, faience (2,340 *livres*)
> Jewelry (400 *livres*)
> Crockery, cutlery from kitchen (500 *livres*)
> Furniture (2,000 *livres*)
> Books (3,500 *livres*)
> Stores of wheat and oats (740 *livres*)
> 18 *queues* of wine (260 *livres*)
> Stable replacement (1,000 *livres*)
> Chimneys, doors, and windows (3,600 *livres*)
> Relocating expenses during renovation (800 *livres*)
> **TOTAL: 21,881 *livres***

Townhouse of Chrêtien Martin, Lawyer

> Tapestries (1,300 *livres*)
> Books (3,500 *livres*)
> His bedroom furniture and clothes (500 *livres*)
> Other cabinets and wardrobes (900 *livres*)
> Other things itemized by room (5,120 *livres*)
> Father-in-law's bedroom (6,000 *livres*)
> [Father-in-law was a *maître d'hôtel* of the king's brother]
> **TOTAL: 17,398 *livres***

Townhouse of Jean Le Grand, First President in the Chamber of Accounts

> Papers, family documents, and cash (17,519 *livres*)
> Gold and silver plated dishes (6,000 *livres*)
> Jewelry (5,697 *livres*)
> His clothes (3,000 *livres*)
> Wife's clothes (1,600 *livres*)
> Weapons including firearms (515 *livres*)
> Books (2,434 *livres*)
> Tapestries from Portugal and Turkey (5,640 *livres*)
> Furniture (3,985 *livres*)
> Daughter's clothes (852 *livres*)
> Linens, some gold-embroidered (5,400 *livres*)
> Dutch tiles (793 *livres*)
> English pewter (1,484 *livres*)
> Wine, grain, oil in cellar (1,300 *livres*)
> "Several curiosities" (3,000 *livres*)
> **TOTAL: 90,000 *livres***

Townhouse of Antoine Joly, Lawyer and Chief Clerk of the Parlement

> "The ruin of the entire house" (6,000 *livres*)
> Tapestries (1,400 *livres*)
> 8 feather beds (450 *livres*)

Table 8.1 *(cont.)*

Bedcovers and curtains (1,000 *livres*)
Chairs covered in silk and leather (700 *livres*)
Other furniture (600 *livres*)
5 pairs of leather shoes (250 *livres*)
Several pictures and a chandelier (400 *livres*)
Linens and clothes of family and servants (2000 *livres*)
Books and two large globes (600 *livres*)
Weapons including firearms (200 *livres*)
Carriage and harnesses (600 *livres*)
Wine, grain, lard, candles, etc. in cellar (1,000 *livres*)
Family papers and "a large sum of money" (1,000 *livres*)
TOTAL: 18,000 *livres*

Townhouse of Etienne de Loisie, President in the Chamber of Accounts

Jewelry (544 *livres*)
Gold box with gold coins (523 *livres*)
Various furniture (786 *livres*)
Cabinet: statues, bronzes, medals, vases, etc. (5,241 *livres*)
Books and manuscripts (1,500 *livres*)
Weapons including firearms (882 *livres*)
Pieces of marble, shells from Levant, red and white coral (160 *livres*)
Contents of the cellar: wine, grain, wood, candles, etc. (806 *livres*)
Loss of family papers (300 *livres*)
TOTAL: 13,521 *livres*

Sources: AMD, I 117, March 8–11, April 10, and May 9, 1631.

The lifestyles lived by these wealthy men of the law seems obvious from such inventories, and they contrasted sharply with the average daily wage of a poorer vigneron or journeyman artisan who made up the bulk of the rioters, which was barely 5 *sous* per day.[63] And so many of these luxury items would have been completely absent from the homes of the rioters, such as tapestries on the walls or silk-covered furniture. Most notable of all were the books these men of the law had in their libraries. The most extensive library of the houses whose inventories have survived was that of Nicolas Gagne:

> The library of the aforesaid Sieur Gagne consisted of a large quantity of fine books ... Among these were included the works of most of the church fathers, such as St. Augustine, St. Gregory, St. Bernard, and the ecclesiastical histories of Baronius, St. Denis, Gennadius, and other doctors [of the church]. There were also a number of law books, such as those by Cujas,

---

[63] See Farr, *Hands of Honor*, 106.

Du Moulin, Choppin, Bodrienne, Menoclime, and Justinian, as well as . . . the works of Seneca, Titus Livy, Cornelius, Tacitus, Plutarch, Justinian and others.[64]

Even this vast collection of books was not the largest personal library in the city, as that was almost certainly the library of Etienne Bouhier, a judge in the Parlement of Dijon from 1611 to 1635, whose family held a judgeship in the court from 1512 right up to the French Revolution. Bouhier's library totaled 1,325 books, with many in multiple volumes.[65] Nevertheless, Gagne's library was probably the most books any vigneron had ever seen. The total sum of more than 400,000 *livres* was so great that the city was still trying to pay back the owners of the sacked townhouses more than a year and a half after the riot.

The king's displeasure with the city's magistrates resulted in swift punishment. Louis XIII, accompanied by the chancellor and keeper of the seals, Michel de Marillac, the king's royal governor in Burgundy, Roger de Bellegarde, along with a dozen other noblemen from the court, arrived in Dijon on April 27, exactly two months after the riot. The king was installed in the ducal palace, and ordered the mayor and *échevins* to appear before him, along with the captains, lieutenants, and ensigns of each parish, and about 200 other notables from the city of Dijon.[66] Jacques Fevret, a judge in the Parlement of Dijon, addressed the king in a formal speech imploring him to pardon and forgive the city's magistrates, who, he claimed, did all they could to prevent the riot and then to stop it once it got started. The riot and sedition, he went on, were caused "by some miserable and desperate people, for the most part unknown, and the enemies of the peace and tranquility in which we give life to the very humble service and obedience owed to Your Majesty . . . Now, Sire, we are here with tears in our eyes and our knees on the ground, our hearts pierced to the quick with sadness and despair to bear witness to Your Majesty that we detest with horror and execration the crime of these miserable people [*ces miserables*]."[67] Louis XIII responded that he was greatly displeased with what happened in Dijon, and that the chancellor and keeper of the seals would respond on his behalf. Michel de Marillac then stood and read from a prepared text,

---

[64] AMD, I 117, inventory of Nicolas Gagne dated March 8, 1631.

[65] Albert Ronsin, *La Bibliothèque Bouhier: Histoire d'une collection formée du XVI au XVIIIe siècle par une famille de magistrats bourguignons* (Dijon: Bibliothèque municipale, 1971), especially 28 and 84–87.

[66] AMD, B 267, fol. 224r, April 28, 1630.

[67] Fevret's speech is in *De la sedition arrivée en la ville de Dijon le 28. Fevrier 1630. & Iugement rendu par le Roy sur icelle* (Lyon: Irenée Barlet, 1630), 10–17, quotes on 12 and 13.

opening with some absolutist rhetoric. Marillac explicitly tied the king to the state, pointing out that to rebel against the king was to commit a heinous crime against the state. No rhetoric about crimes against the public welfare (*le bien public*), but simply crimes against the king and the state.

The chancellor then unequivocally denied that the king had any intention of introducing new taxes (*aides*) on wine along with the *élections*. He only wanted to control the abuses in the system of tax collection. Thus, the rioters based all their actions entirely on "false rumors (*bruits faux*)," and the entire escapade was completely unnecessary. Marillac then addressed the local magistrates the king considered most responsible for the riot, the mayor and *échevins*:

> You are supposed to safeguard the peace and tranquility of this city. If you fall asleep on the job, however, you are delinquent. If any one of you were to make the rounds of the city at night and you found a sentinel who was asleep, you would rightly take out your sword and kill him. You are the sentinels under whose vigilance all the people sleep soundly; and while they were under your care, you have allowed someone to put a dagger to their throats. Your fault is without any excuse whatsoever. But this affair is even worse still, since you had known about this disorder for some time. You were not taken by surprise, but you saw this gestate and grow little by little. You had the means to deal with it, but you did nothing. That is what makes you most guilty of all.[68]

Finally, Marillac informed the city, its leaders as well as its inhabitants, of the various punishments the king had deemed appropriate. First, the captains, lieutenants, and ensigns of the seven parishes – that is, the leaders of the civic militia that was so slow to put down the riot – were to be dismissed and their replacements would be named by the king. Second, the city council was to be reduced from twenty to only six *échevins*, a reduction that most other major cities of the realm had already experienced, including Paris. Indeed, this was yet another absolutist reform for which Louis XIII was blamed, but his father actually initiated. For example, Henry IV reduced the size of municipal governments in a number of Leaguer towns such as Amiens, Troyes, Abbeville, and Doullens at the end of the Wars of Religion by reducing the number of *échevins* just as Louis XIII did in Dijon in 1630.[69] Third, Dijon would

---

[68] The full text of Marillac's speech is in AMD, I 118, April 28, 1630; and it is printed in *De la sédition arrivée en la ville de Dijon*, 17–31 (quotes on 19–21 and 27–31).
[69] S. Annette Finley-Croswhite, *Henry IV and the Towns: The Pursuit of Legitimacy in French Urban Society, 1589–1610* (Cambridge: Cambridge University Press, 1999), 79–86.

no longer elect its mayors by a popular vote of male property owners as it traditionally had done, but by a special council of 24 former mayors and *échevins*, plus another group of representatives from the church and law courts. Moreover, these electors would send three names to the king, who would then select the mayor for the coming year. Fourth, all the vignerons of the city were required to move out of the city and live in the neighboring villages until further notice "on pain of corporal punishment." Because of its members' close ties to the vignerons, the Mother Folly troupe of lawyers who performed plays in the streets (*la Mère Folle*) was ordered to be disbanded. Fifth, all the city's cannon and artillery stored in the Château were to be reduced to just six pieces: four culverins and two smaller guns. Finally, the king required the city to pay damages to the owners of the seven ransacked townhouses for all property lost or destroyed.[70] None of the judges in the Parlement of Dijon – the king's own officers – were mentioned at all, despite the fact that everyone knew that some of them had openly sided with the rioters and may have even organized them.[71] Ultimately, the mayor and *échevins* as well as the city's vignerons took all the blame for the Lanturelu riot. And the former group even had to suffer the humiliation of listening to these chastisements being read aloud to them by the chancellor while they were on their knees in the presence of the king.

But what did the riot achieve? In one sense, the city's magistrates and the vignerons, despite the punishments inflicted on them, actually won. The feared and hated *élections* were never installed in Burgundy, no new aides on wine were introduced, and the *octroi* on wine entering the city was not raised. The Chamber of Accounts ultimately backed down from registering the edict creating the new *élections* as a result of the riot. This was only a temporary reprise, however, as an angry Louis XIII stripped the Chamber of Accounts of the Court of Aids – including the power to register the Edict of *Élections* – and gave it to the Parlement of Dijon in return for a promise to register the Edict of *Élections* immediately.[72] But the edict's registration in the Parlement of Dijon in the spring of 1630 was not the end of the affair. Before the newly appointed *élus* could take up their duties, two events transformed the situation and saved the provincial estates of Burgundy. First, on November 10 and 11, 1630, the king did an about face and fired his chancellor Michel de Marillac

---

[70] AMD, I 118, April 28, 1630; and AMD, B 267, fol. 226v–227v, April 28, 1630.
[71] Fleutelot certainly thought so. See BMD, Ms. 2098, fol. 907.
[72] AMD, B 267, fol. 237, May 7, 1630; and Garnier, ed., *Correspondance de la mairie de Dijon*, 3: lxxxviii.

and dismissed him along with his own mother, Marie de Medici, from the royal council. The so-called Day of Dupes brought Armand-Jean du Plessis, Cardinal Richelieu, to power as the head of the king's council and his de facto first minster.[73] Unlike Marillac, Richelieu strongly favored allowing the *pays d'états* to keep their provincial estates if they were willing to make more regular payments to the crown, and he informed the city in January that the king was now open to a deal to accept a large payment in return for revoking the edict.[74] Second, Burgundy's royal governor, the Duke of Bellegarde, recklessly joined the king's brother, Gaston, Duke of Orléans, in a revolt against the crown in March 1631, so Louis fired him and replaced him as governor in the province with Henry of Bourbon, Prince of Condé. Condé, seeking to cement his power as patron in his new jurisdiction, like Richelieu, sought to suppress the Edict of *Élections* as well. Thus, on May 7 the provincial estates opened with an offer from the king to revoke the hated *élections* in return for a sum of 2 million *livres* to be paid every three years, which Condé managed to bargain down to 1.6 million *livres*, ironically 200,000 *livres* less than Louis had turned down just the year before.[75] Thus, the estates continued to meet and administered the assessment and collection of this large triennial sum. Moreover, the new governor also managed to get the king to allow the city to return to its traditional format of mayoral elections, which occurred in June 1631 after the previous year's election had been first postponed, then forced to follow the king's new format in August 1630.[76] Finally, Condé intervened with the king to restore Dijon's city council to its full capacity of twenty *échevins* instead of the reduction to six that Louis ordered in April 1630. And the vignerons were also allowed to return to their homes in the city. As Barthélemy Morisot noted, "Henry of Bourbon [Prince of] Condé, governor after the Duke of Bellegarde, was received in Dijon on 26 March 1631. He obtained the revocation of the Edict of *Élections*, the reestablishment of the privileges of the city, and the election of the *échevins* in the accustomed manner. It is by these

---

[73] For more on the Day of Dupes, see Victor-L. Tapié, *France in the Age of Louis XIII and Richelieu*, trans. and ed. D. McN. Lockie (London: Macmillan, 1974), 234–239; and A. Lloyd Moote, *Louis XIII: The Just* (Berkeley, CA: University of California Press, 1989), 216–219.

[74] Major, *Representative Government in Early Modern France*, 583.

[75] AMD, B 445, fol. 105; and Garnier, ed., Correspondance de la mairie de Dijon, *3:xciii–xciv; and Jérôme Loiseau, "Elle fera ce que l'on voudra": la noblesse aux états de Bourgogne et la monarchie d'Henri IV à Louis XIV, 1602–1715* (Besançon: Presses universitaires de Franche-Comte, 2014), 76.

[76] For the mayoral elections of 1630 and 1631, see AMD, B 268, fols. 1r–5v, August 2, 1630; and AMD, B 269, fols. 1–24, June 20, 1631.

bienfaits that he signaled the foundation of his government."[77] But why did Louis XIII so quickly abandon the harsh punishments he inflicted on the city and its inhabitants just one year earlier? The principal reason was that with the Huguenots having been defeated, Richelieu wanted to turn his attention fully to foreign affairs, and especially to the menacing Habsburgs. Dijon was a frontier province directly on the border with Habsburg-controlled Franche-Comté. As long as the Burgundians were content to pay their fair share of taxes, their loyalty to the crown mattered much more than reform of the tax collection system.[78] And the very same thing happened in other provinces that had provincial estates, such as Provence and Languedoc: They were allowed to buy back the right to assess their own taxes in return for more regular payments to the crown.[79]

If Dijon's vignerons won in the political sense of preventing the *élections* and halting new taxes on wine, they were also the biggest losers in the aftermath of the Lanturelu riot. For a start, once Dijon's mayoral elections returned to normal after 1631, the vignerons were now forbidden from participating at all in the mayoral elections, even if they met the tax requirements of paying at least 30 *sous* of tax during the three previous years.[80] To be sure, only the wealthiest vignerons had been able to vote in these elections since 1612 when the tax requirements were first introduced. But after 1631, all vignerons were barred from participating in the annual civic rituals altogether, a political event that they once dominated. A far greater loss, however, was their economic status and standing in the city. As already discussed, by 1630, even among the well-off vignerons, many had to sell off portions of their vineyard holdings in order to pay their debts. And they were selling them largely to the city's judicial elites in the Parlement, to other wealthy bourgeois, and even to some wealthy master artisans. As Gaston Roupnel pointed out, in the 107 villages closest to Dijon, by the mid-seventeenth century more than half had no peasant landowners at all, with Dijon's wealthiest citizens having bought them out. And in many of the others, only a handful of vignerons still owned any land.[81] Thus, the vignerons' political influence and ability to influence affairs in the city as they had done in the sixteenth century was on the wane. Thus, absolute monarchy in practice

---

[77] BMD, Ms. 1642, fol. 2r.   [78] Tapié, *France in the Age of Louis XIII and Richelieu*, 235.

[79] Major, *Representative Government in Early Modern France*, 581–599.

[80] AMD, B 267, fol. 294r, June 21, 1630.

[81] Gaston Roupnel, *La ville et la campagne au XVII* siècle: Étude sur les populations du pays dijonnais* (Paris: Armand Colin, 1955), especially 205–211. Also, see Farr, *Hands of Honor*, 98–101.

was always a process of negotiation. Short-term outcomes often gave way to longer term change, and this change would continue in Burgundy throughout the rest of the seventeenth century. But by 1630 the heyday of the vignerons was in the past. And because the goals and ends of government were no longer the public good but the royal state, they no longer had such a significant role to play.

Conclusion

The narrative arc of political history in Burgundy from 1477 to 1630 must surely begin with the negotiation that the former duchy's leaders made with King Louis XI in 1477 to give up its independence under the Valois dukes of Burgundy to become part of the kingdom of France under the jurisdiction of a new king. In return for its loyalty and obedience to their new king, the Burgundians received a royal promise that they would continue to enjoy the traditional liberties, privileges, and franchises that they had enjoyed under the Valois dukes, above all the right to elect their own mayors and to assess and collect their own taxes through the provincial estates. Moreover, the French king also created a series of sovereign courts including a Parlement in the Burgundian capital of Dijon, providing a new area of professional advancement through the legal profession for the duchy's elites as well as bringing prestige and significance to this new addition to the kingdom. The loyalties of Burgundians were tested throughout the Wars of Religion, though it was not until the last civil war (1588–1598) during the period of domination by the Catholic League that the city of Dijon and the province as a whole largely rejected the authority of a king who was a Protestant.

Indeed, Henry himself eventually came to the same conclusion when he abjured his Protestant faith in 1593. When the cities of Burgundy finally submitted to his authority in 1595, the king had to renegotiate his compact with the province and his Burgundian subjects. This he did with great success, and he was remembered even two decades after his death as a good king who safeguarded Burgundian privileges and liberties. This image contrasted sharply with that of his son Louis XIII, who simply took advantage of the innovations his father had put into place. When Louis attempted to interfere in Dijon's mayoral elections, to replace the provincial estates with royal *élections*, and to reduce the number of Dijon's *échevins* from twenty to six, he was simply taking advantage of the changes his father introduced. To most Burgundians, however, Henry IV was a defender of the *foy de Bourgogne*, while his son was viewed as an oppressor and despot. By focusing on the process of negotiations between crown and province rather than strictly on immediate outcomes, we see a different picture. In any case, the process of negotiation was never linear nor did it always lead to suppression of local rights and privileges. And the same was true of the slow transformation from a kingdom in which protecting the public good (*le bien public*) was the king's principal duty to one in which the king's only duty was to defend the royal state.

A related aspect of the political history of Burgundy in this period was the sudden rise – and equally sudden decline – in the participation of the popular classes, and especially the vignerons, in local politics. Whereas their numbers grew in the early sixteenth century, meaning the vignerons formed between a fourth and a fifth of all the heads of households in the city of Dijon, it was only natural that they should participate in giving their voices at the annual elections in equally greater numbers. By the time of the beginning of the Wars of Religion in 1562, they stood firm against the advent of Protestantism in the city, and they worked together with the elites to extirpate it. They also came to dominate the elections, as the elite candidates canvassed for their votes in the parishes offering food and drink for their support. Despite the efforts of the Parlement to suppress this style of canvassing for votes by attempting to eliminate the participation of vignerons in the elections, they continued to turn out every year in significant numbers until the reforms of Marie de Medici and Louis XIII in 1612 introduced a minimum tax requirement that eliminated all but the wealthiest vignerons from participating. And in the aftermath of the Lanturelu riot of 1630, all vigneron participation was curtailed. During the Wars of Religion, however, their influence was felt far beyond the casting of their voices in the Jacobin convent on election day every year. They supervised the policing of the vineyards and the annual grape harvest every year, they helped shape public opinion to support Henry IV during the period of the League, and they maintained throughout close ties and relations with the city's elites through business and personal ties such as god-parentage. Indeed, as Chapter 8 demonstrated, their ties and communication with many of the political elites of the city remained intact even during the Lanturelu riot of 1630. But by 1630, the elites of the province saw that their political futures as mayors, *échevins*, judges, and other royal officials rested solely in the hands of the king. They were now beholden to the royal state for their careers, and the vignerons soon discovered as well that their former local patrons and protectors were no longer as interested as they once were in looking after their needs and remedying their problems.

One final aspect of the history of Burgundy in the period 1477–1630 is the afterlife of the Lanturelu riot. As noted in Chapter 8, their new royal governor, the Prince of Condé, bargained with Louis XIII to restore all the privileges and liberties that had been taken away in the aftermath of the riot. But this was not the end of the story. To be sure, the provincial estates of Burgundy continued to meet once every three years to assess and collect taxes in the province as before, and they even thrived during the absolute monarchy of Louis XIV (1643–1715). Yet the deputies' desire to protect their privileges and even extend their authority further resulted in their being just as beholden to the king as the judges, barristers, and solicitors in the Parlement. Like them, the deputies of the Burgundian estates maintained their careers by collaborating with the monarchy rather than trying to resist it, but they could no longer claim to protect the taxpayers and the public good they claimed to serve.[1]

The mayor and *échevins* in the Hôtel de Ville were not nearly so lucky, however, as the restoration of the mayoral elections to their traditional format and the number of *échevins* to 20 by Condé in 1631 lasted only until 1668. Then, abruptly and without warning, a new crown official, the royal intendant, Claude Bouchu, stepped in to announce that in future the mayors would be nominated by the crown through either the royal governor or the intendant, that the *échevins* would be reduced in number to six, with strict term limits and elected only every two years rather than annually, and that although they would be appointed by the mayor, they were to be nominated by the crown. Michael Breen is surely right that after 1668, "Dijon's once-powerful city government would be gradually transformed into an arm of the local royal administration."[2] For so long able to fend off royal interference in local elections, the city's elites were now powerless to stop the advancing royal state. And despite being perceived by the city's inhabitants as the defenders of public welfare in Dijon for so long, after 1668 they became civil servants working for the king who chose them rather than the people who used to elect them. By the 1680s, Dijon's annual elections for mayor took place only once every three years with

---

[1] Julian Swann, *Provincial Power and Absolute Monarchy: The Estates General of Burgundy, 1661–1789* (Cambridge: Cambridge University Press, 2003); and Jérôme Loiseau, *"Elle fera ce que l'on voudra": La noblesse aux états de Bourgogne et la monarchie d'Henri IV à Louis XIV (1602–1715)* (Besançon: Presses universitaires de Franche-Comté, 2014).

[2] Michael P. Breen, *Law, City, and King: Legal Culture, Municipal Politics, and State Formation in Early Modern Dijon* (Rochester, NY: University of Rochester Press, 2007), 114–119, quote on 119.

mayors and *échevins* serving three-year terms, and from 1692 when the king transformed the office of viscount-mayor into a venal office, the city was required to pay the crown 100,000 *livres* or more every time they wanted to hold a new election.[3] Thus, the influence and participation of the vignerons and other members of the popular classes in local politics had declined precipitously from its apex a century earlier during the Wars of Religion.

But let us give the final word to the characters in a play performed by the Mère Folle in the presence of the Prince of Condé upon his entry into Dijon on October 3, 1632. The play was "Return of Good Times (*Retour de Bontemps*)," and it was an allusion to the restoration of Dijon's privileges, including the Mère Folle's right to perform plays in public after the public humiliation and scolding by Louis XIII after the Lanturelu riot. In the play two vignerons engaged in conversation with the character called Father Good Times, who had been away from the city for some time. The vignerons, speaking in their local patois, were skeptical that peace and good order were on the horizon, so Good Times turned to an astrologer to confirm his favorable prognostication for the city's future. The astrologer recounted for them in formal French all the wonderful things that were in store: "The [good] things that I have related go well beyond your gates. This is enough for you, my friends, that all good fortune is promised to you, as well as to all of France."[4] The vignerons then queried if there would be a good grape harvest that year, to which the astrologer replied: "Before I depart I want to make one more useful prediction for this leap year; the spring will bring flowers, the summer great heat, the autumn fruits of all varieties, and the winter great frosts. Well, what more could you ask for?"[5] We might doubt whether the real vignerons in the audience actually believed this rosy scenario, since all the lost privileges returned to the city were those of the elites. It seems clear that the authors of the play, the *échevins* Etienne Bréchillet and Bénigne Pérard, were attempting to restore relations with the popular classes, which had broken down with the Lanturelu riot two years earlier. To be sure, they wanted to present to the Prince of Condé that the city was now both united and loyal to His Highness the Prince as well as to His Majesty the King. But they also hoped to restore relations with the popular classes, whose support they realized they needed.[6] Though they

---

[3] Ibid., 136–137.
[4] Juliette Valcke, "La société joyeuse de la Mère Folle de Dijon: Histoire (xve–xviie s.) et édition du répertoire," 3 vols., PhD. thesis Université de Montréal, 1997, 3: 629.
[5] Ibid., 3: 640.
[6] Michael P. Breen, "Addressing *La Ville des Dieux*: Entry Ceremonies and Urban Audiences in Seventeenth-Century Dijon," *Journal of Social History* 38 (2004): 341–364.

probably did not realize it at the time, however, the future of the *échevins* and the Hôtel de Ville, like that of the members of the Parlement and other sovereign courts, depended on the monarchial state rather than on popular support. For the vignerons and artisans of the city, they would not enjoy the political and religious influence they experienced during the Wars of Religion again until 1789.

Bibliography

Primary Sources

Archives

Archives départementales de la Côte-d'Or, Dijon (ADCO)

B 1807 Criminal records
B II 60/44 to 45 Criminal records against Protestants
B II 360/29 to 32 Criminal records
C 3015 to 3017 Deliberations of the Estates of Burgundy (1475–1631)
E 2225 Notarial records
G 3573 to 3581 Foundation of masses and *rentes*
G 3947 to 4044 Foundation of masses

Archives municipales, Dijon (AMD)

B 1 to 4 Privileges of the city of Dijon
B 9 Confraternities
B 11 to 13 Documents pertaining to the election of mayors of Dijon
B 19 and 20 Ecclesiastical *échevins*
B 95 Payment for the Painted Gospel of St. John
B 117 Papers of the Hôtel de Ville
B 164 to 268 Deliberations of the Hôtel de Ville (1477–1630)
B 445 *Cens*
B 490 to 506 *État civil*: Baptismal records
D 2 to 4 Religious processions
D 11 Religious processions
D 21 Funds for the distribution of *pain bénit*
D 28 Religious processions
D 63 to 65 Protestants
I 6 Entry of Charles the Bold into Dijon, 1474
I 8 Entry of Louis XI into Dijon, 1479
I 117 and 118 Lanturelu riot, 1630
I 130 Cabarets and taverns

I 147 to 152 Viticulture
I 152 Grape harvests
L 161 to 229 Tax rolls for the *taille* and the *taillon*

Bibliothèque municipale, Dijon (BMD)

Fonds Bossuet The siege of Dijon, 1513
Fonds Saverot 1490 to 1494 Registers of the Parlement of Dijon
Ms. 1012 Patent letters of Louis XIII
Ms. 1070 Entry of Henry IV into Dijon, 1595
Ms. 1642 Edict of *Élections*, 1630
Ms. 2098 Lanturelu riot, 1630

Bibliothèque nationale de France, Paris (BNF)

Fonds français 22302 Copies of the registers of the Parlement of Dijon

Primary Published Sources

Bailey, Donald A. ed. *Histoire de la vie de Michel de Marillac (1560–1632): Garde des sceaux de France sous Louis XIII*. Québec: Presses de l'Université de Laval, 2007.

Calvin, John. "Short Treatise on the Holy Supper of Our Lord and Only Saviour Jesus Christ," in J. K. S. Reid, ed. and trans. *Calvin: Theological Treatises*. Philadelphia, PA: The Westminster Press, 1954.

"Ordinances for the Supervision of the Churches Dependent on the Seigneury of Geneva [February 3, 1547]," in J. K. S. Reid, ed. and trans. *Calvin: Theological Treatises*. Philadelphia, PA: Westminster John Knox Press, 1954.

Chantal, Jeanne-Françoise Frémyot de. *Correspondance*, 6 vols., ed. Marie-Patricia Burns. Paris: Cerf, 1986–1996.

Chasseneux, Bartélemy de. *Catalogus gloriae mundi*. Lyon: Vicentius, 1546; orig. edn. 1529.

De Bèze, Theodore, et al. *Histoire ecclésiastique des églises réformées au royaume de France*, eds. G. Baum and E. Cunitz, 3 vols. Paris: Librairie Fischbacher, 1883–1889.

De la sedition arrivée en la ville de Dijon le 28. Fevrier 1630. & Iugement rendu par le Roy sur icelle. Lyon: Irenée Barlet, 1630.

De Serres, Olivier. *Le Théâtre d'agriculture et mesnage des champs*, ed. Hubert Nyssen. Arles: Actes Sud, 1996.

Du Tilliot, Jean-Baptiste Lucotte, ed. *Mémoires pour servir à l'histoire de la fête des fous qui se faisait autrefois dans plusieurs églises*. Lausanne and Geneva: Marc-Michel Bousquet, 1741.

Fournier, Édouard, ed. *Variétés historique et littéraires*, 10 vols. Paris: P. Jannet, 1855–1863.

Garnier, Joseph, ed. *Correspondance de la mairie de Dijon extraite des archives de cette ville*, 3 vols. Dijon: Rabutot, 1868–1870.

Journal de Gabriel Breunot conseiller du parlement de Dijon précédé du livre de souvenance de Pepin chanoine de la Sainte-Chapelle, 3 vols. Dijon: J.-E. Rabutot, 1864.

Gregory of Tours, *The History of the Franks*, trans. Lewis Thorpe. Harmondsworth, Middlesex: Penguin, 1974.

Isambert, F. A. et al., eds. *Recueil général des anciennes lois françaises, depuis l'an 420 jusqu'à la Révolution*, 29 vols. Paris: Balin-Leprieur, 1821–1833.

Jeannin, Pierre. "Discours apologétique fait par M. le président Jeannin, de sa conduicte durant les troubles de la Ligue, et depuis sous les règnes du feu roi Henry-le-Grand et du roi à present régnant, 1622," in M. Petitot, ed., *Collection des mémoires relatifs à l'histoire de France depuis l'avènement de Henri IV jusqu'à la paix de Paris conclue en 1763*, vol. 16, 2nd series. Paris: Foucault, 1822, 128–148.

Lanturelu: Pièces contenant la relation d'une sedition arrive à Dijon le 28 février 1630. Dijon: Darantière, 1884.

L'Estoile, Pierre de. *Journal de l'Estoile pour le règne de Henri IV*, eds. L.-R. Lefèvre and André Martin, 3 vols. Paris: Gallimard, 1948–1960.

Journal pour le règne de Henri III (1574–1589), ed. Louis-Raymond Lefèvre. Paris: Gallimard, 1943.

"Le livre de la famille Robert: Notes sur le village de Couchey," in Charles Oursel, ed., *Deux livres de raison bourguignons*. Dijon: Mémoires de la Société bourguignonne de géographie et d'histoire, 1908.

Mémoires de Condé, ou recueil pour servir à l'histoire de France sous le règne de François II, et sous une partie de celui de Charles IX, 6 vols., D. F. Secousse and Lenglet Dufresnoy, eds., The Hague and Paris: Jean Néaulme, 1743.

"Le monologue du bon vigneron sortant de sa vigne, et retournant soupper en sa maison," in Charles Moiset, ed., "La poesie auxerroise au XVIe siècle," *Annuaire historique du département de l'Yonne* 21 (1857), 73–78.

Sainte Jeanne-Françoise Frémyot de Chantal, sa vie et ses oeuvres, 8 vols., ed. the Sisters of the Order of the Visitation of Annecy. Paris: Plon, 1874–1879.

Saulx, Gaspard de, seigneur de Tavanes. "Mémoires de très-noble et très-illustre Gaspard de Saulx, seigneur de Tavanes," in C. B. Petitot, ed., *Collection complète des mémoires relatifs à l'histoire de France depuis le règne de Philippe-Auguste jusqu'au commencement du dix-septième siècle*, 1st series, 52 vols., 23. Paris: Foucault, 1822, 5–45.

Schroeder, H. J. ed. and trans. *The Canons and Decrees of the Council of Trent*. Rockford, IL: Tan Books, 1978.

Valois, Noel. éd. *Inventaire des arrêts du conseil d'état (règne de Henri IV)*, 2 vols. Paris: Imprimerie Nationale, 1866–1893.

Voragine, Jacobus de. *The Golden Legend: Readings on the Saints*, trans. William Granger Ryan, 2 vols. Princeton, NJ: Princeton University Press, 1993.

Wright, Wendy M. and Joseph F. Power, eds. *Francis de Sales, Jane de Chantal: Letters of Spiritual Direction*, trans. Péronne Marie Thibert. New York, NY: Paulist Press, 1988.

Xivrey, J. Berger de and J. Gaudet, eds. *Recueil des lettres missives de Henri IV*, 9 vols. Paris: Imprimerie nationale, 1843–1856.

Zamet, Sébastien. *Conférences sprituelles sur divers sujets*. Dijon: J. Ressayre, 1705.

Lettres spirituelles de Sébastien Zamet, évêque-duc de Langres, pair de France, et précedées des Avis spirituels du même prélat, ed. Louis N. Prunel. Paris: Alphonse Picard et fils, 1912.

Secondary Sources

Amanton, Ferdinand. "Précis historique et chronologique sur l'établissement de la commune et des vicomte mayeurs ou maires de Dijon," *Mémoires de la Commission des Antiquités du département de la Côte-d'Or* 8 (1873): 1–142.

Barnavi, Elie. *Le Parti du Dieu: Étude sociale et politique des chefs de la Ligue parisienne, 1585–1594*. Brussels and Louvain: Nauwelaerts, 1980.

Baudouin, P. M. *Histoire du protestantisme et la Ligue en Bourgogne*, 2 vols. Auxerre: Imprimerie Vosgien et Chambon, 1881–1884.

Baumgartner, Frederic J. *Change and Continuity in the French Episcopate: The Bishops and the Wars of Religion, 1547–1610*. Durham, NC: Duke University Press, 1986.

Radical Reactionaries: The Political Thought of the French Catholic League. Geneva: Droz, 1976.

Beam, Sara. *Laughing Matters: Farce and the Making of Absolutism in France*. Ithaca, NY: Cornell University Press, 2007.

Beaune, Colette. *The Birth of an Ideology: Myths and Symbols of Nation in Late Medieval France*, trans. Susan Ross Huston. Berkeley, CA: University of California Press, 1991.

Beik, William. *Absolutism and Society in Seventeenth-Century France: State Power and Provincial Aristocracy in Languedoc*. Cambridge: Cambridge University Press, 1985.

A Social and Cultural History of Early Modern France. Cambridge: Cambridge University Press, 2009.

Urban Protest in Seventeenth-Century France: The Culture of Retribution. Cambridge: Cambridge University Press, 1997.

Belle, Edmond. "Les libraires dijonnais et les débuts de la Réforme à Dijon," *Bulletin de la Société de l'histoire du protestantisme francais* 59 (1910): 481–495.

La Réforme à Dijon des origins à la fin de la lieutenance générale de Gaspard de Saulx-Tavanes, 1530–1570. Dijon: Damidot, 1911.

Benedict, Philip. *The Faith and Fortunes of France's Huguenots, 1559–1685*. Aldershot: Ashgate, 2001.

Benedict, Philip. "Civil War and Natural Disaster in Northern France," in Peter Clarke, ed., *The European Crisis of the 1590s*. London: George Allen and Unwin, 1985, 84–105.

Rouen during the Wars of Religion. Cambridge: Cambridge University Press, 1981.

Bereiter, Gregory. "'Ils ne tendent pas à la defense de la Ligue': Discerner la opposition ecclésiastique de la Sainte Union," in Sylvie Daubresse and Bertrand Haan, eds., *La Ligue et ses frontiers: Engagements catholiques à distance du radicalism à la fin des guerres de Religion*. Rennes: Presses Universitaires de Rennes, 2016.

Bergin, Joseph. *The Making of the French Episcopate, 1589–1661*. New Haven, CT: Yale University Press, 1996.

The Politics of Religion in Early Modern France. New Haven, CT: Yale University Press, 2014.

Berlow, Rosalind Kent. "The 'Disloyal' Grape: The Agrarian Crisis of Late Fourteenth-Century Burgundy," *Agricultural History* 56 (1982): 426–438.

Bernstein, Hilary J. *Between Crown and Community: Politics and Civic Culture in Sixteenth-Century Poitiers*. Ithaca, NY: Cornell University Press, 2004.

Bertucat, Charles. *La juridiction municipale de Dijon: Son étendue*. Dijon: J. Nourry, 1911.

Bissey, Abbé. "Précis historique sur les Legoux de la Berchère et en particulier sur Pierre Legoux, comte de Rochefort," *Société d'histoire, d'archéologie et de littérature de l'arrondissement de Beaune: Mémoires année 1886*. Beaune: Arthur Batault, 1887, 195–293.

Blondeau, G. "Claude Bretagne, conseiller au Parlement. De Bourgogne: Son portrait et ceux de sa famille au muse de Dijon," *Annales de Bourgogne* 5 (1933): 101–129.

Bonney, Richard. *Political Change in France under Richelieu and Mazarin, 1624–1661*. Oxford: Oxford University Press, 1978.

Bossy, John. *Christianity in the West, 1400–1700*. Oxford: Oxford University Press, 1986.

"The Mass as a Social Institution, 1200–1700," *Past & Present* 100 (1983): 29–61.

"The Social History of Confession in the Age of Reformation," *Transactions of the Royal Historical Society*, 5th series 25 (1975): 21–38.

Bourcier, F. "Le régime municipal à Dijon sous Henri IV," *Revue d'histoire moderne* 10 (1935): 97–120.

Bourély, Béatrice. *Vignes et vins de l'abbaye de Cîteaux en Bourgogne*. Nuits St. Georges: Editions de Tastevin, 1998.

Bouwsma, William J. *John Calvin: A Sixteenth-Century Portrait*. Oxford and New York, NY: Oxford University Press, 1988.

"Lawyers and Early Modern Culture," *The American Historical Review* 78 (1973): 303–327.

Breen, Michael P. "Addressing *La Ville des Dieux*: Entry Ceremonies and Urban Audiences in Early Modern Dijon," *The Journal of Social History* 38 (2004): 341–364.

Law, City, and King: Legal Culture, Municipal Politics, and State Formation in Early Modern Dijon. Rochester, NY: University of Rochester Press, 2007.

Brunet, Serge. ed. *La Sainte Union des catholiques de France et la fin des guerre de Religion (1585–1629)*. Paris: Classiques Garnier, 2016.

Bryant, Lawrence M. *The King and the City in the French Royal Entry Ceremony: Politics, Ritual, and Art in the Renaissance*. Geneva: Droz, 1986.

Burke, Peter. *Popular Culture in Early Modern Europe*. Aldershot: Scolar Press, 1994 rev. edn.

Burnett, Amy Nelson. "The Social History of Communion and the Reformation of the Eucharist," *Past & Present* 211 (May 2011): 77–119.

Cabourdin, Guy and Georges Viard, eds. *Lexique historique de la France d'Ancien Régime*. Paris: Armand Colin, 1978.

Carpi, Olivia. *Une République imaginaire: Amiens pendant les troubles de religion, 1559–1597*. Paris: Belin, 2005.

Carroll, Michael P. *The Cult of the Virgin Mary: Psychological Origins*. Princeton, NJ: Princeton University Press, 1986.

Carroll, Stuart. *Noble Power during the French Wars of Religion: The Guise Affinity and the Catholic Cause in Normandy*. Cambridge: Cambridge University Press, 1998.

Cassan, Michel. *Le temps des guerres de religion: Le cas du Limousin, vers 1530–vers 1630*. Paris: Publisud, 1996.

Chabeuf, Henri. *Dijon: Monuments et souvenirs*. Dijon: Damidot, 1894.

Chartier, Roger. *Cultural History: Between Practices and Representations*, trans. Lydia G. Cochrane. Ithaca, NY: Cornell University Press, 1988.

The Cultural Uses of Print in Early Modern France, trans., Lydia G. Cochrane. Princeton, NJ: Princeton University Press, 1987.

"Texts, Printing, Readings," in Lynn Hunt, ed., *The New Cultural History*. Berkeley, CA: University of California Press, 1989, 154–175.

Chaume, Maurice. "Le finage et la banlieue de Dijon," *Mémoires de la Commission des Antiquités de la Côte-d'Or* 21 (1939–1941): 342–344.

Les origines du duché de Bourgogne, 2 vols. Dijon: Académie des Sciences, Arts et Belles Lettres, 1925–1927.

Chevalier, Bernard. *Les bonnes villes de France du XIVème au XVIème siecles*. Paris: Aubier, 1982.

Chiffoleau, Jacques. *La Comptabilité de l'au-delà: Les hommes, la mort et la religion d'Avignon à la fin du Moyen Age, vers 1320–vers 1480*. Rome: Ecole française de Rome, 1980.

Clamageran, Jean-Jules. *Histoire de l'impôt en France*, 3 vols. Paris: Librairie de Guillaumin, 1867–1876.

Collins, James B. *Classes, Estates, and Orders in Early Modern Brittany*. Cambridge: Cambridge University Press, 1994.

"De la république française à l'état français: Duplessis-Mornay et la transformation de la citoyenneté en France," in Hugues Daussy and Veronique Ferrer, eds., *Servir Dieu, le roi et l'état: Philippe Duplessy-Mornay (1549–1623), Albineana* 18. Niort: Cahiers d'Aubigné, 2006, 325–339.

La Monarchie républicaine: État et société dans la France moderne. Paris: Odile Jacob, 2016.

The State in Early Modern France, 2nd edn. Cambridge: Cambridge University Press, 2009.

Collins, Samuel W. *The Medieval Debate Over Sacred Space*. New York, NY: Palgrave Macmillan, 2012.

Constant, Jean-Marie. *La Ligue*. Paris: Fayard, 1995.

Cosandey, Fanny and Robert Descimon. *L'absolutisme en France: Histoire et historiographie*. Paris: Editions du Seuil, 2002.

Courtépée, Claude and Edme Béguillet. *Description générale et particulière du duché de Bourgogne*, 5 vols. Avallon and Paris: F. E. R. N., 3rd edn. 1967–2010.

Crouzet, Denis. *Dieu en ses royaumes: Une histoire des guerres de religion*. Seyssel: Champ Vallon, 2008.

La genèse de la Réforme française, 1520–1562. Paris: SEDES, 1996.

Les guerriers de Dieu: La violence au temps des troubles de religion, vers 1525–vers 1610, 2 vols. Seyssel: Champ Vallon, 1990.

"Recherches sur les processions blanches, 1583–1584," *Histoire, économie et société* 1 (1982): 511–563.

D'Arbaumont, Jules. *Armorial de la Chambre des comptes de Dijon*. Dijon: Lamarche, 1881.

Daubresse, Sylvie. *Le Parlement de Paris ou la voix de raison (1559–1589)*. Geneva: Librairie Droz, 2005.

David, Henri. *De Sluter à Sambin: Essai critique sur la sculpture monumental en Bourgogne au XVe et au XVIe siècles*, 2 vols. Paris: Leroux, 1933.

Davis, Natalie Zemon. "The Rites of Violence," in *Society and Culture in Early Modern France*. Stanford, CA: Stanford University Press, 1975, 97–123.

Dayton, Cornelia Hughes. "Rethinking Agency, Recovering Voices," *American Historical Review* 109 (June 2004): 827–843.

Delumeau, Jean. *Le catholicisme entre Luther et Voltaire*. Paris: Presses universitaires de France, 1971.

Rassurer et protéger: Le sentiment de sécurité dans l'Occident d'autrefois. Paris: Fayard, 1980.

Descimon, Robert. "The Birth of the Nobility of the Robe," in Michael Wolfe, ed., *Changing Identities in Early Modern France*. Durham, NC: Duke University Press, 1997, 95–123.

"The 'Bourgeoisie Seconde': Social Differentiation in the Parisian Municipal Oligarchy in the Sixteenth Century, 1500–1610," *French History* 17 (2003): 388–424.

"Le catholicisme corporative des temps de la Ligue: Témoignages de testaments parisiens des XVIe et XVIIe siècles," in Jean-Pierre Bardet, Denis Crouzet, and Anne Molinié-Bertrand, eds., *Pierre Chaunu historien*. Paris: Presses de l'Université de Paris-Sorbonne, 2012, 169–188.

"Le corps de ville et les élections échevinales à Paris aux XVIe et XVIIe siècles: Codification coutumière et pratiques sociales," *Histoire, économie et société* 13 (1994): 507–530.

"L'échevinage parisien sous Henri IV (1594–1609): Autonomie urbaine, conflits politiques et exclusives sociales," in Neithard Bulst and Jean-Philippe Genet, eds., *La ville, la bourgeoisie et la genèse de l'état moderne (XIIe-XVIIIe siècle)*. Paris: C.N.R.S., 1988, 113–150.

"La Ligue à Paris (1585–1594): Une révision," *Annales: E.S.C.* 37 (January–February 1982): 72–111.

Qui étaient les Seize? Mythes et réalités de la Ligue parisienne (1585–1594) Paris: Librairie Klincksieck, 1983.

Descimon, Robert and Elie Barnavi. *La Sainte Ligue, le juge et la potence: L'assassinat du president Brisson, 15 novembre 1591*. Paris: Hachette, 1985.

Descimon, Robert and Elie Haddad, eds. *Épreuves de noblesse: Les expériences nobiliares de la haute robe parisienne (XVIe-XVIIIe siècles)*. Paris: Les Belles Lettres, 2010.

Desplat, Christian. "Louis XIII and the Union of Béarn to France," in Mark Greengrass, ed., *Conquest and Coalescence: The Shaping of the State in Early Modern Europe*. London: Edward Arnold, 1991, 68–83.

De Waele, Michel. "De Paris à Tours: La crise d'identité des magistrats parisiens de 1589 à 1594," *Revue historique* 299 (1999): 549–577.

Diefendorf, Barbara B. *Beneath the Cross: Catholics and Huguenots in Sixteenth-Century Paris*. New York, NY: Oxford University Press, 1991.

From Penitence to Charity: Pious Women and the Catholic Reformation in Paris. New York, NY: Oxford University Press, 2004.

Diefendorf, Barbara B. ed. *Social Relations, Politics, and Power in Early Modern France: Robert Descimon and the Historian's Craft*. Kirksville, MO: Truman State University Press, 2016.

Dion, Roger. *Historie de la vigne at du vin en France aux origins au XIXe siècle*. Paris: Flammarion, 1990 ed., orig. edn. 1959.

Dix, Gregory. *The Shape of the Liturgy*. London: Dacre Press, 1945.

Drouot, Henri. "Un crime dans la ville bloquée: Notes sur une situation et des mentalités de 1591," *Annales de Bourgogne* 21 (1949): 261–284.

Un épisode de la Ligue à Dijon: L'Affaire La Verne (1594) et notes sur la Ligue en Bourgogne. Dijon: La Revue bourguignonne, 1910.

"Flavigny contre Dijon: Notes sur le schisme dijonnais de 1589," *Mémoires de l'Académie de Dijon* (1922): 47–120.

"Hostelleries dijonnaises en 1593," *Revue de Bourgogne* 3 (1915): 473–476.

Mayenne et la Bourgogne: Étude sur la Ligue (1587–1596), 2 vols. Dijon: Bernigaud et Privat, 1937.

"Le serment de fidélité des Dijonnais à Henri IV (1595)," *Mémoires de l'Académie des sciences, arts et belles lettres de Dijon* (1924): 269–274.

"Vin, vignes et vignerons de la côte dijonnaise pendant la Ligue," *Revue de Bourgogne* 1 (1911): 343–361.

Durandeau, Joachim. *Histoire de la Mère Folle laïque de Dijon*. Dijon: Réveil Bourguignon, 1911.

Dutour, Thierry. *Une société de l'honneur: Les notables et leur monde à Dijon à la fin du Moyen Age*. Paris: Honoré Champion, 1998.

Edwards, Kathryn A. *Families and Frontiers: Recreating Communities and Boundaries in the Early Modern Burgundies*. Leiden: Brill, 2002.

El Kenz, David. "Une mariophanie martiale a Dijon," *Annales de Bourgogne* 87 (2015): 47–57.

"La Saint-Barthélemy à Dijon: Un non-événement?" *Annales de Bourgogne*, 74 (2002): 139–157.

Ellington, Donna Spivey. *From Sacred Body to Angelic Soul: Understanding Mary in Late Medieval and Early Modern Europe*. Washington, DC: Catholic University of America Press, 2001.

Elwood, Christopher. *The Body Broken: The Calvinist Doctrine of the Eucharist and the Symbolization of Power in Sixteenth-Century France*. Oxford: Oxford University Press, 1999.

Evennett, H. Outram. *The Spirit of the Counter-Reformation*. Notre Dame, IN: University of Notre Dame Press, 1970.

Farr, James R. *Artisans in Europe, 1300–1914*. Cambridge: Cambridge University Press, 2000.

Authority and Sexuality in Early Modern Burgundy, 1550–1730. New York, NY: Oxford University Press, 1995.

"Consumers, Commerce, and the Craftsmen of Dijon: The Changing Social and Economic Structure of a Provincial Capital, 1450–1750," in Philip Benedict, ed., *Cities and Social Change in Early Modern France*. London: Unwin Hyman, 1989, 134–173.

Hands of Honor: Artisans and Their World in Dijon, 1550–1650. Ithaca, NY: Cornell University Press, 1988.

"Popular Religious Solidarity in Sixteenth-Century Dijon," *French Historical Studies* 14 (1985): 192–214.

Finley-Croswhite, S. Annette. "Engendering the Wars of Religion: Female Agency during the Catholic League in Dijon," *French Historical Studies* 20 (Spring 1997): 127–154.

Henry IV and the Towns: The Pursuit of Legitimacy in French Urban Society. Cambridge: Cambridge University Press, 1999.

Fontaine, Laurence. *The Moral Economy: Poverty Credit, and Trust in Early Modern Europe*. Cambridge: Cambridge University Press, 2014.

Fromental, Jacques. *La Réforme en Bourgogne aux XVIe et XVIIe siècles*. Paris: Les Belles Lettres, 1968.

Fyot, Eugène. "L'Architecture à Dijon sous la Renaissance: Hugues Sambin," *Revue de Bourgogne* 12 (December 1925): 5–27.

Dijon, son passé évoqué par ses rues. Dijon: Damidot, 1927.

Gal, Stèphane. *Grenoble au temps de la Ligue: Étude politique, sociale et religieuse d'une cité en crise, vers 1562-vers 1598*. Grenoble: Presses Universitaires de Grenoble, 2000.

Galanaud, Anne and Henri Labesse. "Les vignerons à Dijon au début du XVIe siècle," *Cahiers d'histoire de la vigne et du vin* 3 (2002): 79–99.

Galet, Pierre. *Les maladies et parasites de la vigne*, 2 vols. Montpellier: Galet, 1977–1982.

Garnier, Joseph. *Le feu de la Saint-Jean à Dijon*. Dijon: Jobard, 1890.

Garnier, Joseph and Ernest Champeux. *Chartes de commune et d'affranchisements en Bourgogne.* Dijon: Rabutot and Garantière, 1918.

Garrier, Gilbert. *Histoire sociale et culturelle du vin.* Paris: Bordas, 1995.

Gazin-Goussel, J. "Un contre-coup de la Ligue en Bourgogne: L'expulsion et le retour des Jésuites de Dijon," *Revue de l'histoire de l'Eglise de France* 1 (1910): 515–526.

Gordon, F. Bruce. *Calvin.* New Haven, CT: Yale University Press, 2009.

Gourdin, Henri. *Olivier de Serres: Science, expérience, diligence en agriculture au temps de Henri IV.* Arles: Actes Sud, 2001.

Gras, Pierre, ed. *Histoire de Dijon.* Toulouse: Privat, 1987.

Greengrass, Mark. *France in the Age of Henri IV: The Struggle for Stability.* London: Longman, 1984.

Governing Passions: Peace and Reform in the French Kingdom, 1576–1585. Oxford: Oxford University Press, 2007.

"The Later Wars of Religion in the French Midi," in Peter Clarke, ed., *The European Crisis of the 1590s.* London: George Allen and Unwin, 1985, 106–134.

"The Sainte Union in the Provinces: The Case of Toulouse," *Sixteenth Century Journal* 14 (1983): 469–496.

Gros, Louis. *Le Parlement et la Ligue en Bourgogne.* Dijon and Paris: Damidot and H. Champion, 1910.

Grosse, Christian. *Les Rituels de la céne: La culte eucharistique réformé à Genève, XVIe-XVIIe siècles.* Geneva: Droz, 2008.

Guillaume, Marguerite. *La Peinture en Bourgogne au XVIe siècle.* Dijon: Musée des Beaux-Arts de Dijon, 1990.

Haag, E *La France protestante*, 10 vols. Paris: Sandoz et Fischbacher, 2nd edn. 1877–1888.

Harding, Robert R. *Anatomy of a Power Elite: The Provincial Governors of Early Modern France.* New Haven, CT: Yale University Press, 1978.

"The Mobilization of Confraternities against the Reformation in France," *Sixteenth Century Journal* XI (1980): 85–107.

Hauser, Henri. "Olivier de Serres et la Bourgogne," *Annales de Bourgogne* 13 (December 1941): 306–307.

"L'Organisation du travail à Dijon et en Bourgogne au XVIe et dans la première moitié du XVIIe siècle," in H. Hauser, ed., *Les débuts du capitalism.* Paris: Alcan, 1927.

"Le Traité de Madrid et la cession de la Bourgogne à Charles Quint: Etude sur le sentiment national bourguignon en 1525–26," *Revue bourguignonne* 22 (1912): 1–182.

Hayden, J. Michael. *France and the Estates General of 1614.* Cambridge: Cambridge University Press, 1974.

Holt, Mack P. "Burgundians into Frenchmen: Catholic Identity in Sixteenth-Century Burgundy," in Michael Wolfe, ed., *Changing Identities in Early Modern France.* Durham, NC: Duke University Press, 1997, 345–370.

"Culture populaire et culture politique au XVIIe siècle: L'émeute de Lanturelu à Dijon en fèvrier 1630," *Histoire, économie et société* 16 (1997): 597–616.

The French Wars of Religion, 1562–1629. Cambridge: Cambridge University Press, 2nd edn. 2005.

"From Burgundian Netherlands to Dutch Republic: Tradition and Innovation in Sixteenth-Century Europe," *History Review*, 23 (December 1995): 4–8.

"The Memory of All Things Past: The Provisions of the Edict of Nantes," in Richard L. Goodbar, ed., *The Edict of Nantes: Five Essays and a New Translation*. Bloomington, MN: National Huguenot Society, 1998, 28–32.

"Patterns of Clientèle and Economic Opportunity at Court: The Household of François, Duke of Anjou," *French Historical Studies* 13 (Spring 1984): 305–322.

"Popular Political Culture and Mayoral Elections in Sixteenth-Century Dijon," in Mack P. Holt, ed., *Society and Institutions in Early Modern France*. Athens, GA: University of Georgia Press, 1991, 98–116.

"Les Réseaux d'autorité et de pouvoir a l'Hôtel de Ville et au Parlement de Dijon entre 1580 et 1630," *Annales de Bourgogne* 85 (2013): 19–35.

"Wine, Community and Reformation in Sixteenth-Century Burgundy," *Past & Present* 138 (February 1993): 58–93.

"Wine, Life, and Death in Early Modern Burgundy," *Food and Foodways: Explorations in the History and Culture of Human Nourishment* 8 (Fall 1999): 73–98.

Horn, Jeff. *Economic Development in Early Modern France: The Privilege of Liberty, 1650–1820*. Cambridge: Cambridge University Press, 2015.

Houllemare, Marie. *Politiques de la parole: Le Parlement de Paris au XVIe siècle*. Geneva: Librairie Droz, 2011.

Hurt, John J. *Louis XIV and the Parlements: The Assertion of Royal Authority*. Manchester: Manchester University Press, 2002.

Iogna-Prat, Dominique. *Maison Dieu: Une histoire monumentale de l'Eglise au Moyen Age*. Paris: Seuil, 2006.

Iogna-Prat, Dominique, Eric Palazzo, and Daniel Russo, eds. *Marie: Le culte de la Vierge dans la société médiévale*. Paris: Beauchesne, 1996.

James, Mervyn. "Ritual, Drama and Social Body in the Late Medieval English Town," *Past & Present* 98 (February 1983): 3–29.

Jansen, Katherine Ludwig. *The Making of the Magdalen: Preaching and Popular Devotion in the Later Middle Ages*. Princeton, NJ: Princeton University Press, 2000.

Johnson, Hugh. *The Story of Wine*. London: Mandarin Paperbacks, 1991.

Jouanna, Arlette. *Le devoir de révolte: La noblesse française et la gestation de l'État moderne, 1559–1661*. Paris: Fayard, 1989.

Jungmann, Joseph A. *The Mass of the Roman Rite: Its Origins and Development*, trans. Francis A. Brunner, 2 vols. Allen, TX: Christian Classics, 1986; orig. edn. 1951–1955.

Kaiser, Wolfgang. *Marseille au temps des troubles, 1559–1596: Morphologie sociale et luttes de faction*. Paris: E.H.E.S.S., 1992.

Kermina, Françoise. *Jeanne de Chantal, 1572–1641*. Paris: Perrin, 2000.

Kettering, Sharon. *Patrons, Brokers, and Clients in Seventeenth-Century France.* New York, NY: Oxford University Press, 1986.

Kierstead, Raymond. F. *Pomponne de Bellièvre: A Study of the King's Men in the Age of Henry IV.* Evanston, IL: Northwestern University Press, 1968.

Kingdon, Robert M. *Geneva and the Coming of the Wars of Religion in France, 1555–1563.* Geneva: Droz, 1956; 2nd edn. 2007.

Kishlansky, Mark A. *Parliamentary Selection: Social and Political Choice in Early Modern England.* Cambridge: Cambridge University Press, 1986.

Klauser, T. *A Short History of the Western Liturgy,* trans. J. Halliburton. Oxford: Oxford University Press, 1969.

Knecht, R. J. *Francis I.* Cambridge: Cambridge University Press, 1982.
Renaissance Warrior and Patron: The Reign of Francis I. Cambridge: Cambridge University Press, 1994.

Konnert, Mark W. *Local Politics in the French Wars of Religion: The Towns of Champagne, the Duc de Guise, and the Catholic League, 1560–1595.* Aldershot: Ashgate, 2006.

Labbé, Thomas. "Le vin de Dijon du XIVe au XVIIIe siècle: trajectoire historique d'un cru (presque) disparu," in Jean-Pierre Garcia and Jacky Rigaux, eds., *Vignes et vins du Dijonnois: Oubli et renaissance.* Clemencey: Terre en Vues, 2012, 81–87.

Labbé, Thomas and Fabien Gaveau. "Les dates de bans de vendange à Dijon: Établissement critique et révision archivistique d'une série ancienne," *Revue historique* 657 (2011): 19–51.

Lachiver, Marcel. *Vins, vignes et vignerons: Histoire du vignoble français.* Paris: Fayard, 1988.

La Cuisine, Elisabeth-François de. *Le Parlement de Bourgogne depuis son origine jusqu'à sa chute,* 3 vols. Dijon and Paris: Rabutot and A. Durand, 1864.

Lafon, Jean, Pierre Couillaud, and Roger Hyde. *Maladies et parasites de la vigne,* 2 vols. Paris: Baillière et Fils, 3rd edn., 1966–1970.

Lagrandré, Aline. "Les vignerons de Cîteaux dans la Côte de Beaune au Moyen Age," *Annales de Bourgogne* 73 (2001): 95–101.

Lagrange, André. "Musée du Vin de Bourgogne à Beaune: Salles des travaux de la vigne et du vin et des métiers auxiliaires," *Arts et traditions populaires* 13 (1965): 107–180.

Lamarre, Christine. "Les Lanturelus de Dijon en 1630: le peuple en rébellion?" in Philippe Guignet, ed., *Le peuple des villes dans l"Europe du Nord-Ouest (fin du moyen âge-1945),* vol. 1. Villeneuve d'Ascq: Centre de recherché sur l'histoire de l'Europe du Nord-Ouest, 2003, 29–41.

Lamy, Marielle. "Une siege levé par l'intervention de Marie? La dévotion à Notre Dame de Bon-Espoir," in Jonathan Dumont, Alain Marchandisse, and Laurent Vissière, eds., *1513 L'année terrible: Le siege de Dijon.* Dijon: Faton, 2013, 212–217.

Lane, Anthony N. S. *A Reader's Guide to Calvin's Institutes.* Grand Rapids, MI: Baker Academic, 2009.

Lange, Tyler. *The First French Reformation: Church Reform and the Origins of the Old Regime.* Cambridge: Cambridge University Press, 2014.

Lebeau, Marcel. *Essai sur les vignes de Cîteaux aux origins à 1789.* Dijon: Académie de Dijon, 1986.

Le Goff, Hervé. *La Ligue en Bretagne: Guerre civile et conflit international, 1588–1598.* Rennes: Presses Universitaires de Rennes, 2006.

Leguai, André. "La conquête de la Bourgogne par Louis XI," *Annales de Bourgogne* 49 (1977): 87–92.

Dijon et Louis XI, 1461–1483. Dijon, 1947.

Le Person, Xavier. *"Pratiques" et "pratiquers": La vie politique à la fin du règne de Henri III, 1584–1589.* Geneva: Droz, 2002.

Le Roux, Nicolas. *1er août. Un régicide au nom de Dieu. L'Assassinat d'Henri III.* Paris: Gallimard, 2006.

Le Roy Ladurie, Emmanuel. *The French Peasantry, 1450–1660,* trans. Alan Sheridan. Berkeley, CA: University of California Press, 1987.

"Les masses profondes: La paysannerie," in E. Le Roy Ladurie and Michel Morineau, eds., *Histoire économique et sociale de la France,* vol. 1, 1450–1660 in 2 parts. Paris: Presses universitaires de France, 1977, 1, ii: 483–865.

Lierheimer, "Gender, Resistance, and the Limits of Episcopal Authority: Sébastien Zamet's Reationship with Nuns, 1615–1655," in Jennifer Maria DeSilva, ed., *Episcopal Reform and Politics in Early Modern Europe.* Kirksville, MO: Truman State University Press, 2012.

Lietzman, Hans. *Mass and Lord's Supper: A Study in the History of the Liturgy,* trans. Dorothy H. G. Reeve. Leiden: Brill, 1979.

Lignereux, Yann. *Lyon et le roi: De la bonne ville à l'absolutisme municipal, 1594–1654.* Seyssel: Champs Vallon, 2003.

Loiseau, Jérôme. *"Elle fera ce que l'on voudra": La noblesse aux états de Bourgogne et la monarchie d'Henri IV à Louis XIV, 1602–1715.* Besançon: Presses universitaires de Franche-Comté, 2014.

Lualdi, Katharine Jackson. "A Body of Beliefs and Believers: Sacramental Confession and Parish Worship in Reformation France," in Katherine Jackson Lualdi and Anne T. Thayer, eds., *Penitence in the Age of Reformations.* Aldershot: Ashgate, 2000, 134–151.

Maes, Bruno. *Le Roi, la Vièrge et la nation: Pèlerinages et identité nationale entre guerre de Cents Ans et Révolution.* Paris: Editions Publisud, 2003.

Major, J. Russell. *From Renaissance Monarchy to Absolute Monarchy: French Kings, Nobles, and Estates.* Baltimore, MD: Johns Hopkins University Press, 1994.

"Henry IV and Guyenne: A Study Concerning the Origins of Royal Absolutism," *French Historical Studies* 4 (1966): 363–383.

Representative Government in Early Modern France. New Haven, CT: Yale University Press, 1980.

Mâle, Émile. *Religious Art in France, the Late Middle Ages: A Study of Medieval Iconography and Its Sources,* ed. Harry Bober, trans. Marthiel Mathews. Princeton: Princeton University Press, 1986.

Manning, Ruth. "Breaking the Rules: The Emergence of the Active Female Apostolate in Seventeenth-Century France." Ph.D. thesis, University of Oxford, 2006.

"A Confessor and His Spiritual Child: François de Sales, Jeanne de Chantal, and the Foundation of the Order of the Visitation," in Ruth Harris and Lyndal Roper, eds., *The Art of Survival: Gender and History in Europe, 1450–2000*. Oxford: Oxford University Press, 2006, 101–117.

Mariéjol, J. H. *La Réforme et la Ligue: L'Edit de Nantes, 1559–1598*, vol. 6, part 1 of *L'Histoire de France des origins à la Révolution*, ed. Ernest Lavisse. Paris: Hachette, 1904.

Marlier, Jean, ed. *Charetes et documents concernant l'abbaye de Cîteaux, 1098–1790*. Rome: Cistercienses, 1961.

"Le vin de Cîtreaux au XIIe siècle," *Mémoires de l'Académie des sciences, arts et belles lettres de Dijon* (1943–1946): 267–272.

Mathieu, Jean-Baptiste-Joseph. *Abrégé chronologique de l'histoire des évêques de Langres*. Langres: Laurent et Fils, 1844.

Metman, Étienne. *L'Église Saint-Michel de Dijon*. Dijon: Ratel-Cotosset, 1914.

Michel, Guy J. *La Franche-Comté sous les Habsbourg, 1493–1678*. Wettolsheim: Mars et Mercure, 1978.

Monget, Cyprian. *La Chartreuse de Dijon d'après les documents des archives de Bourgogne*, 3 vols. Montreuil-sur-Mer and Tournai: Imprimerie Notre-Dame des Près, 1898–1905.

Monter, E. William. *Calvin's Geneva*. New York, NY: Wiley, 1967.

Moote, A. Lloyd. *Louis XIII: The Just*. Berkeley, CA: University of California Press, 1989.

Mousnier, Roland. *The Assassination of Henry IV: The Tyrannicide Problem and the Consolidation of the French Absolute Monarchy in the Early Seventeenth Century*, trans. Joan Spencer. London: Faber and Faber, 1973.

Murphy, Neil. *Ceremonial Entries, Municipal Liberties and the Negotiation of Power in Valois France, 1328–1589*. Leiden and Boston, MA: Brill, 2016.

Nelson, Eric. *The Jesuits and the Monarchy: Catholic Reform and Political Authority in France, 1590–1615*. Aldershot: Ashgate, 2005.

Nolin, E. "Episodes de la lutte des classes à Dijon au XVIe siècle," *Annales de Bourgogne*, 36 (1964): 270–275.

O'Malley, John W. *Trent: What Happened at the Council*. Cambridge, MA: Harvard University Press, 2013.

Pallier, Denis. *Recherches sur l'imprimerie à Paris pendant la Ligue, 1585–1594*. Geneva: Librairie Droz, 1976.

Parker, David. *La Rochelle and the French Monarchy: Conflict and Order in Seventeenth-Century France*. London: Royal Historical Society, 1980.

The Making of French Absolutism. London: Edward Arnold, 1983.

Patouillet, Xavière. *"L'Émeute des Lanturelus à Dijon en 1630,"* Mémoire de maîtrise, Université de Dijon, 1971.

Peignot, Gabriel. *Nouveaux details historiques sur le siège de Dijon en 1513, sur le traité qui l'a terminé et sur la tapisserie qui le représente*. Dijon: Douvillier, 1837.

Pelican, Jaroslav. *Mary through the Centuries: Her Place in the History of Culture.* New Haven, CT: Yale University Press, 1996.

Pepke-Duix, Hannelore. "L'économie des vignes et du vin autour de Dijon au Moyen Âge," in Jean-Pierre Garcia and Jacky Rigaux, eds., *Vignes et vins du Dijonnois: Oubli et renaissance.* Clemencey: Terre en Vues, 2012, 57–63.

"Les raisins de la crise: Vignes et vin en Bourgogne aux XIVe et XVe siècles," *Cahiers d'histoire de la vigne et du vin* 1 (2000): 23–49.

Perdrizet, Paul. *La Vierge de miséricorde: Etude d'un thème iconographique.* Paris: Albert Fontemoing, 1908.

Phillips, Rod. *A Short History of Wine.* London: Penguin Press, 2000.

Pitiot, Sylvain and Jean-Charles Servant. *Les vins de Bourgogne.* Paris: Presses universitaires de France, 11th edn. 1992.

Plancher, Dom Urbain. *Histoire générale et particulière de Bourgogne,* 4 vols. Dijon: Antoine De Fay, 1739–1781.

Prunel, Louis-Narcisse. *Sébastien Zamet (1588–1655), Évêque-Duc de Langres, Pair de France: sa vie et ses oeuvres, les origins du jansénisme.* Paris: Alphonse Picard, 1912.

Quale, H. J. "A New Root Pest of the Vine in California," *Journal of Economic Entomology* 1 (June 1908): 175–176.

Quarré, Pierre. "La joyeuse entrée de Charles le Téméraire à Dijon en 1474," *Bulletin de l'Académie Royale de Belgique: Classe des Beaux-Arts,* 51 (1969): 326–340.

La Sainte-Chapelle de Dijon: Siège de l'Ordre de la Toison d'Or. Dijon: Musée des Beaux-Arts, 1962.

"La tapisserie du siege de Dijon en 1513," *Plaisir de France* 431 (July–August 1975): 44–77.

Ramsey, Ann W. *Liturgy, Politics, and Salvation: The Catholic League in Paris and the Nature of Catholic Reform, 1540–1630.* Rochester, NY: University of Rochester Press, 1999.

Rapley, Elizabeth. *The Dévotes: Women and Church in Seventeenth-Century France.* Montreal: McGill University Press, 1990.

Reinburg, Virginia. *French Books of Hours: Making an Archive of Prayer, c. 1400–1600.* Cambridge: Cambridge University Press, 2012.

"Liturgy and the Laity in Late Medieval and Reformation France," *Sixteenth Century Journal* 23 (1992): 526–547.

Reynes-Meyer, Marie-Josèphe. "Dijon sous Charles VIII," *Annales de Bourgogne,* 50 (1978): 85–102.

Richard, Jean. "Les quêtes de l'église Notre-Dame et la diffusion du protestantisme à Dijon vers 1562," *Annales de Bourgogne* 32 (1960): 183–189.

"Le vignoble et les vins de Bourgogne au Moyen Age: un état de la recherche," *Annales de Bourgogne* 73 (2001): 9–17.

Richet, Denis. *De la Réforme à la Révolution: Études sur la France modern.* Paris: Aubier, 1991

"Sociocultural Aspects of Religious Conflicts in Paris in the Second Half of the Sixteenth Century," in Robert Forster and Orest Ranum, eds., *Religion, Ritual, and the Sacred: Selections from the Annales*. Baltimore, MD: Johns Hopkins University Press, 1982, 182–212.

Rigault, Jean. "L'ancienne confrérie des Rois à Saint-Michel de Dijon," *Mémoires de l'Académie des sciences, arts et belles-lettres de Dijon* 117 (1969): 81–85.

Robbins, Kevin C. *City on the Ocean Sea, La Rochelle, 1530–1650: Urban Society, Religion, and Politics on the French Atlantic Frontier*. Leiden: Brill, 1997.

Roberts, Penny. *A City in Conflict: Troyes during the French Wars of Religion*. Manchester: Manchester University Press, 1996.

"Peace, Ritual and Sexual Violence during the Religious Wars," in Graeme Murdock, Andrew Spicer, and Penny Roberts, eds., *Ritual and Violence: Natalie Zemon Davis and Early Modern France*. Oxford: Oxford University Press, 2012, 75–99.

Ronsin, Albert. *La Bibliothèque Bouhier: Histoire d'une collection formée du XVI au XVIIIe siècle par une famille de magistrats bourguignons*. Dijon: Bibliothèque municipale, 1971.

Rossiaud, Jacques. "Fraternités de jeunesse et et niveaux de culture dans les villes du sud- est à la fin du moyen âge," *Cahiers d'histoire* 1–2 (1976): 67–102.

Medieval Prostitution, trans. Lydia Cochrane. Oxford: Blackwell, 1988.

"Prostitution, Youth, and Society in the Towns of Southeastern France in the Fifteenth Century," in Robert Forster and Orest Ranum, eds., *Deviants and the Abandoned in French Society: Selections from the Annales*, vol. 4, trans. Elborg Forster and Patricia Ranum. Baltimore, MD: Johns Hopkins University Press, 1978.

Roupnel, Gaston. *La Ville et la campagne au XVIIe siècle: Etude sur la populations du pays dijonnais*. Paris: Armand Colin, 1955.

Rowan, Herbert H. *The King's State: Proprietary Dynasticism in Early Modern France*. New Brunswick, NJ: Rutgers University Press, 1980.

Rubin, Miri. *Corpus Christi: The Eucharist in Late Medieval Culture*. Cambridge: Cambridge University Press, 1991.

The Mother of God: A History of the Virgin Mary. New Haven, CT, and London: Yale University Press, 2009.

Saenger, Paul. "Burgundy and the Inalienability of Appanages in the Reign of Louis XI," *French Historical Studies*, 10 (Spring 1977): 1–26.

Saint-Jacob, Pierre de. "Mutations économiques et sociales dans les campagnes bourguinonnes à la fin du XVIe siècle," *Études rurales* 1 (1961): 35–49.

Salmon, J. H. M. "The Paris Sixteen, 1584–1594: The Social Analysis of a Revolutionary Movement," in his *Renaissance and Revolt: Essays in the Intellectual and Social History of Early Modern France*. Cambridge: Cambridge University Press, 1987, 235–266.

Society in Crisis: France in the Sixteenth Century. London: Ernest Benn, 1975.

Schnapper, Bernard. *Les Rentes au XVIe siècle: Histoire d'un instrument de credit*. Paris: S.E.V.P.E.N., 1957.

Senault, Jean-François. *La Vie de Madame Catherine de Montholon, veuve de Monsieur de Sanzelles, maistre des requestes, et fondatrice des Ursulines de Dijon*. Paris: Pierre Le Petit, 1653.

Sutherland, N. M. *Henry IV of France and the Politics of Religion, 1572–1596*, 2 vols. Bristol: Elm Bank, 2002.

The Huguenot Struggle for Recognition. New Haven, CT: Yale University Press, 1980.

Swann, Julian. *Provincial Power and Absolute Monarchy: The Estates General of Burgundy, 1661–1790*. Cambridge: Cambridge University Press, 2003.

Tallon, Alain. *La France et le Concile de Trent (1518–1563)*. Rome: École française de Rome, 1997.

Tapié, Victor-L. *France in the Age of Louis XIII and Richelieu*, trans. and ed. D. McN. Lockie. London: Macmillan, 1974.

Taylor, Larissa. *Soldiers of Christ: Preaching in Late Medieval and Reformation France*. New York, NY: Oxford University Press, 1992.

Thayer, Anne T. "Learning to Worship in the Later Middle Ages: Enacting Symbolism, Fighting the Devil, and Receiving Grace," *Archiv für Reformationsgeschichte* 99 (2008): 36–65.

Thévenot, E. "Les origines du vignoble bourguignon d'après les documents archéologiques," *Annales de Bourgogne* 23 (1951): 253–266.

Thomas, Danièle. *Henry IV: Images d'un roi entre mythe et réalité*. Bizanos: Héraclès, 1996.

Thomas, Jules. *La délivrance de Dijon en 1513 d'après les documents contemporains*. Dijon: Chez tous les libraires, 1898.

Thompson, E. P. *Customs in Common*. London: Penguin Books, 1993.

"The Moral Economy of the English Crowd in the Eighteenth Century," *Past & Present* 50 (1971): 76–136.

Tingle, Elizabeth C. *Authority and Society in Nantes during the French Wars of Religion, 1559–1598*. Manchester: University of Manchester Press, 2006.

Tournier, Claude. "Notes sur la culture de la vigne et les vignerons à Dijon entre 1430 et 1560," *Annales de Bourgogne* 24 (1952): 141–159.

"Le vin à Dijon de 1430 à 1560: Production et commerce," *Annales de Bourgogne* 22 (1950): 7–32.

"Le vin à Dijon de 1430 à 1560: Ravitaillement et commerce," *Annales de Bourgogne* 22 (1950): 161–186.

Unwin, Tim. *Wine and the Vine: An Historical Geography of Viticulture and the Wine Trade*. London: Routledge, 1991.

Valcke, Juliette. "De l'intermède comique à la leçon de morale: polyvalence des dialogues des vignerons dans le théâtre de la Mère Folle de Dijon," in Corrine Denoyelle, ed., *Le dialogue en question*. Orléans: Paradigm, 2013, 269–282.

"La satire sociale dans le repertoire de la Mère Folle de Dijon," in Konrad Eisenbichler and Wim Hüsken, eds., *Carnival and the Carnivalesque: The Fool, the Reformer, the Wildman, and Others in Early Modern Theatre*. Amsterdam: Rodolphi, 1999, 147–163.

"La société joyeuse de la Mère Folle de Dijon: Histoire (xve–xviie s.) et édition du répertoire," 3 vols., Ph.D. thesis Université de Montréal, 1997.

Théâtre de la Mère Folle de Dijon XVIᵉ–XVIIᵉ siècles. Orléans: Paradigme, 2012.

"Théâtre et spectacle chez la Mère Folle de Dijon (XVᵉ–XVIᵉ s.)," in Marie-France Wagner and Claire Le Brun-Gouanvic, eds., *Les arts du spectacle dans la ville (1404–1721)*. Paris: Champion, 2001.

van Gennep, Arnold. *Manuel de folklore français contemporain*, Part I, 8 vols. Paris: A. and J. Picard, 1943–1988.

Verhaeghe, Luc. "Vers composés pour les enfants de la Mère-Folle de Dijon vers la fin du XVIᵉ siècle," Mémoire de licence, University of Ghent, 1969.

Viaux, Dominique. "Eglises rurales en Bourgogne aux XVe et XVIe siècles," *Annales de Bourgogne* 60 (1988): 111–137.

La Vie paroissiale à Dijon à la fin du Moyen Age. Dijon: Editions Universitaires de Dijon, 1988.

Vincent, Catherine. *Fiat Lux: Lumière et luminaires dans la vie religieuse du XIIIe au XVIe siècle*. Paris: Editions du Cerf, 2004.

Vissière, Laurent. *Louis II de la Trémoïlle (1460–1525): Sans poinct sortir hors de l'ornière*. Paris: Honoré Champion, 2008.

Vissière, Laurent, Alain Marchandisse, and Jonathan Dumont, eds. *1513 l'année terrible: Le siège de Dijon*. Dijon: Éditions Faton, 2013.

Voisin, A. "La mutemaque du 26 juin 1477: Notes sur l'opinion à Dijon au lendemain de la Réunion," *Annales de Bourgogne*, 7 (1935): 337–356.

Walsham, Alexandra. "The Pope's Merchandise and the Jesuits' Trumpery: Catholic Relics and Protestant Polemic in Post-Reformation England," in Jenifer Spinks and Dagmar Eichberger, eds., *Religion, the Supernatural and Visual Culture in Early Modern Europe*. Leiden: Brill, 2015, 370–409.

Wandel, Lee Palmer. *The Eucharist in the Reformation: Incarnation and Liturgy*. Cambridge: Cambridge University Press, 2006.

Winkler, A. J., J. A. Cook, W. M. Kliewer, and L. A. Lider. *General Viticulture*. Berkeley, CA: University of California Press, 2nd edn. 1974.

Wolfe, Martin. *The Fiscal System of Renaissance France*. New Haven, CT: Yale University Press, 1972.

Wolfe, Michael. *The Conversion of Henri IV: Politics, Power, and Religious Belief in Early Modern France*. Cambridge, MA: Harvard University Press, 1993.

Yardeni, Myriam. "Histoires de villes, histoires de provinces et naissance d'une identité française au XVIe siècle," *Journal des savants* (1993): 111–134.

Young, Karl. *The Drama of the Medieval Church*, 2 vols. Oxford: The Clarendon Press, 1933.

Zachman, Randall C. *Image and Word in the Theology of John Calvin*. Notre Dame, IN: University of Notre Dame Press, 2007.

John Calvin as Teacher, Pastor, and Theologian: The Shape of His Writings and Thought. Grand Rapids, MI: Baker Academic, 2006.

Zaluska, Yolanda. *Manuscrits enluminés de Dijon*. Paris: Centre Nationale de la Recherche Scientifique, 1991.

Index

9 781108 456814